inspiring

WOMEN

OF THE FAITH

SOJOURNER TRUTH · FLORENCE NIGHTINGALE · AMY CARMICHAEL · CORRIE TEN BOOM

Published by Barbour Publishing, Inc., P.O. Box 719, Uhrichsville, Ohio 44683, www.barbourbooks.com

Our mission is to publish and distribute inspirational products offering exceptional value and biblical encouragement to the masses.

 Member of the
Evangelical Christian
Publishers Association

Printed in the United States of America.

inspiring

WOMEN
OF THE FAITH

SOJOURNER TRUTH · FLORENCE NIGHTINGALE · AMY CARMICHAEL · CORRIE TEN BOOM

BARBOUR
PUBLISHING

SOJOURNER TRUTH

LIBERATED IN CHRIST

W. TERRY WHALIN

PROLOGUE

The sun was bright that cloudless day in 1851. Hundreds of men and women were settling into their seats in an Akron, Ohio, church. Normally the building was reserved for prayer, but during the next few days, it would serve as the meeting place for an annual convention on women's rights.

Should women have the same political and social rights as men? That question was the burning issue of the day, and people had traveled hundreds of miles to hear the discussion. As they waited for the opening session, a striking black woman entered the auditorium. Wearing a plain gray dress, wire-rimmed glasses, and an oversized sunbonnet, the woman stood over six feet tall and looked more than fifty years old.

Seeing no empty seats in the back of the church, the woman walked slowly past the crowd of white people to the front. She stepped in a proud, almost defiant, manner. At the front of the church, the woman sat alone on one of the steps that led to the pulpit.

"Who is that?"

"Where did she come from?" The people craned their heads to see the figure.

"She looks like an abolitionist to me," someone surmised, familiar with former slaves such as Frederick Douglass, who traveled from town to town and spoke against the injustices of slavery.

At that moment, Frances Gage, who was to preside over the convention, stood on the platform. The crowd's speculation died down, and Gage introduced the first speaker. Throughout the morning, the audience heard a variety of speakers. Some were in favor of the women's rights movement, and others were against it.

The black woman with the sunbonnet sat on the pulpit steps with her face sunk into her hands. Even though she seemed distracted, she listened to every word.

At about midday, Gage called for an intermission. During the break, the black woman stood and walked among the audience. She offered to sell them copies of her book, *The Narrative of Sojourner Truth*. The book had been dictated to a friend, because Sojourner couldn't read or write. It told how she had been freed from slavery and had committed her life to helping other slaves gain freedom. While working for the freedom of slaves, Sojourner Truth had realized that women also needed liberation and that her cause could be broadened to include them. During the late 1840s, Sojourner joined the fight.

At first, the abolitionist and women's rights movements joined forces. Then people known as "Separatists" wanted to split the two movements.

When some of these separatists in Akron learned that Sojourner Truth was attending the women's rights convention, they determined that Sojourner should not speak. Several separatists gathered around Frances Gage during the lunch break and asked her to prevent Sojourner from speaking. "It will ruin our convention in the newspapers," one of them said. "Those reporters will say we are a bunch of agitators."

Gage carefully listened to each person but made no promises. "When the time comes, we'll see," she said. As it turned out, Gage didn't have to make a decision about Sojourner Truth speaking that afternoon, because the former slave returned to her place on the pulpit steps and silently continued listening to the speakers. The next morning, she again appeared content to listen to the speakers, several of whom were ministers.

The first minister told the convention that men deserved greater rights and privileges because they were more intelligent than women. When the next minister spoke, he told the audience, "Men should rule over women because Jesus Christ was a man. If God wanted women to be equal with men, then He would have given some sign of His will through the birth, life, and death of the Savior."

Another preacher told the convention that women had a lower status because Eve, the first woman, had committed the original sin in the Garden of Eden. Finally, a minister described how women were born inferior to men because they needed to have a man hold the door open for them. "Women don't deserve the same rights as men," the minister proclaimed, "because they are so much weaker." All of these speakers believed the Bible supported their claims that men were better than women.

A mixture of men and women were in the audience, and many of the women were visibly upset as minister after minister spoke against the rights of women. Although upset, none of these women were prepared to argue in public with such well-respected clergymen.

Then Sojourner Truth stood and walked to the pulpit. "Don't let her speak!" several men cried who sat near Frances Gage. Sojourner removed her sunbonnet and turned toward the moderator for permission to address the audience. For a brief moment, Frances Gage hesitated. Then she introduced the black woman to the audience.

Sojourner was determined to speak against these ministers. Even though she couldn't read or write, she had memorized a great deal of the Bible. She was certain that the Bible did not say women were less than men—any more than the Bible said that blacks should be slaves. She began to speak in a low, soft voice.

"Well, children, where there is so much racket, there must be something out of kilter." That "something," she said, was the domination of blacks and women by white men. "It will be fixed pretty soon," she promised the crowd.

First, Sojourner addressed the concerns of the minister who had declared women too weak to have equal rights. She explained how no one had helped her into a carriage or carried her across a mud puddle. In her entire life, no one had ever given her the best place to sit. As she spoke, Sojourner straightened her back. Her tall frame gave her words greater impact. To some people, her voice sounded like rolling thunder.

"And ain't I a woman? Look at me!" she proclaimed. "Look at my arm." Then she rolled up the sleeve on her dress. Unlike the plump arms of many women in the audience, Sojourner's arm was lean from years of hard labor.

"I have plowed and planted and gathered into barns, and no man could have done as much," she declared. "And ain't I a woman?"

She went on to describe the many times she had gone hungry, and she told about bearing children, only to watch them be sold into slavery. When she missed those children, only Jesus had been there to dry her tears.

Sojourner turned to the minister who had argued that women were less intelligent than men and therefore didn't deserve equal treatment. "What does intelligence have to do with rights?" she asked with a pointed finger and an angry stare.

Next, she addressed the minister who had argued that men should be superior because Jesus Christ was a man. "Where did your Christ come from?" she asked. The minister didn't answer. Sojourner repeated the question and answered, "From God and a woman. Man had nothing to do with the birth of Jesus Christ."

Finally, she confronted the minister who had discussed Eve and the origin of sin. In defense of women, Sojourner said, "If the first woman God ever made was strong enough to turn the world upside down, all alone, these together—" she motioned toward the women in the audience—"ought to be able to turn it back and get it right side up again." Most of the audience broke out in applause. As the noise died down, she concluded, "Now old Sojourner hasn't got nothing more to say."

Many people in the audience left their seats to congratulate the black woman. She thanked them for their kind words and encouragement. For years, Sojourner Truth had traveled the country speaking on issues of freedom. And from the beginning, it had often been a long and lonely road.

ONE

Colonel Johannes Hardenbergh made the customary visit to the slave quarters on his farm near the Hudson River in upstate New York. Whenever there was a new birth on his plantation—a calf, a lamb, or a slave—the colonel inspected the new property that increased his wealth. In this case, a daughter had been born to his slaves, James and Betsey. They had named her Isabella, a name Colonel Hardenbergh liked, but in private, James and Betsey called her Belle.

In 1626, Dutch settlers had come to the United States and gathered in a colony they called New Netherland. They began importing slaves from Africa to work their farms. Thirty-eight years later, the British seized the colony, changed the name to New York, and continued to bring slaves into the area. By 1723, blacks composed about 15 percent of New York's population—making them a critical part of the local economy.

The Hardenbergh estate was in a hilly neighborhood called by the Dutch name Swartekill (now just north of Rifton), part of the town of Hurley. It was within sight of the Catskill Mountains and near two small rivers, the Swartekill and the Wallkill, which spilled into the larger Rondout Creek about six miles before it flowed into the Hudson River.

Johannes Hardenbergh, the owner of the infant Isabella, had been a member of the New York Colonial Assembly and a colonel in the Revolutionary War. He operated a gristmill and was a large landowner. His land reached from Swartekill south for several miles along the Wallkill River. Although most of Ulster County did not have slaves, the Hardenberghs were wealthier than most families and owned seven slaves.

Although Dutch descendants like Colonel Hardenbergh learned English, they clung to their native language. They taught their slaves only Dutch so that they could better control the slaves' behavior. If the slaves couldn't speak English, they couldn't communicate with the majority of the people around them.

Belle's parents had served Hardenbergh faithfully for many years, and Belle was their eleventh child. Belle's father was a tall, strong man who was proud of his ability to do hard work. James was called Baumfree, a Low Dutch word that meant "tree." But years of hard work had taken a toll on this big man.

Betsey, Belle's mother, was a big, stocky woman with large hands. She was called Mau Mau Brett. Mau Mau Brett was much younger than Baumfree, but they loved each other and had a good marriage. Each of their other children had died or been sold into slavery. Belle's parents worried that she might be sold, as well.

The exact date of her birth is unknown because slave births weren't recorded. Some people claimed she was born in either 1776 or 1777, but it is more likely that she was born about 1797.

Slavery cast a long shadow over the lives of slave parents and their children. They had no control over their families. Children often were taken and sold from their families. Their parents couldn't protect them. The best that Baumfree and Mau Mau Brett could do for Belle was to teach her how to handle her life.

If a slave disobeyed, punishment was often harsh, so at an early age, Belle was taught obedience. Her parents also instilled in Belle the importance of hard work, honesty, and loyalty. Another value they taught was suffering in silence. "Never make a fuss in front of the white folk," her mother told Belle. "When you've got to cry, cry alone."

When Belle was about three years old, Colonel Hardenbergh died. His son Charles had recently built a large limestone house in the nearby hills. He moved his inheritance of livestock and ten slaves, including Belle and her parents, to his new home. The new property had no slave housing, so Charles moved his slaves into the damp cellar of the stone house to eat and sleep together.

During the day, only a small amount of light came in through the tiny cellar window. At night the slaves lit a fire in the room and slept on hard wooden pallets. If it rained, water seeped through cracks in the walls and turned the floor into a pool of mud. During the winter, the slaves huddled together around a fire to escape the bitter cold and wrapped worn-out blankets around themselves as they tried to sleep on their pallets. In the summer, the cellar was hot, humid, and smelly; so most of the time, the slaves slept outside.

In spite of the harsh living conditions, Belle's parents remained obedient to their new master and worked hard at plowing and harvesting the crops in his fields. Consequently, their master developed some affection for the couple and eventually gave them their own land. Then Baumfree and Mau Mau Brett could raise their own corn, tobacco, and other crops to trade with their neighbors for additional food and clothing.

Soon after Belle and her parents moved to the Hardenbergh farm, her brother Peter was born. Now there was someone else for the little girl to love. One night when both children were still very young, their mother took them outside and told them to sit under a tree.

"My children," she said to them, "there is a God who hears and sees you." The two small children looked around them, but they couldn't see God.

"Where does God live?" Belle asked her mother.

"He lives in the sky," their mother answered, "and when you are beaten or cruelly treated or fall into any trouble, you must ask His help, and He will always hear and help you."

Clinging to the promise of a powerful guardian in the sky, Belle faced the difficulties in her life with increased confidence. This confidence continued to grow as Belle grew older and learned new things. On Sundays, Belle and the other slaves didn't have to work in their master's orchards or fields. Belle learned how to row a boat and ride a horse. Her mother taught her to obey her master, to recite the Lord's Prayer every day, and never to steal or lie.

Later Belle's mother told her how—many years earlier—Michael and Nancy, Belle's older brother and sister, had been snatched from their family. One snowy winter morning, some men in a horse-drawn sled stopped at the cabin where Belle's family lived. Michael was delighted when the men told him that he was going for a ride on the sled. Quickly the boy jumped onto the sled. Suddenly, his joy turned to fear. One of the men walked out of the cabin with a large box containing his sister, Nancy. She was screaming.

Afraid of these men, Michael jumped off the sled, ran inside the cabin, and hid under a bed. The men came into the cabin, dragged Michael outside, put him on the sled, and then drove away. Their master had sold these children. Belle's parents never saw Michael or Nancy again.

Despite her mother's fears that Belle would be snatched away and sold to someone else, the family remained together until she was about eleven years old. In 1808, Charles Hardenbergh suddenly died, and his heirs decided to auction off his horses, cattle, and slaves.

The day of the auction, the Stone Ridge Farm was crowded with people. Belle stood trembling beside her mother. "I don't want to leave you, Mau Mau! What if they beat me? Why can't I go free like you and Baumfree?"

"Hush, Belle," her mother said softly in Dutch.

Then Belle's father, Baumfree said, "Nobody would buy a broken-down old horse like me. The law says Old Master's kin have to take care of me, so they're letting me and Mau Mau go free to get rid of us."

Almost thirty years earlier, a New York law had been passed that allowed any slave over fifty years old to be freed. The law also required that the freed slave be able to earn a living. Years of living in the cold, damp cellar had crippled Baumfree's legs and hands with arthritis. He was unable to work.

Even so, Hardenbergh's heirs decided to free both Baumfree and Mau Mau. Younger and in better health, Mau Mau could support both of them. The couple was allowed to continue living in the dark cellar as long as Mau Mau continued to work for the family. Baumfree and Mau Mau had no choice but to accept the offer and stay in the cellar. They couldn't speak any English, so they could not function in the English-speaking world around them. The couple knew Belle and Peter were headed to the slave auction.

With tears in her eyes, Mau Mau told Belle, "Child, you can't stay with us. All our other children were sold. Now it's your turn and your little brother's."

"Just remember what we've taught you, Belle," Baumfree said. "Obey your master and work hard."

Mau Mau chimed in, "And if you pray to God, He'll see that you're treated right."

A white man motioned for Belle. It was time for her to be auctioned. "Good-bye, Mau Mau. Good-bye, Baumfree."

Belle and her brother Peter stood in the auction area. Peter was sold first to a man who didn't live in the area. Although Belle felt like crying, she stood in stony silence. Over and over, she repeated the Lord's Prayer to herself.

The auctioneer called out, "Hardenbergh's Belle, age eleven, good strong body." The girl couldn't understand the words since they were in English, but she knew it meant that she was being sold. At first no one in the crowd offered a bid. Belle thought maybe she would be allowed to stay on the farm with her parents. Then the auctioneer ordered Belle to turn to the right. When the girl did not move, the man grabbed her and turned her. "Look how tall she is, even now. She'll be a big woman in maturity, have lots of children, and be able to do a lot of work."

Still no one offered to buy Belle. She continued to pray that she would not be sold. Then the auctioneer threw in a flock of sheep, saying, "They go with the girl."

John Neely, a shopkeeper from Kingston Landing, New York, stood in the audience and recognized a bargain that he couldn't pass up. He offered one hundred dollars, and with a crack from the auctioneer's gavel, the sheep and Belle were sold. Belle had a new master.

While Neely thought he had struck a good deal, his wife was not impressed. When Belle couldn't understand Mrs. Neely's instructions and responded in Dutch, Mrs. Neely beat Belle. Belle tried to learn English from her new masters, but Mrs. Neely had no patience for teaching. War was declared between Mrs. Neely and her young slave, and Belle had no chance of winning. Mrs. Neely repeatedly slapped Belle. One day Mrs. Neely's frustrations grew unbearable. That Sunday morning, she sent her slave out to the barn where Mr. Neely was waiting for her. In the barn, Belle found her master heating some metal rods over red-hot coals. Without offering any explanation, Mr. Neely grabbed Belle's hands and tied them together. He tore Belle's shirt off her back and began to beat the girl's back with the rods. Belle pleaded with her master to stop and called out to God for help. Finally, she fainted. Belle lay in the straw, soaked with her own blood, and wept bitterly. It was her first beating, and she determined to do whatever was necessary to avoid another one.

Afterward Belle crept off into the woods and cried out to God. "Was it right for them to beat me, God? You've got to get me a new master. You have to help me, God." But Belle's prayers were not instantly answered.

Mrs. Neely continued to scream at her young slave with confusing instructions, but Belle learned how to cope. On her own initiative, Belle scrubbed the floors so clean that Mrs. Neely had no cause to complain. Slowly, Belle learned to speak some English, but her first language, Dutch, always showed in her accented speech.

As Belle worked for the Neelys, she sometimes wondered, *Will I ever see my family again?* One winter evening, when Belle had almost lost hope of seeing her family, her father arrived at the Neely home. Baumfree looked old and very sick. He told Belle how a family named Simmons had rented the big house but permitted her parents to continue living in the cellar. Mau Mau worked hard, but they barely had enough money to buy food or clothing.

Belle listened to her father and didn't mention her own struggles. Baumfree noticed that despite the deep snow on the ground, his daughter didn't have warm clothing or shoes. When he asked about it, Belle explained, "I can't wear Mrs. Neely's hand-me-downs. They are too small."

As her father prepared to leave, he hugged Belle, but she drew back in pain. Baumfree walked out to the gate of the property. Belle followed her father through the snow by stepping in his large footprints. Once the pair was out of the Neelys' sight, Belle showed him her scarred back. Baumfree was filled with rage at her beating, but even worse was the knowledge that he hadn't been able to protect his daughter. Although Baumfree was old and crippled, he was free. He vowed to use his freedom to help his daughter.

As he left, Baumfree promised Belle that he would try to help her. Unfortunately, for Belle, change took time. She continued working for the Neely family.

After about two years with the Neelys, God answered what Belle later called a "desperate prayer." Somehow old Baumfree persuaded Martin Schryver to purchase Belle from the Neelys for $105. The fisherman didn't own any other slaves but had a farm and a tavern on the Rondout Creek. This new location was only about five miles from the Neely farm.

Belle worked hard for her new owner, partially from gratitude but partially from fear of receiving another beating. The Schryvers were a coarse and uneducated couple, but they weren't cruel. They spoke both English and Dutch, so Belle could easily talk with them. Without someone yelling at her constantly, Belle's English became much more fluent.

The Schryvers treated Belle well, although sometimes she felt uncomfortable around the coarse men who frequented their tavern. A hard worker, Belle hoed cornfields, hauled in fish, and gathered roots and herbs for the homemade beer sold in the tavern. She had a great deal of freedom to roam outdoors. With her new owners, Belle had plenty to eat. She grew almost six feet tall before she turned fourteen years old. During the winter, Belle had a warm shawl and even shoes—a cast-off pair from her master because women's shoes were too small for her large feet.

Unfortunately, Belle's parents were doing poorly as freed slaves. They found it difficult to get enough food to eat and grew ill. Too soon, Mau Mau Brett grew sick and died. Belle and her brother Peter were both able to attend their mother's funeral and visit their father. Poor Baumfree was grief-stricken. Despite Belle's concern for her father, she couldn't do anything for Baumfree. She had to return to the Schryver family. She prayed that God would give her a means to help her father.

While working at the tavern, Belle overheard many conversations about slavery. Her ears perked up whenever the people began talking about abolition. It was a new English word that Belle had learned. The abolitionists were people who wanted to end slavery. While Belle did not understand much about it, she knew that if she were free, she'd go straight to Baumfree.

Soon afterward, Belle received a message that her father, Baumfree, had starved to death. After Mau Mau's death, Baumfree had been allowed to continue living on the Hardenbergh estate along with two other slaves. But soon the other slaves died, and Baumfree was left in the cellar alone. Too sick to care for himself, Baumfree lived his last few months cold, filthy, and forgotten.

When the Hardenbergh family learned of the old man's death, they donated a pine box and a jug of whiskey for mourners. It was their final tribute to a man who had been a faithful, kind, and honest servant.

Other than Peter, Belle had no known immediate family still living. She felt alone, and God seemed so distant. In her own determined way, Belle decided to pray for the only thing left: her freedom.

TWO

One day in 1810, a short, ruddy-faced man came into the tavern. As Belle served the various customers, this man began a conversation with Schryver.

"I need this girl to help out on my farm in New Paltz," the man said. "I'll buy her for three hundred dollars."

The price was three times what the Schryvers had paid. Although the couple didn't approve of slavery and had plans to free Belle when she reached eighteen, three hundred dollars was a lot of money in those days. The Schryvers accepted the offer, and Belle had a new master, John Dumont.

When Belle came to the Dumonts' farm, the ten other slaves welcomed her and gave the new slave a quick description of her new master.

According to the slaves, Mr. Dumont was a decent man and didn't deal out excessive punishment. They said, "He doesn't believe in separating families, and if you do your work and don't make trouble, then you'll get along fine."

When the slaves began to talk about the mistress of the house, they told a completely different story. "She's got a spiteful tongue and a sour temperament. As much as possible, keep away from her because it will only get you into trouble."

Keeping away from Mrs. Dumont was impossible for Belle because she worked part-time in the big house, and Mrs. Dumont took an instant dislike to her quiet-spoken new slave. Mrs. Dumont pulled the two white maids aside and told them, "Isabella should be taught a lesson. Make sure you grind down her proud attitude."

Despite the harsh treatment from her mistress and coworkers in the Dumont house, Belle remembered her mother's lessons on obedience, so she always tried hard to please her owners. Throughout her childhood, Belle had been taught to repay evil with good. She had developed a deep belief that her hard work would eventually be rewarded.

Belle was growing into a teenager, and while she had the body of a woman, she had the mind of a young girl. Since there weren't any adults whom Belle felt she could confide in, she made her own decisions and solved her own problems. Sometimes these decisions were incorrect or based on faulty beliefs.

Belle decided that Master Dumont was a god. She reasoned that God knew everything, so He must know about slavery. And if the Lord of the

Universe knew about slavery and didn't—or couldn't—stop it, then her master had to be very powerful—almost a god himself.

Convinced that her master was an all-seeing and all-knowing god, Belle was driven by fear. To gain favor with Dumont, Belle often worked until she dropped from exhaustion. Convinced that her master could know her thoughts, Belle told him everything—even reporting the actions of her fellow slaves.

The other slaves grew impatient and critical of her. They called her, "white folks' nigger," and drove her out of their circle of friends. The other slaves couldn't understand Belle's confusion and hurt.

From Cato, the Dumonts' driver who also served as the slaves' preacher, Belle learned that God didn't always answer prayers immediately or stop evil people in their tracks. Cato told Belle, "He studies on the situation, hoping the evildoers will make a change of heart and correct themselves." Through her talk with Cato, Belle began to understand the human side of her master. Dumont wasn't a god, and if he wasn't a god, then Belle didn't need to be afraid all the time. She could talk to the great God in the sky without her master hearing her pleas for help and understanding. For a while, this conversation with Cato lifted the heavy burden of confusion from Belle's heart.

When Belle's attitude toward Dumont changed, the other slaves began to trust her again. But she still felt lonely without any family around. Through her years with Dumont, Belle came to accept that loneliness would be her companion.

One day, as John Dumont stood in the distance watching his slaves, he thought, *It's time for Belle to get married and begin to have children. Tom would make a good husband for her.* Dumont had purchased Tom as a young man, and he had worked many years on the farm. To Dumont, it made no difference that Belle and Tom did not love each other. They were just two slaves.

When Belle learned of her master's decision, she insisted that a real preacher marry them. Dumont must have seen Belle's determination, because he agreed to the request, and a black preacher married the couple.

Belle could see that her husband had at one time been a good-looking man, but when she married him, he was stooped and old from his years of hard labor in the fields. Before long, the young bride learned that Tom had also suffered heartache and loss. Years earlier, his love had been sold away from him to a family in New York City. Enraged and hurt by the sudden loss of his wife, Tom ran away on foot to the large city so he could find her. With the help of freed slaves in the city, Tom managed to stay away from the Dumont farm for a month. He never located his wife, but slave trackers caught Tom and returned him to the estate.

Belle reached out and gently touched the scars on her husband's back and neck. She wept from the memory of her own beatings. The wounds from their terrible whippings had scarred over, but the memories were seared into their minds forever.

In their own way, Tom and Belle loved each other. Belle was considerate and caring for her husband, and Tom was quiet and agreeable. After a year of marriage, the couple had a daughter named Diana. During the next twelve years, Belle gave birth to four more children: Elizabeth, Hannah, Peter, and Sophia. Each child learned the lessons that Belle had learned from her mother: Never steal, never lie, and always obey your master.

While taking on the duties of a mother and wife, Belle continued her hard work for the Dumonts. Her life was increasingly complicated with nursing and caring for her children. Sometimes she strapped one of her children to her back as she hoed a field. Other times she tied an old sheet to the branch of a tree and had the older children watch the younger child in a makeshift swing. Other slaves on the Dumont farm also helped raise each other's children.

Year after year, Belle chopped wood, planted corn, and hauled buckets of water for the Dumonts, but she never gave up hope that one day she would be free. In 1824, she finally learned the good news. Pressured by abolitionist groups, the New York State legislature had passed an emancipation law. The law required that all slaves born before July 4, 1799, be freed on July 4, 1827. Male slaves born after that date were to gain their freedom when they turned twenty-eight, and female slaves were to be freed after their twenty-fifth birthday.

Belle struggled over the date of her birthday. No one was certain of the exact day, but the Dumonts agreed that Belle would be eligible for freedom in 1827. The slaves looked forward to what they called "Freedom Day." Even though three years stood between her and Freedom Day, just the idea of freedom put a bounce in Belle's step. She sang while she worked and kept her sights set unswervingly on freedom.

One day in 1825, Dumont came to Belle with an offer for her freedom. He complimented her on her hard work for the past fifteen years. Two more years remained until he was required by law to set Belle free.

"I'll let you go a year earlier than the law says I need to if you promise to work extra hard for me," Dumont said. "And as a bonus, I'll let Tom go free with you, and you can live in the cabin that I own down the road."

Belle accepted the offer. Over the next several months, she put in extra-long hours of hard work—planting, washing, cooking, cleaning. Then in the spring, Belle cut her hand on the blade of a scythe. Because she didn't slow down and care for the wound, it didn't heal properly. Despite the way the wound bled and hurt, Belle never missed a day's work. The thought of freedom kept her going. When the year ended, Belle had fulfilled her promise to Dumont.

She waited for Dumont to free her, but he didn't say a word about the agreement. Finally, she could stand it no longer. She burst into the house and confronted her master.

With arrogance in his voice and a wave of his hand, Dumont told Belle, "Our deal is off. Go back to work." Dumont had probably originally planned to free Belle as he had said. That year, however, the Hessian fly had killed most of his crops, and he was facing financial ruin and needed all his slaves—especially Belle—to plant the spring crops and make a new start.

Belle was furious at the curt dismissal from her master. "Why won't you honor your word?"

Dumont searched for any excuse. Then he noticed her bandaged hand and said, "You can't expect me to free you. With a hurt hand, you can't expect me to believe that you've put in extra work."

Belle touched her injured hand, stiff and twisted from hard work and neglect. Anger exploded like the steam roaring from a kettle on a hot stove. She saw a true picture of her master—a little man whose words were small and meaningless. Without bothering to argue or defend herself, Belle turned and walked away. In her mind, she was a free woman and had stopped being Dumonts' Belle. Belle decided to run away. When she escaped, she wouldn't be able to take her children with her, and she wanted to leave on somewhat good terms with Dumont. So she decided that she would first finish spinning the annual harvest of wool.

THREE

Early one fall morning, Belle gathered together her five children, ranging in age from twelve years to less than a year. It was time for a serious talk with them and her husband. Diana, Elizabeth, Hannah, Peter, and baby Sophia listened quietly to their mother.

"Mr. Dumont has cheated me out of my freedom, and I'll not let him get away with it," Belle explained to Tom and her children. "I've got to run away, and I can't take you with me, but I'll be back for you. Someday we'll be together again."

Tom objected to his wife's attitude. "Belle, calm down. It's not worth trying to escape, because we'll be free anyway in another year." But Tom couldn't dissuade his wife. Belle was determined to escape.

Fearing that her plans might be discovered, Belle told no one her exact plans for escape—not even Tom and her children.

On the morning of her escape, Belle woke up before dawn, gathered together some food and clothing, and wrapped them in a large piece of cloth. Next Belle bundled up Sophia, whom she'd decided to take with her. Belle left the Dumont farm just as the sun was starting to light the sky. When full daylight arrived, she was far from her master's house.

At the top of a hill, Belle stopped to rest and scan the horizon. No one was following her, yet she was still troubled. She had no idea where to go or what to do to be safe from Dumont. She turned to God for direction.

While Belle was praying, a memory flickered into her mind. Long ago, she had been walking along the road when a stranger stopped her. He'd said, "It's not right that you should be a slave. God does not want it." Now, as she walked along the road and prayed, Belle remembered the man, Levi Rowe, a Quaker who lived down the road from the Dumont estate. Generally, Quakers were active abolitionists—a word that Belle had never forgotten.

She decided to ask Rowe for help. In the early morning light, Belle walked to his house and knocked on his door. It took a long time for him to answer because he was old and very ill.

In quick bursts of emotion, the frightened runaway slave poured out her story, and Levi Rowe patiently listened. Rowe was too ill to help Belle, but he directed her to the home of a Quaker couple named Isaac and Maria Van Wagener. Belle thanked Mr. Rowe for his advice and continued her journey with fresh hope. She had known the Van Wageners since her childhood. A few miles down the road, Belle reached their home. After hearing Belle's story, the couple welcomed Belle inside and offered her a job and place to stay.

A short time later, Dumont arrived at the Van Wagener home. He was searching for his slave and suspected the Quakers had offered her shelter. Confronting his longtime slave, Dumont threatened Belle with harsh punishment for running away. "I insist that you return at once."

Belle refused. Dumont tried another tactic. "I know where you are, Belle. When you are not looking, I'll steal Sophia, and then you'll come back."

As the Van Wageners watched the struggle between Belle and her master, Mr. Van Wagener offered to buy Belle for twenty dollars and her baby for five dollars. Dumont could see that Belle wasn't going to return to his farm, and even if she did return, she wouldn't work hard for him as she had in the past. He accepted Van Wagener's offer and left in a huff.

Through the winter, Belle worked for the Van Wageners. The kind and gentle couple welcomed her in all ways. They lived simply, without a lot of frills. Often they sat for hours meditating on the Bible and praying—never saying a word. Such a life marked a sharp contrast to the storytelling and constant chatter in the Dumont slave quarters. On the Dumont estate, slaves never went to church or read the Bible.

Although content to stay with the Van Wageners, the thought of losing her children tempted Belle to return to the Dumont estate. Years later, Belle told friends that a powerful force turned her around whenever she tried to leave.

Freedom Day, when all of the slaves would be freed, was getting closer every day.

But Freedom Day didn't arrive soon enough. One day Belle learned that Dumont had sold her only son, Peter, to a Dr. Gedney. The new owner planned to take the boy to England with him as a body servant. Mr. Van Wagener learned that Dr. Gedney had taken Peter to New York City before discovering that the boy was too young to serve him properly. So Dr. Gedney had gone on alone to England. Before leaving, he'd sent the boy to his brother, Solomon Gedney, in New Paltz. Solomon had sold Peter to a wealthy Alabama planter named Fowler, who had just married the Gedneys' sister Liza.

When Belle heard that Peter was headed to the South, she was furious. She hurried to the Dumonts and confronted her old master with anger and determination. From Belle's perspective, Dumont had started the chain of events with his initial sale.

Mr. Dumont contended that he knew nothing about Peter's move to Alabama. He had sold Peter to Dr. Gedney as a body servant, and that was all he knew about the situation.

Because Belle got no aid from her former master, she turned to Solomon Gedney's mother, from whom she received even less compassion.

Belle walked along the road and prayed, "Show those around me that You are my helper!" She turned once again to the Quaker abolitionists for help. A number of them met at the Van Wageners' home to discuss her plight and what they could do to help.

A New York law forbade selling slaves out of state. If Solomon Gedney was found guilty, he would face a fourteen-year jail sentence and perhaps a stiff financial penalty. Peter would immediately be freed.

The Van Wageners recommended that Belle seek help from their friends in Poppletown, a town near Kingston, New York. She would need to file suit against Solomon Gedney.

When the grand jury heard Belle's case, they decided in her favor. Belle's Quaker friends had helped her hire a lawyer, Esquire Chipp, and he helped Belle make out a writ. She took the legal document to the constable of New Paltz. The document ordered Solomon Gedney to appear before the court with Peter.

Unfortunately, the constable served the document on the wrong man. This gave Solomon Gedney advance warning. Gedney slipped away to Mobile, Alabama, before the constable realized his mistake with the paperwork. For months, all Belle could do was wait.

In the spring, Belle heard that Gedney had returned to New Paltz, so she went to his home to claim her son. "That boy is mine," Gedney barked, slamming the door in her face.

Belle refused to back down. She visited Attorney Chipp again. This time, the writ was properly served on the right man. Gedney appeared in court and paid a six-hundred-dollar bond, promising to appear in court and face the charges that he had sold Peter out of state.

Just when things looked promising, Belle faced another delay. Her attorney told Belle that her case would have to wait several months until court was in session. Belle complained about this new delay, but Chipp asked her to be patient with the court system.

Chipp could think of nothing else that could be done to speed up Belle's case, so he sent her away.

While walking back to the Van Wageners' home, Belle met a man on the road. He greeted her and asked, "Have they returned your son to you yet?"

Belle told the man the latest news and that she didn't know what else to do.

The man pointed to a stone house. "The lawyer Demain lives there. Go to him and tell him your case with Peter. I think he'll help you with it."

After Demain heard the details of Belle's case, he promised to return Peter within twenty-four hours for a fee of five dollars. Belle's Quaker friends gave her the money, and Demain went to the courthouse. He quickly returned with bad news. Peter didn't want to return to his mother. The next morning, everyone involved in the case appeared before the judge in his chambers.

"No, she's not my mother!" Peter told the judge.

The judge wasn't fooled for a minute. One look into the boy's eyes made it clear that he was terrified of his master.

The judge awarded the boy to his mother. It was official. After Gedney left the room and Peter was reassured that he didn't have to go with his former master, the boy cautiously changed his story. Belle had won freedom for her son and could take Peter home. That evening, as she prepared Peter for bed, Belle noticed that his back was streaked with old and fresh wounds. "Peter," Belle whispered gently to her son, "what kind of monster would do this to a six-year-old?"

Peter finally told the truth. "Master Gedney told me to say that I didn't know you," he explained as tears ran down his cheeks. "He said that if I didn't say what he wanted, then I would get the worst whipping I've ever had."

Belle touched the scarred back of her small son. She was angry about his beatings and treatment. She called on God to give them a double portion of what had been taken away.

Belle didn't think about the fact that she was one of the first black women in the United States to win a court case. She was simply happy to have her son restored to her.

FOUR

After Belle gained Peter's freedom, she stayed in Kingston, New York, where she found work with a family named Latin. Peter continued living with Belle, but Sophia, at about age two, went to live with her other sisters, who were still on the Dumont estate.

On July 4, 1827, Tom, Belle's husband, was freed. Belle was still in Kingston, and Tom lived in the town of New Paltz. The couple found it impossible to build a home together, and in time they grew apart. Until his health failed, Tom did odd jobs in the area, but he died before the end of the year.

While Belle lived in Kingston, she did laundry for one of Solomon Gedney's relatives. One day, as she hung out the wash on the clothesline, Belle heard a scream from inside the house. She listened as a letter was read aloud from the Alabama authorities. Liza Fowler's husband had beaten his wife to death. The letter explained that Fowler had gone mad and would be kept locked up, "for the rest of his unhappy life."

Before long, Belle and Peter left Kingston and returned to the Van Wageners. The couple welcomed them back and provided work for Belle. She clung to her dream of having all her children under one roof; but for the time being, all she could do was be near them. She settled her differences with the Dumonts, and they allowed her to visit her daughters regularly.

While living with the Van Wageners, Belle became so comfortable that she nearly forgot about God. In her way of thinking, God was someone a person called on for help in trouble. But as her 1850 narrative reports, "God revealed Himself to me with all of the suddenness of lightning." She cried out, "Oh God, how big You be!" Being overwhelmed with the presence of God's greatness, Belle fell on her hands and knees, trying to crawl away from the Almighty, but she could find no place to hide.

Then Belle felt the wickedness of her life and the need for someone to speak to God for her. Years later, Belle described this moment as her conversion to Christ. A space opened between her and God, and in the space she suddenly saw Jesus. She said later, "I felt Jesus come between God and me as sensibly as I ever felt an umbrella raised over my head. . . . I saw the hair on His head, and I saw His cheek, and I saw Him smile, and I have seen the same smile on people since."

Belle's conversion not only saved her life, but it also drastically changed how she related to other people. Later in her life, she explained, "I was civilized not by people, but by Jesus. When I got religion, I found some work to do to benefit somebody."

Belle remembered her time with the Van Wageners as some of the happiest months of her life. When the work for the day was finished, Mr. Van Wagener pulled out his Bible and read aloud to Belle and the others. These lessons from God's Word gave Belle a better understanding of the relationship between God and humanity.

During those months at the Van Wageners, Peter's body began to heal, but Belle realized he also needed emotional healing. As a child, Peter enjoyed running and playing along the wharves in New Paltz. Huge ships came into port, to Peter's great excitement. He thrilled at the sailors' stories of adventures.

Then Peter began to steal and, when caught, lie about it. At first, Belle wasn't too hard on her son because of his difficult past. She tried to keep Peter occupied by having him work for a man who managed the river locks on Rondout Creek. She thought it would fill Peter's days and keep him out of trouble. Instead, Peter grew worse.

Then Belle tried to locate a church home for Peter. A new Methodist church had opened in New Paltz. The Methodist meeting was held in a private house. Knowing that it was not customary for blacks to enter white meetings unless they sat in a separate "Negro pew," Belle was afraid to enter the house. So she stood outside the house and peered in through the open window.

The preacher, a circuit rider named Mr. Ferriss, read the words of a hymn, "There is a holy city, a world of light above," that described the immortal life that awaited the faithful. Line by line, he sang it and thumped the floor with its rhythm. The congregation sang after him. Outside, Belle also learned the hymn and remembered it for the rest of her life.

While Belle delighted in the music, she still wondered if she should walk inside with Peter. Then she remembered 1 Chronicles 29:15–16: "For we are strangers before thee, and sojourners, as were all our fathers. . . . We have prepared to build thee an house for thine holy name cometh of thine hand, and is all thine own." Belle found new strength from God to enter the church, and the congregation welcomed mother and son to their meetings.

Methodists were members of a new, populist denomination that was disdained by the more formal, elite Dutch Reformed who tended to dominate the area. Kingston Methodist, like many Methodist churches elsewhere, welcomed blacks. The Methodists emphasized direct, personal experience with God; they witnessed and spoke without preparation; and they liked to sing—all of which suited Belle. She took her children with her to church as often as possible.

At one of these church meetings, Belle met Miss Geer, a vacationing schoolteacher from New York City. While Miss Geer related well to Belle, the schoolteacher was struck by Peter's inquisitive nature and bright mind. She told Belle, "There are many jobs available in New York City and a world of opportunities for Peter in terms of his education. You should consider moving to New York when you can."

The idea opened Belle's mind to all kinds of possibilities. Why shouldn't she move to New York City? She might find a better-paying job and be able to save money for a home. Then as her children reached twenty-one and were freed by Dumont, they would have a place to live in New York City.

At the end of the summer of 1829, Belle and Peter said a tearful good-bye to the rest of their family and left New Paltz. They promised to keep in touch with the Van Wageners, then boarded a boat to carry them down the Hudson River to New York City.

When the boat pulled into New York Harbor, Belle presented an imposing figure. She stood six feet tall and was dressed in a plain gray dress with a white bandanna tied around her head. Before leaving New Paltz, Belle had a cobbler make her first pair of shoes. Usually she walked barefoot or wore men's boots because her feet were size twelve.

Miss Geer met Belle and Peter at the docks with her carriage. As the carriage rolled over the cobblestone streets, Peter clung to his mother and looked wide-eyed at the new and interesting sights. The busy streets and masses of people amazed Belle, who had only known small-town life. The clutter and the noise of the city bombarded her senses and confused her. People were everywhere and in constant motion. When their carriage passed some buildings that were several stories high, Belle looked up and felt dizzy.

Miss Geer had arranged for Belle to begin working for the Whitings, the Garfield family, and later a prominent newspaper family. She enrolled Peter in a navigation school, which captured his interest in ships and sailing.

Through wandering around the neighborhoods, Belle began to learn her way around New York City. She often listened as people stood talking outside a shop or market. Before long, she learned that Five Points was the poorest section of the city. Widowed mothers with children and people down on their luck lived with the murderers, thieves, and prostitutes. Thousands of Irish immigrants flooded the city on an almost-daily basis. Belle saw how many of these new arrivals didn't have a job or place to live, so they crowded into dirty conditions that were worse than any night she'd spent in the Hardenberghs' cellar. Belle was handicapped because she didn't know how to read and write. She could not read the Bible, even though she believed that knowing the Bible was important. She could not guide Peter in his schoolwork at the navigation school. She did not know for a long time that Peter was only pretending to attend school. Belle had a bank account but could not read the bank records.

There is some evidence that friends tried to teach Belle to read and write. Much later in her life, Belle said, "When I was liberated, there was an attempt made to educate me, but I could not get beyond the ABCs."

While Belle remained illiterate, she became a zealous Methodist. Before long, Belle discovered the long-standing free black community in New York, and she proudly joined their growing ranks. One day Belle was told that whites and blacks worshipped in separate services at the Methodist church on John Street. To see it for herself, Belle visited the Mother Zion African Methodist Episcopal (AME) Church.

The AME church was the oldest African American organization in the United States. During her days in New York City, Belle was a loved member of this AME church and known for her spirit-filled prayers and original hymns.

According to a newsman who befriended Belle later, she believed what she was taught at the church; she outprayed and outpreached her fellows; she "became the means of converting some by her zeal, and was much respected." Still Belle wanted to learn, especially from whites.

Belle, at about the age of thirty-three, was looking for someone to guide her, someone educated and who seemed to be in touch with God.

One Sunday a few months later, a man and a woman approached Belle after the AME services. The woman told her, "I am your sister Sophia, and this is your brother Michael. We are also the children of Mau Mau Brett and Baumfree. Some of our friends told us that you worshipped in this church, so we came here to find you." Incredible joy filled Belle as she was reunited with one of her older sisters and with the brother who had been snatched away on a sled as a child and sold into slavery.

The three siblings spent the entire day talking and catching up on their lives. Sophia was living in Newburgh, New York, while Michael had moved to New York City. Belle asked about their other sister, Nancy, who was sold at the same time as Michael.

"Nancy lived here in New York," Michael said. "In fact, she attended Mother Zion until her recent death." Then Michael described Nancy's appearance, and Belle shrieked with surprise and delight. Nancy had been one of the elderly mothers in the congregation. Belle had prayed alongside Nancy at the altar, and they had sung hymns together. The women had never known that they were sisters.

Miss Geer continued to encourage Belle and Peter as they adjusted to life in New York City. She invited Belle to join her and some others who went into the Five Points area of New York where they told people about the changing power of Jesus Christ. A few times, Belle went with the small group of Christians into this poor section of the city. They greeted people on the street corners and sang hymns in the street. But Belle wondered why they did it. *The people who live in Five Points need food, decent houses, and clothing,* she thought. *There must be another way to show Christ's love.*

When Belle heard about the Magdalene Asylum, a shelter for homeless women, she offered to help out. Elijah Pierson ran the shelter at a large gray house on Bowery Hill. Unknown to Belle and his followers, Pierson was a religious fake. Several years earlier, Pierson had been a merchant, but after an intensely spiritual experience, Pierson had become religious. The Piersons sold their home and started the Magdalene Asylum for homeless women. He claimed to run the Magdalene Asylum with instructions directly from God. Such a claim wasn't hard for Belle to believe, because she felt God directly guided her decisions and life. Belle liked Pierson and agreed to work part-time and often participated in his religious services.

The Piersons became noted for their unusual religious practices, such as going without food or water for four days or longer while holding prayer sessions. They hoped that such long fasts would win favor in God's eyes. The couple encouraged others like Belle to follow their example.

Pierson's wife, Sara, discovered the dangers of fasting too late. After a prolonged fast in 1830, she died. Her illness and death deeply affected her husband. Pierson was so convinced that God had given him supernatural powers that he called his followers together and attempted to bring Sara back to life.

When their attempt to bring back his wife failed, Elijah Pierson again claimed that he had been given divine powers and God had chosen him to start a kingdom of God on earth. One Sunday morning, Belle answered the front door of the asylum. She was startled to see a long-bearded figure in a flowing robe. His eyes were piercing, and Belle thought the man might be an angel. He wore his beard long because Matthias believed that no man who shaved could be a true Christian. In actuality, Matthias was a middle-aged hustler named Robert Matthews who had arrived in the city with a new scheme to steal money from people.

In Albany, New York, Matthias had a wife and children. His wife, who believed him to be honest, nevertheless opposed his calling himself a Jew. She rejected his beliefs and declined to travel with him on his trips to convert the world. Matthias abandoned his wife and family for long periods.

Within months, Pierson and Matthias had become partners in a wicked plan of deceit. Pierson now claimed to be John the Baptist, while Matthias claimed to be God on earth. Belle listened to these men, and their smooth talk convinced her that they were exactly who they claimed.

The two men founded their community, called "The Kingdom," on a farm owned by a married couple, Benjamin and Ann Folger. The farm was located near the Hudson River, about thirty miles north of New York City. Every member of the Kingdom donated all their worldly possessions and money. Pierson and Matthias were the only ones who controlled the finances, and they didn't have to report on how the funds were used. Since Belle didn't have much money, the men accepted her into the group on the basis that she would do the washing, ironing, cooking, and cleaning. For her hard work, Belle would gain the privilege of worshipping with the others in the Kingdom.

At the farm, Belle did more than her share of the work. Besides cooking and cleaning, she helped care for the sick. In his Kingdom, Matthias preached and prayed but scarcely allowed anyone else to do so—and certainly not women. He believed the correct role of women was to be obedient and stay at home. Although Belle was accustomed to preaching and praying in public, she seemed to find Matthias's frank insistence on the lower role of women acceptable. She was fascinated with Matthias's openness, and she could not believe that anyone so open could have an evil side to his nature.

Matthias insisted on being called the head of the Kingdom household. He expected to be called Father. Under his firm authority, the house was clean and orderly. At meals, he presided and served all the food. All of the members drank water, but Matthias drank from a silver goblet while the rest of the group drank from ordinary glass tumblers. Except for Matthias's fine clothes and carriage, their lives were generally plain, so their expenses were not great. Belle didn't rebel against Matthias's authority. She accepted Matthias as ordained by God and was devoted to him.

One day the family of one of Matthias's followers brought a charge against him for lunacy. The police came to the house and roughly arrested Matthias. They stripped him, took his money, and cut off his beard. Matthias submitted to the treatment, but Belle offered some resistance to the police. One of the family members who brought the charges against Matthias struck Belle. The police continued to try to put Belle outside of the house, but she continued to return inside.

Some people in the crowd called out that Matthias was an impostor. Belle didn't believe them. The experience drew her closer to Matthias.

The police took Matthias to the Bellevue prison and put him in the section for the insane; but Pierson, supported by Belle, arranged for Matthias's release.

For a while, the members of the community lived in peace and harmony. Then Matthias began to exert complete control over the community, and his unusual teaching caused a great deal of tension in the group. He claimed that every person had a soul that needed to have a spiritual bond with his or her marriage partner. According to Matthias, if their souls matched, then the people should be married and have sexual relations.

Matthias determined that Ann Folger's soul didn't match her husband's soul. Then Matthias issued a divorce (even though he didn't have any legal authority to do so) and married Ann Folger himself. Benjamin Folger was extremely upset over these actions and began to feud with Matthias.

Belle began to tire of the constant bickering and strange religious rituals. She decided that Matthias and Pierson didn't deserve her trust and confidence. While she had no proof of their dishonesty, Belle decided that she didn't want any part of deceiving others, so she prepared to leave.

In August 1834, Belle returned to New York City, and with Miss Geer's help, she got her old job back with the Whiting family. Back in the city, Belle learned that not only had Peter dropped out of school and hired out as a coachman for one of Miss Geer's friends, but also that Peter was running around with a rough crowd. This disturbing turn of events gave her further incentive to break her relationship with the Kingdom.

Belle made a brief trip to the farm to gather her possessions and tell the leaders that she was leaving. Suddenly, Pierson stiffened and collapsed on the floor. By the next morning, he was dead.

Pierson's relatives and friends, as well as people in the neighborhood, raised questions about his death. Suspecting murder, the local coroner asked doctors to examine Pierson's body. A jury investigated and enjoyed the opportunity to poke into the affairs of the Kingdom.

The trial turned into a media circus, and every day the newspapers featured stories about the strange religious group and their two leaders who had used money for their own greedy desires. When the newspapers described the strange worship practices, Belle felt betrayed and hurt. These articles told about cheating, lying, and other evil practices such as adultery. She was as shocked as anyone on the street about these matters. In the aftermath of the trial, the Kingdom began to fall apart. Westchester County seized the Folgers' farm, forcing all of the members to move. Mrs. Folger decided to return to her husband, and the Folgers moved back to their house in New York City. Belle, along with Matthias and his children, moved in with the Folgers, although they were not welcome houseguests.

In September 1834, the Folgers, who were facing business losses and financial trouble, explained to Matthias that they could no longer afford to support the Kingdom. This led to a painful argument between the Folgers and Matthias. Then the Folgers, hoping that it would encourage Belle to leave, paid her twenty-five dollars as wages. Still loyal to Matthias, Belle turned over the money to him and made it clear that she wanted to stay with him. But Matthias returned the money to her.

The Folgers were also hoping to fend off Matthias, so they gave him $530 with the expectation, according to Belle, that he would use it to carry out his dream of buying a farm in the West. By the end of September 1834, Matthias had left the Folger house and gone to Albany to prepare to move West.

Belle expected to go west with Matthias, even if it meant leaving her children behind. On the day that Matthias left the Folger house, Belle also left, taking her luggage with her. She assumed she left the Folgers on good terms.

Traveling north, Belle visited those of her children who were still at the Dumont estate in New Paltz, then took a steamboat up the Hudson River to Albany where she joined Matthias at his wife's house. While there, Belle was surprised to learn that the Folgers had brought charges against Matthias. The police were about to arrest him for stealing the $530 that Belle had understood the Folgers had given him. Confused and upset, Belle returned to New York City.

Once Matthias had left the city, the Folgers had complained to the police that he had obtained the money from them under false pretenses. The Folgers also circulated other charges and fed the suspicions of the community about the Kingdom. They charged that Matthias, with Belle's help, had murdered Pierson by serving him poisoned blackberries. Also the Folgers claimed that Matthias and Belle had tried to murder them by serving them poisoned coffee.

In response to these new charges, the police ordered that Pierson's body be taken out of its grave and reexamined by doctors. Benjamin and Ann Folger took advantage of the publicity and wrote a novel about their experiences, which was thinly based on fact. In this novel, the Folgers blamed a maid for introducing the evil in their holy community. In the story, this "black witch" murdered the leader of the organization, and the book detailed how the murder was accomplished. The public read the novel and believed the story was about Belle. Newspapers published excerpts from the novel and continued to spread the false story.

Gilbert Vale was a friend of Mr. Whiting, Belle's employer. Both men were journalists, and Whiting was convinced that Belle was incapable of any of the crimes that the Folgers had described. Vale was persuaded to take up Belle's cause; and in 1835, he published a pamphlet called *Fanaticism: Its Source and Influence, Illustrated by the Simple Narrative of Isabella*. The pamphlet gave Belle a chance to tell her story to the public. Vale suggested that Belle might sue the Folgers for their published lies, as well as sue the newspapers that had published the novel.

She returned to New Paltz and Kingston to gather character statements from her employers. Her old master John Dumont praised Belle as being "perfectly honest." Isaac Van Wagener described Belle as "a faithful servant, honest and industrious."

Finally, her most recent employer, Mrs. Whiting, wrote a glowing statement about Belle, saying, "I do state unequivocally that we never have had such a servant that did all her work so faithfully, and one in whom we could place such implicit confidence. In fact, we did, and do still believe her to be a woman of extraordinary moral purity."

Henry M. Western, a lawyer, advised Belle to prosecute the Folgers for slander, that it was the only way to clear her name.

The murder trial of Matthias finally came to the courts in April 1835. State Circuit Judge Charles H. Ruggles presided. When the trial proceeded, Matthias pronounced a curse of God on the jury, for which he was examined for insanity but declared sane. Doctors testified that they had not clearly found poison in Pierson's stomach. Lawyer Western argued that Pierson had died of epilepsy. The prosecution could offer no substantial evidence that Pierson had been murdered, nor that Pierson, even if he had received adequate medical care, would not have died soon from epilepsy anyway. Judge Ruggles advised the jury that in the absence of adequate evidence, Matthias should be acquitted. The jury promptly agreed.

The district attorney, sympathetic with the public's feeling that Matthias was a rogue who should be convicted of something, immediately charged Matthias with assaulting his own daughter. The pretty young Mrs. Charles Laisdell asked the court to drop this charge, but her husband, Charles Laisdell, insisted that the case go forward. The daughter testified that her father had whipped her with his cowhide across her shoulders and arms because he had intended to find her another husband, and she had refused to accept.

Judge Ruggles instructed the jury that because Mrs. Laisdell was legally married, Matthias could not legally whip her. The jury convicted Matthias of assaulting his daughter. The judge sentenced him to three months in prison for this conviction, plus one more month for contempt of court for cursing the jury. In sentencing him, Judge Ruggles called Matthias a "barefaced impostor" who had tried to tell his daughter her marriage was void.

After coming out of prison, Matthias moved west without Belle. It was not clear at this time whether Belle wanted to go with Matthias.

The suit Belle had brought against Benjamin Folger for slander soon came to trial. Her employer, Perez Whiting, testified that Folger, after charging that Belle had tried to help murder both Pierson and the Folgers, had admitted to Whiting that his charge was not true. Folger offered no defense, so Belle won, but without having her opportunity to testify in court. The court awarded her $125 in damages plus costs.

For Belle, little victory was in the money that she gained. Instead, she felt that for three years (from 1832 to 1835) she had wasted her life and time. In God's economy, however, these years were not wasted. Never again was Belle so easily taken in by fast-talking men who mistook honesty and sincerity for weakness.

FIVE

Belle had won the fight of her life and had preserved her reputation, but in a different part of her life, a new battle was already brewing. According to Belle, her son Peter had "gone to seed." For a while, through using firm discipline, she had been able to keep Peter under control, but when she had moved to the Kingdom and left Peter in the city, he had dropped out of navigation school and also refused to attend grammar school.

The city around Peter was bursting with violence that, to the young boy, looked like great adventure. Instead of learning in the classroom, Peter wanted to hang out with his friends—mostly street thugs. Although only eleven years old, Peter was tall for his age, so the street boys accepted him into their group. He liked being with the older boys and stole things to win their approval.

Because Peter wasn't in school, his mother insisted that he find work. Earlier, the boy had been working as a coachman for Mr. Jones. Then one day Peter disappeared with Mr. Jones's best saddle. A few days later, Peter showed up for work again. He confessed that he had sold the saddle then used the money for a good time with his friends. Miss Geer and Belle pleaded with Mr. Jones not to press charges against Peter. Mr. Jones allowed himself to be persuaded, but he fired Peter and turned him out on the streets.

For his mother and Miss Geer, Peter flashed his charming smile and promised never to steal again, but a day or two later, Peter had forgotten his promise. Throughout New York City, blacks and Irish competed for jobs during the day and fought for control of territory at night. Peter often got into these nighttime fights and would come home for Belle to patch his injuries. Each time, she would scold Peter and lecture him about fighting. Then Peter would plead for another chance to correct his wrongdoings. His promise never lasted more than a few days. Soon Peter was in trouble again.

Several times Peter got in trouble with the police, and they threw the boy into jail. On two different occasions, Belle asked for advances on her salary so she could pay Peter's fines and get him out of jail. She always believed in her son. Then Belle found Peter a job in a livery stable. Peter had to take care of the horses, rake out the stalls, and clean the harnesses and bridles. About half the time, Peter didn't go to work, and when he did, he fought with his boss. When Peter stole a bridle and sold it on the streets, the boss pressed charges against him.

Belle knew that she had lost control of her son. He was on a crash course with disaster, and she couldn't help him. The only way that Peter could change would be from his own desire for help. So when the messenger came to tell Belle that Peter had been thrown into the Tombs, New York's dreaded jail-house, she refused to help. Because Belle had warned Peter over and over, she decided to "give Peter up to God."

The boy couldn't believe his mother's reaction. Belle had always been there for him. Even after Peter had spent an entire day in jail, his mother had not come. He was so frightened at the idea of staying in the jailhouse that he created a clever plan. Sometimes Peter used the name of Peter Williams. In the city, there was a minister by the same name, so Peter sent a message of help to his "namesake." For some reason, the elderly Williams decided to help the boy, but first he visited with his mother. Together Williams and Belle agreed that Peter needed discipline—and that the best place for that discipline was at sea as a sailor. They convinced the local judge to agree with their plan and sentence Peter to work as a sailor.

In August 1839, Peter signed up as a crew member aboard the *Zone of Nantucket*. A year later, Belle received a letter from her son, which Mrs. Whiting read to her.

> *My dear and beloved Mother,*
>
> *I take this opportunity to write to you and inform you that I am well and in hopes for to find you the same. I am got on board the same unlucky ship* Zone of Nantucket. *I am sorry for to say that I have been punished once severely, for shoving my head in the fire for other folks. I would like to know how my sisters are. I wish you would write me an answer as soon as possible. I am your son that is so far from home in the wide briny ocean. Mother, I hope you do not forget me, your dear and only son. I hope you all will forgive me for all that I have done.*
>
> *Your son,*
> *Peter Van Wagener*

Belle dictated letters back to Peter. No one knows what Belle wrote to Peter in these letters, but they were likely about family, friends, and activities in the community. Many of Peter's old friends were dead or in jail, so she thanked God that her son had escaped such an ending to his young life.

Belle didn't want to write Peter about the ugly side of New York, because her son had seen enough of that life when he had lived there. Every day Belle watched for letters from Peter. She missed him deeply. A second letter came, and then five months later—September 19, 1841—a third letter arrived. Peter told his mother how his ship had fallen on bad luck, but he was certain that his luck was about to change.

He wrote, "This is the fifth letter that I have wrote to you and have received no answer and it makes me uneasy. So pray write as quick as you can."

The letter continued, "I should be home in fifteen months. I have not much to say, but tell me if you have been at home since I left or not. I want to know what sort of a time is at home. So write as soon as you can, won't you?"

The letter was signed, "Your only son, Peter Van Wagener."

Immediately Belle wrote Peter and told him about her dream to rent a house where the entire family could live together and share life. Months passed, but Belle never heard from Peter again. Many years later, she was told Peter's ship, the *Zone*, had returned to New York Harbor, but it had no crew member by the name of Peter Williams or Peter Van Wagener.

As Belle thought about her son, she remembered the words of her mother, Mau Mau Brett: "Those are the same stars, and that is the same moon, that look down upon your brothers and sisters, and which they see as they look up at them, though they are ever so far away from us, and each other."

Years passed, and Belle continued to live and work in New York City for Mrs. Whiting. Soon it was 1843. All of Belle's daughters had grown up and married—even started their own families. When she thought about it, Belle was sad that she had not spent more time with her daughters as they had grown up, but she could do little to change the past. Now she wondered how to make her future better.

After living fourteen years in or near New York City, Belle decided that New York was no longer the place for her. She felt it was "a wicked city"—a "Sodom." She became convinced that she herself had been robbing the poor because she had been taking on extra jobs that she did not really need, that she had been unfeeling, selfish, and wicked.

In addition, Belle believed that everything she had undertaken in the city had failed. She had tried to preach, but the blacks, whom she especially wanted to reach, had rejected her. She had tried to help build the kingdom of God on earth through Matthias's community, but it had blown up into a scandal and damaged her good name. She had attempted to save enough money for her own home but had failed. She had tried to raise her son, Peter, to be honest and industrious like herself, but he had fallen into stealing and been imprisoned several times.

Because of her uneasy feelings about herself, Belle decided that she must leave the city; but for some time, she didn't say anything to anyone about her plans. She was afraid that if her children and friends knew about it, they would object and make things unpleasant. Belle was, at this time, about forty-six years old.

Belle decided to become a traveling evangelist. Although it was unusual for women to preach, there were several black women in the Northeast who had become traveling evangelists, such as Rebecca Jackson and Jarena Lee from Philadelphia and Julia Foote from Boston, Massachusetts, and Binghamton, New York. Before becoming traveling evangelists, each of these women had gained experience as preachers among the Methodists. Several of them had become widowed or otherwise separated from their husbands, so they were free from any conventional constraints on their preaching. As far as it is known, Belle didn't receive any assistance in her desire to become a traveling evangelist. She left without the promise of support from any church or denomination and with no one advising her.

When she began to dream about a new life away from New York City, Belle understood that her perspective as a freed slave, a mother, and a devout Christian gave her a different viewpoint about human rights and spiritual well-being. She wanted to tell others about her experiences. During one of her times in prayer, Belle thought she received a message from God, *"Go east."* Belle made a decision to follow the Lord to the East—wherever He took her.

For any woman just to wander and speak as the way opened was both unusual and dangerous, but Belle believed that God had called her to leave her unhappy life in New York, begin a dangerous mission, and speak for Him. One thing still bothered her though: her name. The name that she had been given as a slave seemed inappropriate for a person beginning a new life as God's pilgrim. She wanted a new name for a free woman.

Calling on God for help in selecting a name, Belle remembered Psalm 39:12: "Hear my prayer, O Lord, and give ear unto my cry. . .for I am a stranger with thee, and a sojourner, as all my fathers were." To Belle, Sojourner was a good name for someone whom God had called to travel up and down the land, showing the people their sins and being a sign to them. The name also reminded Belle of the holy people described in the Bible who traveled to foreign countries and preached the Word of God.

On June 1, 1843, as the first light shone over the horizon, Belle was already awake and stuffing her few dresses into an old pillowcase. At last the day of her departure had arrived. About an hour before she left, she informed the Whitings, where she had been working as a live-in domestic, that she was quitting. The Whitings were stunned that Belle was leaving and inquired where she would be staying.

Belle explained to Mrs. Whiting that she had taken the name of "Sojourner." Because Belle was traveling, Mrs. Whiting understood that Sojourner was an appropriate name. With those words, Belle flung her pillowcase of belongings across her shoulder and said, "Farewell, friends. I must be about my Father's business."

First, Belle walked to the ferry that was going to Brooklyn. She paid twenty-five cents for the crossing and continued walking toward Long Island. After nearly seventeen years since she'd escaped from slavery, Belle was once again traveling—except this time she truly felt free. In her customary style, Belle left New York City and never looked back.

By evening, she had walked well out of the city. Stopping at a Quaker farm, Sojourner asked for a drink of water. The woman gave it to her and asked for her name.

"My name is Sojourner," she replied with firmness.

But the first name wasn't enough for the woman. "Sojourner what?" she asked.

"My name is Sojourner," the former slave answered and continued on her trip. But the woman's question continued to nag at her. In prayer, Sojourner remembered another Bible verse, John 8:32: "And ye shall know the truth, and the truth shall make you free."

"I've only got one master now—the God of the universe—and His name is Truth. My name is Sojourner Truth," she said to herself, "because from this day I will walk in the light of His truth." It seemed a perfect name for one of God's pilgrims.

Years later, Sojourner explained to Harriet Beecher Stowe how her name had changed. "When I left the house of bondage, I left everything behind. I wasn't going to keep anything from Egypt on me, so I went to the Lord and asked Him to give me a new name. The Lord gave me the name Sojourner, because I was to travel up and down the land, showing people their sins and being a sign unto them. Afterwards I told the Lord I wanted another name, because everybody else had two names; and the Lord gave me Truth, because I was to declare the truth to the people."

SIX

"Go east," was Sojourner's only direction from God, so she continued walking east across Long Island. She preached on the farms and in the villages she passed. These white farmers stopped their work to listen to Sojourner. They were enthralled with her powerful speaking voice and manners. To their amazement, she seemed to know every word in the Bible even though she was illiterate.

As Sojourner traveled, she was often invited to stay with people who gathered to hear her speak. To repay their acts of kindness, she washed their clothes and scrubbed their floors. Throughout Long Island, word spread about the fiery preacher.

One evening Sojourner walked to a large outdoor religious meeting. Hundreds of families were camped in wagons and tents, so she stayed the night and all the next day. The people ate, sang, prayed, and listened to speakers. Everyone seemed so happy and yet very spiritual.

Wearing her black Quaker dress and white shawl, one afternoon Sojourner approached the group and asked if she could speak to them. She climbed the platform, and the people gathered to hear her speak. A black woman as a speaker was unusual, so their curiosity quieted them. Clearly this was no ordinary woman, because Sojourner stood tall, strong-boned, and proud.

Sojourner began to speak in a deep melodious voice, "Well, children, I speaks to God and God speaks to me." As she paused, a murmur spread throughout the crowd. Standing in the late afternoon sunshine, talking about God's love, glory, and protection, the black woman must have looked like she came from another world. She concluded her message with a hymn, "In my trials, Lord, walk with me. In my trials, Lord, walk with me. When my heart is almost breaking, Lord, walk with me. . . ."

After this introduction to many different people in the area, Sojourner traveled and spoke from meeting to meeting. People began to whisper, "It must be Sojourner Truth," whenever she appeared at a religious meeting in a new neighborhood.

Once someone asked Sojourner to speak about her life as a slave. It marked the first time for her to speak to such a large group of white people about her background.

Soon word spread throughout the region that she was an inspirational speaker with a stirring message. Whenever she arrived at a camp meeting, people rushed to greet her. After people heard her speak, they were often so filled with emotion that they cried or cheered.

During the early days of her speaking, Sojourner was amazed that white people would sit still and listen to anything she said. Later, her goal for speaking became clearer. Throughout her life, she had been a victim of oppression. She had been despised because of her race and ignored because she was a woman. Now at age forty-six, she was dedicated to eliminating human suffering and speaking out against slavery. To speak against slavery became the central focus of her ministry.

Once in her travels, Sojourner came across a temperance meeting. She contributed to the meeting by helping to concoct some New York dishes of food to the satisfaction of everyone in attendance. Temperance, or the abstinence of using alcoholic beverages, became a subject that she was also comfortable speaking about. Her experience with the Methodists and with Pierson and Matthias prepared her to be comfortable speaking about this social cause.

During her travels, Sojourner stayed with whoever offered her food and lodging. Usually she found that the poor, not the rich, made such offers. She did not seem afraid to live this way. If she needed money, she stopped and did domestic work for a while.

Sojourner believed that the world was wicked; often she would say that it would look much better if we could see it right side up. She began to denounce the foolishness of following the crowd—a theme that she later developed in her preaching. During her travels, she attended evangelical meetings; and if the opportunity was offered, she spoke, prayed, and sang. Sometimes she held meetings of her own, or friends that she met through her travels arranged the meetings. Sojourner believed that if people had faith, they could withstand any punishing fire that God might send into their lives. Although she was a Christian, she didn't agree with the practices of every group that labeled itself as Christian.

The theme of her speeches during these days was "God's mercy will be shown to those who show mercy." The crowd marveled at this simple black woman speaker. She couldn't read, yet she could flawlessly quote scripture word for word and then apply it in an appropriate manner. For years, Sojourner had heard passages of the Bible and committed them to memory—solely through listening.

The sincerity of her message combined with the simplicity of her language and the courage of her convictions. Many people began to seek out Sojourner Truth as a speaker for their meetings. The farmers left their fields to hear her tell stories about when she was beaten for not understanding English.

They laughed and cried as they heard her personal stories about life as a slave and the poor treatment that she had received as a free woman of color.

Sojourner continued to wander from place to place throughout the area and speak to anyone who would listen. Eventually, she decided that she should follow God's call and move to another area. She took a ship across Long Island Sound and walked on through Connecticut and Massachusetts. Wherever she went, people flocked to hear her preach.

When winter came, Sojourner was ready to settle down for a while. For some time, she had been in the region of Springfield, Massachusetts. She looked for a quiet place where a worn traveler could rest.

After several months of traveling, she arrived in Northampton, a town located along the Connecticut River in the heart of Massachusetts. Her friends described her as a "commanding figure" with a dignified manner. She "hushed every trifler into silence," and "whole audiences were melted into tears by her touching stories."

While in Northampton, Sojourner visited the Northampton Association of Education and Industry, a cooperative community that operated a silk-worm farm and made silk. She was impressed with how the people worked together.

The Northampton Association had been founded in 1842 and was led by two advocates of the abolition of slavery, Samuel L. Hill, an ex-Quaker, and George Benson, who was William Lloyd Garrison's brother-in-law. Garrison, who edited an abolitionist weekly newspaper in Boston, was a frequent visitor. In the eyes of some people, Garrison was the leader of the anti-slavery movement.

Hill and Benson had heard about Sojourner Truth from friends and asked her to stay in their community at Northampton. Although these leaders were nothing like Matthias and Pierson, Sojourner was cautious before getting involved with them too quickly. Since her experience with the Kingdom, she had avoided any weird religious practices.

Despite her uneasy feelings about a community lifestyle, Sojourner stayed in Northampton. She was attracted to the group because of their spirit of fellowship and idealism. They were a friendly haven for leading abolitionists. Her days at Northampton turned into the perfect training ground for her work as an abolitionist and feminist.

One of the frequent visitors at the community was Wendell Phillips. Sojourner learned that Phillips was called "Abolition's Golden Trumpet" because of his powerful speaking abilities.

Another distinguished speaker was Parker Pillsbury, who visited the community on a regular basis. When Sojourner first heard Pillsbury, she was intimidated by this big, red-bearded man whose booming voice shook the chandeliers. He had earned a reputation for being an uncompromising abolitionist. Another person Sojourner met at Northampton was David Ruggles, who also lived in the community. Both had spent many years in New York City but had never met. While at Northampton, they became good friends.

Ruggles had been born free in Norwich, Connecticut, but had worked most of his life in New York for the abolitionist movement. As a writer and editor, he fought slavery legally by donating his skills to the quarterly magazine, *The Mirror of Liberty*. In private, Ruggles served as secretary for the underground New York Vigilance Committee, which illegally helped runaway slaves escape. Along with his friend William Sill, Ruggles is credited with helping more than six hundred fugitive slaves while serving as conductors on the Underground Railroad.

While living in New York City, Ruggles had gone blind and undoubtedly would have ended up living on the streets if not for the help of his friends at Northampton. Frederick Douglass was another frequent visitor to the Northampton community. He became an active member of the abolitionist movement and gained a reputation for outstanding speaking. In fact, his voice and perfect diction were so respected that he was at a disadvantage. Southerners began to spread rumors that Douglass had never been a slave. To prove he wasn't a phony, Frederick wrote his autobiography in 1845, which gave names, dates, and events relevant to his life. While Sojourner couldn't read *Narrative of Frederick Douglass*, someone in Northampton read the book aloud to her.

Still a runaway, Douglass could have been recaptured and returned to the South in accordance with the Fugitive Slave Law of 1793. So for a while, Douglass left the United States and only returned when his freedom had been secured by abolitionists in England.

Frederick Douglass was the only black representative in the Anti-Slavery Society. Other blacks were involved in different abolitionist organizations. Garrison and Douglass pushed the society to seek peaceful solutions to the slavery problems, but other blacks disagreed with this approach.

At the 1843 National Negro Convention in Buffalo, New York, twenty-seven-year-old Henry Highland Garnet, a Presbyterian minister, gave a stirring speech at the convention where seventy blacks attended. Garnet called for his black brothers to rise up in revolt and hold general strikes. Douglass answered Garnet's speech and called for moral persuasion rather than violence to end slavery. Back in Northampton, Sojourner listened as the newspaper accounts of this debate were read to her. As much as she despised and hated slavery, Sojourner could not support violence in any form, so she made a choice to stay in the Douglass-Garrison camp.

During her stay in the Northampton community, Sojourner heard lecturers who advocated that women should be given the same political and legal rights as men. Recognizing that she and the women's rights speakers were kindred spirits, she decided to join their ranks and take on this new battle for freedom. After all, throughout her entire life, she had struggled with a double burden, being both a black and a woman in a society that imposed severe restrictions on both groups.

In the 1840s, a woman in the United States could not vote or hold political office. She was paid far less than a man for the same work. If she was fortunate enough to receive an education, usually she was taught in a separate classroom from the male students.

When a woman married, her property and earnings came under her husband's control. She could not initiate a divorce, but her husband could divorce her and she couldn't testify against him. Priests and ministers commonly told women that they were inferior to men.

The first significant opposition to this situation was organized by women such as Susan B. Anthony, Lucy Stone, and Angelina and Sarah Grimke, who had earlier worked to help abolish slavery in the North. From their participation in the abolitionist movement, these women had become experts at organizing meetings, collecting signatures for petitions, and speaking in public.

At Northampton, Sojourner was introduced to this growing movement for the equality of women. Olive Gilbert, an early feminist and a member of the Northampton society, read Sojourner an article in the *Liberator*, which reported on the first women's rights convention in Seneca Falls, New York, July 19–20, 1848. Douglass was the only man to play a prominent role in this convention for women's rights.

The convention had been planned by two women from New England, Elizabeth Cady Stanton and Lucretia Coffin Mott. During the second session of the convention, Stanton submitted a resolution that called for women to have the right to vote. William Lloyd Garrison disapproved of the resolution, and even Lucretia Mott differed with Stanton about pushing women's rights to this extent. Mott was afraid that to push for women's voting rights would cost the movement some valuable support, but Stanton insisted that this resolution remain a part of the convention. During the conference, every resolution passed without a hitch; but the women's voting resolution, which had the support of Frederick Douglass, only passed by a narrow margin. Disregarding the jeers of male opponents in the audience, the delegates issued a Declaration of Sentiments and Resolutions, a document that was based to a great extent on the Declaration of Independence. The convention's declaration proposed an eleven-point plan for helping women achieve equality with men.

While it was true that in the nineteenth century, white women had few political rights, black free women had even fewer rights. A slave woman had no rights. She was not only brutally mistreated by white men and women, but often the black men would also abuse her, modeling their actions after their white masters.

White women were in a larger cage than slave women. They were controlled by the men in their lives—fathers, brothers, and uncles—who trained them to believe they were too "fragile" to make social or political decisions.

Although white women had some rights, they couldn't serve on juries, hold public office, or even manage their own finances (if they had any money to manage). In the case of a divorce, the husband was automatically given custody of the children because, as one judge said, "If she had been a good wife and mother, sharp on her duties, then her husband wouldn't be seeking separation."

Women would never be able to change these practices in the United States without the legal power to vote for elected officials. With the status quo, they remained powerless.

As Sojourner listened and saw the struggle of all women for freedom, she decided that women's rights was a cause worth fighting for.

After Olive Gilbert read Frederick Douglass's autobiography to Sojourner, she encouraged her to write her own story. "I'll write it for you," Gilbert volunteered. "You dictate it to me."

Garrison encouraged the publication of Sojourner's story because he saw it would add to the growing number of anti-slavery stories. Her story would reveal how slaves in the North were treated. He offered to print the book and even wrote the introduction to *The Narrative of Sojourner Truth: A Northern Slave*.

The book was printed in 1850, the same year that Congress passed a more rigid version of the Fugitive Slave Act as part of the Compromise of 1850. After the Mexican War, Representative David Wilmot of Pennsylvania introduced an amendment to a bill in Congress that prohibited slavery in any territory acquired as a result of the Mexican War, or the Southwest Territory. The House passed this amendment, but the Senate defeated it. Bitter debates followed the vote, and fistfights broke out on the Senate floor. The debate was over the fate of two possible new states—California and New Mexico (New Mexico, then including present-day Arizona, southern Colorado, southern Utah, and southern Nevada, was designated a territory but denied statehood). If even one state was admitted to the United States as a free state, the balance of power between Northern and Southern senators would be upset. At that time, the power was evenly divided at fifteen Southern states and fifteen Northern states.

In September 1850, Congress passed the famous compromise. The second largest state in terms of total area, California was admitted to the Union as a free state in exchange for a law to replace the poorly enforced Fugitive Slave Law of 1793. The new Fugitive Slave Act of 1850 required Northern states to return runaway slaves to their masters.

But this compromise settled nothing. The Southerners continued to hide behind states' rights to protect slavery, and the abolitionists of the North were more determined than ever to fight slavery in the West. Angry and upset by the new Fugitive Slave Act, anti-slavery sympathizers expanded the Underground Railroad network, which each year helped more than a thousand slaves to escape from the South. In some communities in the North, slave catchers began to meet armed resistance when they confronted runaway slaves and their supporters.

Not every Northerner supported the anti-slavery people. Many people in the North maintained that the Fugitive Slave Act had to be obeyed so peace could be maintained between the North and the South. These people accused the abolitionists of trying to divide the nation. They hated the blacks and wanted all freed slaves to be returned to the South or shipped to Africa.

The next month, October, Sojourner traveled to Worcester, Massachusetts, to speak at that year's national women's rights convention. There she listened—along with a thousand others—to such distinguished speakers as Stanton, Mott, Stone, Douglass, and Garrison.

Most of the clergy took an active role in resisting the women's meeting. The male-dominated press that reported on the convention called the conference a hen party and chided the women, saying they were "fe-he-males" or "hens that wanted to crow."

Yet on that day in late October 1850, over a thousand people from eleven states participated in the conference. Several men, such as Douglass, Garrison, Pillsbury, and Phillips, had come to the conference to throw their support to the women's cause. As Sojourner looked around the audience, she noticed that she was the only black woman.

A self-educated physician, Helen Hunt officially opened the meeting by reading a statement from Elizabeth Cady Stanton. Stanton regretted that she could not attend the conference, because she was at home awaiting the birth of her fourth child. Then the chairwoman of the conference gave a powerful speech that concluded, "We claim for women all blessings which the other sex has, solely, or by her aid, achieved for itself."

It took all of the patience that Sojourner could muster to listen to the various speakers. Some of them discussed whether women should be able to keep their jewelry after a divorce or whether women were more liberated by wearing bloomers, a pant-type dress, which had supposedly freed the body and allowed more physical exercise. To Sojourner's way of thinking, these issues were irrelevant. She was more concerned about whether a divorced mother should be allowed to keep her children.

Then Lucretia Mott, a young schoolteacher, addressed the conference. She spoke passionately about being paid less than a male teacher only because she was a woman. Lucy Stone, a graduate from Oberlin College, spoke and was equally concerned with this issue of equal pay for equal work. Stone told about refusing to use her husband's last name so she could show people that he was not her "master." Self-worth and equal pay for equal work were issues that Sojourner could understand and identify with. Her interest in the speeches increased. As different people spoke, she made mental notes about issues that she would like to address.

Toward the conclusion of the conference, Sojourner was asked to speak to the convention. She began, "Sisters, I am not clear on what you be after. If women want any rights more than they've got, why don't they just take them and not be talking about it?"

While the goals for the conference may have been fuzzy at first, by the conclusion of the convention, the women had clarified their goals. Their motto clearly stated their primary objective, "Equality before the law without distinction of sex or color." Sojourner left the conference feeling inspired and motivated. From that time on, she included equality for women in her speeches.

Sojourner's defiant message at the 1850 women's rights convention stirred the ranks of the nation's feminists and abolitionists, as well as any oppressed person who wanted equality. "Why not just take your rights?" Sojourner had asked. Many Americans who had been deprived of their rights were beginning to ask the same question.

SEVEN

After Sojourner Truth published her autobiography in 1850, she became well-known to both the anti-slavery and the women's rights movements. William Lloyd Garrison and his associate Wendell Phillips convinced Sojourner to lend her splendid speaking voice to the abolitionist cause. Soon she was traveling with other lecturers throughout New England. While traveling on the lecture circuit, Sojourner sold many copies of her book, and with the proceeds she continued to pay on her home in Northampton.

By the time Sojourner joined the lecture circuit, she looked much older than her fifty-three years. Her black hair had turned gray, her forehead had become deeply lined with wrinkles, and she wore metal-rimmed glasses to help her fading eyesight. For almost every occasion, Sojourner wore a plain black dress and a long white shawl. A white handkerchief wrapped around her head formed a turban. From her appearance, some people guessed that she was in her nineties.

As a result, the crowds at the abolitionist meetings were astonished at the vigor with which Sojourner Truth attacked the institution of slavery. In her lectures, she denounced slave owners as sinners who would someday soon feel God's wrath. Most of these audiences were filled with white people—mostly men—and few of them had ever heard a black speaker other than Frederick Douglass give a public address. They found it interesting that a black woman would publicly state her views on slavery.

Audiences were surprised at Sojourner's speaking style. Most speakers tried to pronounce their words beautifully and often used formal and flowery speech, but Sojourner didn't try to imitate that style. Instead, she cast a spell over her listeners with the rough, uneducated manner and language of an unschooled slave girl who had never learned to read or write. Unlike some speakers who droned on for hours, she impressed her listeners with her ability to cut to the heart of a complex issue in just a few words.

Soon Sojourner became known for her simple but moving anti-slavery speeches and her witty, biting attacks on people who continued to own slaves yet said they were Christians. She knew that many Northerners wanted to pretend that slavery was strictly a problem in the South. To these people, millions of black slaves were practically invisible. Sojourner believed it was her mission to force all Americans to confront the nationwide moral problem of slavery.

Throughout the nation, people were divided on the issue of slavery. Whether in the North or South, opinions varied. Sometimes people were hostile to Sojourner's messages. Some of them threatened her life with angry mobs. During such occasions, she mustered all her courage, stood her ground, and continued speaking. She was surprised at the angry reactions. They had forgotten that the United States had been founded by people who were themselves fleeing the tyranny of others.

One evening, during a meeting in the late 1850s, Garrison saw his friend Sojourner in the audience and said with a matter-of-fact tone, "Sojourner will say a few words, after which Wendell Phillips will follow."

Sojourner hadn't come to the meeting prepared to speak, but she couldn't pass up the opportunity. When she stood, her tall presence commanded attention. Then, as she had done at the camp meetings, Sojourner used the strength of her voice to capture the attention of her audience. She began by singing one of her original hymns:

"I am pleading for my people,
A poor downtrodden race,
Who dwell in freedom's boasted land
With no abiding place.

"I am pleading that my people
May have their rights restored;
For they have long been toiling,
And yet have no reward.

"They are forced the crops to culture,
But not for them they yield,
Although both late and early
They labor in the field.

"Whilst I bear upon my body
The scars of many a gash,
I am pleading for my people
Who groan beneath the lash."

Then, without any fanfare, Truth began her speech, making each point simply yet eloquently. "Well, children," she began, "I was born a slave in Ulster

County, New York. I don't know if it was summer or winter, fall or spring. I don't even know what day of the week it was. They don't care when a slave is born or when he dies. . .just how much work they can do."

After telling the tragic story of her father's death and her struggle to get her son, Peter, back, she closed her message, saying, "God will not make His face shine upon a nation that holds with slavery." The crowd applauded and cheered. Some of the people cried while others sat stunned and silent. It was a hard act for even Wendell Phillips to follow.

That evening, Sojourner sold twice as many books as before. She decided to go on a speaking tour. . .to sell books and to spread the "truth" as she understood it. After people had asked about her hymns, she made some of them into a booklet and sold them along with her biography. After each evening of selling books, Sojourner dutifully put aside some of the money to pay for the printing of her book and some to pay Sam Hill for building her home.

For a while, Sojourner traveled and spoke with Garrison and George Thompson, an English abolitionist. Often they reached places where their figures had been burned in effigy. Sojourner's messages always managed to stir the emotions of a sympathetic gathering or inflame the tempers of a hostile group. No one could be passive when listening to Sojourner Truth.

Sometimes Sojourner had confrontations with individual preachers. At an anti-slavery meeting, when abolitionists were attacking the church for its reluctance to fight slavery, a clergyman said that he was afraid God might knock him down at any moment for listening to such blasphemy. According to a friend, Sojourner told that clergyman, "Don't be scared. I don't expect God has ever heard of you!"

And at a different anti-slavery meeting, an orthodox clergyman who was visiting the meeting protested that the anti-slavery speakers were "women and donkeys." Sojourner replied that in a Bible story another minister, Balaam, also got "mighty mad" at a donkey, the one he was riding on, because it carried him off the road. But the reason the donkey went off the road was that God had sent an angel to direct them not to go any farther. Only the donkey, not the minister, was able to understand what the angel was directing them to do.

In spite of these confrontations, Sojourner found it natural to associate with ministers. Several clergyman wrote sympathetic articles about her in the newspapers. Despite her outward appearance of simplicity, she understood how churches could help pull people along toward what she considered to be the necessary remaking of both individuals and society. Once in a discussion among Progressive Friends, the radical abolitionist Henry C. Wright insisted on attacking churches bitterly for their cooperation with slavery. Wright urged that these places be named "so-called" churches. Sojourner disagreed with Wright. "We ought to be like Christ," she argued. "He said, 'Father, forgive them; for they know not what they do.' If we want to lead the people, we must not be out of their sight." Sojourner believed in approaching the public with a hopeful attitude and in using widely acceptable, noncontroversial Christian teaching in her public appeals.

At one meeting in Syracuse in 1850, the crowd had come to hear George Thompson speak and was angered when Sojourner came to the podium first. She quieted the crowd by saying, "I'll tell you what Thompson is going to say to you. He is going to argue that the poor Negroes ought to be out of slavery and in the heavenly state of freedom. But, children, I'm against slavery because I want to keep the white folks who hold slaves from getting sent to hell." Sojourner's basic concerns undoubtedly involved her fellow blacks, but she was so perceptive that she spoke directly to the needs of her white audience. The meeting was saved, and the crowd listened with interest to Sojourner and then to Thompson.

Early in 1851, Garrison planned an anti-slavery speaking trip with Thompson. He invited Sojourner to accompany them and explained that the meetings would give her a chance to sell her books. Many years later, Sojourner recalled for Garrison the meaning of those days of travel. "My heart is glowing with the remembrance of George Thompson's kindness to me. I had been publishing my Narrative and owed for the entire edition. It was a great debt for me, and every cent that I could obtain went to pay for it. You [Garrison] said to me, 'I am going on a lecture tour. Come with us and you will have a good chance to dispose of your book.' You generously offered to bear my expenses, and it was arranged that I should meet you in Springfield.

"On the appointed day, I was there, but you were not at the hotel. I inquired for Mr. Thompson and was shown into his room. He received me and seated me with as much courtesy and cordiality as if I had been the highest lady in the land. Then he informed me that you were too ill to leave home, but if I would go with himself and Mr. G. W. Putman, it would be all the same. 'But,' I said, 'I have no money,' and Mr. Garrison offered to pay my passage.

"He said, 'I'll bear your expenses, Sojourner. Come with us!' And so I went.

"Mr. Thompson accompanied me to the cars and carried my bag. At the hotel tables, he seated me beside himself and never seemed to know that I was poor and a black woman. At the meetings, he recommended my books, saying, 'Sojourner Truth has a narrative of her life. It is very interesting. Buy largely, friends!' Good man! Genuine gentleman! God bless George Thompson, the great-hearted friend of my race!"

During February and March of 1851, Sojourner traveled with Thompson, Putman, and others as they made their way by train from Springfield, Massachusetts, west into New York State. They spoke at a series of anti-slavery conventions. Sometimes they were joined by Frederick Douglass. At each meeting, Sojourner sold her books.

Thompson, Sojourner, and others traveled throughout western New York during 1851, speaking to various kinds of audiences. Many of these were unruly mobs whose primary purpose was to disrupt the meetings or fluster or injure the speakers. At all times, Sojourner maintained her dignity and never showed any fear before the greater strength and numbers of her opponents.

By the time the traveling speakers reached Rochester, New York, where they ended their trip, Putnam had become enthusiastic about Sojourner. Though she could neither read nor write, he reported, "She will often speak with an ability [that] surprises the educated and refined. She possesses a mind of rare power, and often, in the course of her short speeches, will throw out gems of thought. But the truly Christian spirit [that] pervades all she says endears her to all who know her. Though she has suffered all the ills of slavery, she forgives all who have wronged her most freely."

In mid-1853, after a successful tour through the Midwest and a fall filled with travel and speeches, Sojourner Truth was tired of traveling and decided to take a period for rest. That winter she stayed with Isaac and Amy Post, well-known Quaker abolitionists in Rochester, New York. At the Posts' home, letters from her children finally caught up with her. The letters made Sojourner want to see them even more. Diana wrote about how Dumont had "gone west" with some of his sons, but that before leaving he had become a strong abolitionist and told them "slavery was an evil institution." The change didn't surprise Sojourner, because the last time she had seen her old master, his attitude had been changing.

After reading these letters from her children, Sojourner made a trip to visit them. Her daughters were living in New York and New England; some had married and had children. Truth's oldest grandchild, Hannah's son, James Caldwell, was already nine years old. After enjoying a pleasant stay with her daughters' families, Sojourner set out for her house in Northampton, with a brief stopover in Andover, Massachusetts, the home of abolitionist writer Harriet Beecher Stowe.

Sojourner's meeting with Stowe was a memorable occasion for both the small white novelist and the tall black preacher. They immediately liked each other and respected the work that each was doing to end slavery. One evening Sojourner spoke to a gathering at Mrs. Stowe's home. Later Stowe wrote about the meetings, saying, "I do not recollect ever to have been conversant with any-one who had more of that silent subtle power which we call personal presence than this woman. No princess could have received a drawing room with more composed dignity than Sojourner her audience. She stood among them, calm, erect, as one of her own native palm trees waving alone in the desert."

Regretting the human loss that occurred when some people enslaved other human beings, Stowe wrote, "I can not but think that Sojourner with the same culture might have spoken as eloquent and undying as the African St. Augustine or Tertullian. How grand and queenly a woman she might have been, with her wonderful physical vigor, her great heaving seas of emotion, her power of spiritual conception, her quick penetration, and her boundless energy!"

After returning home, Sojourner decided to continue her speaking tours. At each of the abolitionist meetings she attended, she always brought along several copies of her autobiography to sell as well as a new item: postcards that bore her photograph and the legend "I Sell the Shadow to Support the Substance." She called these cards her *cartes de visite*, which is French for "calling cards." She also brought her "Book of Life," an album in which she collected short notes and autographs from many people she had met through her travels.

By the mid-1850s, Sojourner Truth had become known throughout much of the United States. However, she wasn't the only black woman whose anti-slavery efforts drew attention. During this period, Harriet Tubman, the poet Frances E. W. Harper, and the abolitionist Sarah Remond often addressed women's anti-slavery conventions and women's rights meetings as well.

As Sojourner continued to speak out in favor of the end of slavery, she insisted that freedom for blacks must be accompanied by freedom for women. "If colored men get their rights and not colored women," she explained to the audience of a women's rights conference, "colored men will be masters over the women, and it will be just as bad as before."

This kind of uncompromising attitude eventually enabled Sojourner and other feminists to bring about some reforms for women. In New York, Susan B. Anthony collected ten thousand signatures for a petition requesting that married women be allowed to control their own property. The state legislature ultimately approved Anthony's petition and also gave divorced women the right to share custody of their children.

Throughout this period, Sojourner continued to travel and speak at different conventions. She felt that God was telling her to go west, and as always, she obeyed. She went to Ohio, which was a free state and one of the main arteries on the Underground Railroad. Despite the strong anti-slavery movement in Ohio, there were also a lot of pro-slavery feelings, especially in the rural areas.

Audience reaction to Sojourner varied greatly. Sometimes she was well received, but more often than not, she ended up hoarse from yelling her speech over the jeers and hoots from protesters. One day she was met outside a city by an angry mob. They told her in clear terms, "Go somewhere else." She walked away from the mob but circled around the town and came in from another direction. On another occasion, a sheriff came to arrest Sojourner and her companion to protect their lives from the angry crowd. For her to give up was out of the question, despite the growing danger.

While lecturing in Ohio, Sojourner learned about a woman's rights convention in Akron, Ohio, which was organized by Frances Gage. Truth decided to attend.

Hundreds of women and men gathered at a local church so they could hear various speakers. Clearly, the audience had mixed opinions about this topic of women's rights. Most of the men had come with firm prejudices against the movement. Many of the men were ministers committed to discrediting the movement as anti-Christian. A few women attended with their husbands, who supported the women's rights position. Finally, the seasoned feminists were also in attendance, because their goals and aspirations were being addressed.

For the most part, the gathering of these different viewpoints was congenial. Suddenly, the doors to the church swung open, and a tall, proud figure stood framed in the doorway. "It's Sojourner Truth," someone whispered. Slowly Sojourner walked to the front of the auditorium. She soon noticed that she was the only black person in the room. Since every seat was filled, she took a seat on the steps leading to the pulpit. As she sat, Sojourner folded her arms and listened.

Soon the people in the room were buzzing with excitement. Would this black woman be permitted to speak to the convention?

The convention listened to speaker after speaker. Each one tried to impress the crowd with his or her opinion. Several ministers tried to disrupt the meeting by encouraging women who "feared God" to immediately leave. When this technique didn't succeed, the clergymen used the same worn-out logic that mankind had used for centuries to oppress women and blacks— God created women to be weak and blacks to be a subservient race.

The entire first day, Sojourner simply listened. Then during the second day, she turned to the chairwoman and asked for permission to speak. For a moment, Frances Gage hesitated; then she simply introduced the black woman as "Sojourner Truth." No other introduction was required.

Sojourner had garnered a great deal of experience speaking to hostile crowds. As she looked around the room, she could see the anger and resentment on the faces of some of the people. Fearlessly but gently, Sojourner took control of the situation. First, as she stood at the podium, she removed her sunbonnet, folded it neatly, and set it aside. These slow and deliberate actions had a calming effect on the crowd.

Throughout the day before and that morning, Sojourner had heard preachers—men who were supposed to know better—use the Bible to support their own purposes. She had heard enough of such talk and had grown angry and ready to do battle using God's own truth. With no prepared speech, Sojourner began to speak in her deep, husky voice.

"Well, children, where there is so much racket, there must be somethin' out of kilter. . . . The white men will be in a fix pretty soon. But what's all this about anyway?

"That man over there. . . ," Sojourner said as she pointed to a minister who had said a woman's place was to be a mother, wife and companion, good sister, and loving niece. "He says women need to be helped into carriages and lifted over ditches and to have the best everywhere. Nobody ever helps me into carriages, over mud puddles, or gets me any best places."

The black woman pulled her frame to her entire height and looked out over the crowd with a defiant gesture and said, "And ain't I a woman?"

Then she turned to face the men who were sitting on the platform behind her. She said, "Look at me!" Then she pulled back her sleeve and showed her right arm and raised it into the air. As though with a single voice, the audience gasped. Her dark arm was muscular and made strong from years of hard work. "I have plowed, and I have planted." She was recalling her years as a slave on the Dumont estate, where she had worked for her freedom. "And I have gathered the crops into the barns. And no man could work stronger than me." She paused and once again asked the audience, "And ain't I a woman?

"I have borne twelve children and watched them be sold into slavery, and when I cried out in a mother's grief, no one heard me but Jesus. And ain't I a woman?" Without a doubt, Sojourner was referring to her mother, Mau Mau, because Sojourner had only had five children.

Then point by point, Sojourner took on the religious speakers. "You say Jesus was a man, so that means God favors men over women. Where did your Christ come from?" Then she answered her own question. "From God and a woman. Man had nothing to do with Him."

Sojourner challenged the widely held belief that women were less intelligent than men and blacks had no intellect at all. "Suppose a man's mind holds a quart, and a woman's mind doesn't hold more than a pint; if her pint is full, it's as good as a quart." With straightforward common sense, Sojourner ripped at the heart of the various arguments.

She then directed her comments to the women in the audience. "If the first woman God ever made was strong enough to turn the world upside down all alone, these women together ought to be able to turn it back and get it right side up again, and now that they are asking to do it, the men better let 'em."

Few of the listeners could understand the full meaning of Sojourner's hard-hitting speech. It was doubtful that the rural Ohio community was ready to accept the claim that took women's rights across the boundaries of race, class, and the bondage of slavery.

Sojourner proclaimed the truth in simple terms. For people who had good reason, racism and sexism were unacceptable.

EIGHT

Sojourner left the Akron conference with a new banner that a friend of hers had made. It stated, "Proclaim liberty throughout all the land unto all the inhabitants thereof." She loaded up with six hundred copies of her book and traveled around Indiana and Ohio in a borrowed horse and buggy. Sojourner made speeches against slavery and in support of the women's rights movement. She never planned her route or worried about food, clothing, or shelter. Often she permitted her horse to choose the direction that she would travel. "The Lord will guide and protect me," she insisted.

The Fugitive Slave Act continued to stir controversy. During an anniversary convention of the Anti-Slavery Society in Salem, Ohio, Frederick Douglass told the audience that he believed a war was the only lasting means for freedom. This stance was a marked change from his previous nonviolent position and strained his relationship with Garrison.

Sojourner was in the audience, and his words struck her heart. *There is no hope. . . . There is no hope!* she thought. Leaping to her feet, she called out to her old friend in a voice that trembled with emotion, "Frederick, is God dead?"

Douglass understood what his old friend meant—she was asking if he had completely lost his faith. "No," Douglass answered quickly, "and because God is not dead, slavery can only end in blood."

Sojourner disagreed with this outlook on slavery. She was convinced that slavery could end without violence.

From her travels and speeches, Sojourner Truth's fame and stature grew as an abolitionist and feminist who had wit and wisdom. As the word spread across the Midwestern countryside, even her opponents respected her.

Not every audience that Sojourner faced was friendly, but over and over she proved how her quick wit could quiet any disruptions from a hostile crowd. In 1853, she attended the women's rights convention held at the Broadway Tabernacle in New York. The hall was packed with hecklers and opponents to women's rights. Chroniclers of the movement called this meeting "the Mob Convention." When Sojourner stood to speak, the crowd roared in reaction to her skin color.

She began her remarks by referring to the noisy audience as people with either the spirit of geese or of snakes. She proceeded to speak above the roar and finally managed to quiet the crowd. "I know that it feels a-kind of hissing and tickling-like to see a colored woman get up and tell you about things and women's rights," she said. "We have all been thrown down so low that nobody thought we'd ever get up again, but we have been long enough trodden now; we will come up again, and now here I am." The crowd responded to her speech with loud applause. It was a huge success.

Throughout the Midwest, Sojourner continued to travel and speak against slavery. At times she felt pressed to defend her stance against the onslaught of criticism hurled at blacks from Northern "meddlers." Many of these opponents quoted George Fitzhugh, a Virginia slaveholder, who wrote in 1854 that blacks were better off as slaves in America than in "a far more cruel slavery in Africa, or from idolatry and cannibalism, and every brutal vice and crime that can disgrace humanity."

Sojourner was quick to respond to those who used Fitzhugh's error-filled material. "Be careful," she'd say forcefully. "God will not stand with wrong; never mind how right you think you be."

Sojourner never permitted herself to be intimidated or put down but rose to every occasion and gracefully withdrew if she felt it was wise. Time and time again, she showed her courage as she traveled through New Jersey, New York, Ohio, Indiana, Michigan, and many other states.

As she addressed her audiences, Sojourner blended tones of pride and modesty. She addressed her audience as "children" and individuals as "honey," showing affection for all sympathizers, and it endeared her to many people. The salty wit, characteristic of her speaking, appeared on many occasions. She was full of amusing sayings, some of which have survived and been used by other speakers. On one occasion, she began her talk by saying, "Children, I've come here like the rest of you to hear what I have to say," an opening line that a distinguished lecturer borrowed many years later. Sometimes she coined new expressions. Instead of saying that every person had to stand on his or her own two feet, Sojourner said, "Every tub has to stand on its own bottom."

Not only did her humor and sharpness make Sojourner an effective speaker against slavery, but her experience of having felt the whip's lash influenced her delivery. But more than this, she had the ability to appeal to white people by shaming them or encouraging them—or even complimenting them.

While Frederick Douglass or Harriet Tubman did a vital job of speaking to black people, Sojourner took a different role. She was one of the few black people who spoke almost exclusively to white people, individually or in groups, and few blacks worked as closely as she did with the white abolitionists. A number of stories demonstrate her talent for subduing racist mobs and destroying racists' arguments. She could deal with white people from all persuasions.

As Sojourner continued to travel, her passion against slavery gave her the energy to continue attacking it as inhuman, unchristian, and intolerable. She was not always kind or moderate. Sometimes she gave vent to her anger when she thought about what slavery had done. On one occasion, she declared, "All the gold in California, all the wealth of this nation could not restore to me that which the white people have taken from me." Although Sojourner spoke to white people, she never diluted her criticism and opposition to the white people who had enslaved her and her fellow blacks.

When Sojourner was sixty years old, she decided it was time to retire and enjoy the life she'd dreamed of for years. In 1857, she sold her Northampton house for $750 and moved to Harmonia, Michigan, a short distance from Battle Creek.

Sojourner's daughter Elizabeth Banks also moved to Harmonia along with her son Sammy. They were joined by Diana and her husband, Jacob Corbin, who was a hotel clerk. They had one son, Frank.

In 1857, fifty-four other African Americans lived in the Battle Creek area, and the mayor was a conductor on the Underground Railroad. The people in the town felt pleased and honored to have such a famous person as Sojourner Truth living among them. They helped her change an old barn on College Street into a comfortable house. There she planned to spend her final days enjoying her grandchildren.

From the beginning, Sammy Banks, Elizabeth's son from her second marriage, favored his grandmother. He begged to stay with her, and Sojourner welcomed his companionship. When he was young, Sammy ran errands and did various chores for his grandmother. Then when Sammy learned to read, he read the Bible to Sojourner. In many ways, Sammy became a substitute for Sojourner's lost son, Peter.

For days, Sojourner was content to sit on the front porch, telling stories and singing hymns. But just as Sojourner was settling down into retirement, the Supreme Court placed still another wedge in the gulf between the North and the South. Dred Scott, a slave, had sued for his freedom because he had lived in a free state. The court considered the case in 1857 and determined that a slave was "property" and therefore not a citizen. They said that Scott didn't have the right to sue. This decision was a blow to the abolitionists, but it didn't really affect Scott. His "owner" freed him immediately after the case was final.

When Sojourner Truth learned about the Scott decision, she became convinced that it was not the time to retreat. Against her daughters' protests,

Sojourner prepared to begin another speaking tour. Before she left, she had her autobiography updated by her friend and neighbor, Frances Titus, who edited and expanded the narrative six times between 1853 and 1884. Then, taking Sammy with her, sixty-two-year-old Sojourner Truth went back out on the speaking tour.

After traveling for a year, Frances Titus volunteered to become Sojourner's traveling companion and "manager." Together the two women spoke to anti-slavery groups. Sojourner told audiences, "Slavery must be destroyed, root and branch."

Indiana was a difficult place for abolitionists. While speaking in Kosciusko County with her good friend Parker Pillsbury, Sojourner experienced a vicious personal attack. A local doctor who led a pro-slavery group claimed Sojourner wasn't a woman. He insisted that she was a man impersonating a woman.

"We demand," the leader said, "if it be a she, that she expose one of her breasts to the gaze of some of the ladies present so that they may report back and dispel the audience's doubts."

Pillsbury leaped to his friend's defense, but Sojourner stopped him, asking, "Why do you suppose me to be a man?"

"It's your voice," the doctor said. "Your voice is not that of a woman." After a moment of hesitation, Sojourner began to slowly unbutton her blouse. "I will show my breast," she said to the astonishment of the audience, "but to the entire congregation. It is not to my shame but yours that I do this."

At another time, the people told Sojourner that they would burn down the meeting hall where she was scheduled to speak. Without fear or hesitation, she replied, "I'll speak on the ashes."

On that particular trip, Sojourner had grown older. It was difficult for her to get started in the morning. "But once she gets up," it was said, "she can go as long as a woman half her age." Another observer noticed that though Sojourner had aged, "There was both power and sweetness in that great warm soul and that vigorous frame." Much as her hard life was affecting her health, she was still able to keep the crowd on the edges of their seats to catch her every word.

NINE

Between 1800 and 1859, bold black leaders led at least two hundred slave uprisings. Three different leaders were prominent during this period: Gabriel Prosser, Denmark Vesey, and Nat Turner.

Merely mentioning those names to slaveholders was to strike fear into their hearts. In 1800, Prosser had organized and armed slaves who were prepared to take Richmond, Virginia, by force. Before Prosser could carry out his plan, however, he was betrayed and hanged. In 1822, Vesey, a free black man, recruited nine thousand slaves to take part in an attack on Charleston, South Carolina. He, too, was betrayed and hanged along with many of his followers. Then, in 1831, Turner, a Virginia slave, led a revolt in which sixty whites were killed. The authorities captured Turner and hanged him, as well.

The people who lived in the South knew that blacks outnumbered whites three to one, so they had reason to worry about rebellions. A female relative of George Washington put it simply: "We know that death in the most horrid form threatens us." Such fear may be part of the reason why slaves received swift and severe punishment for any form of disloyalty to their masters.

Sojourner argued that slave masters had much more to fear than slave insurrections. "It is God the slave owner will answer to on the day of judgment."

While Prosser, Vesey, and Turner caused a rip in the fabric of American politics, John Brown's 1859 raid on Harpers Ferry, Virginia (now West Virginia), caused a great upheaval. Brown was a radical who advocated an armed attack against the South to free the slaves and train them as soldiers to free other slaves. Often Brown said that slaveholders had "forfeited their right to live."

Brown planned to capture arms at the military arsenal at Harpers Ferry, then free slaves through force. But the plan failed. Brown was captured and hanged on December 2, 1859.

Although Sojourner was illiterate, her grandson Sammy kept her well informed about the political affairs of the day. Sammy read aloud every detail of Brown's trial and execution. Southerners accused Brown of being a maniacal murderer, and at first, more than a few moderate abolitionists tried to distance themselves from Brown's firebrand methods. But the grassroots support for Brown was overwhelming. While Brown represented only a small faction of the movement during his life, every abolitionist embraced him in death. Brown became a martyred folk hero, a symbol of the cause of freedom. Sammy also kept his grandmother informed about the upcoming presidential election. Sojourner was particularly interested in Abraham Lincoln and the new Republican Party. She asked her grandson to read articles about Lincoln whenever he found them. Sojourner liked what she learned about the former Illinois congressman and his stance on slavery.

During a debate with Senator Douglas in 1858, Lincoln proclaimed, "A house divided against itself cannot stand! I believe this government cannot endure permanently half slave and half free. I do not expect the Union to be dissolved; I do not expect the house to fall; but I do expect it will cease to be divided. It will become all one thing or all the other." When Lincoln was a congressman, he introduced a bill providing for the gradual emancipation of slaves in Washington, D.C. He opposed the opening of territories to slavery, and he spoke out against the Dred Scott decision. Sojourner was convinced that Lincoln would be a good president but waited to endorse him.

Most abolitionists were being cautious about Lincoln because he hadn't called for the immediate elimination of slavery. Fiercely defending its right to treat people as property, the South threatened to establish its own slave-holding nation if Lincoln was elected president.

When Lincoln won the presidency in the November election, a wide-scale rebellion broke out in the South. By February 1861, seven states had broken off from the Union and formed a Confederate government. Four of the other eight slave states soon joined the Confederacy, and the North and South prepared for war. On April 12, 1861, the Civil War broke out when Confederate units attacked Union troops stationed at Fort Sumter, in Charleston, South Carolina.

Sojourner was in Michigan when she got word that a rebel general had fired on Fort Sumter. She hadn't wanted a war; but once it started, she gave her full support to the Union soldiers. Like Frederick Douglass, Sojourner was concerned that blacks weren't given an opportunity to fight for their freedom. The anti-slavery society and the blacks hailed the war as a struggle to end slavery, but many Americans viewed it as chiefly a battle to reunite the country. Early in the war, Union armies suffered a string of defeats, and anger about even being in a war ran high in many areas of the North.

Immediately after the battle at Fort Sumter, many blacks volunteered for service, but they were turned away. As the war progressed, Lincoln was bombarded with requests from black and white leaders to create a "colored unit" and to allow blacks to serve in ways other than as cooks and laborers.

During the fall of 1862, Lincoln finally yielded to the pressure and ordered an all-black unit to be established with white officers. The 54th Massachusetts Volunteer Infantry was a "test" for the black soldier's ability in combat.

Would these blacks run under fire? Would they follow orders from their officers? Could they be disciplined? The men of the 54th proved that they could be excellent combat soldiers.

The African American response to the 54th was phenomenal. From all over the country, young blacks came to Boston and signed up. Two of Douglass's sons joined, along with nineteen-year-old James Caldwell, one of Sojourner's grandsons. Her only regret was that she couldn't join herself. Sojourner Truth decided to make a tour of the Midwest and rouse support for the Union's war effort. As Sojourner traveled on this speaking tour, angry mobs greeted her in some places and bands of supporters in others. The anti-war and anti-black feelings ran especially high in Indiana, where the state legislature had passed a law forbidding blacks from entering the state. Sojourner defied the law and campaigned throughout the state for the Union cause. She was arrested numerous times. On each occasion, friendly crowds gathered to defend her with shouts of "Sojourner, free speech, and the Union!"

The rigors of such conflict exhausted Sojourner, and she returned home to recover. To have her immediate family nearby served as a great source of comfort to Sojourner, but it also meant that each of her children was free from the bonds of slavery.

Despite her feelings of comfort, Sojourner still had to find the means to support herself financially. In her sixties, she could no longer do the strenuous work of cleaning and cooking for people in Battle Creek. Nor could she continue selling her armloads of books at anti-slavery conventions. Her years of such work had weakened her.

Josephine Griffing, a feminist and abolitionist friend of Sojourner's, came to visit her in Michigan. "I've come to beg your help," Griffing said. "As you know, the president promised to free the slaves the first part of the year. The war effort is not going well. . .anti-slavery speakers are needed more than ever to rally people to our cause. I have been asked to go into Indiana, and I want you to come with me."

Sojourner smiled and said, "Let me get my hat."

Throughout the rest of 1862, Josephine and Sojourner traveled together and urged people to push for the end of slavery. In the *National Anti-Slavery Standard* in New York, Josephine wrote an article, which said in part, "Our meetings are largely attended by persons from every part of the country. . . . Slavery made a conquest in this country by the suppression of free speech, and freedom must make her conquest by the steadfast support of free speech. There are a hundred men now who would spill their blood sooner than surrender the rights of Sojourner."

Articles reporting on Sojourner's "lectures" and other activities that supported the abolitionist cause often made references to her encounters with "Negro haters" and "mobocrats." These loud-voiced opponents of black freedom tried repeatedly to disrupt her meetings and drown out her truths. Some of these conflicts were described by eyewitnesses, and others were just hinted at by writers.

As Sojourner traveled through Indiana with her friend Josephine Griffing, Sojourner and her friends were arrested several times. Sojourner was arrested for entering the state, and her friends were arrested for welcoming her into their homes. In each case, Sojourner managed to outwit the authorities or shame them into releasing her. Often Sojourner's meetings in Indiana were disrupted with loud and insulting shouts, such as, "Down with you! We think the niggers have done enough! We will not hear you speak! Stop your mouth!"

At one meeting, the situation became so dangerous that Sojourner's friends dressed her in military clothing to put the fear of God into her enemies. Sojourner was taken to the meeting in a carriage and surrounded by an army of soldiers. A mob was gathered around the courthouse where she was scheduled to speak. When they saw the crowd of supporters following Sojourner's carriage, they quickly left, described by some as "looking like a flock of frightened crows." No one was left but a small boy who sat on a fence crying, "Nigger, nigger!" The meeting went as planned without interruption.

On January 1, 1863, President Abraham Lincoln signed an executive order ending slavery in the rebel states. The Emancipation Proclamation read, "All persons held as slaves within any State, or designated part of a State the people whereof shall then be in rebellion against the United States, shall be then, thenceforward, and forever free."

The proclamation was received across the North with cheers and tears. Thousands of churches rang their church bells. People danced in the streets. Sojourner gathered her friends in Battle Creek and celebrated with cheering, singing, and long speeches. In her mind, no festival could compare to the joy and enthusiasm that people shared who had dedicated their lives to freedom.

Several days after the emancipation, Sojourner had a stroke. Somehow the rumor spread that she had died. The editor at the *Anti-Slavery Standard*, Oliver Johnson, believed the rumor and printed a story about her death. Author Harriet Beecher Stowe wrote about her 1853 meeting with Sojourner and Sojourner's accomplishments as a tribute to her life. The article was published in the April 1863 issue of *Atlantic Monthly* magazine. People who had never heard of Sojourner were introduced to the amazing exploits of the woman who Stowe called the "The Libyan (African) Sibyl," which referred to a prophetess from ancient times. Stowe was amazed at Sojourner's great intellectual abilities and wondered what other feats this illiterate former slave would have accomplished if she had learned how to read and write.

But the great lady wasn't dead. With the help of her friends and family, Sojourner recovered quickly. Sojourner had been active all of her life, and it was almost impossible for her to sit still. Besides, now was no time for a seasoned abolitionist to quit. Sojourner plunged back into her work, even though her daughters urged her at least to slow down. "There's a war going on," Sojourner said, "and I mean to be a part of it."

After the Emancipation Proclamation was issued, the North began to recruit blacks to serve in racially-segregated units. Fifteen hundred black troops enlisted in the 1st Michigan Volunteer Black Infantry. These black soldiers weren't paid the same as whites, and sometimes their white officers mistreated them. Sojourner spoke out against this injustice, pointing out that if black soldiers were dying equally, why weren't they paid equally for living?

By Thanksgiving of 1863, Sojourner received the news that her grandson, James Caldwell, was missing in action. He had not been seen since the morning of July 16, 1863, when the 54th had seen action on Majes Island. Two days later, the regiment had attacked Fort Wagner, South Carolina. Sammy had read the details to Sojourner from the *Standard*: "The Charleston papers all say that 650 of our dead were buried on the Sunday morning after the assault. . . . Unofficial reports say the Negroes have been sold into slavery and that white officers are treated with unmeasurable abuse."

Sojourner traveled to Camp Ward, an army base located near Detroit, Michigan. Over fifteen hundred black troops were stationed at Camp Ward. Truth brought food donated from the residents of Battle Creek so the soldiers could enjoy a proper Thanksgiving dinner. When she arrived, the regiment's commanding officer ordered his men to stand at attention. Then Sojourner spoke to the men about patriotism, and when she finished, the men gave her a rousing cheer.

After the official ceremony, Sojourner remained to help prepare the Thanksgiving meal, and while the men ate, she sang a hymn that she'd composed especially for the Michigan Infantry to be sung to the tune of "John Brown's Body":

We are the hardy soldiers of the
  First of Michigan;
We're fighting for the union and

for the rights of man.
And when the battle wages
you'll find us in the van,
As we go marching on.

We are the valiant soldiers who
'listed for the war;
We are fighting for the Union;
we are fighting for the law.
We can shoot a rebel farther than
a white man ever saw;
As we go marching on.

They will have to pay us wages,
the wages of their sin;
They will have to bow their foreheads
to their colored kith and kin;
They will have to give us houseroom,
or the roof will tumble in,
As we go marching on.

The bespectacled elderly woman moved from soldier to soldier and served them a proper Thanksgiving dinner. She talked with them about parents and home. "Can you write, son?" she asked a soldier. "Yes," came the response. Sojourner quickly continued, "Have you sent your folks word of your whereabouts?" If the soldier responded, "No," Sojourner admonished him, saying, "Don't grieve your parents. Write them now."

During the spring of 1864, Sojourner decided to visit President Lincoln in Washington, D.C. Although many of her abolitionist friends believed President Lincoln was moving too slowly to bring about an end to slavery, Sojourner greatly respected the president. "Have patience!" she told her friends. "It takes a great while to turn about this great ship of state." In the meantime, she believed that Lincoln could use some encouragement.

Accompanied by her grandson, Sammy Banks, Sojourner boarded the train for the nation's capital, stopping in several towns along the route to give speeches. In September 1864, she reached Washington, D.C. In a little more than a month, Americans would vote about whether President Lincoln would serve a second term of office.

Parts of Washington reminded her of the Five Points district in New York City. The streets of Washington were filled with slaves who had poured into the city after their freedom. They lived in unhealthy conditions and were surrounded by despair and filth. Sojourner's heart went out to them, and she helped them whenever she could.

Freeing the slaves had created another problem: What was to be done with the millions of people who had no education or money and only limited skills? Congress had set aside funds to establish the Freedman's Bureau, which was designed to help freed slaves make the transition from slavery to freedom. Sojourner hoped that there might be some job for her within the Bureau.

When Sojourner learned that her good friend and former traveling companion, Josephine Griffing, was in Washington, she went to see her right away. Griffing had become the local agent of the National Freedman's Relief Association. When Sojourner expressed her concerns about the condition of the newly freed slaves, Josephine said, "I know just the place for you: Freedman's Village."

Constructed by the army as a model village, Freedman's Village was a series of neat cottages, a great improvement over the shacks the slaves had lived in during slavery. The village was located in Arlington, Virginia, just outside Washington, on the old estate of General Robert E. Lee.

Sojourner, along with her grandson Sammy, moved into the village. There Sojourner moved around like a woman half her age. She helped the other women learn how to sew, cook, clean, comb hair, and take care of their children. She sent Sammy to the village school and encouraged mothers not only to send their children but also to attend adult classes themselves.

Although Sojourner had been in Washington, D.C., several weeks, she still hadn't gotten a chance to meet with President Lincoln. When she'd first arrived, she'd tried to secure an appointment with Lincoln but had found that on her own, she was unable to do so. Then she asked Lucy Colman—a white, Massachusetts-born abolitionist, whose permanent home was in Rochester and who at the time was teaching freed slaves in Washington—to arrange an appointment for her. Colman admired Sojourner, once saying that Sojourner never "disgraced" her name, and was willing to help her. After some time, Colman, using Mrs. Lincoln's black dressmaker, Elizabeth Keckley, as a go-between, succeeded in arranging an appointment. When Colman finally took Sojourner to the White House on October 29, 1864, the two women had to wait several hours until it was their turn to see the busy president.

From time to time as the women waited, the president appeared to usher someone into his office. Truth was pleased to see that he treated his black guests with the same courtesy that he showed to the white visitors.

Finally, Truth gained her turn to go into the president's office. She had planned to speak with him about improving the conditions of former slaves; but when she was introduced to the president, she looked at his weary face and his shoulders, which seemed to sag heavily with the burden they carried. Sojourner's heart was moved by the great sadness of this man who had freed her people. She decided not to add yet another complaint to his load. Instead, she kept the conversation light.

After she had sat down, Sojourner told him bluntly, "I never heard of you before you were put in for president."

Lincoln laughed at the comment and replied, "I heard of you years and years before I ever thought of being president. Your name is well-known in the Midwest."

President Lincoln showed her around his office and pointed out a Bible that a group of Baltimore blacks had presented to him. She held the book in her hands and traced the big gold letters—the Bible—with her finger. Remembering one of her favorite Bible stories, Sojourner reminded President Lincoln that he was like Daniel in the lions' den; but with God on his side, he'd win, just like Daniel. Then she told the president that in her opinion, he was the best president the country had ever had.

Then Sojourner thanked the president for his efforts to help black Americans and advised him not to worry about the blustering attacks of his critics. The people in the nation were behind him and would support him in the upcoming election, she said. Lincoln, in turn, thanked her for the encouragement. When it was time to leave, Sojourner asked Lincoln to sign her "Book of Life." For Sojourner, the "Book of Life" was a combination scrapbook and autograph book. Throughout her travels, she collected the signatures of the great people she had met and respected. She also kept personal letters and newspaper clippings. Everywhere Sojourner went, she took her "Book of Life" with her.

She watched with great pride as the president signed, "For Aunty Sojourner Truth, A. Lincoln, October 29, 1864." (Years later, the terms "Aunty" and "Uncle" became words that black women and men resented. During the time of Lincoln, however, they were terms of endearment. For instance, General William T. Sherman was affectionately known as "Uncle Billy," and General Robert E. Lee's soldiers called him "Uncle Bobby.")

In November, as Sojourner had predicted, Lincoln was swept back into office by an overwhelming margin in the wake of several victories by the Union army. By that time, Sojourner had discovered that she enjoyed the busy atmosphere in the nation's capital. Instead of returning to Battle Creek, she decided to stay in Washington, D.C., and see what she could do to assist the Union's war effort.

At the invitation of prominent black minister Henry Highland Garnet, Sojourner spoke at a local charity benefit to help raise money for black soldiers. In addition, she joined a group of women who were feeding and nursing thousands of former slaves who had fled the South. Many of the escaped slaves settled in Washington, D.C., which had become a free area in April 1862 after Lincoln had signed a bill that outlawed slavery in the capital.

These recently freed slaves endured harsh conditions in Washington. The men and women covered themselves with rags to keep warm in the winter, and they ate scraps gleaned from garbage dumps to keep from starving. Many of them became sick and died.

Besides their physical living conditions, freed slaves also had to hide from the bands of slave traders who kidnapped blacks and smuggled them into the Confederate states. The kidnappers threatened to kill anyone who gave information about the illegal slave trade to the federal marshals. Most freedmen were afraid to say anything in protest.

Sojourner, however, refused to be silenced. She marched through the freedmen's villages and told the freed slaves, "The law is for you. Take refuge in it."

As she attacked the injustices for blacks in the nation's capital, the morale of the African American community rose. Toward the end of 1864, a public welfare organization called the National Freedman's Relief Association asked Sojourner to work as a counselor to former slaves who were living at a camp in Arlington Heights, Virginia. There she educated the freedmen about the need to locate work and housing and about the other responsibilities that came with their newly won freedom.

Sojourner was still working at the Freedman's Village when General Robert E. Lee surrendered to General Ulysses S. Grant at Appomattox Courthouse in Virginia on April 9, 1865. The surrender ended the war, leaving more than half a million people dead.

Six days after the surrender, President Lincoln's name was added to the list of victims. A freezing drizzle was falling on Washington the night it was announced that Lincoln had been assassinated during a play at the Ford Theater. Actor John Wilkes Booth had shot the president. Although Lincoln was taken to the home of William Peterson at 453 Tenth Street, he died at 7:22 the next morning.

That same evening in a separate incident, Secretary of State William

Seward was stabbed, but he survived. Vice President Andrew Johnson became president of the United States. Sojourner, believing that no one had done more for the cause of black Americans than Lincoln, was devastated by his sudden death.

Sojourner and Sammy joined thousands of people who walked through the East Room of the White House where Lincoln's body lay in state. For the last time, Sojourner looked at the president who would be remembered as "the Emancipator."

In the month following Lincoln's death, the last of the Confederate armies surrendered to Union forces. The Civil War was over. It had spanned four years and taken hundreds of thousands of lives, but the battle against slavery had been won. Sojourner's prayers had been answered. She had lived to see the end of slavery.

On December 12, 1865, Sojourner and millions of other Americans celebrated as Congress ratified the Thirteenth Amendment to the Constitution. It declared that "Neither slavery, nor involuntary servitude. . .shall exist within the United States, or any place subject to their jurisdiction." At last, slavery had officially ended.

Returning to the Freedman's Village, Sojourner spent hours trying to convince former slaves that Lincoln's death didn't mean reenslavement and that Vice President Johnson, from Tennessee, wouldn't turn back the hands of time. Even though Sojourner sounded convincing, she had her private doubts.

During the summer of 1865, she met with President Andrew Johnson. "Please be seated, Mrs. Truth," said the president.

"Sit down yourself, Mr. President," Sojourner replied. "I'm used to standing because I've been lecturing for many years." Then she talked with the president about her concerns and the problems that her people faced, based on firsthand information from Freedman's Village. While the president listened politely, he made no commitment. Sojourner carried her "Book of Life" that day, but she didn't ask President Johnson to sign it. She never explained whether it was oversight or intention.

Not long after her visit with Johnson, the War Department assigned Sojourner to work at the Freedman's Hospital. They needed her to help "promote order, cleanliness, industry, and virtue among the patients." Although Sojourner was seventy years old, she accepted the position. She did her best to ensure that proper medical care was given to the hospital's black patients. Her work gave her a renewed sense of purpose, and she began to have greater energy than she had for some time.

Since Sammy was helping at the Freedman's Village, he and Sojourner continued to live there. Also, he continued to keep in communication with the family back in Battle Creek. By this time, Sojourner's grandson James had returned home from the Civil War. He had survived months as a prisoner of war.

To get to and from her work at the hospital, Sojourner often walked; but one day she decided to take a streetcar. She signaled a car to stop. When it kept going, she ran after it, yelling. The conductor kept ringing his bell so that he could pretend that he had not heard her. When at last the conductor had to stop the car to take on white passengers, Sojourner climbed into the car, scolding the conductor. "It is a shame to make a lady run so." He replied that if she said another word to him, he would put her off. She threatened him, "If you attempt that, it will cost you more than your car and horses are worth." When a dignified man in the uniform of a general intervened on her behalf, the conductor left her alone.

Sojourner was keenly aware that the law was on her side. She did not try to organize blacks to join her, but when circumstances seemed to suggest it, she acted directly and on her own.

A few weeks later, Sojourner and her white friend Laura Haviland were boarding a streetcar together. Sojourner stepped ahead of her friend, but the conductor snatched her out of the way. "Let the lady on before you," he snapped.

"I'm a lady, too," Sojourner snapped back. The conductor pushed Sojourner off the streetcar.

Mrs. Haviland stopped the man. "Don't you put her off," she said.

"Why? Does she belong to you?" the conductor asked angrily.

"No," Mrs. Haviland replied. "She belongs to humanity."

"Then take her and go!" The conductor slammed Sojourner against the door and bruised her shoulder. After Sojourner asked Haviland to jot down the number of the car, the conductor left them alone. "It is hard for the old slaveholding spirit to die," Sojourner reflected, "but die it must."

Back at the hospital, when the two women asked a surgeon to examine Sojourner's shoulder, he found it swollen. Then the two women reported the incident to the president of the streetcar company. He promptly fired the conductor.

This company president also advised Sojourner to have the conductor arrested for assault, which she did with the help of the Freedman's Bureau, who furnished her with a lawyer. A few days later, Justice William Thompson held a hearing for the conductor, as reported in a curious article published in at least four Washington newspapers.

Sojourner won her case in court. As she said about the incident, "Before the trial was over, so many blacks were now daring to ride in the cars that the inside of the cars looked like pepper and salt." Soon the conductors who had cursed Sojourner for wanting to ride would stop for both black and white women and even condescend to say, "Walk in, ladies." Sojourner later claimed that her Washington ride-ins had changed the city. The old warrior marked another victory in her struggle for equality.

TEN

Sojourner's victory over the streetcars, however, was short-lived. Soon laws were passed across the nation that made it illegal for blacks and whites to ride together. These "Jim Crow" laws stayed in force until the modern civil rights movement.

Meanwhile, Sojourner continued speaking out about women's rights. When she addressed an audience, Frederick Douglass said, "She seemed to please herself and others best when she put her ideas in the oddest forms." In 1867, she complained to a New York newspaperman that he was not reporting her words accurately, but she admitted "good-naturedly," he said, that her speech was difficult to record because she "was speaking in an unknown tongue."

Largely, Sojourner spoke from her own experiences, but what she said reflected an awareness of the current clash of thought. She was able to cut through the debate with startling flashes of insight. She was very articulate, even though not in as ordered a fashion as Douglass. Her thinking was more spontaneous. It lent itself to sudden leaps, poetry, and parable.

Sojourner spoke extemporaneously, she said, not knowing what the Lord would put into her mouth. Some phrases she spoke deliberately, while others she raced through. Often she interrupted herself with droll asides. According to a Quaker friend, Sojourner had a "magnetic power over an audience." The *Detroit Advertiser* wrote that she "had a heart of love" and a "tongue of fire." Her friend Lucy Stone said that Sojourner spoke "with direct and terrible force, moving friend and foe alike."

In other aspects of her life, illiteracy continued to handicap Sojourner. Once she conceded that it was "hard work" to get as many letters written for her as she wanted. In another instance, thanking a correspondent for "her kind words," she replied as a friend wrote down her response, "Oh, if I could but write and answer them myself." More important, Sojourner's illiteracy limited her opportunities for leadership. She never became part of the decision-making inner circles of either the abolitionists or women's rights movement as Frederick Douglass sometimes did. Also, her illiteracy kept Sojourner poor because it limited her job opportunities. But her overwhelming faith that God had called her to a special mission to set the world right side up seemed to convince Sojourner that her illiteracy was another God-given trait, like her blackness and womanhood, which fashioned her beautifully to carry out her mission.

Whenever Sojourner spoke, she usually sang—sometimes with difficulty as she grew older. At an 1867 equal rights convention in New York, she said she had not heard any singing at the convention, but "there ought to be singing here." Though she admitted, "I can't sing as well as I used to," she proceeded to sing, and the audience responded with hearty applause. One newspaper reporter at the conference reported on the singing as "a weird, wailing song, with a very queer tune, an odd though clear pronunciation of words, and her old head swaying to and fro in harmony."

For years, abolitionists and women's rights activists had worked together and supported each other's cause. In 1869, the Fifteenth Amendment to the Constitution was passed, giving black men the right to vote, but women were still excluded. It said, "The right of citizens of the United States to vote shall not be denied or abridged by the United States or by any State on account of race, color, or previous condition of servitude."

Women abolitionists felt betrayed by black men who benefited from their efforts and then seemed to desert them. Even Frederick Douglass, who had been the first to back women's rights to vote, said, "This hour belongs to the Negro."

After hearing this statement, Elizabeth Cady Stanton retorted, "My question is this: Do you believe the African race is composed entirely of males?"

The argument divided women into two different camps. The National Woman Suffrage Association (NWSA), which was founded in 1869 by Elizabeth Cady Stanton and Susan B. Anthony, devoted their efforts to women's suffrage through constitutional amendment. The American Woman Suffrage Association (AWSA), founded a few months later by Lucy Stone and Henry Blackwell, believed women's suffrage was best achieved through state actions.

Each organization looked for allies among the former women's abolitionists. Since Sojourner had always championed the cause of women's suffrage, Susan B. Anthony wrote her a letter with a petition listing demands for women's rights and asked her to sign it. Sojourner responded, "I feel that if I have to answer for the deeds done in my body just as much as a man, I have a right to have just as much as a man. There is a great stir about colored men getting their rights, but not a word about the colored women; and if colored men get their rights, and not colored women theirs, you see the colored men will be masters over the women, and it will be just as bad as it was before. So I am for keeping the thing going while things are stirring; because if we wait till it is still, it will take a great while to get it going again."

Sojourner's prophecy about the future of the women's suffrage movement came true. The movement lost momentum during the next few years. Stanton,

Stone, Truth, and others died before women won the right to vote.

—— Before long, black male voters began to make their numbers felt and increased their representation in state legislatures. In addition, more than twenty black leaders—including Blanche K. Bruce, P. B. S. Pinchback, Joseph Rainey, and Hiram Revels—were elected to Congress during the Reconstruction era. The work of these legislators helped to end more than two hundred years of enforced ignorance as blacks throughout the South began to attend free schools and acquire knowledge that could help them succeed in a free society.

Another theme of Sojourner's speeches during this period was equal pay for equal work. She told her audiences, "I have done a great deal of work, as much as a man, but did not get as much pay. I used to work in the field and bind grain, keeping up with the cradler; but men doing no more got twice as much pay. . . . We do as much; we eat as much; we want as much."

Sojourner felt strongly about the women's suffrage issue. She not only spoke about it, but she acted on her beliefs. Some report that Sojourner tried to vote for Ulysses S. Grant in 1868. Four years later, in Battle Creek, she attempted to register to vote in the third ward, where she lived. Of course, she was refused, but nevertheless, she appeared the following week on election day and tried to vote. Once again, she was refused, but she remained at the polls all day and lectured the authorities on the issue of women's rights. The newspaper that reported this incident concluded their article, "It is Sojourner's determination to continue the assertion of her rights until she gains them."

Not only Sojourner's personal feelings inspired her fight to express her political opinion through the ballot. As in her fight for the end of slavery, Sojourner truly believed that she was doing the work of God and that somehow her person and her actions embodied God's will. Thus, when she addressed the equal righters in New York, she declared (perpetuating the myth about her age), "I am above eighty years old; it is about time for me to be going. . . . I suppose I am kept here because something remains for me to do; I suppose I am yet to help to break the chain." Unfortunately, she never lived to see women voting. The chain to which she referred didn't break until the ratification of the Nineteenth Amendment, which granted women the right to vote in 1920.

Although Sojourner Truth was over seventy years old, she took up one more cause—land rights. Besides continuing her ongoing cause of women's rights, she worked for government-sponsored black homesteads out West. Sojourner argued that blacks had been forced to work with no profit from their own labor, yet no slave had ever been compensated. It was too late to pay back with money, but by setting aside land for each slave—"Twenty acres and a mule"—the government, in her opinion, could pay the debt in full.

Sojourner began to talk up the idea of a land grant program for former slave families. Since farming was what these people knew best, why not provide them with a means to become productive, self-sufficient citizens?

As Sojourner spent more and more time among the freed slaves, she saw their lives had been used for the enrichment of others, their labor had been taken from them, and their children stolen away. She became angry. Looking at the large, white buildings around Washington, she exclaimed, "We helped pay this cost." Then she detailed with painful accuracy the vast and various contributions black people had made to the welfare and development of the United States. She made certain to point out that their efforts were yet to be acknowledged and rewarded.

Sojourner knew that the government owned vast lands in the West and was giving many acres to the large and rapidly expanding railroad companies. She wondered why some of these acres could not go to the women and men whose bondage had served to increase the nation's wealth. She didn't ask for all of the land, merely enough on which black people could build the new life they so badly needed.

Sojourner's job at the Freedman's Hospital had finished, so she and Sammy traveled the nation to lecture for equal women's rights and newly freed blacks. Her lectures often succeeded in helping people throw off their prejudice and hatred.

On March 31, 1870, Sojourner returned to Washington, D.C., and along with Giles Stebbins of Detroit, visited the newly elected president, Ulysses S. Grant. Through talking with the president, she hoped to gain support for her land grant proposal.

As the meeting began, both Sojourner and the president were stiff and very formal with each other, but by the end of the meeting, Sojourner, her eyes glowing with emotion, thanked Grant for his efforts to secure new guarantees of justice for blacks. The president was moved. He replied that he hoped to be wise and firm and to remember that everybody deserved full rights. Then he signed Sojourner's "Book of Life" and took one of her calling cards as a memento of their meeting.

Later, in the *Detroit Tribune*, Stebbins captured the meeting in an article about Sojourner.

> She expressed her pleasure in meeting him, yet I could see it was not quite easy on either side. She had met Abraham Lincoln, and he, born a Kentuckian, could call her "Aunty" in the old familiar way, while Grant

was reticent yet kindly. But a happy thought came to her. It was the civil rights bill days, and not long before he had signed some act of Congress giving new guarantees of justice to the colored people. She spoke of this gracefully and the thin ice broke. Standing there, tall and erect while stirred in soul by the occasion, her wonderful eyes glowed with emotion as she thanked him for his good deed to the once enslaved race to which she belonged. . . . Words followed freely on both sides—she telling him how his tasks and trials were appreciated, and how much faith was placed in his upright doing of duty to the oppressed, and he quietly, yet with much feeling, expressing the hope that he might be wise and firm and never forget the unalienable rights of all.

The meeting with Grant capped a memorable pair of days for Sojourner. On the previous day, the Fifteenth Amendment had been ratified, guaranteeing the right to vote for all men regardless of "race, color, or previous condition of servitude." The right to vote was crucial to the welfare of blacks, who made up a sizable portion of the Southern population and composed the majority in some states.

But when the help that Sojourner expected from Grant was not forthcoming, she took her request to Congress. Arriving at the Capitol one morning dressed in her usual white cap, gray dress, and white shawl, Sojourner cut a striking figure as she addressed a group of senators.

"We have been a source of wealth to this republic," she said, eloquently defending her position. "Our labor supplied the country with cotton, until villages and cities dotted the enterprising North for its manufacture, and furnished employment and support for a multitude, thereby becoming a revenue to the government. . . . Our nerves and sinews, our tears and blood have been sacrificed on the altar of this nation's avarice. Our unpaid labor has been a stepping-stone to its financial success. Some of its dividends must surely be ours."

Fourteen senators signed Sojourner's "Book of Life" even though they weren't supportive of her land grant proposal. Senator Charles Sumner of Massachusetts, however, took more than a casual interest in her ideas. He promised to sponsor a bill if she could show him that there was widespread support for such a plan. Sojourner had the following petition drawn up:

To the Senate and House of Representatives, in Congress Assembled:
Whereas, from the faithful and earnest representatives of Sojourner Truth (who has personally investigated the matter) we believe that the freed colored people in and about Washington, dependent upon government

for support, would be greatly benefited and might become useful citizens by being placed in a position to support themselves;

We, the undersigned, therefore earnestly request your honorable body to set apart for them a portion of the public land in the West and erect buildings thereon for the aged and infirm, and otherwise legislate so as to secure the desired results.

With her petition in hand, Sojourner, her grandson Sammy, and another grandson set out across the nation to collect signatures.

On January 1, 1871, the eighth anniversary of the Emancipation Proclamation, Sojourner celebrated at Tremont Hall in Boston. She spoke about beginning life in a cellar, suffering beatings with a rod, and enduring other indignities during slavery. She said in part, "Now some people say, 'Let the blacks take care of themselves.' But you've taken everything away from them. They don't have anything left! I say, get the black people out of Washington! Get them off the government! Get the old people out and build them homes in the West where they can feed themselves. Lift up those people and put them there. Teach them to read part of the time, and teach them to work the other part of the time. Do that, and they will soon be a people among you. That is my commission!"

When they heard Sojourner speak, the people gladly signed her petition—even those people who initially opposed the proposal. After listening to her, they were convinced.

While in Massachusetts, Sojourner went to visit her friend Olive Gilbert, the woman who had written her autobiography while they had been in Northampton, Massachusetts. Olive helped her gather more signatures for her petition. She also spoke in Rochester while with Olive, eloquently painting a picture of the degradation in which the capital's black population lived. Once again she appealed for the granting of land by the government and for her audience's support of her petition.

"You owe it to them," she said to the audience, "because you took away from them all they earned and made them what they are. You take no interest in the colored people. . . . You are the cause of the brutality of these poor creatures, for you are the children of those who enslaved them." Then, recalling how eagerly people in those days helped the poor and oppressed outside of the United States, she said, "You are ready to help the heathen in foreign lands, but you don't care for the heathen right around you. I want you to sign petitions to send to Washington. . . ."

Many of the newspaper reports of her speeches during this period were friendly, but there were some that opposed her support of unpopular causes and mocked her uneducated speech and often unconventional ways. Sojourner never grew discouraged in her fight for freedom and women's rights. Not only did she make her own gestures toward exercising her rights, but she also encouraged others to exercise their rights. In 1871, she heard that her friend Nannette Gardner had actually succeed in voting in Detroit. She asked for a written statement from Gardner to substantiate the story, and she kept the letter of response among her treasured autographs and papers until her death.

Speaking in Detroit in the campaign for the reelection of President Grant in 1872, Sojourner was about seventy-five years old. She "sang several of her original songs, all of which," according to the newspaper, "were received with applause." When she was speaking in a small Pennsylvania town in 1874, a newspaper reported that Sojourner sang "right sweetly a Negro melody. . .giving just enough of a southern Negro double-demi-semi-quaver to it, to make it interesting."

Another newspaper from Springfield declared, "We do most decidedly dislike the complexion and everything else appertaining to Mrs. Truth, the radical—the renowned, saintly, liberated, oratorical, pious slave. . . . She is a crazy, ignorant, repelling negress, and her guardians would do a Christian act to restrict her entirely to private life."

Despite these attacks, which showed the poorest side of society during this period, Sojourner refused to give up her fight to get land for indigent black people. Her advancing age, precarious health, and the threats and jibes of people notwithstanding, Sojourner continued to travel and preach. She passed through Massachusetts, western New York, Michigan, Kansas, Iowa, Illinois, Missouri, Wisconsin, Washington, Ohio, New Jersey, and Kentucky during the last ten years of her life. On each of these trips, she met with old and new friends, sang her songs, and continued entertaining and enlightening people on a variety of topics—all connected to the well-being and liberation of black people and women.

A year after leaving Washington, Sojourner returned with a thousand signatures. She hurried to Sumner's office and was told by his secretary that the great senator had recently died. No other person would help Sojourner with her cause. Her hopes of getting a bill introduced into the Senate evaporated. The tide of black progress continued to be blocked by conservative whites. More and more, she began to realize that the battle for black freedom had only begun.

Sojourner fought for abolition, equality, and suffrage, but she also moved into other fields of struggle. Like many feminists and abolitionists, Sojourner was attracted to the temperance movement. This movement called for voluntary abstinence from drinking alcoholic beverages. Many references were made to her speaking before temperance groups, either on this subject or on other questions that interested her. Like other black leaders, Sojourner felt alcohol was fast becoming a serious social problem among poor blacks. She believed that only complete sobriety would enable her people to pull themselves up fully from the mire of a past as slaves.

At last, Sojourner decided to return home to Michigan. She missed Battle Creek and her family there, but more important, Sammy was ill. At first his condition didn't seem serious, but his fever grew worse along with his cough. Worried about her favorite grandson's illness and suffering with an ulcer on her leg, Sojourner grew depressed. When Sammy died in February 1875, her condition worsened. Sammy hadn't even reached his twenty-fifth birthday. To Sojourner, Sammy's death was worse than losing her son, Peter, because Sammy had been such a good and faithful companion. She never stopped mourning his death.

No matter what Sojourner did, she couldn't work away her hurt. She missed Sammy terribly and without him felt handicapped. He had read to her, taken care of all her correspondence, and looked after her affairs. She had written to her family that she was going back to Battle Creek to die, but she outlived her grandson by nine years.

Meanwhile, conflict throughout the nation continued. In the South, many whites rebelled against the Reconstruction laws by forming white-supremacist groups such as the Ku Klux Klan, which kidnapped and murdered blacks without fear of punishment. White insurrectionists conspired to overthrow the Southern state governments in which blacks had succeeded in marshaling a great deal of power. Blacks armed themselves and fought back, and Grant was forced to send regiments of federal troops to South Carolina and other troubled areas to restore order.

The Supreme Court supported the anti-Reconstruction sentiment by issuing rulings that weakened the effects of the Fourteenth and Fifteenth Amendments. The justices ruled that the federal government had only limited power to protect Southern black voters. By July 4, 1876—the hundred-year anniversary of the signing of the Declaration of Independence—white Americans had still not decided if they really believed that "all men are created equal." By the end of that year, they had, in effect, decided—but Sojourner could not have liked their decision.

The initial results of the 1876 presidential election indicated that the victor, by a narrow margin, was Democratic candidate Samuel Tilden. However, Republicans bribed the electoral officers of Louisiana and Florida to change their voting tallies and thus switch their states' electoral votes to the Republican candidate, Rutherford Hayes. These Republicans promised that the new administration would let conservative whites regain control of the South.

With a change in the electoral vote, Hayes became the nineteenth president of the United States. One of his first acts as president was to withdraw the federal troops that were helping to protect the civil rights of Southern blacks. The action signaled that the Reconstruction era was over, and the gains that blacks had won after the Civil War would be rolled back. Despite the significance of this action, Sojourner did not have the strength to go on a speaking tour to protest against the new attempts to deprive blacks of their rights.

Rumors began to circulate that she had died or that she was too old to travel, having already celebrated her one hundredth birthday. Actually, she was nearing eighty years old and living at her home in Battle Creek. Her hair had turned gray thirty years before, and now her hearing and sight had almost completely failed. The once tall and strong Sojourner Truth needed the support of a cane to walk.

In 1877, according to some accounts, Sojourner's health mysteriously improved. Perhaps her spirit was strengthened by the knowledge that wherever there was oppression, courageous people like herself were rising up to carry on the battle for freedom. In any case, her hearing returned and her eyesight sharpened dramatically. That next year, Sojourner went on another speaking tour, covering thirty-six different towns in Michigan. Then, at eighty-one years old, she was one of three Michigan delegates to the Woman's Rights Convention in Rochester. Later, after a grueling trip to Kansas where she spoke to newly freed slaves who were planning to homestead, Sojourner returned home for good.

Four years before Sojourner died, a Louisville, Kentucky, newspaper wrote, "The oldest truth nowadays is Sojourner." And so it seemed to the nation, because for many decades, they had heard the name of Sojourner Truth. To the general public, she seemed blessed with boundless energy, subject to rules of existence that were other than human. Despite the great age that she claimed, she never seemed to tire and would pick up new causes to champion with a vigor unknown in most people of her years. The general perception of Sojourner was wrong, however. She was very human, and her health was steadily declining.

Many people were misled about Sojourner's age. They believed that she was almost a second Methuselah: One person said that she was 82 in 1868; when she met with President Grant and the senators in 1870, she was reportedly 90; close to death, she herself declared that her age was 114; her obituary put it as 108; on her gravestone, which was carved years later, her age was listed as 105. In fact, when Sojourner Truth died in 1883, she was approximately 86 years old.

In the introduction to the 1878 edition of Sojourner's *Narrative*, Frances Titus wrote that despite various rumors of Sojourner's death, her "mind is as clear and vigorous as in middle age." She reported, however, that as far back as 1863, Sojourner had complained, "Lord, I'm too old to work—I'm too sick to hold meetings and speak to people and sell my books." What a great tribute to Sojourner's determination that despite her ill health, she was able to devote herself so tirelessly to the various causes that occupied her final years.

By the beginning of 1882, Sojourner had become gravely ill. Painful ulcers covered her arms and legs, and she became too weak to get up from her bed. She remained this way for the next year and a half. Dr. John Harvey Kellogg, director of the Battle Creek Sanitarium, admitted her because she was near death. Even in her pain and close to death, Sojourner was able to display that spirit that had become so familiar to her admirers and friends. She spoke weakly to visitors, mostly on religious subjects. She seemed completely at ease with her imminent death, feeling that God's glory was awaiting her.

One morning early in November 1883, Gilbert visited Sojourner and found her in extreme pain. Yet when Sojourner saw her old friend, she smiled and, with a faraway look in her eyes, began to sing her favorite hymn, which she had often used to gather crowds for her speeches:

> *It was early in the morning,*
> *It was early in the morning,*
> *Just at the break of day,*
> *When He rose, when He rose, when He rose,*
> *And went to heaven on a cloud.*

Two weeks later, at her home in Battle Creek, Sojourner Truth sank into a deep coma. She died at three o'clock on the morning of November 26, 1883. She did not fear death, she had said, for she was confident that she would be happy in heaven.

At the time of Sojourner's death, a Battle Creek newspaper reported, "This country has lost one of its most remarkable personages." A New York paper reminded its readers that "she did not seek the applause of her fellow beings, but worked quietly and with modesty."

More personal expressions of sadness about Sojourner's death came from her old colleagues Wendell Phillips and Frederick Douglass. Phillips wrote that Sojourner "was a remarkable figure in the anti-slavery movement, almost the only speaker in it who had once been a slave in a Northern state." Douglass wrote that she had been "venerable for age, distinguished for insight into human nature, remarkable for independence and courageous self-assertion."

Two days after Sojourner Truth's death, nearly a thousand people gathered at her house and formed a procession behind the black-plumed hearse that bore her body. Her coffin was decorated with the images of a cross, a sheaf of ripe grain, a sickle, and a crown. It was carried by white residents of Battle Creek to the Congregational and Presbyterian Church, and many of her fellow activists in the women's rights and abolitionist movements spoke about her "rare qualities of head and heart." At her funeral, Sojourner was remembered as a dynamic woman with strength, integrity, poise, and wit. Her friend the Reverend Reed Stuart delivered the funeral sermon.

The sun was setting in Battle Creek's Oakhill Cemetery as Sojourner Truth was lowered into her final resting place. Crimson and gold lit up the western horizon. When the sun finally set, millions of stars lit up the heavens in which Sojourner had found assurance that God was watching over her. She was buried near her grandson Sammy.

In return for God's guidance, Sojourner Truth became His faithful servant, continually ignoring personal hardship in her pursuit of freedom for blacks and women. Deeply devoted to turning the world "right side up," she traveled far and wide to leave an inspiring legacy to all those who face a long and difficult journey when fighting for justice and respect.

ELEVEN

During her lifetime, few tributes to Sojourner Truth's life were written. Fewer yet survived her into history. Sojourner's *Narrative* and her "Book of Life" were carefully recorded and printed by Olive Gilbert and Frances Titus. In these human documents, the reader can sense the love and respect Sojourner earned from many of her contemporaries.

The visual arts also paid tribute to Sojourner Truth. The sculptor William Wetmore Story heard Harriet Beecher Stowe's account of her meeting with Sojourner in her Andover, Massachusetts, home. He was inspired to make a statue he called the *Sibilla Libica*, which was shown in the World's Exhibition in London in 1862 and attracted much critical attention.

In 1892, Frances Titus commissioned a posthumous portrait of Sojourner to be painted by the artist Frank C. Courter from the photograph on Sojourner's *carte de visite*. This painting shows Truth seated with Lincoln, both of them looking at the Bible that the black residents of Baltimore had given the president. The painting was exhibited in the Michigan building at the 1893 World's Fair in Chicago and later hung in the Battle Creek Sanitarium until the building burned down in 1902. In 1913, an artist named Jackson, working from a photograph of Courter's work, produced another canvas of Sojourner and Lincoln, which now hangs in the Detroit Historical Museum.

Beyond these few memorials, few people carried Sojourner's memory into this century. Even in Battle Creek, where many prominent residents attended her funeral and where they held her up as the city's foremost and first famous citizen, her grave remained unmarked for thirty-three years. The only identification was the number 9 in lot 634. In 1904, the Daughters of the American Revolution launched a movement to have Sojourner Truth's grave properly marked, and in 1916, a marble headstone was finally placed on the site. When the harsh winter weather in Michigan had eroded it, the marker was replaced with a granite tombstone in 1946, which today marks Sojourner's grave.

Almost eighty years after her death, the Sojourner Truth Memorial Association of Battle Creek placed a historical marker beside her grave. This memorial association had been formed in the 1920s to raise five thousand dollars to perpetuate Sojourner's name. Dissolved during the 1930s, the group appeared later under different leadership and was responsible for providing the funds for both the historical marker and the Sojourner Truth Room in Battle Creek's Kimball House Museum.

Battle Creek is also home to Truth Drive, a road that connects streets in a housing project. Bernice Lowe, a dedicated historian who devoted more than twenty years of her life to research Sojourner Truth, makes her home in Battle Creek.

Outside Battle Creek, Sojourner Truth has received little of the national attention she deserves. The Soldiers and Sailors Monument in Detroit shows the figure of a black woman crowning soldiers and sailors. Some people say that the statue represents the black people's gratitude for emancipation. Legend has it that the black woman is Sojourner, but this has not been confirmed.

In 1942, the federal government built a housing project in Detroit and named two hundred units of it the Sojourner Truth Houses. On February 28, 1942, three black families were to move into the otherwise unoccupied buildings. A mob of twelve hundred whites, armed with knives, bottles, clubs, rifles, and shotguns, prevented the families from moving into the units. Three times the police used tear gas to disperse the crowd. Dozens of people were injured, and over a hundred were arrested. Not until April of that year, with the protection of eight hundred state police troopers, were twelve black families able to occupy their apartments.

At least two libraries in other parts of the country have rooms named for Sojourner Truth.

Former New York congresswoman Shirley Chisholm visited Sojourner's grave in April 1972 as an act of tribute from one black woman to another.

Sojourner Truth believed in peaceful dialogue and energetic persuasion. She surely would weep to see the degree of intolerance that persists more than one hundred years after her death.

When Belle became Sojourner Truth, she declared that her devotion to the truth would never die: "And the truth shall be my abiding name," she promised. Whenever people speak out against injustice and scorn oppression, they keep Sojourner Truth's ideals of justice and freedom alive.

FLORENCE NIGHTINGALE

LADY WITH THE LAMP

Sam Wellman

ONE

August 22, 1827, was both the happiest and the unhappiest day that seven-year-old Florence Nightingale had ever spent at Tapton in Yorkshire, England. The day began in her grandmother's fine house with a breakfast so wonderful that Florence lost her usual reticence.

As Florence savored each bite of her meal, the discussion at the table centered on the unusual wedding that was to take place that afternoon.

"Flo will soon have a double-uncle and a double-aunt," quipped a grown-up at the far end of the long dining table, using Florence's nickname. Almost everyone called her Flo. Her sister's name, Parthenope, was usually reduced to the two-syllable "Parthe," which rhymes with Marthy.

As it happened, the bride, this particular day, was the sister of Flo's father, William, and the groom was the brother of Flo's mother, Fanny. So Flo would indeed have Aunt Mai as an aunt twice over, and Uncle Sam would be her uncle twice over. Any children they had in the future would be Flo's and Parthe's double-cousins.

The wedding turned out to be a nightmare for Flo. When Aunt Mai and Uncle Sam were kneeling at the altar, Flo suddenly felt her mother's strong hand on her shoulder, pulling her back into one of the first pews. Goodness! Had she actually kneeled between Aunt Mai and Uncle Sam? She couldn't remember doing it. But she must have.

Though only seven years old, Flo already had a history of other nightmarish moments. Strange things had haunted her earliest years, frightening her very much. In fact, at times it seemed as though something was inside her. She thought she might be "possessed." She couldn't remember where she might have gotten such an insane notion. Certainly no fairy tale or Bible story would have planted an idea like that. She feared being found out and avoided everyone, throwing tantrums if asked to do anything in the presence of others. At times she had fought to stay in the nursery rather than attend meals.

When Flo was young, social etiquette among the upper class in England was complicated, demanding, and troubling. And yet the fears—if not the discomfort—had almost gone away. By the age of seven, Flo no longer feared social occasions as much. In fact, she had even begun to appreciate the rigidity of upper-class English manners.

The social skills exhibited by Mama and Parthe were exemplary. Though only one year older than Flo, Parthe had always laughed easily through dinners and parties and visits. Mama did not laugh so gaily as Parthe, but she labored lightly through her social obligations nevertheless. Young Flo endured society, even losing her fear of socializing, but she did not gain peace of mind. She was restless, though she didn't yet consider that an affliction.

As a child educated by governesses, she was impressed that the great poet George Herbert had lived a scant fifteen miles or so from the Nightingales' Embley Park estate, and she was very familiar with Herbert's poem "Pulley":

> When God at first made man,
>   Having a glass of blessings standing by,
>   "Let us," said He, "pour on all we can:
> Let the world's riches, which dispersed lie,
>   Contract into a span."
>   So strength first made a way;
> Then beauty flowed, then wisdom, honor, pleasure:
> When almost all was out, God made a stay,
> Perceiving that alone of all his treasure
>   Rest in the bottom lay.
>   "For if I should," said He,
> "Bestow this jewel also on my creature,
> He would adore my gifts instead of me,
> And rest in nature, not the God of nature;
>   So both should losers be.
>   Yet let him keep the rest,
> But keep them with repining restlessness:
> Let him be rich and weary, that at least,
> If goodness lead him not, yet weariness
> May toss him to my breast."

Herbert's poem rang true for Flo, for she was very restless and she was drawn to God. Her restlessness was not satisfied by simply keeping on the go—unlike Mama, for whom activity was the balm of life.

Soon after the wedding, Mama, along with her daughters and servants, left the Nightingales' summer home, Lea Hurst in Derbyshire near Tapton, to journey south to their winter home at Embley Park in Hampshire. Their route from year to year couldn't have been more varied. Even when a broken axle waylaid their enormous carriage one time, the incident just seemed part of Mama's eccentric itinerary. Flo recorded every incident in her journal.

In Staffordshire, they were guests for several days at Betley Hall, where

Flo and Parthe had the privilege of socializing with twelve-year-old Miss Caroline, who was so gracious she not only pretended they were sisters, but treated them as equals. The Nightingale sisters were in awe of Caroline's huge doll, with its own canopied bed and wardrobe beside her own bed and wardrobe. On the grounds, Caroline showed them how to shake inedible nuts from the great spreading crown of a horse chestnut. Then Caroline's older brother took them rowing on a lake.

Next, Mama and the girls were guests at Castle Downton. Here Flo encountered a modern wonder: a bathtub with taps. But when the Nightingales' French maid, Agathe, turned on the faucet, she somehow jammed it and flooded the room with water. After that crisis, Flo broke down one of the beds by jumping on it. It took all of Mama's social skills to smooth over their barbaric entry.

Boultibooke was their next stop. Flo was surprised when Sir Harford Brydges spoke to her as if she were an adult—especially when one of her front teeth came out during the visit.

After Boultibooke, the entourage moved on to the heights of Herefordshire and the ruins of the twelfth-century Goodrich Castle. The old bastion received many visitors, though its stone floors were shot full of thistles. The arched gateway was still intact, as were some of the walls with their loopholes for firing weapons. All around the castle were white wildflowers called traveler's joy. Blackberry vines abounded, and once again silly Agathe distinguished herself by eating so much of the sweet, dark fruit that she became sick. Flo wondered how long Mama would tolerate the young French maid's poor judgment. Mama seemed to shrug off the incident.

The journey continued as Mama led the travelers into Wales to explore Tintern Abbey, another ruin. The girls were shown the mundane aspects, like the hole through which a cook passed meals to the monks and the large prayer room now floored with grass. The famous poet William Wordsworth—still very much alive at fifty-seven—had been here, and Mama recited his poem "Tintern Abbey." Flo was struck most of all by verses that said:

> *And I have felt*
> *A presence that disturbs me with the joy*
> *Of elevated thoughts; a sense sublime*
> *Of something far more deeply interfused,*
> *Whose dwelling is the light of setting suns,*
> *And the round ocean and the living air,*
> *And the blue sky, and in the mind of man:*

A motion and a spirit, that impels
All thinking things, all objects of all thought,
And rolls through all things.

Flo had noticed lately that grown-ups seemed reluctant to speak of God. Why did they always allude to God rather than speak His holy names? Outside the church service, God was rarely mentioned. Oh, the poor people in the village were likely to speak directly of God. But the well-to-do, the powerful ladies and gentlemen, rarely spoke like that. It almost seemed a sign of good breeding that one did not mention God. But why?

Mama, the girls, and their retinue of servants traveled by carriage on to Monmouth, then by boat on the River Wye to Chepstow. Again they visited a castle, but by now Flo was so bored with ruins that she quickly forgot its name. From there they departed Wales on a steamship that plied the Severn River, taking their huge carriage aboard, as well. At Bristol, they disembarked and had to try seven hotels before they found one suitable. Flo carefully noted the number in her journal. After Bristol, they rolled on to Bath, the fashionable resort.

Aunt Julia was already in Bath, having gone there directly from the wedding. She was in town to learn how a certain home for elderly women operated. Aunt Julia, sensing that the girls were tired of history and literature, tried to entertain them, amusing them with stories and allowing them to play with a dog. Yet Flo could not quite warm to her. Papa admired Aunt Julia, and Flo's dear cousin Hilary Carter counted Aunt Julia her favorite aunt, emphasizing how hard Julia tried to be "good" and how hard she and the other spinster aunt, Patty, worked to care for Grandpapa and Grandmama Smith. But even Hilary and Papa could not persuade Flo to really love Julia. After all, reasoned Flo, if Aunt Julia really cared for the elderly Smiths in far-off Essex, then why was she always somewhere else?

Flo was even unmoved by Aunt Julia's old sketch of the two Nightingale daughters toddling beside their tall, lanky father on a stroll. Aunt Julia confided to Flo, "You see that your sister, Parthe, clung to your Papa's hand, whereas you—though younger by one year—independently stumped along by yourself!" Aunt Julia loved independence. So did Flo. And yet Flo much preferred Aunt Mai. After Bath, the girls and their entourage, with Mama directing the travel, trundled across fifty miles of forests and meadows to Embley Park, their winter estate in Hampshire near Romsey.

TWO

At breakfast, the one meal that allowed the informality of family and guests strolling into the dining room at varying times, Flo was startled to see an unfamiliar young lady walk to the sideboard with Mama. Parthe watched wide-eyed as the young woman put dainty portions of ham and eggs on her plate. Who was this modestly dressed woman? No servants ate with the family, except—

"This is Miss Christie, girls," announced Mama. "She is your new governess." Of all the servants, only the governess dined with the family. How many more changes could Flo live through? She had only recently learned that Agathe had been replaced by another French maid, Clemence. Mama hadn't tolerated Agathe's mishaps after all. And now there was a new governess. That had to be Papa's doing. He had said he was very unhappy with the girls' lack of Latin, even though Flo had learned a smattering from her cousin Henry Nicholson. Inasmuch as the girls were fluent in French, because of the ever-present French maids, they thought their foreign language skills were more than adequate. Apparently, Papa didn't agree.

But by the time 1828 arrived, several months later, Flo adored Miss Sara Christie. Miss Christie made her want to be "good." Flo enjoyed her studies because Miss Christie knew how to make learning fun.

When Mama took the girls on their customary spring visit to London, Flo became very unsettled. Miss Christie no longer stayed with them but with her own family in London. Flo resented seeing Miss Christie only during the day for lessons. The Nightingales were hosted by the Bonham Carters, so Flo had cousin Hilary for company—although this time there was no way to exclude Parthe. The year before, Flo had been frightfully lucky when Hilary came down with the whooping cough. Because Flo had suffered it already and her older sister had not, Parthe was excluded from the company of Flo and Hilary. It had been heavenly. This year Flo did her best not to let Parthe spoil her pleasure in hearing Tyrolean singers imported by King George IV himself or in seeing the fabulous relics of ancient Egypt in the British Museum.

After London, the family went to Lea Hurst, their summer home in the heights of Derbyshire. During their stay, Aunt Mai took the girls to Grandmama Shore's house in Tapton, then to the original Shore home in Norton. Thus Flo learned that Lea Hurst was not the original family home but came from the estate of Peter Nightingale. Flo's father had been born William Edward Shore but took the name of Nightingale at his uncle Peter's request. In return, as "William Nightingale," he became heir to Uncle Peter's fortune. Flo's father not only received an enormous annual income—many thousands of pounds sterling per year—but he had added to it through his own enterprise.

The winter back at Embley Park began with a visit from cousin Laura Nicholson. The Nicholsons were also quite wealthy and lived at Waverly Park, less than forty miles northeast of Embley Park. The main winter socializing among the families now revolved around the Nightingales at Embley Park, the Nicholsons at Waverly Park, the Bonham Carters at Fair Oak near Winchester, and the estate of Uncle Sam and Aunt Mai at Combe Hurst in Surrey. All the relatives were quite wealthy and lived within a half-day's carriage ride of each other.

Although Laura, or Lolli, was a red-haired, snub-nosed delight, she was only five. Flo would have much preferred the company of Lolli's older siblings—if not Marianne, then Henry. But remembering Miss Caroline's gracious hospitality at Betley Hall, Flo was inspired to make every effort to include Lolli. It was common practice to send siblings alone to visit, on the theory they needed a break from each other. Flo couldn't argue with that. Nothing pleased her more than to be apart from Parthe.

Soon Flo was allowed to visit the Carters at Fair Oak. There she indulged her friendship with Hilary. An unexpected event of that stay was accompanying Hilary's governess, Miss Johnson, when she visited cottages in the nearby villages. The damp, dimly lit cottages repelled Flo at first. She had gone around with Mama to leave food at cottages before, but she had never gone inside to help the sick. Mama said Aunt Julia did that sort of thing because the villagers could not afford medical care. Flo had never understood what was involved. Now, when Miss Johnson helped a villager with a sick baby, Flo was seized by the importance of helping. And the essence of the act went beyond importance. The help seemed an act of love. Never had Flo felt so radiant.

Flo suddenly realized she was experiencing the gospel of Jesus Christ as she never had before. Of helping the poor, the Lord had said, "Verily I say unto you, Inasmuch as ye have done it unto one of the least of these my brethren, ye have done it unto me."

Flo was by nature meticulous, so she recorded just which medical powder Miss Johnson used for each ailment. She recorded how many grains of the medical powder were needed for patients of differing ages. Never had she felt so useful. She didn't want her visit to Fair Oak to end. Still, the moment Flo returned to Embley Park, she received great news. Mama had to take Parthe to London for dental work. Flo now had Miss Christie all to herself, which meant her schooling could be more rigorous—without Parthe, who resisted difficult, repetitive lessons.

For one of her exercises, Flo perfected her handwriting by compiling moral sayings, such as "Avoid lying; it leads to every other vice," "Conscience is a faithful and prudent monitor," and "Temperance in prosperity indicates wisdom."[1]

And so Flo labored happily through her penmanship. But such copying was laborious, even for Flo, after a while. Finally, Miss Christie allowed her to compose letters. Of course, Flo had written letters before, but she had not reflected much on their composition. In no time at all, Miss Christie pronounced her quite a polished correspondent. Flo wrote to everyone. Because the Nightingales moved around so much, often the recipients of her letters were Papa, Mama, and Parthe! But also she wrote to her grandparents, her many aunts and uncles, and her even more numerous cousins. Flo loved to write. She went beyond letters and began to write stories. Miss Christie encouraged her to record the life of her maid, Clemence. The exercise was a revelation. Clemence's father had been a loyal coachman for King Louis XVI, the French king beheaded in the French Revolution! Flo learned an important lesson from Miss Johnson: Never underestimate people because they appear to occupy a low station. Clemence related some narrow escapes of her own from death, which Flo suspected were mostly imaginary, but which made very lively reading.

"Why not write of your own exciting life?" asked Clemence in French.

"Exciting life" seemed a preposterous exaggeration, but slowly Flo warmed to the notion. To allow Clemence to read it, Flo wrote her *Life of Florence Nightingale* in French. *La Vie de Florence Rossignol* was launched January 1829. She was fortunate that there was an exact French word for Nightingale. Rossignol appeared to be a good omen. She not only labored on her autobiography, which she took back to her earliest memories at Lea Hurst, but attacked geography and history, too. And her journal was sprinkled with Bible quotations, such as "The Lord is with thee." She soon became confident enough to discuss her studies with Papa.

Papa was a reflective man, who loved to talk about history and politics. And here was his eight-year-old daughter suddenly speaking of such things. He didn't hide his pleasure, which only made Flo work harder on her subjects.

When Flo again joined Parthe in London in the spring, Miss Christie lightened the subjects. The two sisters devoted themselves to physical exercise and music. They later left London with heavy hearts, because their cousin Bonham Carter Junior, whom everyone called Bonny, was seriously ill. Shortly after their departure, Flo learned that Hilary's older brother had died. At Lea Hurst, Miss Christie tried hard to keep the girls busy so they would not brood over Bonny's death. She devised projects for the girls to earn their own money so they could help the poor. The highlight of their effort was a party for poor village children, complete with food and cakes and gifts. But Flo also visited cottages and began again to record illnesses in her notebook, how they were being treated, and the results. In fact, by this time, Flo was recording in her notebooks nearly everything that happened to her each day. The character of individuals—rich and poor—she also carefully noted. Was her subject cheerful? Merely agreeable? Morose? Tolerant with children? Playful?

When Flo returned to Embley Park for the winter, she discovered that her father had been bestowed the honor of being named high sheriff for the county of Hampshire. Once a position of enormous power, it was now a symbolic position bestowed for one year. Flo was nevertheless enthralled to see Papa as high sheriff ride out in ceremonial robes to meet the king's judges, whom he then escorted to Winchester Cathedral before the judges began their trials. Flo was allowed to witness a trial, a very sad case of a farm worker's stealing beans from the owner. For this egregious offense, the worker was "transported" to Australia, with no chance to return for fourteen years! The punishment far exceeded the crime, and Flo thought it was no wonder poor people feared the law. Other astonishing things happened that winter. Sir Nicholas Tindall came to their estate in a hot air balloon, the first Flo had ever seen. Then Mama took the girls south to enjoy the warm breezes off the English Channel. At Portsmouth, they saw a yacht race and boarded the warship *Victory*, the great flagship of Lord Nelson's British fleet. Farther west along the channel, Mama rented a cottage. The girls combed the beach, collecting seashells. The most exciting event was when Mama rode a fat pony onto a mudflat along the beach. The pony sank! Featherlight Mama jumped off and skipped across the mudflat, but it took their coachman, Joseph, with four other men and their horses to pull the poor animal out of the mud. They said that if the animal had struggled, it would have been buried alive.

When they returned to Embley Park, an endless stream of visitors began. Flo's favorite was Aunt Mai, who now proudly doted on a baby girl, Flo's double-cousin, Blanche. To Flo, she was double precious. Also with Aunt Mai was Grandaunt Maria, who read aloud to the girls every evening. Then Hilary Carter came. Not every day was fun for Flo, though, as she recorded November 15, 1829:

I, obliged to sit still by Miss Christie, till I had the spirit of obedience. Carters and Blanche here, not allowed to be with them. Mama at Fair Oak ill. Myself unhappy, bad eyes, shade and cold.[2]

But Flo's pain shrank to insignificance when Miss Christie had to abruptly return to her family in London. Miss Christie's brother Robert was dying! When Mama saw Flo's unhappiness, she packed her off to the Bonham Carters, who had returned to Fair Oak. Along the way, Flo's spirits rose.

THREE

"Why aren't you ready for your piano lesson, Hilary?" crackled a nasty voice one day. "Just because precious Cousin Flo is visiting us doesn't mean you can shirk your duty."

Flo looked up from Hilary's desk. Yes, it was her cousin's thirteen-year-old brother, Jack, standing in the doorway. Flo didn't think Jack cared anything at all about duty. He just wanted to antagonize them. "Pray, respect our privacy, Jack."

"You get more like your imperious sister, Parthe, every day," snarled Jack.

Flo had to admit that looking at Parthe was almost like looking at herself in the mirror. Both girls were long-faced, sharp-nosed, rosebud-mouthed, tall and willowy—for ten and nine, that is. Parthe also wore colorful satiny dresses, so all-covering that the only exposed skin was her hands and face. About the only physical difference between the two sisters was the color of their long locks. Flo's hair was reddish brown—thick and glossy and wavy. Parthe's was drab and straight as straw.

Suddenly, Flo was distracted by a form flitting down the hallway outside Hilary's bedroom. "What are you gawking at?" demanded Jack, swirling around to look.

"It's just the maid, Molly," soothed Flo.

"Do you know her name?" asked Jack in astonishment.

Soon Flo was alone in the bedroom. She was pleased to be alone. Now there was no need to explain to Jack or Hilary how intensely interested she was in the servants. The two wouldn't understand. Oh, Flo wasn't such a foolish girl to think she would be a close friend with any servant other than her governess or her own personal maid. A servant was to be seen as seldom as possible by the betters. A servant never spoke to a better unless the servant was spoken to first. What Flo really liked was making their acquaintance so she could find out how they kept the house so wonderfully in order.

In any respectable manor the rules of "service" were rigid. The three at the top of the hierarchy—the butler, the housekeeper, and the cook—were military in their demands. Each servant not only had to do his or her duties proficiently, but precisely when required. Timing was essential. Long before the betters arose in the morning, the servants scurried about stoking fireplaces and stoves, then delivering trays of coffee and hot chocolate to their betters' bedroom suites. While the betters rose from bed and dressed, with the help of their ladies' maids and valets, of course, the other servants busily laid out breakfast in the dining area. Then, while the betters chatted and dined, served by the butler and the footmen, the other servants rushed to the bedrooms to clean them, make beds, and empty chamber pots. Custom was so rigid that Molly wore a dress of pale lilac before noon, indicating she was a housemaid. In the afternoon, she wore the black dress of a parlor maid. Also required were an apron and cap of white, but stockings and boots that were black. Except for those directly attending their masters and mistresses, all day long the servants busied themselves, always one step ahead of the betters. Their very regimented service didn't let up until after the final evening meal was served and cleared.

The staff of servants at Fair Oak, the country manor of her uncle Bonham Carter, was very similar to the staff that ran Papa's Embley Park. Including scullery maids, gardeners, stable hands, coachmen, and such, the number probably reached forty—which wasn't too many, reflected Flo, considering that on special occasions Fair Oak slept up to eighty guests! Aunt Mai could accommodate just as many at Combe Hurst. And at the Nicholson's Waverly Abbey estate, the number of guests often exceeded that. After all, Flo's extended family was enormous. If one counted up all the grandmamas and grandpapas, twenty-five or so uncles and aunts, dozens of cousins, and hundreds of servants, Flo's family was quite overwhelming!

On the other hand, her father's summer estate way up north in Derbyshire— Lea Hurst—was a reprieve from such an army. Nearby relatives were not nearly so numerous, and Lea Hurst had a mere fifteen bedrooms. Nearly half the staff was left behind at Embley Park to keep it immaculate for their return. Lea Hurst was a dreamy place, set high above the Derwent River. Mama had never persuaded Flo's father to buy a London residence. So when they went to the city in the spring and fall, as all fashionable people did, they stayed at one of the fine hotels. Of course, the hotel had to be in the West End. All people of prominence knew the West End was the very heart and soul of London—"and all of England," the residents no doubt would have added without hesitation. It was hard to argue with those grand assertions. The West End sprawled from the Houses of Parliament on the Thames River all the way west to Kensington Palace and its spacious gardens. Kensington, the Strand, Hyde Park, Buckingham Palace, Piccadilly, the British Museum, Mayfair, the National Gallery, Westminster Abbey, Trafalgar Square—all were claimed by the West End. Flo had come to know more about Papa now that she could discuss history with him. Papa had gone to Cambridge University, where he mastered Italian, Greek, Latin, German, history, philosophy, and other subjects, all of which gave him entrée to quiet, pleasant indulgences. At thirty-six, Papa gave the appearance of a swaying Lombardy poplar, very tall and slender. He rarely sat, preferring to lean—on mantels, on door frames, on anything vertical. He even had a special desk made with legs so tall he could stand up while working.

Mama, too—the former Fanny Smith—was tall and slender. Yet she was not like a tree at all. Mama was a beauty, but a beauty who worked. Her hospitality was gracious, but it was an obsession. In fact, Flo suspected that Mama rather than Papa was the engine that ran the manors. In the house, Papa appeared to care only for his large library and his gun cases. It was Mama—the "milady" of the manors—who examined the grocery lists, inventoried the china, had the sofa recovered in red silk damask, and commanded the ceilings be painted sky blue and the moldings glossy gold. It was Mama who wrote countless letters of condolence, invitations, dismissals, and referrals. She was as energetic as Papa was casual. The two seemed a strange pairing, but some whispered that when Fanny Smith realized William Nightingale's ambition was minimal, she decided to make up for it by socializing the family into prominence. Such a thing was possible, Flo knew. Perhaps it had not yet happened for the Nightingales, but it would. Mama was a force.

And how nice it was to be away from Parthe, Flo realized as she looked at her unsigned letter to Papa. Parthe was so possessive, so demanding.

Flo's delicious reflections were interrupted when Hilary rejoined her in the bedroom. Hilary was so dear to her that she didn't mind at all. Flo signed the letter to Papa at last and put it aside. No one knew better than Flo, who moved about constantly, that her visit with Hilary would soon end, and so she sought to make the most of each day they had together. Flo was resigned if not pleased when she had to return to Embley Park four weeks later.

Embley Park was an enormous stone mansion, with large, mullioned bay windows and peaked Dutch gables. It gave an impression of loftiness but of earthbound solidity, too. But it was not large enough for Flo's mother. She would not be content until five good-sized families—a dozen per family would be a fair average—could be accommodated at Embley Park. That would require a couple of dozen bedrooms and at least one more kitchen! Happiness to her would be a horde of guests at all times. The house seemed always full of wandering nieces and nephews anyway. Rarely was the baby of a guest not being pampered and coddled. Ecstasy to Mama would be a larger mansion and the arrival of dinner guests every evening that would include lords and ladies, with at least a few barons and baronesses. Flo turned ten on May 12, 1830. The very next month—while she was visiting the Nicholsons—King George IV died at age sixty-seven. He would be followed by his younger brother, William, who was sixty-four. William was not highly regarded, Flo learned.

Although he knew he was next in line to George IV, his life had been spent in seeking pleasure. "But who could blame him?" argued some. His father, George III, had lived to the age of eighty-one, having reigned sixty-seven years! Wasn't there every good reason to expect George IV to reign into his eighties, too? Nevertheless, as King William IV began his reign, the privileged classes speculated about his sympathies.

It might seem strange that Flo, at age ten, could engage in such sophisticated conversations. But by now she had experienced many such discussions with her father and had overheard others discourse about the machinations of power. She was curious, and her mind was like a sponge. But an education had to involve more than snippets of conversation. Flo had already realized she would never attend the great universities at Oxford or Cambridge, a privilege offered only to young men of her wealthy class. It made her heart ache to know she would be excluded.

Her one-month London stay in the spring of 1830 was with Uncle Octavius Smith, whom she called "Uncle Oc," and his wife, Aunt Jane, at their home on the bank of the Thames River. She played with Cousin Freddy, who adored animals as much as she did. The two cousins spent much time rendering an old sheet into a tent. They attached cords to anchor their tent to pegs driven into the lawn. It was Flo's idea to make a standard naming their tent "Brob-dingnag," after the far-off land of giants she had read about in Jonathan Swift's *Gulliver's Travels*.

Such was Flo's world, an odd, rich mixture of imaginative children's games, adult discussions of history or politics, and the privilege of guided tours of the city. While they were in London, Uncle Oc took the two cousins around the marvelous pipe work of a distillery, then to hear the choir at St. Paul's Cathedral, then to a gallery of Sir Thomas Lawrence's portraits. Aunt Julia came to escort Flo to Lea Hurst for the summer. But Aunt Julia's route was no more direct than Mama's would have been. First they stopped at Warwick Castle, where Flo pondered a vase brought from Pompeii that was so large it dwarfed even a tall man. In the same vicinity, they stopped at Stratford-on-Avon to marvel not only at the birthplace of Shakespeare, but also his grave. Later on the trip, they visited the niece of one of Aunt Julia's best friends, Harriet Martineau. Miss Martineau, Aunt Julia told Flo forcefully, was a literary woman who had not yet arrived. But she most certainly would. Before she was through she would be at least as influential as Maria Edgeworth had been. She could write fiction or hard-edged fact. She was all for the rights of women.

Aunt Julia confided to Flo, "But your aunt Patty thinks Miss Martineau 'too positive, too like an uncouth man, to be agreeable, or even to excite much confidence in her opinions.' But I admire Miss Martineau very much."

"Thank you for being so frank with me," responded Flo.

"You have an open mind? Well, then I'll tell you more. Your grandmama says you have the qualities of 'both Martha and Mary, two excellent characters blended.'"

Martha and Mary? What did that mean?

Of course Flo remembered the two sisters of Lazarus in the books of Luke and John. But her opinion of Martha was not favorable. "But how am I like Martha?" she finally asked with a little anger. "Wasn't it Martha the Lord chastised, saying, 'Martha, Martha, thou art careful and troubled about many things: But one thing is needful: and Mary hath chosen that good part, which shall not be taken away from her'?"

"You are quite right about that. Martha had so busied herself with making her guests comfortable that she momentarily lost sight of what was important. But her desire to make everyone comfortable was not a flaw in itself. It was only poor judgment when it distracted her from listening to the Lord. You must remember, my dear, that when Jesus came to Bethany because He had heard Lazarus was dead, it was Martha who first ran to Him and cried, 'Lord, if thou hadst been here, my brother had not died. But I know, that even now, whatsoever thou wilt ask of God, God will give it thee.' So you see, it was Martha who first expressed her faith that the Lord could do the impossible. Mary still sat in the house."

"So Martha and Mary both had their good points."

"That was exactly what Grandmama meant when she said you blended the qualities of the two sisters. You are very active like Martha, but you are also very contemplative like Mary."

Ever so slowly, Flo was beginning to like Aunt Julia.

FOUR

Although Flo began to admire Aunt Julia, she was far from idolizing her like Hilary did. Perhaps Flo was put off by Aunt Julia's talk, which reminded her of some very unpleasant realities for women. Genteel women, Flo was sorry to admit, behaved most strangely. She had heard some of the gentlemen at social occasions say women were pure emotion. It was their nature to react emotionally rather than logically. But Aunt Julia insisted it was artificial. Such behavior had been induced only recently by the popular poets—like the late Lord Byron. "Imagination" was preferred over reason. Ladies expressed this "imagination" by being highly emotional—so much so that it came to be expected they would faint over an adverse letter or a mild argument.

Flo soon realized that such extreme sensitivity was not the least of her concerns about the plight of women. A child as educated and advantaged as she soon realized it was the male gender that enjoyed opportunities. Mama's attitude was that the girls should be thankful they were born into privilege. Yet that was not satisfying to Flo—or Aunt Julia. The more Flo thought about her own future, the more convinced Flo became that she lived in the worst time in history for women. A privileged girl could be taught Greek and Latin and logic—as the Wesley sisters had been in the century before—but have no use for it whatever, except to chatter cleverly at the dinner table!

Her woe evaporated, though, when she was reunited in September with Miss Christie at Lea Hurst. Flo's trek from Embley Park to Lea Hurst had taken four months. It seemed the peripatetic Nightingales were never still. As if to prove it, after Flo had been at Lea Hurst only a few weeks, Papa and Mama went south to visit. Aunt Julia remained to run the household. Helping Miss Christie with Flo and Parthe was Mrs. Marsh. Mrs. Marsh had a history of tragedies, the likes of which few could equal. She had lost her husband, then her only daughter, then a niece she adored. Mrs. Marsh had adopted the niece's children and lost them one by one—all five—to tuberculosis! And yet Mrs. Marsh was very kind and cheerful. Flo discovered that if someone broached the subject of her lost ones, Mrs. Marsh broke into tears. Otherwise, she was buoyed by her faith in the Lord. Nothing pleased Flo more than seeing someone actually live in Christ, truly displaying the joy of the Lord. Flo delighted in seeing someone who was "good." She longed more and more to be that way herself. Miss Christie and Aunt Mai had reinforced her desire.

Flo and Parthe certainly needed the presence of Mrs. Marsh when Miss

Christie had her accident. The day began so innocently. They had gone on one of their picnics, intent on collecting a rare wildflower called Grass of Parnassus. Then, out of the blue, a drunken man lurched his donkey into Miss Christie's pony. She was hurled to the ground, writhing in agony. In much pain, Miss Christie was returned to Lea Hurst, but it was after nightfall before a physician finally came to look at her. Mrs. Marsh finally came to them. "Oh, children, you're so distraught. I was so intent on seeing Miss Christie doctored I forgot you. She is alive and well. Her shoulder was badly dislocated. It took seven people to hold her still while the physician forced her shoulder back in place."

"Pray to God that her shoulder really was dislocated," snapped Flo angrily.

Why did Miss Christie have to suffer so? Why did Mrs. Marsh have to suffer so? Both were the best kind of people. And yet they suffered so much more than other people. Why? Still, Mrs. Marsh remained cheerful and Miss Christie was her old self by the time the Nightingale girls had to head south again.

True to form, the Nightingales took an indirect route. Flo and Parthe accompanied Miss Christie and some servants to Buckenham in Norfolk to stay with Miss Christie's friend, Miss Emily Taylor. Miss Taylor was an advanced woman "doing good" by running a small school for village children. She financed it by selling her own poetry and other writings. The schoolchildren helped by knitting slippers for sale. Flo was soon knitting slippers herself. Oh, how wonderful she felt when she was useful. For one month, she luxuriated in her goodness.

For the next several months, Flo traveled constantly back and forth from Derbyshire in the north of England to Hampshire in the south—with dozens of stops in between. But the news she received in early 1831 was so upsetting that she threw aside her life story, *La Vie de Florence Rossignol*, for good. Her life was ruined. Miss Christie was leaving!

"I am going to be married, Flo," she said, "to a gentleman named Collmann."

And just like that, Miss Christie was gone. It seemed terribly unfair, but could Flo deny Miss Christie a good marriage? Papa now became quite concerned about his daughters' tutoring. Their departing governess had done a fine job of instructing the daughters in arithmetic, art, sewing, music, and numerous concepts from the Bible. Indeed, she had even pushed them further, getting them started in Latin. But she could have taken them only so far. If they were to master the languages necessary to be cosmopolitan readers as well as cosmopolitan travelers, he—the Cambridge scholar—would have to undertake their instruction personally. Under his tutelage, Flo and Parthe would learn Greek, German, French, Italian, and more Latin! Of course they couldn't "travel" as ignoramuses, so Papa would instruct them also in history and philosophy. He would hire another governess, but only to continue their instruction in sewing, music, and art.

The other great event of 1831 was the birth of a son to Papa's sister Aunt Mai. According to the complicated conditions of Peter Nightingale's estate, if William Nightingale had no son of his own, this boy would inherit everything upon Papa's death. Mama was now forty-three. There was little chance of a son. To her family's credit, Flo noticed no resentment at all toward the baby boy. In fact, he was named William Shore Smith—"William Shore" being Papa's name before he took the name Nightingale. No one was affected more by the baby than Flo.

Not only did Flo feel very close to her "boy Shore," but to Aunt Mai, too. Although Aunt Mai was thirty-three at this time, she was much more like an older sister to Flo than an aunt. Even more than Aunt Julia, she treated Flo like an equal, discussing things with Flo as her confidante. Aunt Mai was definitely her brother's sister. Like Papa, she was philosophical and probing. She had sensed for a long time the difference between Parthe and Flo. Flo anticipated with dread the life of a woman. She must have something more than domesticity as a goal. But what? Aunt Mai reasoned with Flo over the possibilities. But the possibilities were few indeed.

"Your father is preparing you," concluded Aunt Mai finally, "with a wide background of disciplines. Wait for inspiration."

That preparation included church. From conversations Flo had overheard, she gathered that many in her family had gone to dissenting churches in the past, churches that had tried to break away from the very rigid service offered by the Church of England, often referred to as Anglican. And yet there was a movement among a handful of English elite, especially at Oxford University, to reintroduce Roman Catholic elements into the Church of England, the very elements the Puritans had removed! Mama was pragmatic; she cared little for theology or doctrine. If one wanted to prosper among the privileged of English society, one went to the Church of England.

Such cynicism did not discourage Flo from studying the Bible and attending to her prayers. In early 1832, while Hilary was visiting Embley Park, Flo awaited word of the first child of Mrs. Collmann, her beloved Miss Christie. When the news arrived, she was devastated. Her Miss Christie had died in childbirth! Flo was reeling. She never thought anything could be worse than Miss Christie's screams at Lea Hurst back in 1830. But this was infinitely worse. Flo tried to console herself by remembering Mrs. Marsh's faith in the Lord. But it was impossible for her to feel cheerful. This injustice would take a great deal of reflection. One of the few things that gave her any relief was wearing mourning clothes as a sign of her grief and her love for Miss Christie. Another thing, as simple as it was, was a visit by a dove to the windowsill of her bedroom each morning at exactly eight o'clock. It was as if the dove were saying, "Life must go on."

Yet Flo remained gloomy.

Hilary, now living in the Carter's new family home at Ditcham near Petersfield, had a baby brother, Hugh. Hugh was Hilary's "baby," just as Shore was Flo's "baby." Hilary wrote Flo that her baby Hugh was very sick. When Grandmama Smith came to visit, this time without Aunt Julia, both Parthe and Flo tried to smother their grief over Miss Christie by attending to her needs. They would care for her just like Aunt Julia did.

Caring for Grandmama led Flo to write to Hilary that she suddenly realized how much she adored Aunt Julia. Surely that would cheer Hilary, who already felt that way about Aunt Julia. But then Flo got the terrible news that little Hugh Carter had died. She consoled Hilary by writing that Hugh was like a little angel now, even being looked after by his big brother Bonny. Yes, even Miss Christie was there to attend him. But this latter consolation brought Flo up short. Wasn't she being a hypocrite comforting Hilary in this way? Why hadn't she been able to console herself with the image of Miss Christie quite happy in heaven? Why couldn't she visualize Miss Christie delighted to see her brother Robert again? And she began to think that her grief for Miss Christie had become an indulgence, her woe actually self-pity. "Well," she asked herself, "do I believe in heavenly bliss or not?" Finally, she decided she did. She took out Miss Christie's letters to read them again. Now she must cherish her friend's memory and not use it to wallow in self-pity. Life does go on.

Aunt Mai and the Nightingales soon celebrated Shore's first birthday, followed twelve days later by Flo's twelfth. Flo had been taught a tradition in which the one who had the birthday gave gifts to family and friends. So through the past year she had carefully stockpiled gifts for the occasion: an ivory letter opener, green silk braid, books lined for writing music, a pair of scissors, and two small elegant purses. Perhaps her own gift was Aunt Mai's leaving Shore with the Nightingales when she and daughter Blanche left for Harrogate. Then, when the Nightingales' own nurse fell ill, it was twelve-year-old Flo who was allowed to care for Shore. Flo felt like she was in heaven. Shore so engrossed her that all her letter writing ceased!

By the spring of 1833, it was clear that Flo's character was very different from her sister, Parthe's. Parthe was never happier than when the Nightingales were socializing or "calling." She was perfectly at ease, whereas Flo was restless after a few minutes. But Flo was not an unhappy child. Life was blissful when she cared for the vulnerable. Babies drew Flo like magnets. Wild birds fascinated her, too. At Embley Park, she was most attracted not to the common white-cheeked sparrows but to the nuthatches that scampered all over the cypress in front of her window. After years of watching, Flo had decided both the tree and the nuthatches were quite peculiar. First of all, the tree, though it looked like an evergreen, dropped its needles in the winter just as an oak or a hawthorn dropped its leaves. The nuthatch was eccentric, too. Although the tiny, black-headed, needle-beaked, blue-backed, fawn-breasted, stunt-tailed birds scampered all over the tree every hour of the day, as if it were their domicile, Flo could never find a nest.

Observing babies of every kind gave her the most tender, most joyous feeling. Was this a reflection of the joy of God in His creatures? Often she reflected on the meaning of her own life. She so wanted now to do good. But how was it all connected? About this time, she found that the poet Felicia Hemans had articulated her feelings almost exactly. Nature seen through the mind of Felicia Hemans agreed exactly with how Flo felt about "all glorious things," the beyond that no eye could see nor any ear could hear. Yes, Flo loved the magical lands Felicia Hemans put to verse. But most of all, Flo wanted confirmation of the connections she felt herself.

Flo knew her Bible well enough to know the source of inspiration. As the apostle Paul said in 1 Corinthians, "God hath revealed them unto us by his Spirit: for the Spirit searcheth all things, yea, the deep things of God." Surely it was the Spirit who moved Felicia Hemans and Flo herself.

Papa was now very involved in Flo's formal education, and Parthe's, as well. In the evenings, he read aloud to both daughters. If he read English classics like Shakespeare's *Hamlet* or modern novels like Sir Walter Scott's *Old Mortality*, Parthe was engrossed. Flo's enjoyment was tainted, because she wanted the book in her own two hands to savor the words and reflect on their meanings. On the other hand, if the reading was in Latin or Greek or history, Parthe only pretended to listen as she sketched, a hobby she loved. Although Flo maintained her interest in Papa's more erudite readings, she was still frustrated at not having control over the words herself.

As time went on, Papa more and more gave Flo and Parthe his precious leather-bound books to read for themselves. Parthe considered this "privilege" drudgery, but to Flo it was heavenly. Increasingly, in the evenings, the four Nightingales paired off: Parthe with Mama to discuss social things, Flo with Papa to discuss philosophy and politics. Politics was an exciting subject in England these days, and Papa's Whig party was pushing for reforms. Grandpapa

Smith—still alive at seventy-seven—had been a Whig, too, but he was a doer rather than a dreamer like Papa. For forty-six years in the House of Commons representing Norwich, William Smith had championed the cause of dissenters and all the oppressed. Although not an Evangelical himself, Grandpapa Smith was a friend and ally of the powerful Evangelical politicians dubbed "the Clapham Sect." Their main champion, William Wilberforce, who had fought slavery and discrimination against Catholics, had died recently, but not before he knew that his bill abolishing slavery in all British dominions was becoming law. The Catholic Emancipation Bill was already law.

All these things Flo discussed with Papa. The Reform Bill they had speculated on so often, which redistributed the seats in Parliament more fairly, had become a reality in 1832. Many tiny boroughs, no more than deceits to give aristocratic landowners—the landed gentry—more votes, were eliminated. Representation of Ireland and Scotland increased as well. The electorate itself was broadened by eliminating restrictive residential and financial requirements. Overall, the reform doubled the number of eligible voters and transferred much political power from the landowning aristocrats to the middle class.

"But nothing for women," commented Flo.

FIVE

Men of England—enlightened and otherwise—were not enthusiastic about rights for women. But problems for other groups abounded, as well. Children labored in factories disgracefully. The poor in general were neglected. And there was the question of Ireland. Would Britain ever give the pesky Irish home rule? Flo became interested in these conundrums. When she spoke of them to Papa, she felt her life meant something. And though she wished she did not have to go calling with Mama and Parthe so often, thus being always short of time, she had the consolation that Papa was not neglecting her studies. Flo was soon studying Cicero in Latin and translating the Italian of Tasso into French.

Flo also studied English giants like Chaucer, Spenser, Milton, and Shakespeare. Parthe rebelled; she saw no purpose at all for such painful learning. But she did see purpose in all of Mama's interests. Thus, Flo became ever more attached to Papa, Parthe ever more to Mama. The Nightingales kept to their routine of Embley Park in winter, London in the spring, Lea Hurst in the summer, and London again in the fall. The daughters were sent often to visit aunts and uncles and grandparents. Flo and Parthe continued to be sent separately. Occasionally they were sent off together. Often now it was in the summer to the Isle of Wight, with their governess along to chaperone.

Most of their time was spent enjoying the sights and pleasures of the resort island. The diamond-shaped island of Wight—its largest dimension twenty-three miles long—was only a couple of miles off the Hampshire coast. The cliffs of Alum Bay flaunted vertical sandstone layers in twelve shades of yellow, red, and brown. The island didn't lack history, with a castle outside Cowes built by wife-slaying Henry VIII. Nor did it lack amenities. Yachting and sunbathing were the chief pursuits of most visitors. Ventnor, a terraced resort village on the south side of the island, was possibly the warmest spot in all of England.

The two sisters were on the Isle of Wight when they received news that Papa was going to run for Parliament in 1835. Parthe was delighted for many reasons, not the least of which was that Papa's victory would mean an end to her severe lessons! He would have no time to teach them if he was elected. Flo was depressed. She had thrived under Papa's tutelage, even laboring dutifully over Italian verbs. The sisters now bickered more than ever. Parthe was imperious and hypersensitive. Flo was well aware that she herself was often self-righteous and too independent, even indifferent to Parthe. On the other hand, Parthe felt no guilt over their fights, whereas Flo was weighed down with guilt. Much of the time now, Flo was introspective. What was her destiny? Just what was it God wanted her to do? Flo formalized her concerns in prayer, too: *"Oh please, God, tell me what to do."* Sometimes she could stifle her discontent and become involved—like Parthe—in what was expected of clever young girls. After all, if a woman had no object in life other than making a good marriage, shouldn't Flo hone her social skills? Yet she felt her greatest pleasure tending to innocents: a pet squirrel, a pigeon, or best of all, a baby.

Her position began to crystallize in 1834. Aunt Jane in London needed help. She was about to have another baby. Son Freddy had fallen and was not well himself. So whom should the Nightingales send to help? Mama bypassed her elder daughter, Parthe, and selected Flo! Flo didn't gloat, because Parthe didn't care, but Flo did battle with pride over being chosen. She really did seem to be growing into another Aunt Julia, whom she now greatly respected. Aunt Julia was universally regarded as good. And more than that, Aunt Julia was a doer. She had a system. Of all the people Flo knew, it was Aunt Julia who visited poor people most often. It was Aunt Julia who knew all the babies. It was Aunt Julia whom the poor people asked Flo about. Yes, it was Aunt Julia who had earned the respect of nearly everyone, family and friends, rich and poor.

In 1835, the great moment came: Papa ran for Parliament. No one was more excited about his prospects than Mama. At last, her dreamer would show everyone he was ready to scale the political heights. But he was resoundingly defeated! To emphasize even more Papa's lack of political fortune, other Whigs won gloriously that year! Some of the Nightingales, Smiths, and Carters lamented that the times were not right for a William Nightingale. He was too honest to be elected. But care had to be taken where such talk was vented. Not that Mama's father, who had served in Parliament for forty-six years, would object. The poor old fellow died that same year. But Mama and many of the other Smiths were touchy about it. Bonham Carter, Hilary's father, was currently in Parliament, too. After his defeat, Papa grew even dreamier and more philosophical. Flo began reading Plato in Greek. The gulfs among the Nightingales widened. Fanny became more aggressive socially. She would definitely have to accomplish socially what Papa had failed to do politically. Their separate callings intensified. Meanwhile Mama and the others had to complete their mourning for Grandpapa Smith.

Men merely wore a black armband, but women had to dress in black, preferably bombazine, because that fabric was not shiny. Parents were mourned for one year, grandparents six months. But Grandmama Smith, as the wife of the deceased, was expected to wear her mourning clothes for two years.

Parthe was sixteen now, very close to coming out. For a while, Mama considered presenting Parthe to the king and his court on the king's birthday in August 1836. She had just the gown in mind for the willowy Parthe. White satin would be covered with *tulle illusion*, or sheer ornamented with tiny pink hyacinths. For herself Mama imagined mouse-colored satin with pink ribbons, or green watered silk with black lace. Finally, she decided her consideration was motivated more by a desire to burst out of her mourning than by any real need for Parthe to come out. Parthe needed more refinement, she decided.

"Europe is just the thing to give both girls that last bit of polish," declared Papa.

"I agree—under one condition," said Mama, still stung by Papa's political defeat. Fanny looked Papa squarely in the eye. "My one condition is that while we're gone we have Embley Park renovated, so that we can entertain properly when we return."

"Agreed," said Papa, his voice subdued.

Flo was more unsettled than ever. Why must she go to Europe? She was becoming more like Aunt Julia every day. More and more often, she was the family member called upon to nurse the sick. More and more often, she visited the cottages of the poor near Embley Park in the winter and near Lea Hurst in the summer. She was at long last feeling useful. Nevertheless, the other three Nightingales planned both the renovation of Embley Park and a trip across Europe. As Mama and Parthe finalized their plans to remodel the exterior, completely redecorate the interior, and add six bedrooms plus two new kitchens, Papa busied himself designing a coach.

Their imminent trip evoked reminiscences of Papa's and Mama's honeymoon in Europe. Mama's family was well known for its social whirl. Pensive William Nightingale, close friend at Cambridge University of Fanny's brother Octavius, had gained entry by his social status and his wealth. It was certainly a measure of Papa's wealth that the newly married Nightingales could leave England and not return for three years! By 1819, Mama had been confined in Naples, where she gave birth to a daughter. The baby was named after the Greek name for that Italian city: Parthenope. One year later, Mama had once again been confined, this time in Florence. On May 12, 1820, their second daughter was born. She, too, received the name of the city of her birth. Neither daughter had any recollection of this "fabled" trip.

But what happened to Flo in February of 1837—before they could leave for the Continent—was even more unbelievable. As always, it was recorded by Flo, the compulsive journalist of thoughts and observations. She had long since abandoned her autobiography, but she still wrote letters by the hundreds, as well as jotting her feelings into journals and diaries—all of which she saved. Moreover, she scribbled down notes on any available scrap of paper. These "scraps" were not discarded, either. No other scrap was so terse yet momentous as the one she recorded before the family left for Europe:

On February 7th, 1837, God spoke to me and called me to His service.[1]

Flo herself could scarcely believe it had happened. And yet, why not? Didn't she pray daily, almost hourly? Hadn't she beseeched God ten thousand times for guidance? Much of what she did—especially the endless social calls—was so boring. And much of what she lacked—time to do "good" things—was so frustrating. Was it any wonder she had retreated into a world of prayer? Who but God would listen to her unceasing complaints? Even Hilary, who felt the same way Flo did, tired of Flo's restlessness. So Flo had learned to vent her frustration to God. And then He spoke to her. It was not a dream. It was not a hallucination. Of that she was certain. God did speak.

But, God, she prayed, *You have not told me what I must do.*

She began to realize that was her cross to bear. Just what was it that she was to do? And why the "call" just before she was off to Europe? Was Europe to be her temptation in the desert? The impending trip had become a sore point to Flo anyway. It seemed so frivolous to her as the other three Nightingales planned and planned. Letters were written. Letters of introduction were acquired. Provisions were discussed and debated. What clothing must be packed? What books must be taken? How hard should the girls study while abroad? Which servants would accompany them? On and on went the debate. Papa's coach grew and grew. Soon it was so enormous it would require six stout horses to move it. At that point, Papa turned his plans over to the coach maker.

Then in June of 1837, King William IV died!

There was much talk of the young Alexandrina Victoria. She had just turned eighteen. She was of age. Wise friends were now calling her Victoria to remove the Russian sound to her name. Czar Nicholas was very unpopular. Victoria was old enough to assume the throne, which should have removed all the titillation about a regency. But it hadn't. Victoria's mother, the Duchess of Kent and the daughter of the Duke of Saxe-Coburg-Saalfield, was involved in an intrigue with the powerful Whig politician Sir John Conroy to assume a regency anyway, assuring everyone the tiny princess was far too young and inexperienced to govern. However, the dying king had made it very clear he expected Victoria to succeed him. Finally, Lord Melbourne, the prime minister, facilitated the claim of the princess. Melbourne, a Whig himself, feared the backlash of the English people against the Whig Conroy—and possibly all Whigs—for trying to deny the throne to the young heir.

About the only intrigues left now were the status of the queen's entourage and the identity of her future husband. The Nightingales were kept well apprised of such events, because Papa had become good friends with a neighbor who was none other than Lord Palmerston. Palmerston was Melbourne's foreign secretary, a very powerful position in government.

But in the meantime, the Nightingales would see Europe in their monstrous carriage. On September 8, 1837, the four Nightingales and their necessary servants departed Embley Park. From Southampton they sailed the English Channel on the *Monarch*. From Le Havre, the Nightingales rumbled south across France to the Mediterranean. Flo's French was fluent, but she felt constrained from engaging in much conversation. More often than not, she and Parthe sat on the box-seat on top of the carriage. Parthe sketched madly. Flo wrote just as energetically in her journal. Never was her methodical nature more obvious. She recorded each sight, the date and time of day, even the miles they had traveled since the last sight. She simply had to record these precious moments as fully as she could. She wanted never to forget spotting across the plain, in spite of the fall of night, the rising spires of the cathedral at Chartres. And in her room at the inn there, she watched almost all night as the moon danced above the spires.

The Nightingales' trip across France was three months of interesting people, inns, rivers, cathedrals, even mountains. Everywhere they had prearranged invitations to well-bred, respectable society. Flo now went to fancy balls. These lasted hours and consisted of more than twenty quadrilles, waltzes, galops, and polkas. To Flo's utter amazement, her dance card was usually full. At seventeen, she was a young woman—and apparently attractive to men!

Finally, Flo saw the Mediterranean as the Nightingales worked their way east along the French coast, eventually into Italy. Not that "Italy" was one political unit. The country was fragmented among several powers, including Austria. Still "Italy" was a definite ideal, displayed in its glory by great artists like Michelangelo and great writers like Dante. Flo was very well versed in the Italian ideal. Liberal thinkers in England—many of whom had visited the Nightingales—often talked of a united Italy as dreamily as they had once welcomed the French Revolution. In Genoa, Papa and Mama had many invitations. The Nightingales themselves held a soiree. Flo was now intoxicated with the social swirl. She fought the dizzying pleasure by trying to insert observations of the poor in her journal. But she felt as if she were losing her desire to be "good."

Florence was special for her. The sight of her birthplace, Villa Colombaia near the Porta Romana, warmed her. In Florence, Flo's pleasures were even more varied and intense. She indulged in lessons in Italian, drawing, perspective, and singing. She visited churches, enjoyed operas, danced at balls, attended functions at the Grandducal Court, and socialized among a large circle of elite acquaintances. In her diary, she wrote about everything as fully as she could. Again she tried to somewhat offset this hedonistic life by observing the less fortunate. She went to a large orphanage run by a man named Guicciardini. Flo, the scholar, was active, too, reading the ponderous *History of the Italian Republics* by Sismondi. She became a devotee of the incomparable Michelangelo, who three hundred years before had also supervised the fortifications of Florence in a war. This she regarded as "good." It was summer when the Nightingales reached Geneva, Switzerland. The English there were all abuzz about Victoria's coronation in Westminster Abbey on June 28, 1838. There had been no such interest in the coronation of King William IV. Somehow this tiny, pinched-faced princess, who stood so erect yet curtsied so very low and with such dignity, was winning the hearts of everyone. Flo met the historian Sismondi in Geneva. Polite to a fault, he offered lectures to anyone who asked. Of course, Flo was quick to ask, scribbling notes at a furious pace. Sismondi's reputation for kindness was so great, he was constantly pestered by beggars. Invariably he handed out his francs until he had none left. While Flo was enjoying Geneva very much, the serenity of the Swiss town was suddenly shattered. One of the Bonapartes—a very real threat to the reign of France's King Louis Philippe—was an exile in Geneva, and now the French had demanded him. Switzerland refused to surrender him. The French army was coming to take him by force!

On the road to Paris, the great carriage of the Nightingales passed the French troops that were marching on Geneva. Later, the Nightingales learned that Bonaparte had fled to England before the French army arrived. The Nightingales' apartment in Paris was well situated. The streets of Paris were far more cosmopolitan than those of London, with faces, languages, and attire from all over the world.

SIX

A widow named Mrs. Clarke lived in a posh apartment on the rue de Bac with her unmarried forty-year-old daughter, Mary, who was said not to like young ladies! Mrs. Clarke was a Scot but was mistress of an estate at Cold Overton, in the Midlands. Flo was startled by the sight of her unmarried daughter. Mary Clarke was short, with a peculiar Dandie Dinmont hairdo heaped up over her forehead yet cascading all around her face in ringlets. A children's soiree was in progress. No one was moving more rapidly than Mary Clarke. She was a small dynamo. Flo joined the activity with gusto. Mary Clarke, whom everyone called Clarkey, introduced visitors, participated in all the activities, all the while firing witty remarks. Flo had never seen anyone so lively and entertaining as Clarkey. And Clarkey seemed to know personally half the important people in England.

Although Clarkey was the epitome of what Parthe wanted to be, Flo was in awe of her. Later the Nightingales received an invitation to visit the Clarkes again. Only then did Flo realize that the spontaneous delight she had shown at the soiree had endeared her to Mary Clarke, who before that moment wanted no more to socialize with an eighteen-year-old than Flo wanted to socialize with a forty-year-old. The second occasion with Clarkey didn't disappoint Flo, either. Again, the older woman was totally spontaneous, saying anything that popped into her head, yet witty and completely original. But now Flo saw another side of Clarkey. Her charm was not just good manners; she was utterly sincere. She urged Flo and Parthe to visit any time they liked.

After this, Paris was a dream. In Clarkey's apartment, Flo found herself talking to historians, artists, actors, and intellectuals of every stripe. Clarkey gave them entrée to all the most entertaining shows, the best restaurants, the finest galleries, and the most high-powered literary meetings. Flo could scarcely believe it one evening as she sat listening to Chateaubriand himself reading his memoirs! But if Clarkey had not done any of that, Flo would have enjoyed her like no other person she had ever met. Clarkey was a complete original. And she was liberated! Nothing was denied her because she was a woman. No gentleman excluded her from conversation. In fact, the gentlemen sought her out. Such a thing Flo had never seen before.

Flo was astonished. Clarkey had made this life for herself. Yes, she was moderately well born but not particularly wealthy. And she had conquered Paris by her own will and wit. She was a real inspiration. What if one had the social skills of Clarkey and the conscience of Aunt Julia? Why, there might be nothing that woman could not accomplish for the "good."

Alas, their time in Paris—and indeed the European trip—finally had to end. The Nightingales returned to England on April 5, 1839. The renovation of Embley Park, which was to make many additions and to transform the style from Georgian to Elizabethan, was not complete. So the Nightingales settled in at the Carlton Hotel in London with the Nicholsons. At last, Flo and Parthe were coming out. The European experience had prepared them well. Already the two were quite comfortable in bustle and glitter. Mementos of the occasion for Mama were her daughters' locks of hair tied with pretty ribbons.

"Coming out" had changed little under Queen Victoria. Although the queen had taken up residence in Buckingham Palace, she still used the drawing rooms of St. James's Palace. There for the queen's twentieth birthday, nineteen-year-old Flo was presented, along with Parthe and dozens of other young debutantes. Flo wore a white gown from Paris. By the queen's command, the young ladies' necks and shoulders had to be bare. The train of the gown had to be exactly three yards long. With her train folded over her right arm, Flo waited with the others in a long gallery. When her time came, she was ushered into the Presence Chamber. She dropped the train, which was spread out immediately by attendants. Then she walked gracefully but breathlessly to the throne. The queen's very large blue eyes studied her. There was the tiniest smile on the cupidlike lips. An attendant barked out Flo's name. Flo curtsied as low to the floor as she could get. Trembling now, she advanced to kiss the queen's outstretched hand, tiny and ivory.

Flo backed off and curtsied again. She backed out of the room, all the while facing the queen. Once back in the gallery, she wanted to scream with relief, but of course she couldn't. That was only the beginning of "coming out." The two sisters then danced and flirted through the "season," enduring more than fifty balls and parties and as many breakfasts and dinners. They also now attended—as fashion required—the great horse races at Derby and Ascot, the rowing regattas, and the most important cricket matches. By the end of the season, Florence Nightingale, the lithe young beauty from Hampshire with the calm gray eyes, sunset tresses, and perfectly sweet smile, was well known among the young gentlemen.

Meanwhile, the young queen's reputation continued to grow, taking on legendary proportions. Flo saw the queen's growing popularity for herself. At the opera, the audience stood to face the queen's box and cheered. When the London season ended, all proper people retired to their summer estates, as did the Nightingales. Life was leisurely at Lea Hurst after the hectic soiree season. Flo's only real pleasures were visiting the poor in the villages, studying mathematics—which she found very satisfying in its certainty—and having Clarkey visit. Clarkey was her usual peppery self, confiding to Flo that while at her ancestral home in Cold Overton she had kept her tongue "nailed." As a guest of the Nightingales, Clarkey was allowed freedoms that rarely came to Flo. If Clarkey wanted to read a book for hours, curled up on a sofa, only occasionally exploding in admiration or fury, no one even hinted that it was unseemly.

Most of Flo's cousins visited that summer, but not Freddy. He was in Australia with the exploration party of George Grey. At the end of the summer, Flo was privileged to ride a railroad train, which from then on would make traveling to and from Lea Hurst both pleasant and very fast.

On the train, the Nightingales chatted with old friend Sir Frederick Stovin, who was now part of the queen's retinue. He told them frankly that the queen was being tutored in politics by the Whig Lord Melbourne. They read the newspaper together and discussed any facet that interested her. Her own father—the Duke of Kent—had died when she was an infant, and now Lord Melbourne was like a father to her; they were that close. Only Lord Melbourne could lose patience with her favorite terrier and openly call him "a frightful little beast." The queen just laughed. Or if Lord Melbourne would slump into a slumber at the end of a long day, the queen couldn't have been more sympathetic. It was impossible not to tell from Sir Frederick's tone that he, too, adored the queen like a daughter.

Back at Embley Park, they discovered that much work still remained of the remodeling. Flo and everyone else were inundated by Mama's plans for decorating. Little else was discussed. Though Flo was not enthralled by such concerns—after all, Parthe was the artist of the two sisters—she did express opinions. To her, the best part of the remodeling was the break in routine. Using her old nursery as the family parlor was wonderfully bizarre. So was sleeping in the attic! And she enjoyed very much recruiting boys in the village for junior servants.

When Hilary visited, she carried much grief with her. She had lost not only two brothers but also her father, Bonham Carter, in February 1838. Still, she carried hope of an independent future, much more so than Flo. Hilary seemed to be escaping the futility of the parlor. She took art lessons from a master in London and attended Miss Rachel Martineau's school in Liverpool. That Hilary would be tutored by the sister of Harriet Martineau, a good friend of Aunt Julia's, was no surprise to Flo. Hilary now read the *Examiner* thoroughly once a week for its politics, a hobby she had enjoyed with her late father. And she rode the railway—but in her case, alone!

Because of Papa's interest in politics and the intrigues surrounding the queen, Flo wanted to be as engrossed as Hilary. But her time was rarely her own now. She very much believed in Socrates's axiom: "A life unexamined is not a living life." More and more she felt captive to her family. There was no hope of college for her. Some men studied on their own like she. But they were given time. Her time was frittered away. As Mama became more and more aggressive socially, Flo had less and less time for serious study.

Visitors constantly called, whether the Nightingales were at Lea Hurst, Embley Park, or London. Young ladies were expected to entertain guests, to converse amiably but not very deeply, or to play on the piano a lively tune, but nothing as serious as Beethoven. Entire days were spent showing guests the grounds at Lea Hurst or Embley Park. Entire days were spent sitting with guests in the drawing room, never broaching any subject that might agitate. Doing fancywork while sitting was allowed, but Flo was not inclined to sew or knit. Parthe had an advantage in that respect, for she could lose herself in her sketchbook. Even if a book was discussed in the evenings, it was generally done with a gentleman reading the book aloud. There were a few odd times— hours, rarely days—between visitors. Then Flo had time of her own. Odd times. Odd times. Flo began to despise those words. And too often the odd times were when she was already exhausted, too exhausted to take on serious study. More and more she longed for time for herself. She wanted to study deeply, with great concentration, things that were important. Politics. History. Religion. But when would she ever find the time? And why would men her own age not talk about anything of substance?

Thomas Macauley, a brilliant essayist as well as a Whig politician, was a visitor. So was their neighbor Lord Palmerston, a very powerful man in government, even more so now that he had married Lord Melbourne's sister. Married to the niece of Lord Melbourne was the young firebrand Lord Ashley, another visitor to Embley Park. Lord Ashley was destined to become Lord Shaftsbury. He had studied the right and true then put his convictions into action. He was determined to prevent mistreatment of women and children in factories. One way was to limit the amount of time they could be worked in one day. He worked ceaselessly on what he called a Ten-Hours Bill. In her heart, Flo knew he would someday succeed. His cause was so right. But would it ever be possible for her to study as Lord Ashley had and then put her conclusions—no matter how right—into action?

Some of their visitors said doctors were advocating public health programs for the poor in East London. This was particularly interesting to Flo.

There was a great need in England to improve the lives of the working poor and the helpless. But perhaps the poor were no longer so hopeless. Or helpless. A coldhearted law passed in 1834 that threw debtors into workhouses had electrified the poor. Only recently the London Working Men's Association had delivered a petition called "The People's Charter" to Parliament with more than one million signatures. Six demands in the petition included voting rights for commoners, secret balloting, and annual elections. When Parliament spurned them, referring to their movement as "Chartism," the workers struck in the fall of 1839. Many strikers had since been jailed.

Then a young writer in London shocked everyone with his monthly installments of a story called *Oliver Twist*. He had begun making a reputation as a writer of humor, but *Oliver Twist* was not humorous. Oliver was "a parish child—the orphan of a workhouse—the humble, half-starved drudge—to be cuffed and buffeted through the world—despised by all, and pitied by none." *Oliver Twist* portrayed the poor of London as no well-to-do person could know. One villain, named Bill Sykes, was chilling. Some doubted the veracity of the story's setting. "Just walk the streets of London if you doubt me," countered the young writer Charles Dickens.

Flo read Thomas Carlyle now, too. A Scot of about forty-five, he had long lived in the Chelsea area of London and was very popular among the literary set. He was great friends with John Stuart Mill and Ralph Waldo Emerson. Carlyle's opinions were a peculiar mix, but often strikingly original. For example, he had recently championed the idea that mankind was advanced by heroes. The hero was one who was able to perceive the intent of God. The greatest hero was Christ. Flo liked this theory very much. It seemed true. Yet Carlyle had a flaw in Flo's view. "He does not prove his arguments with patient reason."

Flo, who was well read in English, French, Italian, German, Latin, and Greek, now read novels, too. The English novel was changing. Dickens was just one example of the new novelist. The best novelist of the previous generation had been Jane Austen. But she had triumphed within the bounds of manners. Her characters, especially the women, had not broken out of those bounds. Now Flo read *Gabriel* by George Sand in French. It was an ingenious story that showed the predicament of women. George Sand was the pen name for a woman who was shocking even Paris society. She not only lived in sin but also wrote about it. Clarkey would not receive Sand in her apartment, but she devoured her novels.

Flo was very troubled by Sand's ideas. "But I am impressed that a woman could take so bold a stand."

Christmas of 1839 should have been joyous, with Embley Park just re-modeled and hosting the Nicholsons and the Carters. But the news that Freddy Smith had died in Australia threw everyone into gloom. After Christmas, Flo left Embley Park to stay with Aunt Mai in Combe Hurst. She was as open with Aunt Mai as with Hilary. What could she pursue to make herself worthy? Aunt Mai was in complete sympathy. Together the two discussed what she might study—as Hilary studied art—and where. In March 1840, Aunt Mai wrote Mama:

> *Hard work is necessary to give zest to life in a character like hers, where there is great power of mind and a more than common inclination to apply. So I write you if you in any way object to a mathematical master.*[1]

Mama did object. How would Flo find the time? And what use is mathematics to a young lady desiring marriage? "I don't think they have any idea of half that is in you," commiserated Aunt Mai to Flo. Aunt Mai persisted, but Mama opposed the idea and raised objection after objection. Where would they find a master who could be trusted with a young lady? Even Papa entered the dispute. "Why mathematics? Why not history or philosophy?" Slowly Mama and Papa strangled Flo's attempt to pursue mathematics. She was more depressed than ever.

But one thing still cheered her: helping out. Aunt Jane, still grieving over Freddy, was expecting a baby. Flo was pleased when opinion prevailed among the aunts that she should be the one to stay with Aunt Jane on the Thames in London. At this time, all London was buzzing about Queen Victoria's wedding. She was marrying her first cousin Prince Albert of Saxe-Coburg-Gotha. Albert was the nephew of Victoria's mother. By custom, the queen proposed marriage, and everyone agreed that the dashing, honorable Albert—born the same year as Victoria—was a superb choice. All England was privy to the fact that Victoria loved Albert very much.

As spring of 1840 arrived, Grandmama Smith died at age eighty-one, freeing Aunt Julia at long last. Now forty-one, Aunt Julia threw her liberated energies into the Anti-Slavery Convention to be held in London that summer. Flo was frightened to think her own future might repeat Aunt Julia's past. Would Flo, too, be forty or older before she was free of the responsibility of aging parents? Often now she brooded over her "call." It had been three years since God called her to His service.

SEVEN

In the summer of 1841, the Carters borrowed Papa's enormous coach to tour France. Once there, Hilary did exactly what Flo had advised. She remained with Clarkey and studied art. She salved Flo's envy by sending her sketches. Meanwhile Mama worked feverishly to attract guests to Embley Park. She could sleep five large families now and intended to do just that at all times. She was beginning to get worried. Flo was twenty-one, Parthe twenty-two. She was not impressed that she herself had been quite happy to wait for marriage until the age of thirty!

One day, at Lord Palmerston's Broadlands estate, Mama thought she had hit pay dirt for Flo. There Flo met Richard Monckton Milnes, an eminently eligible bachelor of thirty-three. Someday he would become Lord Houghton. He claimed to have political ambition, though few believed him. Somehow he had become the center of an elite literary circle in London. Though he had no great talent himself, he drew to "breakfast" at his residence in Pall Mall the likes of Alfred Tennyson, Thomas Carlyle, Robert Peel, William Thackeray, and Alexis de Tocqueville. His chief attraction resembled Clarkey's. He was said to be always amiable, with crackling wit. But unlike Clarkey, Milnes was destined for great money, as heir to an enormous estate, Fryston in Yorkshire. Flo's first impression of him was one of disappointment. He was small and bland.

Yet Mama was not going to miss an opportunity. She invited Milnes to Embley Park, and he accepted. There he came alive. He captivated Flo. He was a wonderful raconteur, telling one story after another. Everyone wanted to listen. Milnes also talked about his visit with the notorious George Sand in Paris, cavalierly defending her. Flo had to admit that Milnes was very entertaining and broadminded.

The next great event socially for the Nightingales was an invitation to meet the Duke of Sussex at the Chatsworth estate of the Duke of Devonshire. The queen's sixty-nine-year-old "Uncle Augustus"—the Duke of Sussex—was highly eccentric. He had worn a black skullcap at her wedding and sobbed uncontrollably through the entire ceremony. The Nightingales spent three busy days at Chatsworth. Entertainment was planned for every moment. Chatsworth had not only a great palace but also immense grounds with elaborate gardens and a renowned glass conservatory. In the conservatory flourished tropical plants, a novel accomplishment at the time.

Mama was ecstatic. Chatsworth was the Nightingales' most important recognition yet by royalty. But after Mama's Chatsworth triumph, Flo was much happier staying with Grandmama Shore and eleven-year-old Shore in Tapton, simply because she was allowed to care for them. Nothing gave her greater peace of mind. And she knew many local villagers. Often they needed care. Among them was Helen Richardson. Helen's sister, Hope, had died in childbirth. Helen was determined to raise Hope's baby herself, although she was almost paralyzed with grief. Flo was expected back in Embley Park, but surely Mama would give her time to help Helen. But Mama refused. Flo went back to the social whirl, but something new developed. She found herself daydreaming constantly of doing "good." Much was vanity, she realized, because in her dreams she was admired by all. This offspring of pride bothered her. And were such daydreams healthy? Perhaps even sinful? What was she going to do?

In 1842, the Prussian ambassador to Queen Victoria visited Embley Park with his English wife. Christian Bunsen was far more than a diplomat. He was a scholar of renown, master of subjects as diverse as Egyptology and philosophy. Flo was as fascinated as Papa by Bunsen's discussion of the German philosophers Schleiermacher and Schopenhauer. Bunsen easily discussed theological developments in England. The Broad Church movement was attracting those not adhering to either the Low Church, the Evangelicals who believed truth was revealed by the Bible and personal experience, or the High Church, the quasi-Catholics who believed truth was revealed by the Bible and church traditions. The Broad Church had no unified theology but challenged the Bible and allowed all free inquiry. This very liberal outlook did not shock any of the Nightingales. They had heard unorthodox opinions discussed all their lives.

Flo trusted Bunsen enough to ask him privately, "What can an individual do toward lifting the load of suffering from the helpless and the miserable?"[1]

The startled Bunsen recommended the good works being done at the Institute of Kaiserswerth in Germany. There Pastor Fliedner trained Protestant women—deaconesses they were called—to be nurses.

But Flo was sure Bunsen didn't believe she was really serious about doing good works. So few people were. Besides, how could she free herself? On went her frustrating life. Yes, she was every bit as restless as Aunt Julia. Sometimes she accepted her restlessness, remembering fondly dear old George Herbert's poem "Pulley." Lack of rest was God's way of pulling the weary heart back to Him. Yet, other times Flo became very angry that she did not know how to satisfy her restlessness.

That next winter, she was down for a time with a chest ailment—not at

Embley Park, but Waverly. While bedridden, she read Harriet Martineau's *Thoughts in a Sick Room*. She found much to agree with. In illness one did realize how an instant of good swallowed up long hours of pain, just as Martineau asserted. How wonderful. What could be more beneficial than doing that kind of good for the suffering? While recovering, she began a friendship with Aunt Hannah, the sister-in-law of Aunt Anne. Aunt Hannah was a mystic who impressed Flo as being more in touch with the unseen than the seen. Flo thought she was the holiest person she had ever met. Flo read books Aunt Hannah recommended, especially those that enlarged on dispensation. These speculated on stages of God's revelations about His plan for mankind. Flo wanted very much to experience a revelation herself, and just as much she wanted to be part of His plan. She rarely forgot her "call," and the mystery that she did not know how to fulfill the call. Yet she was drawn more and more to the plight of the suffering.

Others were concerned, too. Unlike Flo, they were actively researching misery and issuing reports. Flo had no problem acquiring the reports. Finding the time to read them was the problem, but read them she did—even at the expense of her sleep. She digested the *Report of Select Committee on the Health of Towns*, the *Report on Sanitary Condition of Labouring Classes*, and the *Second Report of the Children's Employment Commission*. She found all these concerns compelling. And she was definitely drawn to helping the sick. The summer Flo turned twenty-four, Embley Park was visited by two Unitarians from America, Dr. Howe and his wife, Julia Ward Howe. The first evening, the doctor talked about his institute for the deaf and blind. His greatest challenge was to educate them. But he had other concerns. He wanted to treat the sick and the feebleminded. He also fervently wanted to help prisoners and slaves. Flo could scarcely sleep that night.

Next morning, she drew the doctor aside. "Dr. Howe, do you think it would be unsuitable and unbecoming for a young Englishwoman to devote herself to works of charity in hospitals and elsewhere, as Catholic sisters do? Do you think it would be a dreadful thing?"[2]

"My dear Miss Florence," he said soothingly, "it would be unusual, and in England whatever is unusual is apt to be thought unsuitable; but I say to you, go forward if you have a vocation for that way of life; act up to your inspiration, and you will find that there is never anything unbecoming or unladylike in doing your duty for the good of others. Choose, go on with it wherever it may lead you, and God be with you."[3]

Flo felt like soaring to the heights. In truth, Flo was only at peace now when she was helping the destitute in the nearby villages. In the village of

Wellow near Embley Park, Flo offered her services to the new vicar, Mr. Empson. She knew he was trying to start a school for the poor village children. Flo became more and more introspective. She became more disdainful of the frippery and finery of Mama's world. Once, when she missed a ball, she thought how smashing she would have been in her pink silk dress with the black lace flounces. Then she caught herself. Such pride! Flo longed to agree with 1 John: "For all that is in the world, the lust of the flesh, and the lust of the eyes, and the pride of life, is not of the Father, but is of the world." "Pride of life" especially jolted her. Pride. Pride. Pride. In her heart, she knew she still indulged "pride of life."

Flo adored John, the mystical disciple. She was herself sensing more and more the unseen. After taking Communion with a sick woman in the village, she later wrote:

> [I] suddenly felt that it was like the Upper Chamber when the doors were shut, and He all at once stood in the midst of them. He was the only reality there; she herself and the others in the room were but ghosts who put on form for a moment and would soon vanish into invisibility.[4]

But when the immediate sense of Christ's presence had faded, Flo focused on the sick woman. This, too, was mystical. At that moment, Flo *knew* the woman was dying. She was merely waiting to put on incorruption. Soon she would be a spirit.

God wants me, thought Flo, *to give her eyes, ears, and human reason to understand.* And so she did.

She then wrote to Clarkey:

> I think it is a mistake to say, as Carlyle does, that the end of life is to know ourselves and what we can do, because we may lose all interest in ourselves—so oftenest we wish to forget ourselves, but to know God and all His ways and all His intercourse with us, surely is the end of all our experience—and what really constitutes the "dark mystery" of life and its desolate emptiness is the veil which He has hung over His face. Oh the blessing of a pure heart, for it can only see God.[5]

To know God was all. Flo increasingly felt the presence of Christ. Yet, ironically, during this time she also saw more of Richard Monckton Milnes. She didn't attend his famous breakfast club, but Milnes came often to Embley Park, which Mama had relentlessly promoted into one of England's most sought-after invitations. All the other Nightingales were expected to recruit, as well. Friends were expected to do likewise. At Embley Park, the "picked and chosen of society," as Mama immodestly phrased her guests, wandered sunny velvet-green grounds among laurels, rosebuds, and azaleas.[6] Obligated, of course, to entertain those guests was demure twenty-five-year-old Flo. Flo was not happy, nor was her confidante, Hilary, who had returned from Paris. Hilary was "at home" now and allowed only intermittent art lessons. The leisure of both young ladies was poisoned by knowing the true freedom Clarkey enjoyed. Flo's discontent worsened when Parthe, who enjoyed society immensely, began to needle her. She even chided Flo in letters to others, pointing out her gloominess and calling her "Foe."

Flo continued to daydream and feel guilty about it. Her spiritual quest had increased her sense of guilt in other ways, too. "Wrongs" she had done others haunted her. She blamed her disagreeable relationship with Parthe on herself. New friendships tempted her into "crying on their shoulder." Or, worse yet, she was tempted to impress them with her "goodness." Her guilt and her temptations hung on her like chains. If only she could do something useful. But her constant yearning for good works became an object of guilt, too. Was she motivated by a love of others or by a desire to escape a life that oppressed her? Yet she knew in her heart and mind that there was a world of sickness and poverty out there crying for help. But how would she—woman of privilege but also confinement—ever reach that pain? Her introspection and frustration were harder and harder to manage.

In a letter to Hilary, she expressed her guilt over not answering God's call:

Oh, is our life here merely to deceive and be deceived? . . . There are strange punishments here for those that have made life consist of one idea and that one not God. . . . I often feel how much truth there is in the old myths of strange punishments and bewitchments. . .falling on those who have defied the power of a God. . . . Oh, dearest, pray for me—not for peace, for I have not sufficient interest in myself to care about it; for what does it signify? I can perform my duties as well at home without it; indeed, I am more use to my father and mother than I was five years ago—but for truth, truth, truth and a manifestation of God.[7]

Meanwhile Mama fussed over her. "You know, my dear, Lord Palmerston's daughter Fanny also was very restless. He almost despaired. But she finally accepted reality and stopped looking for the perfect man. Now as Lady Jocelyn, she is so useful in society."

Flo knew perfectly well that Mama wanted her to become Monckton Milnes's wife, a woman destined to be Lady Houghton. Then at Lea Hurst that summer of 1845, the Nightingales received word that Grandmama Shore was gravely ill.

EIGHT

After the family visited Grandmama Shore at Tapton, Flo alone was allowed to stay on. Grandmama was partially paralyzed. Flo could do little that was therapeutic, but by now she knew very well how sick people appreciate the tiniest comforts. Flo found peace of mind at Tapton. Caregiving was so satisfactory all the way around. Even problems seemed God-sent, if only she could be part of their solution, as caregiver or comforter. Grandmama Shore stabilized, much comforted by Flo. But suffering was everywhere for Flo, whether with Aunt Mai's depression over the lameness of one of her youngest daughters or with poor people in the village.

Flo continued to visit the villages, often becoming intimately engrossed in their problems. One man she counseled had accidentally shot and killed his cousin. He was inconsolable. Even the Nightingale household had its suffering. Their elderly family nursemaid became seriously ill at Lea Hurst. But the elderly woman insisted on traveling south to Embley Park with the family. Once there, she lasted only two days. Had the trip killed her? Flo wrote to Hilary:

> *Our dear old friend had left us early that morning. Her Father had sent for her so quietly that, though I held her hand, I could not tell, except for the coldness, the moment when her gallant spirit sped its way on its noiseless journey. She suffered very much on Monday, but on Tuesday it was all over before seven. Upright in her chair she died. . .so short a time before her death her voice was as strong as ever. . .now nothing in her room to remind one of life excepting the tick of her watch, and that stopped just before I came away. . . . [How unpleasant] it is coming out of the room where there is only her and God and me, to come back into the cold and false life of prejudices and hypocrisy and conventionalisms; by which I do not mean to find fault with life but only with the use I make of it. It seems to me to be all deceiving and vanitousness.*[1]

There it was again: Flo's despair with the uselessness of her own life. God had called her nearly eight years before, and still she did not know what to do nor how to do it! Clarkey had suggested writing novels as Jane Austen and other women had done. There was some freedom for women there. But Flo did not want to write plots of the mannered; after all, it was that polite society

126

that smothered her. On the other hand, she certainly could not write steamy novels like George Sand, with whom she did not agree or approve. Oh Lord, what was she to do?

After the death of her old nursemaid, Flo busied herself in the village of Wellow. Besides the usual deaths and births, there was an unusual amount of sickness during the fall of 1845. Three times she was at deathbeds, almost an angelic presence awaiting the end. But one case made her realize that not every death was necessary.

Good heavens, her soul cried after one woman died, *they might as well have poured poison down her throat!*

Some of the poor people had notions about remedies that were not only false, but also deadly! In addition to that, all around her now she saw suffering that could be alleviated—perhaps even prevented—if only the caretakers knew what to do and how to do it. How outrageous it was to have to guess! Such treatment was irrational. Surely she was not the first to think of this paradox. Where could one get real medical training? She had taken many careful notes over the years about ailments and their remedies, but she was by no measure medically trained.

Then she recalled Dr. Fowler, a family friend. More than eighty years old, Dr. Fowler practiced medicine at the Salisbury Infirmary, a mere fifteen miles from Embley Park. The doctor would be a guest at Embley Park during the Christmas season. A plan began to grow in her mind. Why shouldn't she train at Salisbury under Dr. Fowler for several weeks? Then Flo could come back and give qualified care in the village. Not only could she serve, but she could teach others how to help. The more she thought about her idea, the more elaborate became her plan.

Someday, like Aunt Julia, she would be free of family. Then she would most assuredly take a small house in the village and start a Protestant "sisterhood" of caregivers—yes, like the one in Kaiserswerth that Christian Bunsen had talked about. Oh, if only she knew more about Kaiserswerth. If only she could start such an institution herself. What a boon for those who suffered! These thoughts were golden to her. All gloom evaporated. She felt heavenly. She could scarcely wait to broach the subject with Dr. Fowler at Christmastime.

"What an excellent thought," responded Dr. Fowler.

"But isn't that nursing?" screeched Mama as she overheard Flo's remarks to Dr. Fowler.

Flo remained calm. "Yes, in a sense. . ."

"Do you not know about nurses?" hissed Parthe. "They are all low and vulgar."

Parthe, too? But Flo directed her calm toward Mama. "I'm sure the good doctor. . ."

But Mama was almost frantic. Flo had never seen her so irrational. "Nurses are common drunks," muttered Mama. "Do you wish to disgrace your family, Flo? How could you?"

Flo answered, "I've read Charles Dickens, too, Mama. I know he paints a sordid picture of nurses. But I'm sure Dr. Fowler can assure you that caricature is poetic license."

Parthe snapped, "Don't you know most physicians are not gentlemen like Dr. Fowler? They will surely take advantage of you, Flo."

Dr. Fowler's mood had changed. "Perhaps it's best not to pursue this."

Dr. Fowler's wife echoed his advice. Flo had no ally now in her wonderful scheme. It was dead. She had avoided the use of the word *nurse*—but to no avail. After that defeat, Flo turned to theological treatises again for satisfaction. But the vehemence of Mama—and especially Parthe—ate at her. Why should their prejudices have to be hers? For that matter, why should their pleasures have to be hers? She did not begrudge them their pleasures. Papa, too, disappointed her. Would he never stand up to Mama? He was less and less connected to the family. Mama ran everything now. And Parthe was her shadow. After Papa went into London to stay with Aunt Jane, Flo was at Mama's beck and call—and Parthe's. It was certainly no consolation to Flo that Hilary, also at Aunt Jane's, wrote how much she enjoyed dining with Thomas Macauley and in general being immersed in all the politics and literature of London. Hilary also noted that Flo's father complained of England's unfulfilled young ladies. They did not know what to do with themselves, he said.

"But now I do know!" muttered Flo as she read the letter. "And why don't you do something about it, Papa? If our Savior walked the earth now and I went to Him, would He send me back to this life I am leading? No. He would say to me, 'Do this work for Me!' "

Flo agonized more and more over her dilemma. God had called her. And she did nothing, although now she was surer of what she should do. Oh, she knew what Mama and Parthe were saying: "Why does she think she is so special? Her desires are no more than vanity and selfishness." Perhaps Papa felt the same way. It all appeared so hopeless. It was during this time that Flo found another trusted confidante in Selina Bracebridge of Coventry.

By letter of introduction, the Bracebridges had sent the Howes to Embley Park. Flo's pet name for Selina became "Sig," shortened from sigma, the Greek letter for *S*. Sig was a close friend of Clarkey's, too, so it was little wonder that Sig understood completely what Flo was suffering. But could Sig help her? Flo soon realized that Selina Bracebridge was the strongest willed of all her confidantes. She offered not just sympathy but strategies. And she was sly enough to stay on the good side of Mama and Parthe—yet be in complete sympathy with Flo. But as yet Sig could not see a way out for Flo, either.

In June, when Flo returned for the summer stay in Lea Hurst, she noted wearily in her journal:

> *Arrived here tonight. Everything the same. . .yet how much one has thought and suffered since one was last here. All my plans have been wrecked and my hopes destroyed, and yet without any visible, any material change. . . . Our movements are so regular that our year is more marked even than other people's, and often the year returns without having had any visible fruit of all its tribulation but experience. . .and the experience how sad. However, I must not belie St. Paul, who, I believe, saves his truth by saying that it is the experience of patience which worketh hope.*[2]

Yes, hope was one of the three great Christian virtues. She must never give up hope, or faith, or love. Yet she fluctuated back and forth between that hope and despair. How tedious the whole process was, how melancholy, perhaps even self-pitying. *Lord, free me from this,* she prayed. She read the Bible and Homer. She had little use for novels at this time of her life, often setting aside her reading and thinking of angels. Wouldn't one come with a message for her? She meditated more and more. Lying in bed in an upper-floor bedroom at Lea Hurst one night, she gazed at a flickering candle. The candle was like human reason, she thought. Its glare prevented her from seeing the moonlit landscape outside her window. That invisible landscape was the spiritual world—yes, the real world.

She made July 7 her self-examination day. This self-appraisal was profoundly depressing. She realized how much the family consumed her. Much, if not all, of her activity was trivial. She had resumed her Greek lessons to please Papa. She also rode with him in the hills to give him companionship. Each day she had to read her friends' letters aloud to Mama. Mama also had her reading novels aloud for her. Flo always had to be ready to amuse poor, sensitive Parthe. Lately, Flo had been reading a novel aloud to her, too. And each day Flo wrote letters to her friends, often lamenting her own woes. She regretted her complaining. It was vanity.

But then there was the nearby village of Holloway. In its gabled, gray stone cottages hugging the hill slopes, her heart filled once again with purpose. For a while she felt as if she existed only to relieve the suffering of those poor unfortunates. On July 16, she wrote in her journal:

> *I can do without marriage. . .or any of the things that people sigh after.*
> *My imagination is so filled with the misery of the world, that the only*
> *thing worth trouble seems to me to be helping or sympathizing there—*
> *the only thing where labor brings any return. When I am driving about*
> *a town, all the faces I see seem to me either anxious or depressed or*
> *diseased, and my soul flings itself forth to meet them, to "pledge them in*
> *the cup of grief." My mind is absorbed with the idea of the sufferings of*
> *man; it besets me behind and before. A very one-sided view, but I can*
> *hardly see anything else, and all the poets sing of the glories of this world*
> *seems to me untrue. All the people I see are eaten up with care or poverty*
> *or disease. When I go into a cottage, I long to stop there all day, to wash*
> *the children, relieve the mother, stay by the sick one. And behold there are*
> *a hundred other families unhappy within half a mile.*[3]

Yes! This was her calling—caring for the suffering. She knew that now. At long last, she was certain! Two days later, she wrote in her journal:

> *It satisfies my soul, it supplies every want of my heart and soul and mind.*
> *It heals all my disease. It redeems my life from destruction. . . . I want*
> *nothing else; my heart is filled. I am at home. I want no other heaven. I*
> *can desire no further benefits, as long as Evil has its reign in the world.*[4]

Unfortunately for Flo, the Nightingales were soon heading south again. It tore at Flo's heart to leave her "patients" in Holloway. Two boys dying of consumption she knew she would never see again. Back at Embley Park, as a part of her voracious reading, Flo studied reports on prison reform. She approved some kind of rehabilitation. She had seen the squalor and hopelessness that the poor had to fight. Of course her own great privilege—which she did nothing to merit—made her feel even worse. By now she knew her father's annual income was not much less than Queen Victoria's!

She had another jolt. None other than Richard Monckton Milnes had introduced a bill in Parliament to establish juvenile reformatories, so that the youths would not be thrown in with grizzled criminals. Milnes had surprised everyone by getting elected to Parliament. And he had not settled into being "clubby" about it. He had traveled to Ireland to see the consequences of the potato famine. He was an activist. He also came to Embley Park with ever greater frequency.

Milnes had grown in Flo's eyes. His attention now thrilled her. Could she satisfy her restlessness with such an active man? Or would she become like Mama, merely the chief instigator of all his social activity? And what of her "call"? Wasn't it clear now that she was destined to do something in the medical realm? If only she could be Milnes's closest friend and confidante—but not his wife. But such cerebral relationships between men and women were almost impossible in England.

Meanwhile her relationship with Sig grew. Of Mrs. Bracebridge, Flo wrote in her journal:

> *I wonder whether she knows what a difference she has made in my life. The very fact of there being one person by whom one's thoughts are not pronounced fit only for a dream not worth disputing, who does not look upon one as a fanciful spoilt child who ought to take life as it is and enjoy it—that mere fact changes the whole aspect of things to one. Since one has found that there is one person who does not think that Society ought to make one happy, I have never had that sinking of spirits at the thought of the three winter months of perpetual row.*[5]

Nevertheless, Sig did ask Flo whether she could not find happiness in marriage as she herself had. Flo told her bluntly she believed God "has as clearly marked out some to be single women as He has others to be wives, and has organized them accordingly for their vocation." The truth was that, at twenty-six, Flo had almost resolved not to marry. Flo steeled herself. She had heard a thousand comments—all derogatory—about how Fanny, Lord Palmerston's very difficult daughter, had resisted marriage. So Flo had no illusions about being admired for her desire to be different. But the truth was that now she felt far more guilt about the neglect shown by the upper class to the poor and the sick. *I am like the poor now,* she thought. *We expect little from life, much from God.* Oh, how the poor trusted Flo. What a magnificent responsibility for Flo. Why, it was a thousand times more important than her social obligations to the upper class. And to think that in her own house she was treated like a confused child!

Her thoughts became angrier:

> *This house is the embodiment to me of the drainage of the poor to fill the rich, who, upon the plea of a better bonnet and a better dinner, blurt out "truths" to the poor and expect them to be grateful (without knowing their manners, hardly even their language, certainly not their feelings). . . . I loathe that house.*[6]

Surely these fiery thoughts come from God, she thought. He was sending this heat to Flo until she did His will. On the other hand, if they were not from God, they would die out. But they strengthened. On December 31, 1846, she wrote:

It has often been said: How extraordinary that Jesus Christ should have arisen among the working class! But how much, much more extraordinary if He were to arise among our class. Nay, almost beyond a miracle for Him ever to come to see us. We have no time! . . . We're too busy—we have no time for that (prayer). . .which our Saviour found so necessary that He sat up whole nights for it, having so much to do in the day.[7]

During the daytime, Flo toiled in the muddy lanes of Wellow more and more. Long before dawn, she awoke to study reports. Evenings were almost a dead loss, because she had to sit in the drawing room—young lady-in-waiting—until ten o'clock. She salvaged some of the evenings by retreating into her dreams, not so fuzzy now that Christian Bunsen had sent her a detailed report of the Kaiserswerth Institute. This report confirmed exactly what Flo wished to do in England. Young Protestant maidens served the Lord by nursing and teaching the poor. And after many years, the Kaiserswerth Institute had even been recognized by the Prussian government.

Then a remarkable thought jolted Flo. Why found her own institute in England? Why could she not join the Kaiserswerth Institute? But, oh, how Mama—and her shadow, Parthe—would fight her. Meanwhile, her men friends were changing England. Lord Ashley's Ten-Hours Bill finally was passed into law in May 1847. The future Lord Shaftsbury, Lord Ashley, had fought for many years to protect women and children. Meanwhile, the thrust and parry of "why doesn't Flo marry?" never stopped. Richard Monckton Milnes was more persistent than ever. Then Flo was shocked to learn that Clarkey had married the brilliant Egyptologist Julius Mohl, a German but longtime resident of Paris. Flo had met Julius and knew he was just right for Clarkey. At the age of fifty or so, Clarkey had married. Was it then not still possible for Flo? Should she reward Monckton Milnes for his patient courtship? She searched her heart.

"When I imagine myself as his wife, I am overwhelmed with unhappiness," Flo confided in Sig.

Then at long last, Sig justified Flo's great faith in her.

NINE

Sig hit upon a wonderful scheme to get Flo away from her social bondage—for a while. When the Bracebridges decided to go to Rome for the winter, they invited Flo to go with them. Winter was the time of the most intense stress between Flo and her family. Flo thanked God for Sig's social skills, because Mama and Papa had complete faith in her, too. They agreed without hesitation. Not even Parthe was upset. In fact, she busied herself dictating just what wardrobe Flo would take and just exactly which people Flo must call on once there.

Flo and the Bracebridges arrived in Rome the evening of November 9, 1847. They stayed near the Piazza del Popolo. The next day, long before dawn, Flo awakened, exulting in the thought of seeing St. Peter's Cathedral. Finally, she could not wait for the Bracebridges to arise. She walked furiously along the streets, looking neither left nor right. As she entered St. Peter's Square, framed by its stunning colonnades, the sun was just touching the cathedral. At the entrance, she gathered herself, breath, and mind. When Flo left the cathedral, she was struck by how bitterly cold the air was. She had felt nothing on her way there. For several weeks after that day, Flo was a relentless sightseer. She followed an itinerary Papa had designed for her, ticking off each sight after she visited it. She was happier than she had thought she would ever be again. Always she was drawn back to St. Peter's and the Vatican. One day, in the Vatican's Sistine Chapel, she saw Michelangelo's supreme masterpiece, his depiction of the Old Testament on the enormous ceiling. It had been done in fresco, the most challenging form of art in that it was painted on fresh plaster each day. Revision was virtually impossible. Only the greatest master could attempt such a thing. To Flo, it was the zenith of human art. Flo was enraptured with Isaiah, whose writings she regarded more highly than Shakespeare's. For Flo, Isaiah was the forerunner of Christ. And she was absolutely certain that Michelangelo had captured the true Isaiah. Yet she did not enjoy seeing Michelangelo's *Last Judgment* on the wall behind the altar. She had even hoped the failing afternoon light in the chapel would prevent her seeing the Lord separating the "sheep" from the "goats." But no. Flo could see it all too clearly. This fresco had been just as demanding, with just as dazzling results. But it was depressing, even frightening to Flo. Michelangelo had wanted it so. In the fresco, even St. Peter has fear in his eyes. Eternal damnation awaits some! Flo did not want to believe this.

She and Sig had been in the Sistine Chapel nearly all day. She was glad when they left. Away from the chapel, Flo let the great ceiling dominate her thoughts. Eternal damnation she suppressed.

Rome was truly a delight. She even enjoyed socializing again. One of the first couples Flo met in Rome was the immensely wealthy Herberts of Wilton, only twenty miles from Embley Park. Flo should not have liked Sidney Herbert much, for after all, he was a Tory and very High Church, leaning toward the Catholic traditions. However, she found him not only gracious but sincere in his intentions to do good. He wielded power in the government, too, as Peel's secretary of war. His wife, Elizabeth, was just as open and friendly. Flo welcomed 1848, luxuriating in the grandeur of Rome. But her enjoyment began to wear on her even there. Could she ignore Roman urchins, begging everywhere on the streets, all desperately poor? Why could she not help some of them as she helped children at Wellow and Holloway? It was not long before she had virtually assumed responsibility for a little girl named Felicetta Sensi. Attempting to arrange the education of this child caused Flo to be summoned by Mother Santa Colomba at the Convent of the Trinita dei Monti.

The Mother could not have been kinder. Flo was summoned because the convent ran an orphan school. They would take the child in, but they requested 180 scudi for five years. As wealthy as William Nightingale was, Flo had little money for her own use. Where could she get such a sum? Mulling it over, she decided the money would come out of her clothing allowance. So Flo signed a contract, assuring the child an education. But she avoided talking about her act of charity. That would have made it appear she did it only to make herself look noble.

The incident had another result. Mother Santa Colomba recognized Flo's ravenous spiritual hunger. She encouraged her to participate in the convent. Flo tried it, studying the rule of their Order of the Sacred Heart and trying to understand how these women dealt with the trials of life. Mother Santa Colomba, in bad health and often in pain, insisted this affliction was sent to her by God. She accepted it, just as the apostle Paul had finally accepted the "thorn in his side," with joy. She would die laughing, she told Flo. The only thing—*"unicamente!"*—was to do the will of God. And for her that was to educate the orphans of Rome.

"But how am I to know what His will is for me?" blurted Flo.

"Pray. Ask God, 'Am I to do Your will in a religious order or in the world? If in the world, married or single?' " Then the nun added, "God generally answers."

Flo admired her candor. Mother Santa Colomba had not guaranteed an answer. Ever methodical, Flo recorded everything she saw and heard at the convent, including how the children were educated. The latter information she might use at Wellow. The atmosphere of this orphan school was unlike the clamor and harshness of English schools. The nuns created an atmosphere of calm. The children came in defiant and unruly. Soon they were almost angelic!

"Teachers must be lighthearted," insisted Mother Santa Colomba, "to create an atmosphere of loving kindness."[1]

Flo was shocked to see the little "angels" contradict their teachers. Even the teaching sisters contradicted Mother Santa Colomba. Yet freedom made love blossom everywhere. Flo's idea of oppressive dogma in the Catholic world had been wrong. The children said only short prayers.

Flo, too, was encouraged to criticize. She had been swallowing all her criticism but now spoke out in front of the entire community. The sisters indulged in too many vocal prayers, she said. The sisters accepted her criticism, although one said Flo was a donkey in her spiritual development. Flo rejoiced in the blunt comment! Flo loved the nuns' character, their joyous way of service. Increasingly she compared Mother Santa Colomba to her friend Sig. The two represented the very best women produced by the Protestant and Catholic faiths. They both thought only of pleasing others, never themselves. She revered them both.

But Flo confided to Mother Santa Colomba, "I feel like such a failure."

Mother Santa Colomba told her she must accept failure. God knew she had failed. She must be as joyous in failure as she was in success. It all came from God. Being anxious or miserable pleased no one. Should Flo expect more "success" than the Lord? He was thwarted by everyone in His earthly mission. Even His own apostles understood little of who He was before the Resurrection. And finally, the nun told Flo she had prayed about her many times. She was sure that God was not calling her to become Catholic. But Flo must turn her whole heart to God so that she would be ready to do His will. The nun was certain that Flo was called to do something very special! Then Flo received an exceptional gift from Mother Santa Colomba. She was allowed to make a retreat at the convent. After the retreat, she recorded her final conversation with the nun:

> Mother SC: *Did not God speak to you during this retreat? Did He not ask you anything?*
>
> Flo: *He asked me to surrender my will.*
>
> Mother SC: *And to whom?*
>
> Flo: *To all that is upon the earth.*
>
> Mother SC: *He calls you to a very high degree of perfection. Take care. If you resist, you will be very guilty.*[2]

Vowing to crush her self-will so that she could do only the will of God, Flo said good-bye to her friends in the convent. The Bracebridges and Flo left Rome at the beginning of April. What had affected her more? God revealed through Michelangelo? Or God revealed through a pious nun? Why weigh the difference? Rome had been wonderful. Italy itself was still parceled out and fighting for liberty and unity, but Flo had never been less interested. Still, by habit she called herself a friend of united Italy, and united Germany, or any people united for liberty.

This idealism upset Parthe. "Foreigners are scarcely likely to know what to do with freedom anyway," she sniffed.

Parthe was certainly not alone in her sentiment. She shared the consensus of the "picked and chosen" who strolled the rose-bordered garden paths of Embley Park. "Such arrogance," fumed Flo. Soon she was arguing with Mama, sparring with Parthe. It angered her that Papa, who agreed with her, made himself scarce. Then Flo realized she had resumed all her old angers. Enduring Parthe—and Mama, too—had seemed so simple in the convent. Now at Embley Park, crushing her self-will appeared impossible. How could she do that around people who bullied her? Wouldn't that just mean she would never be able to do the will of God? Oh, how she longed for the peace of the convent and the comfort of like minds.

At least she was allowed to work in the school at Wellow—even instituting some things she had learned at the orphan school in Rome. But so, too, did she endure her monotonous evenings in the drawing room at Embley Park, as well as Mama's never-ending social whirl. How unreal their life at Embley Park was.

In spite of her feelings of futility, she renewed her confidences with Aunt Julia, Aunt Mai, and Hilary. She cultivated her newer friendships: Sig, of course, but also Elizabeth Herbert. Mrs. Herbert, besides being a new mother, was founding a convalescent home at Charmouth. So she was doing what she could within the confines of marriage. The Herberts were Tories, so Flo began to suspect perhaps there was not that much difference in the political parties after all. Queen Victoria had recently come to the same conclusion. Before her marriage to Prince Albert, the tiny, hot-tempered queen had been staunchly Whig. Now it appeared she was leaning toward the Tories. Were Flo and dreamy-eyed Papa being fools to think the political parties were different? Were both parties merely representing the well-to-do, with only the smallest shades of difference?

"Am I going to spend the rest of my life becoming more and more disillusioned?" she asked wearily.

Then Flo learned that Clarkey and her husband, Julius Mohl, had gone to Frankfurt, Germany, to escape political turmoil in Paris. God would not turn France upside down to please Flo, but it was fortuitous. Frankfurt was very near Kaiserswerth! Flo could visit the Mohls in order to visit the Protestant deaconesses at the Kaiserswerth Institute. But Frankfurt itself was soon in turmoil. So that plan—and any vain notion about God's arranging it for her—evaporated.

When the social cycle took her again to London, Flo found good works there to escape to during the day. The reformer Lord Ashley had been promoting for six years what were called "ragged schools" for poor children. By 1849, ragged schools numbered eighty-eight. Of the almost one thousand volunteer teachers, one was Flo. Some of these teachers had the same joy of the teaching she saw at the orphan school in Rome. Life was raw in London. One could see people dying on the streets. Now there was a monstrous problem crying out for her help. It pleased her to educate, she finally admitted to herself, but it did not bring joy. No, teaching was not her calling. And her daydreams had returned. All would admire her, she fancied in her dreams. She still had visions of personal success! How she loathed her own ambition, her restlessness, just as others did.

During the summer of 1849, the Bracebridges introduced Flo to a young woman her same age named Elizabeth Blackwell. Elizabeth had the same fire in her that Flo had. A woman could not attend medical school in England, so Elizabeth had gone to medical school in America! Now she was a certified physician but still unable to practice in England. She only visited England before going to Paris for more training. Eventually, she would return to America to practice medicine. Every step of the way, she had been supported by her father in Bristol. Flo had nothing but admiration for Elizabeth Blackwell's determination, but the more she thought about her own family's lack of support—especially now Papa's—the more depressed she became!

Once again, the Bracebridges sought to remove her from her unhappiness. This winter they were going to Egypt. Would Flo come?

But before she could do anything else, she had to face another quandary. Richard Monckton Milnes pursued her everywhere now: Embley Park, London, Lea Hurst. He wanted an answer. Would she marry him or not? This time, he said it with finality. As much as he wanted her, he could wait no longer. He was nearly forty, Flo nearly thirty. She had to admit his stature grew in her eyes every day. He was now established as a liberal Whig, espousing the very ideals Flo loved. He worked on a biography of the poet John Keats. Why could she not love this gifted Monckton Milnes? She couldn't bear the thought of his one day giving up on her. Was she going to force him to give up on her so that she could preserve her ambition—an ambition that had so little chance of ever happening?

She told him, "I cannot marry you." Her heart remained closed to him.

With that rejection, Mama was furious. She didn't care whether Flo left the country or not. In November 1849, Flo arrived with the Bracebridges at Alexandria, Egypt. She had prepared herself well. She knew some very distinguished Egyptologists in Christian Bunsen and Julius Mohl. She took a small library with her about Egypt. She was determined to take Egypt—called in some circles the "East"—and its ancient mysteries by storm. And with good cheer, too. In Alexandria, Flo was taken inside a mosque—such a terrible affront to Muslims that she had to be heavily disguised. If they had known the masked intruder was a woman, they might have killed her. In another letter home, she would write that the perilous visit to the mosque revealed "what it is to be a woman in these countries, where Christ has not been to raise us. God save them, for it is a hopeless life."[3] Although Cairo stunned her with its alien beauty, the human misery she saw was so appalling she had to turn away and thank God she did not have to stay.

But the worst scene was the surrounding desert. She wrote, "One goes riding out, and one really feels inclined to believe this is the kingdom of the devil."[4]

Up the Nile she toured by ship. As much as she was supposed to admire the pyramids—which they saw from a distance but had not yet visited—she loathed them. She could imagine nothing more vulgar, having nothing to commend them but size and resistance to time. But Egypt was choked with other relics that had also resisted time. So what did the pyramids represent? To Flo they represented tyranny—vain objects built by breaking the backs of slaves!

Frequently they docked and the passengers went ashore to explore. Flo and the Bracebridges had their own escort, Paolo, a very experienced guide of about fifty. To Flo, the desert continued to be diabolical, the killer of life. Ruins were everywhere. Was it any wonder Christ encountered the devil in the desert? The desert constantly reminded her of the struggle between God and Satan. Egypt was fast becoming a potent experience for her, a religious experience.

One day aboard ship, they were struck by a sandstorm so violent that dunes of sand ran across the surface of the Nile. What a sight! Once, in a storm, a boat went careening helplessly past their ship. The wind never let up in its fury until the next morning. Then the entire day they were drenched with rain. When the storm passed, they learned four boats had gone down, every passenger lost. Who could doubt anything in Genesis and Exodus after these violent episodes?

Her letters were no longer perky. The mud huts of the Arabs appalled her:

> *To see human beings choosing darkness rather than light, building their doorways four feet high or less, choosing to crawl upon the ground like reptiles, to live in a place where they could not stand upright. . . . In a cold climate, one could have understood it; but here it seemed as if they did it on purpose to be as like beasts as they could. . . . If they had been deserted, you would have thought it was the dwelling-place of some wild animal. I never before saw any of my fellow creatures [so] degraded.*[5]

Finally, their ship arrived at Thebes, where they could go ashore to explore the grand ruins of Karnak, of Luxor, and of the Valley of Kings. Flo focused her reason and all her preparation for Egypt on this exploration and subsequent long, erudite letters. But in her heart and soul, Flo was profoundly disturbed by Egypt and its satanic desert.

TEN

Flo wrote of the desert "being perpetually restless, of Milton's Satan, turning ceaselessly from side to side in his lake of fire."[1] Another time she described the desert as "a great dragon, putting out his fiery tongue and licking up the green, fertile plain, biting into it."[2] She was frank in her letters, but not as frank as she was in a tiny diary she started on New Year's Day of 1850. Entries in her diary revealed the true depth of her turmoil, "daydreaming" in her mind being a killer of action:

> *1 Jan—(at Luxor) Dreaming.*
> *17 Jan—(at Abu Simbel) Dreamed in the very face of God.*
> *20 Jan—(in temple cave) Oh heavenly fire, purify me—free me from this slavery.*
> *22 Jan—By the temple of Isis with the roar of the Cataract, I thought I should see Him. His shadow in the moonlight.*
> *26 Jan—(at Janeb) I spoiled it all with dreaming. Disappointed with myself & the effect of Egypt on me. Rome was better.*
> *11 Feb—Did not go out—but the demon of dreaming had possession of my weakened head.*
> *16 Feb—Karnak—& where was I? All the while. . .dreaming.*[3]

In February, the life of her soul became truly mystical. God began speaking through the words of Mother Santa Colomba:

> *22 Feb—Long morning by myself. . .on the steps of Portico. . .God spoke to me once again.*
> *28 Feb—(Tombs of the Kings) God called me with. . .[Mother Santa Colomba's] words.*
> *3 Mar—Did not get up in the morning, but God gave me the time. . .to "meditate" on. . .[Mother Santa Colomba's] words.*
> *7 Mar—God called me in the morning and asked me would I do good for Him, for Him alone without the reputation.*
> *8 Mar—Thought much upon. . .[Mother Santa Colomba's words], "Can you hesitate between the God of the whole Earth & your little reputation?"*[4]
> *10 Mar—Every day, during the quarter of an hour I had by myself,*

> *after dinner & after breakfast, in my own cabin,*
> *read. . .[Mother Santa Colomba's] words—Can you give*
> *up the reputation of suffering much &*
> *saying little? they cried to me.*
>
> *15 Mar—God has delivered me from the great offence—& the*
> *constant murderer of my thoughts.*
>
> *16–17 Mar—(in Cairo) God told me what a privilege He had*
> *reserved for me. Kaiserswerth. . . . If I were never think*
> *ing of the reputation, how I should be better able to see*
> *what God intends for me.*

What a spiritual experience! After Egypt and its terrible desert tormented her mind, God had talked to her! God had raised the promise of Kaiserswerth. The process really defied human understanding. But she was more sure than ever that Kaiserswerth held the answer for her. As if to confirm it, just before she left Egypt she visited a dispensary in Alexandria run by Christian sisters who took no vows. As the sisters tended hundreds of poor Arabs, their joy radiated from them.

Yet after leaving Egypt to visit Greece, Flo's spirits sank again. Surely Kaiserswerth was just a dream itself. Hadn't it been eight years since Christian Bunsen had first suggested it? Why did she think Kaiserswerth would materialize now? But in Greece she had a significant event.

> *12 May—Today I am thirty—the age Christ began His mission.*
> *Now no more childish things, no more vain things, no more*
> *love, no more marriage. Now, Lord, let me think*
> *only of Thy Will, what Thou willest me to do—Oh Lord,*
> *Thy Will, Thy Will.*[5]

She tried desperately to crush her own ambition:

> *18 May—My history. . .[is] a history of miserable woe, mistake,*
> *and blinding vanity, of seeking great things for myself.*
>
> *19 May—God, I place myself in Thy Hands. . . . If it be Thy Will*
> *that I should go on suffering, let it be so.*
>
> *21 May—Let me only accomplish the Will of God. Let me not desire*
> *great things for myself.*
>
> *10 June—The Lord spoke to me: He said, "Give five minutes every*
> *hour to the thought of me."*[6]

Still, Flo sank deeper into depression. By the end of June, she could scarcely believe her eyes. The handwriting in her diary was that of an old lady. Was she so heartsick she was dying? *Oh, please save me, God,* she prayed.

Suddenly, she was apprised of Sig's brilliant strategy. On the overland route back to England, they would detour in Germany—where at last Flo would visit Kaiserswerth! Yet Flo felt no joy at all. In fact, she was so apprehensive that this last hope would disappoint her, she was almost paralyzed. Suppose she indeed discovered Kaiserswerth was not her calling? Could she handle a disappointment as enormous as that? Was there any hope beyond Kaiserswerth? In despair, she wrote that she was "lost and past redemption, a slave that could not be set free."[7]

In such a state of mind, she arrived at Kaiserswerth on July 31. Pastor Fliedner and his wife ignored her funk. Energetic and cheerful, the Fliedners appeared overjoyed to show her their institute. Flo was mildly pleased when they insisted she stay in the quarters with the Protestant deaconesses. She had seen nothing yet and felt strange confined in a tiny room that first night. Then Flo was amazed to feel her heart soar again. Surely this was what God intended! The next morning, she was actually helping Sister Katerina bathe a group of boisterous children in the orphanage. Later she observed the sister as she taught the children in the school. Then Flo stayed until long after midnight with a deaconess who nursed in the hospital. Every hour they patrolled the wards together. The wards were squeaky clean, with none of the foul smells usually endured in hospitals. And everything was completely proper. The deaconesses nursed only female patients. Males attended male patients.

All patients received spiritual help as well as medical care. Every facet of the Fliedner institution was carried out in this spirit. The children in the orphanage and the infant school were subjected to both academic and biblical learning. One day Flo was fortunate to see how a new orphan was welcomed. The welcome was like a joyous birthday party. Pastor Fliedner presided, encouraging the new child to choose the songs to be sung. The child even received a modest gift. The welcome ended with all the children joining in to pray for the latest foundling.

Wayward young women were also housed at Kaiserswerth. They, too, were treated with kindness. Unlike other institutions of the day, Kaiserswerth did not give them tedious sewing to occupy endless hours. The young women gardened and did various farm chores. Flo was thrilled to see how the women responded to farm animals. Flo carefully noted the way the Fliedners managed the institute. She could find no fault, other than suspecting that their medical practices were not up-to-date. But that was due to a lack of doctors.

Everything else was perfect. Piety. Cleanliness. Love. Discipline. Work. Trust. She could not have been more at peace. Her joy was unbounded.

For two weeks she had been allowed to observe. When she left for England, she was ebullient, "feeling so brave as if nothing could ever vex me again."[8] Pastor Fliedner had asked Flo to write a report on his institute so the English people would know of their work. She was so focused that she wrote a thirty-two-page tract—specifically for other English women like herself—that described the *Institution of Kaiserswerth on the Rhine for the Practical Training of Deaconesses, under the direction of the Reverend Pastor Fliedner*. Here was an opportunity for all in England like herself to escape the busy idleness in which they were confined at home.

Before they reached Calais to sail for England, she finished her manuscript, which Mr. Bracebridge proofed before sending it off to be printed. How accomplished Flo felt. And yet on August 21, 1850, she had to return to "busy idleness" herself. When she strolled into the drawing room at Lea Hurst, Mama and Parthe were stunned to see her. She introduced them to her owl, Athena. Mama's eyes grew more concerned by the moment as Flo's few belongings—mostly books—were set in the entry by the coachman.

England seemed grim now. Of Flo's confidantes, only Aunt Mai was available. The entire family was jolted by the news that Henry Nicholson had drowned in Spain. Flo went to Waverly to console the family. In her heart, she did not pity Henry. Could one believe the words of Christ and pity those who had died? Death was a door to the kingdom of God. But in consoling others, Flo's spirits sank to the depths again. Why was she alive? Her great plans were forever thwarted.

Seeing Richard Monckton Milnes at parties only depressed her more. He was cordial but cool. What had she expected? Did she actually want to encourage him? Hadn't she put him through enough torment? How could she be so selfish, so foolish? And yet his apparent indifference to her now stung like a whip. She also saw the extraordinary Elizabeth Blackwell again. Blackwell had returned from studying obstetrics in Paris. In the process, she had contracted an eye disease that cost her the sight of one eye. But her sacrifices had paid off. She was an eminently qualified doctor now, even if she would have to go back to America to practice medicine.

It seemed as though everyone Flo saw these days reminded her of her own failure. And her home life was more contentious than ever. Mama was exasperated with her. When was Flo going to outgrow these childish desires! Now Parthe joined Mama in being constantly irritated by Flo.

Flo began to write a very long tract of her unhappiness, her own restlessness.

Perhaps that would give her insight, perhaps justification, or if nothing else, relief in something to do. Her tract grew into a treatise on activism. She talked to the Chartists, to Lord Ashley. Yes, the working people needed all the voices they could find among the aristocracy. England certainly had problems, not unsolvable at all but simply ignored by all the powers but a few. So Flo poured her heart into her tract. She discovered many working men angry with God, and quite a number refused to believe there was a God. Flo felt she had to straighten them out on this. Her tract changed direction. It grew into a treatise on theology.

Flo believed with all her heart that God was benevolent and His very thoughts were expressed as immutable physical laws. These physical laws that the atheistic materialists so cherished were evidence to Flo of His being. Flo even corresponded with a Catholic priest, hinting she might be more suited to Catholicism than Protestantism. But the priest saw that her chief attraction to Catholicism was the freedom of the sisters to nurse in clean, well-run hospitals. So he bluntly wrote her that her beliefs were not compatible with Catholicism.

Flo's relationship with Parthe worsened. Now Parthe was scheming with Mama to prick Flo's conscience and make her feel obligated to care for Grandmama Shore and all other aging relatives. The same technique had been used to divert Aunt Julia from becoming too active. Meanwhile, Parthe's health was getting worse, in no small part due to having a very difficult younger sister, Flo was told. Word that Richard Monckton Milnes was going to marry Annabel Crewe ignited Mama and Parthe for a while, too. "How foolish Flo has been!" they ranted. This type of foolishness only made Parthe's health worse, said Mama. Finally, Mama decided she should take Parthe to Karlsbad for bath treatments. Of course, Flo had to go, too.

Once in Germany, Flo announced, "I'm going to Kaiserswerth while Parthe gets her treatments."

"What injustice!" screamed Parthe. "Flo ruins my health so that I have to come to Karlsbad. And while I'm here, she will go to Kaiserswerth!"

With that, Parthe hurled some jewelry into Flo's face. Mama was shocked. No one must know of this disgrace. Flo agreed to silence, but she did go to Kaiserswerth. Papa had not gone to Europe at all with the three. He was not supporting Flo yet, but he no longer supported Mama and Parthe against Flo. No less than the Bracebridges, the Bunsens, Aunt Mai, and the Sidney Herberts had recently urged Flo to break away from Mama and Parthe—if Papa didn't object. But Flo could not bring herself to make an open break. She had no financial support.

Still, Flo managed to return to Kaiserswerth. This time she worked with the deaconesses as an apprentice. Rising at five in the morning, she was consciously happy every waking moment until she fell asleep at night, exhausted. Four times during the day she was allowed ten minutes to eat: rye tea and bread at 6:00 a.m. and 3:00 p.m., broth and vegetables at noon, and broth only at 7:00 p.m. She would have been unhappy with more. It was weeks later, in October 1851, that she rejoined Mama and Parthe. Their resentment was smoldering. How dare Flo defy them?

Then, back in England, Flo was once again under their oppression. Battling depression and frustration, she wrote *Cassandra*, a plaintive yet very angry eight-thousand-word essay on the frustrations of an English woman, married or unmarried. Among its many bitter complaints, she included:

> *Why have women passion, intellect, moral activity—these three—and a place in society where no one of the three can be exercised?*
>
> *...Women are never supposed to have any occupation of sufficient importance not to be interrupted.*
>
> *...Women long for an education to teach them to teach, to teach them the laws of the human mind and how to apply them.*
>
> *...Dreaming always—never accomplishing; thus women live—too much ashamed of their dreams, which they think "romantic," to tell them where they will be laughed at.*
>
> *...The chances are a thousand to one that, in that small sphere, the task for which that immortal spirit is destined by the qualities and the gifts which its Creator has placed within it, will not be found.*
>
> *...This system dooms some minds to incurable infancy, others to silent misery.*
>
> *...In a few rare, very rare cases...always provided in novels, but seldom to be met with in real life...[marriages] give food and space for the development of character and mutual sympathies.*
>
> *...Jesus Christ raised women above the condition of mere slaves, mere ministers to the passions of the man, raised them by His sympathy.... [Yet] if anyone attempts the real imitation of Him, there are no bounds to the outcry with which the presumption of that person is condemned.*
>
> *...To God alone may women complain without insulting Him!*
>
> *...[The dying woman cries], "Free-free-oh! divine freedom, art thou come at last? Welcome, beautiful death!"*
>
> *...Give us back our suffering, we cry to Heaven in our hearts— suffering rather than indifferentism; for out of nothing comes nothing.*

But out of suffering may come the cure. Better have pain than paralysis!
A hundred struggle and drown in the breakers. One discovers the new
world. But rather, ten times rather, die in the surf, heralding the way to
that new world, than stand idly on the shore![9]

In spite of her unhappiness, Flo now socialized within a very distinguished circle that included the Sidney Herberts, Lord Byron's wife, Elizabeth Barrett Browning, George Eliot, Lord Ashley, William Thackeray, Lord Palmerston, and poet Arthur Hugh Clough. They all acknowledged her insight into medicine and nursing. Yet all her efforts to participate in nursing orders were furiously opposed by Mama and Parthe. Still, Papa was finally stirring, waking up to her dilemma. But would he oppose Mama? Flo could not remember his ever doing that. Flo's only hope might be Parthe's illness, feigned or not. None other than Sir James Clark, the private physician to Queen Victoria, examined Parthe. His diagnosis: Parthe must be separated from Flo because her presence aggravated Parthe's delicate condition!

Could Parthe argue with the distinguished Sir James Clark's diagnosis? Could Mama argue with it? Yes. They remained stubborn. Either Parthe's fits or the fancy that only Flo could nurse some sick relative nearly always managed to foil Flo's plans to visit medical facilities. In early 1853, at Tapton, Flo nursed Grandmama Shore—now ninety-five—through her final days. She felt the dear old lady's pulse die out. All the elderly relatives were now dead, and Mama herself was now sixty-five. Surely she would not hesitate to use her own old age to enslave Flo.

The time had come for Flo. She was almost thirty-three. Her resolve must be solid steel. No longer must she allow any excuse to deter her if an opportunity came.

ELEVEN

In the spring of 1853, Flo's opportunity came.

A group of wealthy aristocratic ladies wanted to create a medical facility: the Institute for the Care of Sick Gentlewomen. Elizabeth Herbert recommended Flo to manage it. On April 18, Flo was interviewed by Lady Canning. Flo backed up her reputation for nursing know-how with calm, articulate answers. Lady Canning seemed awed by the authority in Flo's manner. She could not hide her approval. But she was stunned when Flo set conditions to her acceptance.

"Gentlewomen of all religions must be accepted, not just members of the Church of England," insisted Flo.

Lady Canning presented Flo's demand to the Ladies' Committee. They accepted her terms. But Flo had not extended her conditions as far as she wanted. The institute would not care for poor women. The number of gentlewomen the institute could treat would not be great. Worst of all, Flo detected little enthusiasm in the Ladies' Committee for launching a nursing school. But still the opportunity was great.

Mama did not agree. "How can you think to degrade yourself so?" she stormed.

But that fury was nothing compared to the maelstrom Mama and Parthe raised when they discovered Papa had endowed Flo with a generous annual allowance! And he insisted they accept Flo's decision to head Lady Canning's institute. At last Papa had backed Flo, but the turmoil was so intense in Embley Park that Papa moved to London until things simmered down. Flo was elated. Surely now Mama and Parthe would stop interfering. But she was wrong. The two women worked relentlessly to modify Flo's plans. Why couldn't she start a nursing home near Embley Park?

Flo refused to negotiate. She moved to lodgings in London and planned the institute with the Ladies' Committee. They inspected houses on Upper Harley Street off Regent's Park. Flo knew exactly what she wanted: available hot water, quarters for nurses, and space to accommodate medical necessities. She found one building that was acceptable for a start. She went to Paris to study the medical facilities of the Sisters of St. Vincent, firing back by letter renovations to the Harley Street building. By August 1853, Flo had returned to open the institute, choosing to ignore the continued protests of Mama and Parthe. In the past, she had always answered them out of guilt—but no longer.

Flo's will was hard-forged steel now. Her operation at Harley Street was very sophisticated for its time. Hot water was piped to every floor. Flo had determined it was most efficient to have the water heater on the top floor. Food and all medical supplies were lifted by a windlass to each floor—as well as the patients! "The nurse must not be a pair of legs for running up and down stairs," insisted Flo. In fact, the nurse should not leave her floor at all. She would have sleeping quarters on her floor. Patients could "ring" the nurse by means of a pull rope.

Flo immersed herself completely in the activity. There was no lack of immediate patients. She assisted a surgeon who removed a cancer then supervised the patient's recuperation. They used a new anesthetic called chloroform, recently pioneered by a physician named James Simpson. She nursed women with consumption. She consoled women suffering from hysteria. It was the compassionate but steely Flo who had to tell a woman she must surrender her bed if she appeared to be malingering. Flo nursed, she comforted, she inspired—as well as administered. She ordered and scavenged for furniture. She installed shelves. She kept accounts and inventoried. The institute thrived. The patients wrote her adoring, even loving, notes of thanks. Within a year, Flo had cut the cost of care for each patient by one-half! In the summer of 1854, cholera broke out in London, especially around the notorious slum area of St. Giles. Flo threw herself into the nursing effort, spending her time at Middlesex Hospital. She was committed to helping the sick, no matter how dangerous it was to herself. Her will—which she considered God's will—crushed objections raised by doctors. She did not influence by strident bullying, but calm reason and charm—and intrigue if necessary. She could tell that doctors who were meeting her for the first time expected a burly hellcat. She saw them blink in disbelief as they realized this thin, demure woman in front of them was Florence Nightingale. Then they fell under her spell. Her reputation grew. London had so many problems, she could stay feverishly busy there the rest of her life.

In March 1854, England and France declared war on Russia. Because the notorious Russian czar, Nicholas, was expanding his empire south into Turkey, the English believed that the route to their precious crown jewel, India, was threatened. England had certainly won its share of wars, so the public reacted enthusiastically. The horror of war had been forgotten; after all, it had been thirty-nine years since Waterloo. In September the allies invaded the Crimea, an area of Russia on the Black Sea. At Sebastopol in Crimea, the Russians harbored their fleet. A direct attack on Sebastopol was deemed impossible, so the allies landed sixty-five thousand soldiers many miles north at the River

Alma. But Russian forces, numbering forty thousand men and two hundred cannons, were there, too.

Flo, resting up from the London cholera siege, was somewhat distracted from the Crimean tragedy by a toothache and the presence at Lea Hurst of Susan Gaskell. Mrs. Gaskell was an accomplished writer who was writing a biography on the brilliant Charlotte Brontë. Flo had read Miss Brontë's advanced novels, written under the name Currer Bell, and wanted to know more about her. Instead, she found Mrs. Gaskell was burning with curiosity about *her*. But this interesting domestic situation at Lea Hurst was trumped by developments stemming from the Crimean War. In October, the *London Times* newspaper revealed that it had a reporter on the scene in Crimea. It was the first time ever for such civilian reporting. William Russell's reports were stinging, too. By October 9, he was alerting all England to the horrible realities of war:

> *No sufficient preparations have been made for the care of the wounded. Not only are there not sufficient surgeons. . .not only are there no dressers and nurses. . .there are not even linens to make bandages. . . . Can it be said that the battle of the Alma has been an event to take the world by surprise? Yet. . .there is no preparation for the commonest surgical operations! Not only are the men kept, in some cases for a week, without the hand of a medical man coming near the wounds. . .but. . .the commonest appliances of the workhouse sick ward are wanting, and. . .the men must die through the medical staff of the British Army having forgotten that old rags are necessary for the dressing of wounds.*[1]

Flo received an offer from Lady Forester to finance a mission of mercy to the Crimean conflict. The British wounded were being brought back to Turkey, specifically to a suburb of Constantinople called Scutari. It was far from the combat area, so nurses would surely be accepted there. Flo left for London without hesitation. Besides the obvious need to go, the scathing criticism of the British army fell directly on Flo's good friends. Lord Palmerston was home secretary for Prime Minister Lord Aberdeen. But most affected was Sidney Herbert. He was the secretary of war. In London, Flo used her considerable influence with Lord Palmerston. Within hours, it seemed every powerful lord in the government was clearing a path for Flo's mission of mercy to the Crimea. By the time William Russell reported in the *Times* that the French wounded were very well served by the Sisters of Charity—and the editorial in the *Times* screamed, "Why have we no Sisters of Charity?"—Flo had her expedition of mercy organized!

On October 15, Flo read Sidney Herbert's appeal to her to take a group of nurses to the Crimea:

> *There is but one person in England that I know of who would be capable*
> *of organizing and superintending such a scheme. . . . Would you listen*
> *to the request to go and superintend the whole thing? . . . Deriving your*
> *authority from the Government, your position would secure the respect*
> *and consideration of everyone. . .together with a complete submission to*
> *your orders. I know these things are a matter of indifference to you, except*
> *so far as they may further the great objects you have in view.*[2]

Herbert was angered and perplexed. He had been reassured by the chief medical officers in the Crimea that the facilities were excellent. What was going on? Flo gladly accepted the government endorsement. But as calm as any Duke of Wellington, Flo had already recruited thirty-eight nurses, including ten Catholic nuns, ordered uniforms made, arranged travel, and garnered medical supplies. Even the sudden arrival of Mama and Parthe, ecstatic at her sensation, did not rattle her. But their bad news did. Her owl, Athena, forgotten in all the excitement, had died of starvation.

That was Flo's most traumatic moment in all the hectic preparation. Just six days after her letter from Sidney Herbert, Flo embarked with her contingent as "Superintendent of the female nursing establishment in the English General Military Hospitals in Turkey." Uncle Sam was to go with her as far as Marseilles. The Bracebridges agreed to accompany her all the way to Turkey. What colossal friends she had! The party crossed France by rail. Flo was very attentive to her nurses. She ate with them and pampered them. She promised new warm shoes at Marseilles.

In Marseilles, Flo loaded up on more supplies, in spite of the assurance of government authorities that it was not necessary. Before she boarded ship again on October 27, she was being heralded as a heroine—both in Britain and in France. Crowds gathered to cheer her. How could she ever justify such recognition? Then she learned that the *Times* had started a fund for her mission and had already raised a small fortune!

While crossing the Mediterranean on the *Vectis*, Flo learned more about the battle operations. The commander in chief of the British forces was Lord Raglan. Raglan was sixty-six and had lost an arm at the battle of Waterloo many years before. The gore that awaited her was foreshadowed in a story she was told about Lord Raglan. After his arm was amputated at Waterloo, he yelled at an overeager assistant, "I say, don't throw that arm away just yet! One of the fingers has a ring my wife gave me."

Lord Raglan delegated authority to his field commanders. Queen Victoria's cousin, His Royal Highness the Duke of Cambridge, commanded a five-thousand-man division that included the highly publicized Coldstream Guards, Black Watch, and other elite units. Sir George Brown also commanded a division of five thousand foot soldiers, as did Sir George De Lacy Evans. Cavalry, under Lord Lucan, consisted of the Light Brigade and the Heavy Brigade. Two additional divisions of foot soldiers were held in reserve.

Flo felt as if she were already in battle. The *Vectis* fought storms so severe while crossing the Mediterranean that the cannons aboard had to be jettisoned. But finally on November 4, 1854, the ship anchored off Seraglio Point in the Bosporus, a strait that connected the Mediterranean Sea with the Black Sea. The day was grayed by falling rain. To the west sprawled Constantinople, thoroughly Muslim with its domes and minarets. To the east was Scutari, where the General Hospital and its enormous neighbor of blond brick, Barrack Hospital, sat conspicuously on a hill. According to Sidney Herbert's charge, the nursing in these two hospitals fell under Flo's jurisdiction. The two hospitals were supposed to care for up to three thousand wounded soldiers.

Coming aboard the *Vectis* to greet her was Lord Napier, representing Lord Stratford, the British ambassador to Turkey. Lord Stratford had "reigned" at Constantinople for sixteen years. His residence was virtually a palace, with twenty-five servants. He did not have a good reputation among the well-to-do in England. Some of the nicer things said about him were that he was "lazy, coldhearted, arrogant, and nasty-tempered." Certainly, Flo had not expected the sixty-eight-year-old potentate to greet her personally. And she suspected he would be of little help to her, whether she had powerful friends or not.

After a few pleasantries, Lord Napier's face clouded. "We had another great battle on October 25. The 'Battle of Balaclava' they are calling it. The ships will be bringing the wounded here in a few days."

Flo and her contingent were rowed ashore in the small, local caïques. The sight that greeted them was from hell. The bloated carcass of a horse lay rotting near the dock. Dogs fought each other as they ripped at the reeking flesh. A few soldiers loitered around the rickety wooden dock, undisturbed by the carnage. Wounded soldiers—unassisted—were struggling up the hill toward the hospitals. The hill was a quagmire of mud and garbage. Flo immediately determined that the dock was inadequate for receiving wounded from ships. And bringing them ashore in caïques in rough weather would only worsen their condition.

As Flo neared the Barrack Hospital with her nurses, it loomed up into its true immensity. It was no ancient palace, but the relinquished barracks of the Turkish army. Watchtowers stretched skyward from each corner of the three-storied quadrangle. Someone had said there were several miles of usable corridors inside, despite one entire side having been gutted by fire, and rumor had it that deep in its basements a small town of "camp followers" remained: hundreds of wives, prostitutes, and children.

Flo and the others entered Barrack Hospital through a massive gate. They were greeted by the chief medical officer, Dr. Menzies, and the military commandant, Major Sillery. Every impression after their cordial welcome was unfavorable. The floors in the corridors had loose tiles. The walls ran damp. Flo's contingent was allotted five cramped rooms. One served Flo as her office, although it doubled as Mr. Bracebridge's bedroom. Another of the five rooms was still occupied by the decaying corpse of a Russian general! Furniture was almost nonexistent in every room and corridor. Trash was scattered everywhere. The central yard of the quadrangle was a virtual dump. Rats darted in and out of the refuse.

"You will receive a daily ration of one pint of water per person," advised Dr. Menzies. "I'm terribly sorry there are no cooking facilities for you."

"We'll manage," said Flo, hiding her shock.

How were the wounded being fed? Her search led to a dirty kitchen with thirteen five-gallon copper pots. These pots had to feed more than two thousand men! The cooking techniques were barbaric. Food was prepared by soldiers, not chefs. Chunks of crudely butchered animals were thrown into water that often was not even hot enough to simmer. Vegetables were nowhere to be seen. Eventually, the "broth" was served in bowls. The patients had no other utensils. The army assumed they had utensils with their mess kits, but of course the wounded rarely had more than the clothes on their backs. Ironically, no spoon or fork was necessary, because the bowl rarely contained any meat but the smallest scrap.

As for special rations for those who could not take this broth, they didn't exist. There was no organization to handle such a request. On the other hand, Flo discovered that in most matters the army was bogged down in bureaucracy. Over several decades of peace, the army had implemented hundreds of checks and counterchecks to cut spending. Now they were choking on these precautions. Every request proceeded at a snail's pace. Requisitions needed the signature of two doctors. Then the purveyor processed it, passing it on to the commissariat, who was supposed to negotiate contracts for the purchase.

The hospital operation had a monstrous—possibly deadly—problem, which manifested itself immediately by assaulting the nose. The pervading smell was that of a crowded barnyard on the hottest day. Flo soon discovered that the great building had abominable sewers, which often backed up, spewing human waste out into the wards. To counteract this unspeakable filth, the doctors had started the use of huge chamber pots. One chamber pot served about fifty men. Flo learned that the reeking pots stood unemptied for days at a time.

Then Flo saw the wounded. It was another ghastly scene from hell.

TWELVE

Flo had seen much sickness—yes, even death—in her life, but not of this magnitude, not of this unimaginable gore. Most of the British soldiers were ripped, torn, and mutilated. Arms, legs, eyes, noses, ears, jaws were gone, replaced by filthy, blood-clotted rags! Flo had to fight tears of sympathy then of rage. All but a few of the wounded men sprawled on the broken tile floors. There were few beds, few blankets. No hospital garb was issued, although supposedly hundreds of outfits had been sent from England. No one knew where the outfits were. The men lay in their rotting battle gear, infested head to toe with lice. One doctor had implemented a routine for bathing the men. But it processed only thirty men a day!

Then she noted that one sponge was used for all thirty men. No wonder the hospital was rife with cholera, lice, and fleas. Perhaps it was a blessing not to be washed.

Then Dr. Menzies floored Flo. "The doctors are under orders to allow you to quarter here. But you must not assist them unless they specifically request it."

Flo bit her tongue. She must not label this revelation as the monumental stupidity it was. This shock was as great as any she had suffered. Still, she could keep her nurses occupied for some time making slings, pillows, mattresses, anything to help the wounded. Even a stubborn doctor would use those things if they were lying about available.

Over the next few days, Flo and her contingent settled in. The doctors did indeed resist true nursing care offered by Flo and her nurses. Flo wasted no time, though, procuring vegetables and meat from the local markets with the large fund she had available. With the portable stoves she had brought, her nurses prepared food and managed to dispense it. The doctors didn't object. Perhaps they didn't notice.

"I've received the most distressing news about the Battle of Balaclava," confided Charles Bracebridge.

The Russians had sprung a surprise attack on the British naval base at Balaclava, a mere seven miles from the main Russian naval base at Sebastopol. After already suffering for two weeks, the wounded from the battle began to arrive by ship at Scutari. To compound the problem, another battle took place at Inkerman on November 5. These wounded also were headed for Scutari. Russian wounded were brought to the hospital, too. The resistance of the doctors against

Flo and her nurses evaporated under the onslaught of suffering. Flo wrote a doctor friend in London about events of November 9:

> On Thursday last, we had 1,715 sick and wounded in this Hospital (among whom were 120 cholera patients) and 650 severely wounded in the other building, called the General Hospital, of which we also have charge, when a message came to me to prepare for 510 wounded on our side of the Hospital, who were arriving from the dreadful affair. . .at Balaclava, where were 1,763 wounded and 442 killed besides 96 officers wounded and 38 killed. . . . We had but half an hour's notice before they began landing the wounded. Between one and nine o'clock, we had the mattresses stuffed, sewn up, and laid down. . .the men washed and put to bed, and all their wounds dressed. . . . Twenty-four cases [died] on the day of landing. We now have four miles of beds, and not eighteen inches apart. . . . As I went my night-rounds among the newly-wounded that night, there was not one murmur, not one groan. . . . These poor fellows bear pain and mutilation with an unshrinking heroism which is really superhuman, and die, or are cut up without a complaint. . . . We have all the sick cookery now to do—and I have got in four men for the purpose. . . . I hope in a few days we shall establish a little cleanliness. But we have not a basin, nor a towel, not a bit of soap, not a broom. I have ordered three hundred scrubbing brushes.[1]

The patients in both hospitals almost doubled to nearly four thousand. The surgical operations began immediately. The hospital was so poorly supplied that the surgeons had neither screens nor tables. Flo ordered these things out of her private fund. Instead of pleasing the doctors, this gesture irritated them. Why did she have such resources when they had almost none? Flo chose to be hopeful about the medical staff:

> We are very lucky in our Medical Heads. Two of them are brutes and four are angels—for this work which makes either angels or devils of men and women, too. As for the assistants, they are all Cubs. . . . But unlicked Cubs grow up into good old Bears, though I don't know how.[2]

She appealed to Sidney Herbert to send supplies by comparing the abysmal facilities of British hospitals with the comparatively lavish facilities of the French hospitals. Nothing could make a British politician react more vigorously than that. To be outdone by the French, indeed! If events were not already grim enough for the British army, the Crimea was hammered by a hurricane on November 14. Tents and supplies were whipped into the frozen hinterlands by the wind. The *Prince*, which carried winter clothing and supplies for the British troops, sank in Balaclava harbor. So the soldiers were exposed to the elements with no winter gear. Temperatures in Constantinople and Scutari dropped below freezing many nights from December through February. Snow was common. The Crimea was even colder.

Meanwhile, Flo's request to Lord Stratford, the ambassador to Constantinople, for help at the hospital was answered by Lady Stratford. The fine lady was so appalled by the foulness of the hospital—she had visited it but once—she tried to pull Flo away to "help" her. Flo was forced to ask Sidney Herbert to politely beseech Lady Stratford to stop interfering, because the well-intentioned lady was a "time waster and impediment." Instead of bumbling interference, Flo told Herbert, her nurses—and the doctors—would be greatly helped by an expediter, a man who could cut through the maze of bureaucracy.

Even without such assistance, by mid-December she was able to write Herbert that she had a kitchen set up to provide special diets for those patients who needed it. The wards were at long last being scrubbed by nurses. Both patients and gowns were being regularly washed by nurses. Wounds were dressed daily by nurses. Flo had charmed the assistants in the wards into emptying the chamber pots daily although it was a nauseating chore. She had bought out of her own funds six thousand hospital gowns, two thousand pairs of socks, and hundreds of nightcaps, slippers, plates, cups, and utensils. She hired two hundred Turkish workers, whom she personally directed, to restore the burned-out corridors. Soon those corridors would hold beds for another eight hundred wounded. Nor had she neglected the camp followers living in the basements. Many of these destitute women she employed as laundresses. Her chief complaint was of those who wouldn't work or who prevented others from working.

The situation soon worsened. Late in December, Flo heard that a group of nearly fifty women was arriving to help. They were completely unqualified. Flo was furious. Before she left England, she had specifically asked Sidney Herbert not to send any more nurses until she requested them. She had his agreement in writing. All logic and common sense told Flo that a small number of very disciplined nurses was far better than a large number of undisciplined ones. Soon the fifty newcomers inundated the hospital. Many were aristocratic ladies, more interested in meeting officers than in nursing. Flo loathed amateur nurses, ladies or not. Her pessimism was borne out. The new arrivals disrupted the order she had created in the hospital. They refused to answer to her. She tried to have the newcomers removed from the hospital. Flo's hostility toward the newcomers was seized upon by a few doctors who resented her power. And she had no friends in the purveyor and the commissariat, who considered her pure evil for circumventing their purchasing power. Then came betrayal. One of her own group sent a letter to the *London Times* condemning not only Flo's efforts but her arrogance. The use of nurses, which had appeared so promising, was falling apart.

But if certain enemies thought Flo was in retreat, they could not have been more mistaken. To alleviate the overcrowding of "nurses," she sent ten of her own back to England, including, of course, the letter writer. Flo, who had always been intrigued by the way English servants made a great house run smoothly, next proceeded to take on the hospital bureaucracy. Earlier, she had called for an expediter for her own effort, but since then she had decided that the maze of regulations—indeed, the organization itself—had to be changed. The abysmal state of the hospital when she arrived proved the system did not work. The procedures and the organization were abominations, but none of the doctors or professional soldiers would champion changes.

While she worked out a plan for reform, the wounded kept arriving. On January 2, a contingent of twelve hundred arrived! Besides being wounded and sick, nearly all suffered from scurvy. Lime juice had been sent to the soldiers to prevent this disease, but somehow it had been lost! On January 4, Flo wrote Sidney Herbert that properly executed requisitions to the purveyor at the hospital were nearly futile. Requested but out of stock were gowns, socks, underwear, plates, and drinking cups. The purveyor had only a handful of bedpans to satisfy the need for thousands. There was a shipment of twenty-seven thousand flannel gowns somewhere—but the purveyor did not know where!

By January 28, 1855, Flo was at last ready to take on the bureaucracy of army medical facilities. In her letter to Sidney Herbert, she first apologized for her very unpleasant role; she felt like a spy. But changes had to be made. As secretary of war, he had the power to make changes. She offered as an example of present inefficiency the purchase and distribution of fresh meat. Every morning, orderlies had to requisition rations for the day from the commissariat. Much meat—as precious as it was—spoiled in the delay. Flo recommended that every bed in a ward have a ticket identifying which diet its patient was on. Ward masters, supervised by doctors, should requisition needed food the day before it was distributed. Meat should be sent directly to the kitchen. Also, every patient must have his own bed with all necessary bedding. If blankets or linens wore out, the ward master—a position Flo regarded as the equivalent of a hotel manager or head housekeeper—must requisition replacements. The ward master must also oversee the delivery of incoming patients, cooking, cleaning, and washing. Flo offered numerous other changes and cited examples.

To administer her changes, Flo recommended a "governor," one man instead of a disinterested—usually distant—committee as now. Because it was a military hospital, the governor should be an officer. Under the governor would be four officials: one for administering daily hospital routine, one for procuring food, one for procuring furniture and clothing, and one to be the medical head in charge of the doctors. Flo was diplomatic enough to praise certain enlightened individuals. But she knew well that her recommendations to Sidney Herbert would not be taken kindly by those currently in power at the hospital.

All she could do in the meantime was persist in her battle for progress at Scutari. She continued to chronicle the exasperating deficiencies:

> We have lost the finest opportunity for advancement of the cause of medicine and erecting it into a science which will ever be afforded. Here there is no operating room, no dissecting room, post mortem examinations are seldom made and then in the dead-house, no statistics (the ablest staff surgeon here told me that he considered that he had killed hundreds of men owing to the absence of these) are kept as to what ages most deaths occur, as to modes of treatment, appearance of the body after death. . .[all the] most important points which contribute to making Therapeutics a means of saving life.[3]

Flo had her supporters in England, including the queen. Sidney Herbert wrote Flo that Her Royal Majesty wished Miss Nightingale to tell the noble wounded and sick men that no one took a warmer interest in their recovery or admired their courage more than their Queen Victoria. And the queen wished Herbert to pass on frequently to her the accounts he received from Miss Nightingale. Flo had the chaplains read the queen's words to the men in the wards. But this raised another issue. Though encouraged, the men complained bitterly that the army had cut their pay when they were sick or wounded. Couldn't Queen Victoria do anything about it? Flo relayed their complaint.

Next, Flo learned that Londoners were warring over whether she was a force for good or for evil. She was grateful that Elizabeth Herbert was one of her most enthusiastic defenders. Apparently the queen was, too. The English public was fussing over far more than Florence Nightingale. They were in a fury over the bungled conduct of the war. "Half the British army is dead or in hospital!" some screamed. Others speculated that Prime Minister Lord Aberdeen's government might fall. What if Sidney Herbert was replaced as secretary of war? Flo's entire effort might disintegrate. Who would support her demands for reform then? Which ladies—qualified by nothing more than friendships in the new government—would arrive to take over the "nursing" of the hospital?

To her horror, Lord Aberdeen's government did fall.

THIRTEEN

Lord Aberdeen was replaced by an almost blind, almost deaf man of seventy-one. The new prime minister was openly besmirched by the opposition as an old geezer with false teeth that would fall out of his mouth if he did not speak with such hesitation! Flo knew him well.

"The new prime minister is my neighbor and good friend Lord Palmerston!" celebrated Flo.

Instead of being a disaster, the new government appeared a colossal good fortune for Flo. She regretted losing Sidney Herbert, but with a sponsor like Lord Palmerston, Flo could work with Herbert's replacement, Lord Panmure. Then Flo heard of another change of government. The enemy's leader, Czar Nicholas, had died. Would his successor, Alexander II, be more likely to negotiate peace? Perhaps not. But Flo's optimism about the new British government was borne out. Her entreaties to all her powerful friends led to the formation of a Sanitary Commission. The driving force on the commission was Dr. John Sutherland. This team came to Scutari in early March of 1855.

Dr. Sutherland and his team were appalled by the Barrack Hospital. They judged the sewers murderous. The sewers were so vast and so clogged that the hospital seemed floating in filth. In addition, the water supply, meager though it was, had other problems. It was contaminated. The team found a dead horse in one conduit! They hired workers to flush and clean the sewers. Contaminants in the water supply were removed. All refuse was carried out, and the central yard was cleared. Rotting wood pallets found throughout the hospital were ripped out. Scavenging rats were exterminated. Walls, floors, and ceilings were washed with lime.

Another great contribution by Lord Panmure—or those back in London who influenced him—was the arrival of a master chef to run the kitchens at the hospitals. Alexis Soyer appeared a comic Frenchman, but he was not a gourmet cook. His forte was cooking enormous amounts of simple food that was both nutritious and appetizing. He baked bread. He made soups and stews. He trained soldiers to be cooks. He designed a camp stove for soldiers to cook with.

Flo's first four months at the hospital had been permanently etched in her memory. Misery and hope. Tragedy and triumph. Often she had been on her knees eight hours straight dressing wounds. She comforted men headed for surgery. She had a gift for calming them. Some soldiers called her the

"Lady-in-Chief." Others called her the "lady with the lamp," because she carried a glowing lamp as she made seemingly never-ending rounds in the dark corridors. She personally had attended two thousand men on their deathbeds. She had been told by many of the officers that the common soldier was the scum of the earth. Now she knew the character of the common soldier was in many ways superior to that of the officers. She organized reading rooms. She urged the soldiers not to drink. They told her they drank because they couldn't send their money home. She resolved to change that when she had time. In the meantime, perhaps, she could hire a tutor to teach the illiterate soldiers to read and write.

She admired the common soldiers very much and considered them—just as the common village people in England were—victims of prejudice by the well-to-do. To those in England, she wrote:

> *What the horrors of war are, no one can imagine, they are not wounds and blood and fever, spotted and low, and dysentery chronic and acute, cold and heat and famine. They are intoxication, drunken brutality, demoralization and disorder on the part of the inferior—jealousy, meanness, indifference, selfish brutality on the part of the superior.*[1]

Flo slept behind a screen in a storeroom. About the only responsibility she delegated was management of the "free gift" stores. These were stockpiles of gifts sent by the British people and entrusted to her to distribute to the soldiers. Sig Bracebridge did that chore for her. During the day—her body warmed by a black wool dress with white cuffs, and collar and head covered by a white cap under a black silk handkerchief—Flo nursed, supervised, requisitioned supplies, received callers, and wrote correspondence. Her writing was mountainous: records, reports, requisitions, letters for the men, letters for the nurses, and letters for herself. Often, in the wee hours, she would lurch from her writing desk onto her bed and pass out from exhaustion. Sig would wake her in the morning.

With good sanitation, good food, good nursing, and good morale added to good medical treatment, the mortality rate at the Barrack Hospital began to fall. When Flo first arrived, a man had an even chance he would die if admitted to the hospital! By the end of March, the mortality rate was 15 percent; by the end of April, it reached 10 percent and was still falling. Was her effort appreciated by Dr. Hall, the chief of medical staff of the British army? Not at all, she learned. He felt threatened. Flo wanted to visit the facilities in the Crimea itself, starting with the two hospitals at Balaclava, where Dr. Hall resided. Dr.

Hall insisted she had no authority outside Turkey.

On May 5, 1855, she sailed on the *Robert Lowe* across the Black Sea to Balaclava. Alexis Soyer and Charles Bracebridge were in her party. Aboard ship, she wrote home of the irony of accompanying four hundred of her patients back to the front where they might be shot. Flo arrived in the Balaclava harbor, the main British naval base, with its vast thicket of masts on the ships, only to discover that Lord Raglan was elsewhere. Dr. Sutherland of the Sanitary Commission and John McNeill, representing a second commission investigating the supply protocol and performance of the British army, came to greet her.

Atop fine riding horses, the gentlemen took her out among the fortifications. The British army and its retinue in Balaclava numbered almost two hundred thousand. Tents were still used by many thousands of British soldiers, but wooden barracks were being added as rapidly as they could be built. The route was muddy.

"And the air foul," added the fastidious Soyer.

Flo shuddered to see men marching toward the trenches to watch for a Russian attack from Sebastopol, only seven miles away. A sergeant presented her with a bouquet. She remembered him well. Flo had saved his life at Scutari, after noticing his inert form in the corridor during one of her nocturnal rounds. Thorough to the last, she had examined him under her lamp. Good gracious! The man had never been attended at all. Somehow he had been missed. He was beyond protesting. He was dying, helpless to make a sound. A bullet was in his eye! Praise God, she had found a surgeon, who saved him. And to imagine this same sergeant back on the front! Flo was astonished as more and more soldiers gathered around their small party. At first dozens, then hundreds, then thousands. They began to cheer. For her? Surely not. But for whom? They appeared to be gawking at her.

The soldiers cheered her until it was deafening. More bouquets of wildflowers were presented to her.

The reception overwhelmed her. "Give God the praise," she tried to yell, but emotion choked her voice.

Her reception at the General Hospital the next day was as hostile as the previous one was loving. Not only was Dr. Hall cool, but the nurses were openly unfriendly.

Flo discovered she was the victim of vicious rumors. According to her persecutors, she lived in luxury at Scutari with her own French chef. She plundered the free gifts intended for the soldiers. She was in every way aristocratic and arrogant. But Flo was unflappable. Never did she rise to the bait. She didn't acknowledge rude remarks but stolidly proceeded with her inspection. She went on to Castle Hospital, on the heights outside Balaclava. Both Castle Hospital and General Hospital were filthy and poorly administered, replicas of Scutari before Flo arrived. But the terrible inefficiencies seen here were the direct result of the iron hand of Dr. Hall. He prevented every measure for improvement. He made every requisition as difficult to fill as possible. It was then that Flo realized he was the one who had reassured Sidney Herbert in London the previous fall that the medical facilities for British soldiers were top drawer. But time and the British government were on her side. If the two commissions did their work in Balaclava, the truth would be known in London eventually. And she must do her work now. But her old enemy—disease—intervened.

"Crimea fever" seized her. Her last coherent thought was that the doctor was probably right. She writhed in a hospital bed against a consuming heat. Every bone ached. The medical staff tried to restrain her, but Flo was in a nightmare. She was delirious. She rose against their wishes. She scribbled madly at a desk. She imagined a Persian adventurer coming and getting a draft for three hundred thousand pounds sterling from Charles Bracebridge. Her notes were gibberish. One day the doctors had to shave her head—anything to dissipate the heat. Slowly the maddening heat went away. Gradually, she came to her senses. She had been in her nightmare for two weeks, her nurse said. Flo had no energy to write now. She could not even get out of bed. Her voice was a weak whisper.

On May 24, she heard her nurse say in exasperation, "Well, of course this is Miss Nightingale's room!" Flo heard a scuffle. The nurse gasped, "But you can't come in here!"

It was Lord Raglan, commander in chief of all British forces! The old man didn't look much better than she felt. It was clear he was working himself to death. Nevertheless, he acted delighted to learn she was recovering. He was bubbling over with other good news, too. The allies were moving again, at this very moment attacking the Strait of Kertch, through which Russian supply ships traveled. He had every reason to believe the assault would succeed.

He left her, saying, "I will telegraph Her Majesty that you are out of danger. She inquires about you constantly."

Sig then arrived to help care for Flo. It was decided that Flo would be better off at Scutari. The medical staff of Balaclava arranged for her to be put aboard the *Jura*. But before it sailed, Charles Bracebridge discovered it was the one ship in the fleet that would not stop in Scutari. Once under way, it would go on to England! Hurriedly, Flo and her party transferred to another ship. Flo was utterly convinced the selection of the *Jura* by the medical staff of Balaclava was no accident. Dr. Hall was behind it. He still hadn't learned that Flo had direct lines to the very top of the British Empire!

At Scutari, she was installed in a house to convalesce. Dr. Sutherland told her, "That fever saved your life. You were most assuredly working yourself to death."

In June, Flo was dismayed to hear that Lord Raglan had died. The cause of death was officially deemed cholera, but Flo thought he had worked himself to death, just as she might have. Lord Raglan's replacement, the new commander in chief, took no note whatsoever of Flo. She was effectively being removed from any influence on the medical facilities in his theater of war. Apparently the new commander did not appreciate her lofty connections any more than did Dr. Hall. Yet she knew her work in the Crimea was far from done. Her suggestions for improving conditions at the Balaclava hospitals had not yet been implemented.

The next months—during which Flo visited Balaclava off and on—were very difficult. The Bracebridges—her greatest moral support—sailed back to England at the end of July. The woman Flo picked to replace Sig in running the free gift storehouse in Scutari turned out to be a thief. Her room and her assistants' rooms were bursting with stolen goods. Among the stolen free gifts were articles of Flo's own clothing! Sending the thief away meant Flo had to assume that burdensome duty again herself. When the doctors in both Scutari and Balaclava realized that Dr. Hall considered Flo a nuisance, their attitude toward her changed from cooperation to indifference to hostility. Still, she persisted.

In September, Aunt Mai arrived for a visit.

"Flo!" she gasped, visibly shocked by her niece's appearance.

The long, thick locks were gone. And Flo's trim figure was now cadaverous. Aunt Mai helped her as best she could. That same month, the British took the Russian stronghold at Sebastopol. The war was won, if not over. But Flo's fortunes were not so bright as the British army's. Back in England, the woman Flo had dismissed from the free gift storehouse was libeling Flo as the thief! Then, in a public meeting in October, Charles Bracebridge foolishly attacked the medical establishment of the British army—at the same time lauding Flo. If reporting by the *Times* was accurate, his charges were embarrassingly inexact. Many thought Flo was behind his attack. The medical staff in Scutari and Balaclava became even more hostile. Flo wrote to Bracebridge and urged him to be silent.

Despite the controversy, in November, Flo was feted in England. The

Duke of Cambridge, a powerful royal and veteran of the Crimean War, chaired the occasion. Richard Monckton Milnes, Sidney Herbert, and others started a Florence Nightingale Fund. The fund was intended to help Flo establish a school of nursing after the war. Parthe and Mama were ecstatic in writing Flo about her exalted stature in England.

Then a brooch arrived for Flo in Scutari from Queen Victoria. Prince Albert had personally designed it for her. It was topped by three large diamonds, each the center of a star with five smaller diamonds. The border read, "Blessed Are the Merciful." In the middle of a red cross in the center were a crown and the initials "VR." At the bottom of the brooch a banner declared, "Crimea." On the reverse was etched, "To Miss Florence Nightingale, as a mark of esteem and gratitude for her devotion towards the Queen's brave soldiers from Victoria R. 1855."[2]

The brooch is far too grand, Flo thought. But it presented her with a wonderful opportunity to write to the queen and her consort directly. Along with her thanks, she intended to champion the cause of the common soldier. As she had promised, Flo had already set up a system for sending the soldiers' pay home. She had to do it herself. The army had firmly rejected the idea at the same time they spurned her suggestion that a tutor be hired to teach the soldiers to read and write. In her own system, she kept meticulous records of the money, sending the combined sum of many soldiers' pay to Uncle Sam in England. He parceled out the money to the soldiers' families according to Flo's records. But why should the army itself not offer this convenience to its soldiers? Flo implored the queen to help with the problem. The lack of such a system for sending money home and the lack of schooling were leading contributors to the soldiers' heavy drinking.

Lord Panmure objected that it was nonsense that a system was not in place for soldiers to send their pay home. But he found out he was wrong. And just as he had shown a willingness to send commissioners to investigate army practices, he showed a willingness to institute necessary changes. In the future, strategically located offices would be available to sell money orders to the soldiers. Thus they could safely send money home to their families.

In spite of her many triumphs, Flo felt a failure. The never-ending work—usually under great stress—was gnawing her nerves raw. Factions gossiped and schemed against her.

Although the war ended on February 28, 1856, the men maimed in battle still had to be cared for. Flo remained, though not at peace. Her outrage over the contempt the officers had for the common soldier festered. To Uncle Sam, she wrote:

*I have never seen so teachable and helpful a class as the army [soldier]
generally. Give them opportunity promptly and securely to send money
home—and they will use it. Give them a school and a lecture and they
will come to it. Give them a book and a game and a [slide show]. . .and
they will leave off drinking. Give them suffering and they will bear it.
Give them work and they will do it.*[3]

In January 1856, John McNeill and Colonel Tulloch brought a report
before Parliament. Slowly, it became apparent that the report was a bombshell,
confirming everything Flo had written her friends and superiors in London.
As if Dr. Hall and his colleagues had not been hammered hard enough by
the report, in March they received the final blow. It seemed Lord Panmure
had sent a man—Colonel Lefroy—to secretly investigate the situation in the
Crimea. He was to check not only on the medical staff but also on Flo. His
report to Lord Panmure resulted in a general order to be posted in every barrack and every mess hall in the British army!

*It appears to me that the Medical Authorities of the Army do not cor-
rectly comprehend Miss Nightingale's position as it has been officially
recognized by me. I therefore think it right, to state to you briefly for their
guidance, as well as for the information of the Army, what the position
of this excellent lady is. Miss Nightingale is recognized by Her Majesty's
Government as the General Superintendent of the Female Nursing
Establishment of the military hospitals of the Army. No lady, or sister, or
nurse, is to be transferred from one hospital to another, or introduced into
any hospital without consultation with her. . . . The Principal Medical Officer will communicate with Miss Nightingale upon all subjects
connected with the Female Nursing Establishment, and will give his
directions through that lady.*[4]

Flo's triumph for nursing in the Crimea was officially and utterly complete.

FOURTEEN

The British war machine in the Crimea was slowly disassembled. The sick and the wounded were the last to leave—along with the nurses.

Flo had administered more than one hundred nurses during the war. Six had died. The toll for the soldiers was staggering. Nearly three thousand had died in battle, but another twenty thousand died of wounds or sickness! And of the living—nurses and soldiers alike—who could say how mentally wounded they would be for the rest of their lives? It was not until July 16 that the last patient left the Barrack Hospital in Scutari. Only then could Flo herself leave. Letters from home said England waited impatiently to fete her. She wanted none of it. On the return trip, she and Aunt Mai traveled incognito. From Paris, Flo traveled alone, and upon reaching London, she took the railroad north to the family's summer home. Flo quickly claimed her privacy. She not only refused to make a public appearance but refused to attend any public ceremony. Nor would she issue a statement. Getting credit for God's work shamed her. The Nightingales respected her privacy, but Flo found no peace at Lea Hurst. Her memory of the thousands of dead soldiers prodded her. She must do something for the living soldiers, present and future. At last she endeavored to meet privately with the powers that be. But in the aftermath of the war, no one was eager to discuss such matters. Then in September, a letter arrived.

"Sir James Clark invites me to visit him at his Birk Hall in Scotland," she told Mama and Parthe.

Staying with James Clark was a means for Flo to visit Queen Victoria and Prince Albert discreetly at Balmoral. She flew into action. There was much to do before she went to Scotland. She met with John McNeill, Colonel Tulloch, and Colonel Lefroy. They inundated her with facts about the army. Flo was now very enamored with statistics. This was her outlet for the fondness she had long held for the purity of mathematics. Flo and her allies formulated a very ambitious plan. Flo would solicit the queen to form a royal commission to investigate not only the medical procedures of the army but its education and administration of the common soldier. After all, Queen Victoria said that the welfare of the common soldier was one of her greatest interests.

James Clark prepared Flo for her royal audience. "The queen is quite nervous about meeting you. Almost terrified."

Flo was astounded. The queen now had eight children. She had reigned for nearly twenty years. She had handled so many difficult situations. For years, Flo had heard about the queen's deftness—not only at ceremonies but at social gatherings. And Queen Victoria was almost terrified of *her*? What kind of monstrous heroine had Flo become?

On the afternoon of September 21, James Clark took Flo to Balmoral. Although Prince Albert was calm, Flo could easily see the fear in the queen's large blue eyes. The monarch's fair skin flushed, but within minutes, she relaxed. Flo's demure and gracious demeanor could melt just about anyone. Queen Victoria sounded almost giddy with relief as she asked for the royal children to meet Miss Nightingale. Vicky was the oldest at sixteen. Crown Prince Edward, called "Bertie," was one year younger. The children were very respectful. After the children were dismissed, the queen initiated a conversation.

"You have no self-importance or humbug," said the queen. "No wonder the soldiers love you so."

Flo was encouraged to make her plea. For over an hour she presented her case for reform of the army. Later, at Birk Hall, Flo learned from James Clark that Queen Victoria and Prince Albert were overwhelmed by her. They marveled that she was even more magnificent than her reputation. The queen couldn't get over the fact that Flo traveled around alone, that she refused all public acclaim, and that she was so totally forgiving.

During her stay in Scotland, Flo saw the royals on several occasions. Years had passed since Flo had wrestled with metaphysics; now she renewed that contest with Prince Albert. He loved to talk about metaphysics. Once she accompanied the queen and the royal family to church. But the most surprising event of all was when Queen Victoria, taking her cue from Flo, arrived one day at Birk Hall, quite alone!

Praise meant nothing to Flo, except perhaps that it pleased the person giving the praise or that it was a gauge of what Flo might accomplish toward her goals. Her mission these days was to help the common soldier by means of a royal commission. One man remained to be convinced. The queen could not issue a warrant for a commission to investigate the army unless the secretary of war, Lord Panmure, advised and consented. To this end, the queen informed Flo that Lord Panmure would be at Balmoral the next week. The queen insisted that Flo give her a draft of the main issues. This she would send to Lord Panmure to digest before the meeting.

Lord Panmure was nicknamed the "Bison." At Flo's first encounter with him at Balmoral, on October 5, 1856, she saw why. His head was huge, crowned with unruly tufts of hair. And to make the comparison perfect, he swayed his head from side to side as he talked! But never had Flo been so disappointed in a man's character. He scorned the reports of the commissions he had sent to the Crimea. If their conclusions had not been so devastating, he would have squelched them. After the meeting, she was told by several sources that Lord Panmure had been impressed by her. A royal commission seemed a certainty. Her confidence in success was reinforced when Lord Panmure came to see her privately at Birk Hall. Flo was asked to submit a confidential report outlining the royal commission, even recommending its eight members. She selected James Clark, Dr. Sutherland, and six others, all of whom had much to commend them. Under no circumstances could Dr. Hall, her old nemesis in the Crimea, be included.

She needed facts to back her position. In a frenzy of activity, she compiled a report of nearly one thousand pages, with copious statistics. One fact she uncovered was shocking. Even in peacetime, young soldiers in the prime of life died at twice the rate of average citizens! How could that be, except for negligence on the army's part? Her report included a chilling line: "Our soldiers enlist to death in the barracks." Surely that would sway anyone with a good heart and an open mind!

She sent her report to Lord Panmure. It seemed the naming of a royal commission was imminent, yet weeks passed with no obvious progress. Apparently to mollify her, Lord Panmure sent her blueprints of Britain's first purely military medical facility, Netley Hospital. But he underestimated Flo. She studied the plans, consulted experts, and compiled statistics from British and foreign sources, then issued her response: Netley Hospital was a disaster in the making. Lord Panmure was stunned. The building was well under construction! Alterations now would cost a fortune, he quickly informed Flo.

During Christmastime of 1856, Flo dined with her neighbor Lord Palmerston at Broadlands. He was kind enough to hear her complaints about Netley Hospital. He trusted her judgment and heeded her compelling arguments that the hospital was an architectural marvel but a calamity for patients. Because Lord Palmerston was also the prime minister of Great Britain, he was very upset that such a poor hospital was being built. On January 17, he notified Lord Panmure that construction on the hospital must stop. The secretary of war was stupefied. How would he explain scrapping such a large investment? He decided to expedite construction. Once the hospital was completed, even the prime minister would have to accept it. Maybe even Florence Nightingale.

With reluctance, Flo did accept Netley Hospital. But she was depressed. As champion for the common soldier, she was faring badly. Not only had she lost the battle over the hospital, but she had probably lost the war. Would Lord Panmure now retaliate for her interference by shelving the royal commission?

Assurances from the secretary that the plan was still under way failed to comfort her. She no longer trusted the man. At long last, she decided to draw on her capital with the British people. She would go public, she advised Sidney Herbert, if the royal commission was not launched. Herbert, she assumed, would advise Lord Panmure of her intentions.

On April 27, 1857, Lord Panmure visited her at the Burlington Hotel in London. "Perhaps you would be so kind as to review the plans for the royal commission," he said, "that will be presented to Her Royal Majesty?"

As badly as Flo wanted the commission to convene, she did not rubber-stamp Panmure's plans. The eight members he had picked for the commission were pawns of the army. They were not acceptable. The secretary took a deep breath and changed the composition of the committee. Yes, he would include James Clark, Dr. Sutherland, and so on. Only one army pawn remained on the commission. Flo was pleased. The only thing better would have been for her to chair the commission herself, but Britain was not ready for anything that radical. Instead, her good friend Sidney Herbert would be chairman.

In May, the royal commission was launched with its first meeting. Flo worked tirelessly behind the scenes. She coached witnesses and visited hospitals to gather more statistics. Flo labored the entire summer for the commission while enduring the aggravation of Parthe and Mama in their Burlington Hotel suite. A wealthy widower, Sir Harry Verney of Buckinghamshire, began calling, not hiding his interest in marrying Flo. Although he was an enlightened philanthropist, she rejected him. Mama was quick to see opportunity there for Parthe, who was now thirty-eight.

Irritated by the distractions created by her mother and sister, Flo took one footman and slipped off to lodgings at Malvern, a fashionable resort area in the Midlands. The work of the royal commission was soon completed but not yet presented in final form. Flo began a book on nursing she knew only she could write. Dr. Sutherland visited and found her near a nervous breakdown. By October, Flo had recovered enough to return to the Burlington Hotel. She continued to work on her book. As the months passed, she fretted over the lack of progress of the royal commission. Her worries were borne out in February 1858, when Lord Palmerston's government fell. Then her great friend Alexis Soyer, who had been enlisted to help, died. Sidney Herbert looked sicker every day, and though Flo didn't like to admit it, her own health was precarious.

No one any longer thought reform would be easy. Under the Earl of Derby's new government, the old army stalwarts in the War Office sought to thwart—or at least stall—every reform, much as the medical staff in the

Crimea had hampered Flo's efforts during the war. It was going to be a long battle—perhaps even a losing battle. Flo was elated, though, when Parthe married Sir Harry Verney. The only good thing about having the Earl of Derby as prime minister was the fact that his son, Lord Stanley, was secretary of state for India. Flo knew Lord Stanley well. Soon she was pushing for another royal commission, this one to reform the army in India. The army had an enormous presence in India, virtually running Britain's "crown jewel." In May 1859, the royal commission on India was granted, and Flo threw herself headlong into that endeavor, too! In June 1859, the government fell again. Lord Palmerston returned, this time not with Lord Panmure as secretary of war, but Sidney Herbert!

Flo had proposed an Army Medical School in 1857. In 1859, it was formally initiated and due to receive its first students the next year. In the meantime, Flo's health failed even more. She became breathless. Standing made her faint. Food nauseated her. Some hinted that her illnesses were feigned to avoid visitors, even family. Whatever people thought, she labored on, now usually lying on a couch in a sea of books and notes. Dr. Sutherland served as her legs, helping constantly by gathering data. Flo kept a residence in the suburb of London called Hampstead but kept her address secret from everyone but the closest of family and friends.

In spite of her frailty, she labored incessantly, working on a dozen things at once. When one subject felt stale, she switched to another. She had recently published a 108-page book on hospitals for the public. She worked on projects to support the royal commission on Britain. She compiled statistics for the royal commission on India. She toiled on refinements in the new Army Medical School. She planned a school of nursing with the Florence Nightingale Fund, which had swollen since the end of the Crimean War. She agonized over theology and metaphysics, compiling her thoughts in hundreds of pages.

She also completed her nursing book.

FIFTEEN

Flo poured her knowledge into her book, *Notes On Nursing: What It Is, and What It Is Not* which had chapter headings such as "Ventilation and Warming," "Petty Management," "Taking Food," "What Food?" "Bed and Bedding," "Light," "Cleanliness of Rooms and Walls," "Personal Cleanliness," "Chattering Hopes and Advice," and "Observation of the Sick." Her hundreds of anecdotes, rules, and comments were touted as "gems" by her colleagues:

It has been said and written scores of times, that every woman makes a good nurse. I believe, on the contrary, that the very elements of nursing are all but unknown.

. . . [On the other hand], it is constantly objected, "But how can I obtain this medical knowledge? I am not a doctor. I must leave this to doctors." Oh, mothers of families! You who say this, do you know that one in every seven infants in this civilized land of England perishes before it is one year old?

. . . Symptoms or the sufferings generally considered to be inevitable and incident to the disease are very often not symptoms of the disease at all, but of something quite different—of the want of fresh air, or of light, or of warmth, or of quiet, or of cleanliness, or of punctuality and care in the administration of diet, of each or of all of these.

. . . There are five essential points in securing the health of houses,

1. Pure air.

2. Pure water.

3. Efficient drainage.

4. Cleanliness.

5. Light.

Without these, no house can be healthy. And it will be unhealthy just in proportion as they are deficient.

. . . The very first canon of nursing. . . is this: To keep the air he breathes as pure as the external air, without chilling him.

. . . Second only to their need of fresh air is their need of light.

. . . The amount of relief and comfort experienced by the sick after the skin has been carefully washed and dried, is one of the commonest observations made at a sick bed.

FLORENCE NIGHTINGALE

. . .Every nurse ought to be careful to wash her hands very frequently during the day.[1]

Flo's approach was many pronged. One mandate was a sanitary environment for the patient. Another was consideration for the patient's troubled feelings. A third was for shrewd observations. Flo's book was received with acclaim. It was a masterpiece. She was far too modest, critics said. A woman could indeed learn to be a nurse just from reading her book. Thousands of copies were sold.

Her book on theology and metaphysics was far more imprecise. She titled it *Suggestions for Thought*, and it reflected her dilemma: She had no time to thoroughly synthesize the subjects. She published nearly one thousand pages of her thoughts for private distribution. Her editing was halfhearted, and, in contrast to *Notes on Nursing, Suggestions for Thought* rambled and repeated itself, even contradicting itself. Still, powerhouse intellects like John Stuart Mill glanced through it and praised her efforts. He saw some real nuggets of original wisdom in the pages. But not one reviewer advised her to publish it. It needed strong editing.

Flo sensed that she would never find the time necessary to edit the writings for general publication.

Another of Flo's projects was more fruitful. She had long wanted to start a school of nursing. In her many visits to hospitals, Flo had met Mrs. Sarah Wardroper, matron of St. Thomas Hospital in London. The matron, too, had "no humbug or self-importance" and sparkled with good humor. Best of all, she sounded eminently practical, frankly admitting to Flo that a school for nursing within a hospital would be resisted by many doctors. Nevertheless, Flo knew she had discovered the woman who could start such a venture. In May 1859, she began to work out the funding for a school of nursing at St. Thomas Hospital with money from the Florence Nightingale Fund.

On June 24, 1860—just after her fortieth birthday—the "Nightingale Training School for Nurses" opened with fifteen probationers under their supervisor Mrs. Wardroper. Each woman had a private room in a new wing of St. Thomas Hospital, board, as well as a brown uniform with white cap and apron. In addition to training the probationers to nurse real patients in the wards, three senior doctors gave lectures to ground the women in the medical science of the day. Those trainees who successfully completed the one year of training were certified and registered as nurses.

Flo monitored the school like a hawk. Her complex evaluation system for each candidate had five possible grades for twenty different attributes. Any moral failing, such as drunkenness or excessive flirting, meant immediate dismissal. Flo had a long history of enforcing morality. She had shipped several nurses back from the Crimea for failing to live up to Christian standards. Still, with Flo and Mrs. Wardroper shepherding their flock, only two of the fifteen failed to qualify at the end of the year at St. Thomas. The thirteen successful candidates were snapped up by local hospitals. Flo implored these highly qualified young nurses not to hire out to wealthy private families. They must serve everyone, not just the well-to-do.

Shortly after her school for nurses opened, in September 1860, the Army Medical School opened at long last. In spite of Queen Victoria's backing, indeed Lord Palmerston's backing, too, the battle with the old army officers had been won only because Sidney Herbert had personally hammered it to a conclusion. Even as professors taught the school's first ten students, the old army bureaucracy harassed them over every requisition. In spite of the limited success, Flo had been critical of Sidney Herbert's drive and determination. She often wrote him stinging letters.

But by June of 1861, he told her the army reform was too much for him. He simply had no energy to overcome the constant haggling with the old army establishment. Like Flo, he often spent the entire day on the sofa. Flo refused to admit he was failing and urged him to continue. He declined. Were they to lose their battle for army reform after four hard-fought years? "What about our duty to the common soldier?" she railed. She angrily accused him of having a winning hand yet quitting the game. On July 16, Sidney Herbert informed Flo that he had sent his resignation to Lord Palmerston. His successor was George Lewis. On August 2, at his great Wilton estate, Sidney Herbert died. Flo was devastated. She had belittled his incurable illness. She had prodded him, needled him. Consumed by guilt, she reflected on what she and Sidney Herbert had accomplished. Of course, they had started the Army Medical School. They had the worst barracks demolished and new ones constructed. Kitchen ovens were provided to the common soldiers. Good nutrition was pushed through training schools for cooks. Reading rooms were provided at many bases now. So were recreational facilities. Mortality had dropped markedly where they had been allowed to make improvements. But the improvements were not universal. And so much remained to be done.

Although her goals were frustrated, Flo's relations with her family were excellent now. Her relationship with Parthe's husband, Sir Harry Verney, was warm. At the end of 1861, he helped her move to one of his residences on South Street in London. But December 1861 brought another obstacle to Flo's goals. Prince Albert, only forty-two years old, had died of typhoid fever. Queen Victoria was paralyzed with grief.

SIXTEEN

Flo became even more depressed. Aunt Mai was no longer with her. Hilary had lived with her for a year but was forced to rejoin her family. Flo could not read a newspaper—she could not bear to see the names of those recently lost to her—but she still wrote letters. Reform was at a standstill—or it seemed that way, because for several years, she had advanced a dozen projects at once. Her Training School for Nurses still operated smoothly, but with Sidney Herbert gone, none of her friends had real influence with the War Office. Flo was still much in demand as a source for information, though. She knew the histories of the various departments in the War Office. She knew about hundreds of transactions. She knew where documents could be found. She even had copies of some documents that the War Office had lost! Ministers, clerks, and secretaries deluged her with requests for information.

Reform for India had stalled, too. Flo saw that it would be a very long struggle with but tiny victories. She fought poor health and depression, and she became very difficult. When the queen of Holland wanted to see her, Flo refused. Only Clarkey, the Verneys, and the Nightingales could assume she would receive them. Then, in the summer of 1865, she refused to see even Clarkey.

Only later did Flo realize how rude she had been to her dear old friend. Friends tried to placate her—by letter. She admitted to some—by letter—that, as poor as her physical health was, her mental health was worse. Flo was in no way prepared for the news that Hilary had cancer. She had fallen out with Hilary, who had never escaped her domestic prison. After Hilary's death, Flo suppressed her guilt with anger, writing Clarkey that the Carter family was guilty of the "most monstrous of slow murders."[1]

Few helped her more than Dr. Sutherland, a man whom she had to see because of their work. Yet he had become her "pet aversion."[2] He was going deaf, and his constant "Pardon me, Miss Nightingale?" drove Flo into a rage. She no longer spoke to him. She scribbled exasperated notes, such as, "My dear soul! It's rather late for this," and "You said you were going to lay it before your committee; you had better lay it before me!"[3] She couldn't imagine why he had taken a house farther out of London. Now she couldn't summon him on a moment's notice.

When Papa purchased the 10 South Street house for Flo, it quickly became her very own home, characterized by its brightness and lack of frills. She did, however, grace some walls with prints of Michelangelo's frescoes in the

Sistine Chapel, and her household included her lady's maid, five housemaids, a cook, and a handyman.

Flo still loved to read and take notes. Besides reading medical journals, she corresponded with doctors. The news in medicine these days was very exciting. Chemist Louis Pasteur of France was trying to prove that tiny organisms, or "germs," caused disease. Joseph Lister, a Yorkshire man who doctored in Scotland, was experimenting with the carbolic acid used to disinfect sewers. He applied carbolic acid to his surgical instruments before surgery and to the open wound after surgery. Flo heard that his first results were very encouraging.

She read belated accounts of the Crimean War. Many were self-serving. Few were masterpieces. Ironically the truest was by a Russian artillery officer, Leo Tolstoy, who commanded a cannon battery in the Fourth Bastion, the most forward Russian position during the fall of Sebastopol. His writing of actual combat made other accounts of the war appear to be childish scribbles.

She had no lack of correspondence, no lack of people seeking advice on many topics. She monitored her nursing school and advised those who wanted to start others. She wrote hundreds of letters to her staff and the nurses they had certified. She lauded Agnes Jones's monumental effort in the Liverpool Workhouse Infirmary. But hard-focused projects were a thing of the past for Flo. She tried at one point to resurrect her *Suggestions for Thought* but once again abandoned it. The book of John triumphed over modern rationalism.

Flo was very worn out for her age. And her family and friends were dying. In 1874, Papa died at eighty, which necessitated the vacating of Embley Park so that Shore Smith could at long last inherit it. Mama died in 1880 at ninety-two; Clarkey in 1883 at eighty-six; Richard Monckton Milnes in 1885 at seventy-six; Aunt Mai in 1889 at ninety; Parthe in 1890 at seventy-one; Dr. Sutherland in 1891 at eighty-three; Aunt Julia in 1893 at eighty-four. Sir Harry Verney died in 1894 at ninety-three. Flo's "boy Shore" died that year, too, at a mere sixty years of age.

Flo saw the new century in. So did Queen Victoria, who by now had reigned for more than sixty years! Flo herself had passed into legend as "the lady with the lamp." Some hailed Flo as one of the three greatest figures of nineteenth-century medicine in Britain, along with James Simpson and Joseph Lister. Simpson had pioneered chloroform as an anesthetic. Lister had pioneered carbolic acid as an antiseptic. The contributions of these three had drastically reduced mortality in the sick. But praise meant little to Flo. She was ever restless. Oh, if only she could have done more. There was so much to do. Was it any wonder she was irritable? Could anyone know the frustration she felt when reform stalled? For that matter, could anyone know the frustration she had endured in the earlier years?

She had gained weight with age. She appeared the stolid matron instead of a wiry Joan of Arc. People were still in awe of her. There was little said about her that she didn't eventually hear from her hundreds of correspondents. But by 1906, the queen had died and no one requested any advice from Flo. At eighty-six, her health had failed almost completely. A visitor was never received until her caretaker had coached her first as to the caller's identity and purpose. Flo was very concerned about final arrangements, too. There must be no elaborate burial in some honored place like Westminster Abbey. Besides, nothing could honor her more than common soldiers bearing her coffin to her grave next to Mama and Papa in the St. Margaret Church cemetery at Wellow. She gave specific instructions as to what her epitaph must read. With that, she was satisfied to await the end.

On August 13, 1910, at the ripe old age of ninety, Florence Nightingale fell asleep and passed on into Paradise. The small cross above her grave was inscribed:

FLORENCE NIGHTINGALE
BORN 1820
DIED 1910

FLORENCE NIGHTINGALE

FOR FURTHER READING

I. Excellent biographies:

Huxley, Elspeth. *Florence Nightingale.* New York: Putnam, 1975.

O'Malley, I. B. *Florence Nightingale, 1820–1856.* London: Thornton Butterworth, 1931.

Woodham-Smith, Cecil. *Florence Nightingale: 1820–1910.* New York: McGraw-Hill, 1951.

II. Various collections of Florence Nightingale's many writings:

Calabria, Michael D., ed. *Florence Nightingale in Egypt and Greece: Her Diary and "Visions."* Albany: State University of New York Press, 1997.

Nightingale, Florence. *Notes on Nursing: What It Is, and What It Is Not.* Cutochogue, NY: Buccaneer, 1976 (reprint of 1860 classic).

Poovey, Mary, ed. *Cassandra and Other Selections from Suggestions for Thought.* New York: New York University Press, 1992.

Vicinus, Martha, and Bea Nergaard, eds. *Ever Yours, Florence Nightingale: Selected Letters.* Cambridge, MA: Harvard University Press, 1990.

III. Other relevant readings:

Barbary, James. *The Crimean War.* New York: Hawthorn, 1970.

Longford, Elizabeth. *Queen Victoria: Born to Succeed.* New York: Harper & Row, 1964.

NOTES

Chapter 2

1. I. B. O'Malley, *Florence Nightingale, 1820–1856* (London: Thornton Butterworth, 1931), 23.

2. Ibid., 25–26.

Chapter 5

1. Cecil Woodham-Smith, *Florence Nightingale, 1820–1910* (New York: McGraw-Hill, 1951), 12.

Chapter 6

1. Cecil Woodham-Smith, *Florence Nightingale, 1820–1910* (New York: McGraw-Hill, 1951), 26.

Chapter 7

1. I. B. O'Malley, *Florence Nightingale, 1820–1856* (London: Thornton Butterworth, 1931), 88.

2. Cecil Woodham-Smith, *Florence Nightingale, 1820–1910* (New York: McGraw-Hill, 1951), 34.

3. Ibid.

4. O'Malley, *Florence Nightingale*, 97.

5. Ibid., 100.

6. Ibid., 101.

7. Ibid., 104.

Chapter 8

1. I. B. O'Malley, *Florence Nightingale, 1820–1856* (London: Thornton Butterworth, 1931), 109.

2. Ibid., 116.

3. Ibid., 119.

4. Ibid., 120.

5. Ibid., 125.

6. Ibid., 128.

7. Ibid.

Chapter 9

1. I. B. O'Malley, *Florence Nightingale, 1820–1856* (London: Thornton Butterworth, 1931), 142.

2. Ibid., 144–45.

3. Anthony Sattin, ed., *Florence Nightingale's "Letters from Egypt," 1849–50* (New York: Weidenfeld & Nicolson, 1987), 26.

4. Ibid., 39.

5. Ibid., 81.

Chapter 10

1. Anthony Sattin, ed., *Florence Nightingale's "Letters from Egypt," 1849–50* (New York: Weidenfeld & Nicolson, 1987), 85.

2. Ibid., 63.

3. Michael D. Calabria, *Florence Nightingale in Egypt and Greece: Her Diary and "Visions"* (Albany: State University of New York Press, 1997), 20–48. Used with permission.

4. Ibid.; Martha Vicinus and Bea Nergaard, eds., *Ever Yours, Florence Nightingale: Selected Letters* (Cambridge, MA: Harvard University Press,

1990), 41. Used with permission. Cecil Woodham-Smith, *Florence Nightingale, 1820–1910* (New York: McGraw-Hill, 1951), 53.

    5. Woodham-Smith, *Florence Nightingale*, 53.

    6. Ibid.

    7. Calabria, *Florence Nightingale in Egypt and Greece*, 55.

    8. Ibid.

    9. Raymond G. Herbert, *Florence Nightingale: Saint, Reformer or Rebel?* (Malabar, FL: Robert E. Krieger, 1981), 34–52. Used with permission.

Chapter 11

    1. Cecil Woodham-Smith, *Florence Nightingale, 1820–1910* (New York: McGraw-Hill, 1951), 85.

    2. Ibid., 87–88.

Chapter 12

    1. Martha Vicinus and Bea Nergaard, eds., *Ever Yours, Florence Nightingale: Selected Letters* (Cambridge, MA: Harvard University Press, 1990), 83–84.

    2. Elspeth Huxley, *Florence Nightingale* (New York: Putnam, 1975), 81.

    3. Vicinus and Nergaard, *Ever Yours*, 109.

Chapter 13

    1. Martha Vicinus and Bea Nergaard, eds., *Ever Yours, Florence Nightingale: Selected Letters* (Cambridge, MA: Harvard University Press, 1990), 114.

    2. Cecil Woodham-Smith, *Florence Nightingale, 1820–1910* (New York: McGraw-Hill, 1951), 164.

    3. Vicinus and Nergaard, *Ever Yours*, 148–49.

    4. Woodham-Smith, *Florence Nightingale*, 174.

Chapter 15

    1. Florence Nightingale, *Notes on Nursing: What It Is, and What It Is Not.* Reprinted by Cutochogue (New York: Buccaneer, 1976), 105.

Chapter 16

    1. Martha Vicinus and Bea Nergaard, eds., *Ever Yours, Florence Nightingale: Selected Letters* (Cambridge, MA: Harvard University Press, 1990), 265.

    2. Cecil Woodham-Smith, *Florence Nightingale, 1820–1910* (New York: McGraw-Hill, 1951), 285.

    3. Ibid., 286.

AMY CARMICHAEL

FOR THE CHILDREN OF INDIA

Sam Wellman

ONE

S teady there, girl," murmured twelve-year-old Amy Beatrice Carmichael one summer day in 1880 along the Irish Sea.

She patted her pony's sweaty neck. Its barreled sides heaved. Although most of the shore was rocky, Amy knew the soft spots well. She had ridden the small animal hard through the sandy patches. She surveyed the rubble-strewn shore to make sure Norman and Ernest weren't lurking about. They could be ornery to be sure, especially when trying to even the score with Amy for some delicious trick she had pulled on them. Confident that her two younger brothers were not nearby, Amy dismounted.

Amy loved animals, and as she grew older, Amy found herself returning more often to the beach to ride. While the pony rested, Amy examined the tidal pools. The shoreline seemed to be God's creation in the raw: "Plants," which her father said were really animals, clung to the rocks and swayed in the surging surf; stalk-eyed crabs skittered in the shallow pools left by the retreating tide; mute, blind, deaf clams sent their bubbling breath to the surface of the sand. All these creatures thrived in a sea that appeared chaotic from the distance but on close inspection was clear and teeming with life. Yes, how Amy loved animals. At home she had cleared her dollhouse of the insipid, rosy-cheeked, glassy-eyed dolls, replacing them with beetles and crickets. She had substituted moss and rocks for the tiny chairs and beds that furnished no comfort to her insects. A mouse or a toad would have been a nice addition, but Amy knew that her nursemaid, Bessie, would complain to Mother.

Amy studied the endless sea. She loved the color blue. The sea was so peaceful when it was blue. She remembered watching the sea from her nursery window on the second floor of the old house, when she must have been three years old. A green sea was an angry sea. A gray sea was an anxious sea. But a blue sea was peaceful. The sky was peaceful, too, when it was blue. She had told Norman her great discovery about colors, but he had merely burbled in his crib.

She glanced over at the great mill that sat near a creek that emptied into the sea. There was a second mill half a mile upstream on the same creek. The stream had been dammed just beyond the second mill, creating a pool of slack water. How well she knew that murky vastness. Her father had tied a rope around her waist and held the other end as Amy thrashed about in water that felt as unyielding as a slurry of concrete. But eventually she began to "swim."

Or at least she could dog-paddle to safety in an emergency. Norman and Ernest passed the same ordeal. And so it was with every Carmichael child. Of course, the sea was quite a different challenge. Once Amy and her brothers were rowing a small boat in the long tidal channel near Portaberry, where Grandmother Filson lived. The current caught the boat and swept it toward the open sea. Amy began to beseech God with a hymn:

> *He leadeth me, O blessed thought,*
> > *O words with heavenly comfort fraught;*
> *Whate'er I do, where'er I be,*
> > *Still 'tis God's hand that leadeth me!*[1]

Frightened, Norman and Ernest joined in at the top of their lungs as their small arms cranked the oars against the current. Just as the rowboat seemed destined to cross the bar into the open sea, a coast guard lifeboat rescued them. God had surely answered Amy's plea. Life seemed lost then found again, and Amy would never forget looking death in the face. In the middle of the reservoir at the mill where Amy learned to swim was a tiny one-tree island. This rather insignificant feature gave her home village its name: Millisle. The mills were very old, first bought by James Carmichael, Amy's ancestor, in 1705. James was from Ayr, in southwest Scotland. He was a staunch Presbyterian, too, one of those Scots who defied the English kings who wanted to shove the Church of England down their throats. It was no surprise that the Carmichaels had crossed the Irish Sea to practice their faith in northern Ireland.

The mills were now run by her father, David, and his brother William. They had modernized the mill machinery with steel rollers for milling the hard wheat imported from America, but some of the Irish were now importing American wheat already ground into flour, a development that worried her father and her uncle very much.

"Come on, Fanny; let's ride," Amy said as she remounted the rested beast.

She rode Fanny into a lather again and then trotted the pony back to her home. Most houses in Millisle were tiny-windowed stone cottages. But the two Carmichael clans, David's and William's, lived in two of the three largest houses in Millisle. David's was a two-story house of gray stone, with fireplaces on each end. Bay windows and dormers spoke of money and privilege, almost as much as the walled grounds with apple trees and rosebushes. Amy and her brothers and sisters were taught by a governess. Other than her five cousins— all deemed unruly roughnecks by her mother—she saw other children in the village only when she went to their cottages on a mission of mercy with a pot of soup or when she saw them in the Presbyterian church. The village children must have liked her, because often before church they offered her peppermint candy, which she had to refuse.

The other children not only sucked on candy, but they were also allowed to lie down in the pews. Not Amy, or Norman, Ernest, Eva, Ethel, Walter, or Alfred. The Carmichaels sat upright. It wasn't possible to stretch out, not even if one resolved to suffer the consequences later. Punishment for slouching in church was swift as lightning.

After she led Fanny into the stable, she curried the animal as her father had taught her. Being indifferent to the needs of an animal was a sin. "A righteous man regardeth the life of his beast: but the tender mercies of the wicked are cruel," says Proverbs 12:10. Amy was sure the verse applied to any animal.

One time Amy had thrown a fit when a cousin tortured a frog. That was a memory she could live without. The wicked boy had impaled the frog on some thorns, and the thought of terrible thorns like that tearing the flesh of Jesus sickened her. But, praise God, most of her animal memories were tender ones. Daisy the cat and Gildo the collie had the run of the Carmichael estate. They were family pets, like Fanny and the other pony, Charlie. Amy now noticed that Charlie was gone, which probably meant that pesky Norman and Ernest were being bounced around somewhere in the village. Good. Perhaps she could enjoy some quiet reading at her desk.

Back in her bedroom, which she shared with her two young sisters, Eva and Ethel, she sat at the desk. Long ago, Norman and Ernest had slept in this same room with Amy—the "nursery," Mother called it then—but now the two older brothers slept with the two younger brothers, Walter and Alfred, in the boys' bedroom. Mother was loving but stern, too. Not that Amy herself was some sort of saint, she reflected, but it seemed she had taken more than her share of punishment. "Pink tea" was an ever-looming threat—if Mother had the time. She would watch as Mother mixed a nasty pink powder into a little cup of hot water. It gave quite a stomachache to be sure, but complaining to Mother about the pain did no good at all. The potion was intended to give pain. A lesser punishment was a ruler across the palm, after which Amy was required to politely thank her mother. Another form of correction was standing in a corner with nothing to see but the dreary wall. And, of course, an instant, skin-burning spanking was only an arm's length away, if Mother was pressed for time or really angry.

When Amy looked in the mirror, she saw thick brown hair framing an oval, milky-skinned face with a turned-up nose and brown eyes. This was the demure Amy that her mother wanted other people to see. But did astute observers notice that Amy's eyes were not the placid liquid browns of a deer but the sparkling, mischievous eyes of a fox? With little effort, in private, she could beetle her brows into a face any demon would be pleased to wear or into a mask of trust.

TWO

Although Amy's parents—especially her mother—punished without fail and did not express love in a tender way, the house was full of love. Mr. Carmichael often took his children away from the house and grounds to wander the village of Millisle and its surroundings. He introduced Amy to her first clovered field and her first tidal pool. The children never lacked for pets and toys and books. When Amy was very young, her parents had read to her. When it wasn't the Bible or the Shorter Catechism, it was usually tales of Christian martyrs. Of course, martyrs of Scotland were emphasized, from Patrick Hamilton in 1527 to Walter Mill in 1558. The legends of Robin Hood and King Arthur seemed to have been served to Amy with her mother's milk, as were Mother Goose stories and Aesop's fables. Shakespeare was spoon-fed in the form of Charles Lamb's *Tales of Shakespeare*.

When the children were old enough to read on their own, the richness in the Carmichael library seemed inexhaustible. Among Amy's favorites was *The Pilgrim's Progress*; and the story of its author, John Bunyan, a simple tinker, was almost as uplifting as the Christian allegory of salvation itself. *Robinson Crusoe* was not as essential but contained the stuff of dreams. What to do on a deserted island? *Gulliver's Travels* was available, too; and no child of Amy's day could miss *Alice's Adventures in Wonderland* and *Through the Looking Glass*. And like any good girl of Scottish descent, Amy enjoyed George MacDonald's *At the Back of the North Wind*. Amy knew early on that MacDonald's writing was not the best, yet his storytelling overwhelmed any literary inadequacies. Novels by Sir Walter Scott never raised a parent's eyebrow, but borrowed literature such as the Victorian novels of Jane Eyre and Charlotte Brontë or the American imports *Little Women* and *Tom Sawyer* would draw a suspicious frown from Mother. Any Irish writer, except a Protestant like Maria Edgeworth, would draw an immediate rebuke from Amy's parents.

Poetry thrilled Amy most of all. It soared high above prose in its brilliance. The majestic poetry of John Milton was certainly encouraged. Poetry by Bobby Burns or George Herbert was not suspect. But John Donne and William Blake were close to crossing the line. When occasionally Amy was able to read Irish poets, she was often startled by their fiery hatred of England. She read the works of many suspect poets, as well as all the expected. In addition to the great changes from Milton to Wordsworth and from Wordsworth to Tennyson, she began to discern subtle differences between contemporaries like Robert Browning and Matthew Arnold. Smitten, she wrote poetry herself. Her rhyme and meter clunked woodenly, but she persisted. And the more poetry she read, the better her own poetry became. What a very happy childhood Amy had! And yet she had worried for some time that the end of her childish reverie might soon be approaching. One day late in the summer of 1880, her luggage packed with clothing, Amy said good-bye to her mother and her six brothers and sisters and stepped into a carriage to begin her journey to boarding school. Her father accompanied her to the docks in Belfast, fifteen miles due west. As a poetic device, the direction west was death, and Amy felt its figurative truth. She kissed her father good-bye and was off on a steamship, east as it turned out, across the Irish Sea to England. Well-to-do "British" families deemed such remote schooling necessary.

Upon first seeing her destination, Amy muttered with dread, "Marlborough House."

The girls' boarding school in the large town of Harrogate was run by Methodists. Crossing denominational lines obviously didn't bother Amy's parents. They were from a Presbyterian background, but they were not such staunch Calvinists that they had a problem with John Wesley's Methodism. If one could set aside the question of predestination, both were holy equals. Nor did her parents have a problem with Quakers or any other devout group. Their concerns were to believe God's Word in the Bible and to accept His Son as their Savior.

Harrogate was in the uplands. Mineral springs had been discovered in the area more than three hundred years before, and many came there to enjoy their recuperative powers. Below Harrogate, the rise between the Nidd and the Wharfe rivers slipped down to the larger town of York. The most decisive battle of the English civil war had been fought in nearby Marston Moor, where on July 2, 1644, Oliver Cromwell had thrashed the first King Charles. York also boasted York Minster, an old Gothic cathedral with more medieval glass than any other church in England.

Amy learned much English history from her surroundings. She had been sheltered from much of it in Millisle. Even as Amy went to school, a new chapter in Irish history was being unveiled. She learned that reforms passed in the English Parliament had not satisfied the Irish. They wanted self-rule. Their champion, Charles Parnell, urged the Irish not to pay land rents to the British. For that rebellious act, he was arrested and imprisoned. Then he struck a deal with William Gladstone, the current prime minister of Great Britain, only to have it disintegrate when Irish revolutionaries murdered British officials in Dublin, Ireland.

Among her English schoolmates, Amy preferred to change the subject from politics to something more to her liking.

Her interest in botany blossomed in her dormitory window, where she nurtured lilies and chrysanthemums from her native soil. Of course, as the oldest child, she had been nurturing her whole life in the role of "little mother" to her brothers and sisters, and her habits prevailed in her new environment as well. At school she not only socialized among her peers but regimented them. She led by example. If the girls desired a certain dessert, it was Amy who brashly approached the cook and persuaded her to prepare it. In admiration, the other girls said she was "wild Irish," which amused Amy.

In the spring of 1884, she sang in the choir at the meetings of the Children's Special Service Mission. Mr. Edwin Arrowsmith had them sing a simple hymn—an import from America—that had become popular:

Jesus loves me! This I know,
for the Bible tells me so.
Little ones to Him belong;
they are weak but He is strong.

The first verse sang to Amy's heart like a thousand angels! Did she know she belonged to Jesus? The chorus spoke to her just as grandly:

Yes, Jesus loves me! Yes, Jesus loves me!
Yes, Jesus loves me! The Bible tells me so.

Jesus loved her. Of course the Bible had told her that. But had she accepted that love? She knew by now how the Wesleys had stressed a second sanctification in a Christian's development. But it seemed mumbo jumbo to Amy. The last verse of the hymn resonated in her heart:

Jesus loves me! He will stay
close beside me all the way.
Thou hast bled and died for me;
I will henceforth live for Thee.[1]

After the hymn, Mr. Arrowsmith asked the children to be silent for several minutes. Amy brooded. What if what the Wesleys had said was true? Was this her second chance? Did she have to "accept" Jesus? As far as she could remember, she had not once actually asked Jesus to come into her heart. The pain He bore on the cross seemed to crush her. Yes, she would open her heart to Jesus. Then it happened. Suddenly, her chains fell away! She was soaring. The years in England that had seemed to her so empty, such a void, took on special meaning now. She had come into the desert as a pilgrim; and away from the distractions of human love at home, she had found God.

At the end of that school year in 1884, her father came to the boarding school to take Amy to visit London before they both returned to Ireland. London was the greatest city in the world at that time, in every way. More than three million people inhabited the city, compared to one million in New York City at that time. London had a glorious history many times longer than any American borough, preserved in blood and paper and stone. Amy saw as much as could be seen in a few days, including Westminster Abbey, the British Museum, the Tower of London, St. Paul's Cathedral, Buckingham Palace, and Windsor Castle. She never caught a glimpse of Queen Victoria; but in the houses of Parliament, Father pointed out the white locks and craggy face of Prime Minister William Gladstone.

Amy's father soon revealed the purpose of the trip to London. It was possibly Amy's last chance to see such things. Her school days in England were at an end. The mills in Millisle had become unprofitable. There was no future in grinding American wheat, because the market was flooded with imported American flour. Her father and Uncle William were building a new mill near Belfast; and because the family also had to move to College Gardens to be near the new mill, money would be tight for a while. Norman and Ernest were being withdrawn from their boarding schools as well. Amy now appreciated her schooling as never before.

Amy was ashamed of her performance as a boarding student. She had indulged her "wildness" and wasted her chance at a higher education, a chance her four younger brothers and sisters might never get. She would just as soon forget her shortcomings; but back in Ireland, Amy did not forget her decision to accept Jesus as her Savior. But how was she to serve Him? A girl of sixteen had few options. At home she was once again the "little mother" to Ethel, Alfred, and Walter. Amy went calling socially with Mother, too. She participated in homespun charities, carrying food to the destitute and the elderly.

One experience made her heart ache. Her mother indulged her with a visit to a Belfast tea shop. While sitting at a table sipping tea and sampling sweet delicacies she didn't want, Amy noticed a face pressed against the window. *How charming*, she thought, *to see a little girl peering in at the sweets*. But when they left the tea shop, Amy saw that it was raining, and the girl's dress was very thin and dirty. With shock Amy realized that the ragamuffin girl was barefoot! Barefoot on a cold, drizzly day. So cold, so hungry, so poor, so sad!

In the cozy warmth of her bedroom that night, she set her feelings to verse.

When I grow up and money have,
*   I know what I will do,*
I'll build a great big lovely place
*   For little girls like you.*[2]

Weeks later, she was in Belfast on yet another gray, drizzly day, this time on a Sunday morning. After the service at the Rosemary Street Presbyterian Church, she saw an old lady on the street who was struggling to carry a heavy bundle. "Let's help her," Amy impulsively urged Norman and Ernest. So the three helped, one brother carrying the bundle and the other two escorting the old lady along. But when they ran into more and more people on the street who were leaving church services, Amy became embarrassed. Eyebrows were raised. The old lady was dirty and shabbily dressed. *Surely,* Amy thought, *these well-dressed people don't think we Carmichaels are somehow associated with this wretched old woman.* Oh, why had she been so impulsive? Amy became more and more exasperated, blushing as red as an apple, she was sure, by the time they passed a square with a great fountain.

Then words struck her ears like a thunderclap!

A voice boomed, "'Now if any man build upon this foundation gold, silver, precious stones, wood, hay, stubble; every man's work shall be made manifest: for the day shall declare it, because it shall be revealed by fire; and the fire shall try every man's work of what sort it is. If any man's work abide which he hath built thereupon, he shall receive a reward.'"

First Corinthians 3:12–14, thought Amy numbly.

THREE

Amy glanced around. All she saw were people bustling along the street. Now she was frightened. Was this some kind of mystical experience? Surely such things didn't happen to everyday people like herself. Not voices! Norman and Ernest showed no sign of having heard anything. She had to bite her tongue not to tell them. They would think she was crazy. That afternoon, back in College Gardens, she retired to her room. All the rest of the day she asked herself over and over whether God had spoken to her. Was such a thing possible? Wouldn't a rational person think it was merely Amy scolding herself in her anxiety? But after many hours, she acknowledged that she had heard the voice. She was certain. The incident could mean only one thing: " 'The fire shall try every man's work of what sort it is.' The meaning of that is plain enough," she admitted.

And what had her work been? Gold or stubble? One charitable act had been required of her this day, and she had been mortified with embarrassment! *Stubble!* In His mercy God had warned her. *Oh God, let me serve You with gold,* she prayed. She would tell no one of the experience, but she would immediately begin to offer her gold—if she could presume to call the work she planned such an exalted thing.

First, Amy began to invite children of the neighborhood on Sunday afternoons to her home. There she regaled them with stories. They played games. Bible lessons were woven in the midst of the fun. She was not surprised when the children responded enthusiastically to her efforts. She had much experience entertaining younger children. Ethel, Alfred, and Walter attended, too, just as eagerly awaiting the fun as the others. But in her heart, Amy knew these neighborhood children were privileged. They certainly deserved to know Jesus, but somehow it seemed that other children needed Jesus more. How could she doubt it? Hadn't she seen that innocent urchin peering through the tea-shop window?

Oh, why hadn't she insisted to her mother that they invite the little girl into the tea shop for a sweet? And why did Amy not now invite the poor in to taste the Lord's meat?

Amy went to the Belfast City Mission and volunteered to go into the slums with the Reverend Henry Montgomery on Saturday nights. *Oh God, give me the strength and courage to make a difference,* she prayed. Amy began to approach children who were loitering on the street. "Come with us and let us sing and tell stories," she said to them with a warm smile.

"What for?" they asked suspiciously.

"Fun," she replied with a laugh. A handful of them did come! Of course, the meat of God's Word was always sandwiched in the middle of fun things to do. Oh, indescribable joy! But not indescribable power. Her power came from Jesus. She knew that. The handful grew to dozens as the word spread. Why wander around with nothing to do? There was a young woman over at the City Mission who knew how to have fun! Amy did not even mind being teased a bit. Teasing was just an impish form of friendship. Any difficult children she bore with a loving smile.

But she quickly corrected sins. Even then Amy was smiling.

Her efforts grew, always injecting the Word of God into the fun. Soon she was teaching a group of boys at night. She knew children did not love to be "organized," but they did love to belong to an organization. She started another program she called "Morning Watch," in which the slum children pledged to regularly read the Bible and pray. To seal the bargain, each child signed their very own gilt-edged blue pledge card. Every Saturday morning the Morning Watch children met to discuss their week's successes or failures. And, of course, they had fun, too—so much fun that Alfred and Walter were soon Morning Watchers as well.

Her prayer group for girls soon became so large it had to be moved to Victoria College. Every night, Amy thanked God that He gave her such power with children. And Amy's power also attracted older children, even some young women. These were the mill girls, the girls too poor to wear the fancy hats of the day. They covered their heads in public with their shawls and thus were called "shawlies." Amy drew these girls and young women from the slums to the Presbyterian church on Rosemary Street. Almost hidden in her efforts to teach them hygiene and etiquette, she taught them to read the Bible and pray.

"Ernest," she said one day to her brother, who now worked on the railroad, "what do you know of the shawlies?"

So Ernest told her what he truly knew. That was horrifying enough. Unmarried shawlies with babies were common. Ernest had seen them with his own eyes. And common, too, was the crime of men molesting the shawlies. Often it came down to just how hard the girl could kick and scratch and scream. That Ernest had seen with his own eyes, too. And the gossip he couldn't repeat was a thousand times worse. Many of the shawlies were mired in a living nightmare.

Amy knew she must try harder than ever to give these girls hope, but her own world was shaken again. Her father had looked ill for several months. In the spring of 1885, Amy, who was by now seventeen, saw him talking to Mother in the dining room. The subject was money, and Father had never looked so sick. He had loaned a very large amount of the family money to someone. It seemed now the family would never get it back. That bad judgment seemed to be crushing Amy's father. Soon he was bedridden. On April 8, a Wednesday, the traditional day for singing hymns—he asked his family to sing "My Faith Looks Up to Thee." The last verse ran:

> *When ends life's transient dream,*
> *when death's cold sullen stream*
> *shall o'er me roll,*
> *Blest Savior, then, in love,*
> *fear and distrust remove—*
> *O bear me safe above,*
> *a ransomed soul.*[1]

Was it possible that Amy's father sensed the end? He was only fifty-four years old. She had just traveled the year before with him in England. He seemed all right then. Yet on Sunday morning, April 12, David Carmichael died as the church bells were ringing. It was as if he willed it.

Amy continued her labors, now dressed in the somber winter colors of mourning. The household rose at 4:50 a.m. these days. For breakfast they ate brown and white bread, fresh sliced or toasted, with marmalade. Often they had bacon, too; and on Sundays they had smoked fish called *finnan haddie*. Supper was usually bread, potatoes, and sausage or fish. With every meal they drank tea. Their table had suffered a little since Father's death. No longer were Grandmother's occasional offerings from Portaberry of turkey and such treats taken with an air of nonchalance. Now their arrival was an event of great interest.

But the Carmichaels were scarcely destitute. Many of the truly poor in Ireland virtually lived on potatoes. That was the reason the blight of the 1840s that caused the harvested potatoes to rot in their cellars was so catastrophic. The poor starved by the hundreds of thousands. No, the Carmichaels had never suffered like that.

In September 1886, Amy took a ship across the Irish Sea to Scotland to visit an old school friend.

There Amy learned what "Keswick" meant. In 1875, in Cumberland, one of England's most northern counties, a convention was held in a large tent at Broadlands, the estate of W. Cowper-Temple, in the village of Keswick in England's tranquil lake district. One of the sponsors was Robert Wilson, a man wealthy from his coal mines in Cumberland. Also in attendance in that first meeting had been the writer George MacDonald. The purpose of the convention was a return to holiness and an opportunity for spiritual healing. All discussions of forming a new sect were forbidden. Discussions of doctrine were discouraged, yet an informal "Keswick" doctrine had developed over the ten years since then. Keswick participants generally rejected a common notion that, although the believer is justified in an instant, he must struggle for years for sanctification. Keswick people believed sanctification could come in an instant, too, in a "second blessing."

Amy went with her friend to the meeting in Glasgow, certainly hoping and praying for such a moment. Neither speaker the day she was there affected her at all. But in the closing prayer, the minister paraphrased part of verse 24 of the book of Jude. "Lord, we know Thou art able to keep us from falling."

Yes, "unto him that is able to keep you from falling," she reflected. The rest of the verse in Jude popped into Amy's mind. Yes, the Lord was able to present us in His glory without fault and with exceeding joy, too. Oh yes, glory and majesty, dominion and power, now and forever. Amy left the meeting slightly dazed. It was odd how some things moved her and some did not. It reminded her of the sermon she heard at Harrogate—completely forgotten now—that had been followed by singing the hymn "Jesus Loves Me." That hymn thrilled her every time she thought of it. And sitting in a restaurant with her friend after the Glasgow meeting, the verse she heard struck her again: "Unto him that is able to keep you from falling." Now it seemed momentous. Was this the instant? Was this her second blessing?

In the flyleaf of her Bible, she wrote at the top left the words, "Thou Shalt Remember." Below that line she wrote "Glasgow Sept. 23, 1886." Below that she wrote the part of verse 24 from Jude that now thrilled her so: "Unto him that is able to keep you from falling."

But was she transformed in any way? And how did one know? Long ago Charles Wesley had known his "second blessing," because the next morning he had awakened so full of joy and love he was singing a hymn! But Amy had no such dramatic scene. When Amy returned to Belfast, the season of mourning for her father was over. Her mother took Amy to dress shops to update her wardrobe, but Amy spurned the new clothes. Such finery was vanity. All the frills and sashes and ribbons filled her with revulsion. Amy realized with a start that some very fundamental change had happened to her in Glasgow. She was bent on living and breathing God's Word, bent on leading a new life of discipleship.

Her disdain for "the world and its applause" did not sour her enjoyment of her family. As a recreation, she proposed a family news "magazine" called *Scraps*. All seven siblings had to contribute under pen names. Norman was "Namron," Ernest was "Oddfellow," Eva chose "Lulu," Ethel wrote as "Atom," Walter was "Blanco," and Alfred coined the acronym "SSI," for Silly Silly Idiot. Amy had read somewhere that the "i-a-n" at the end of "Christian" should stand for "I am nobody," so in *Scraps*, Amy became "Nobody."

The seven siblings contributed anecdotes, cartoons, drawings, poetry, and anything else they thought worthy of an evening's discussion. Amy—that is, "Nobody"—especially liked to contribute sketches and poetry. Her sketches were usually botanical: ferns, flowers, and grasses. One sketch revealed an ambition. She designed the dust jacket for a book titled *Mill Girls and All About Them*. Needless to say, she was the author on the cover. One example of her poetry in *Scraps* was:

> *Think truly, and thy thoughts shall be*
> *Spotless with God's own purity.*
> *On every thought–bud let us bear*
> *The stamp of truth, and love and prayer.*[2]

In 1887, many of the "Keswick people" held meetings in Belfast and invited none other than Hudson Taylor. Taylor was the most famous missionary in the world, at least since the great David Livingstone had perished in Africa in 1873. Taylor had gone into China in the 1860s. His mission society was called the China Inland Mission. Most now just referred to it as the CIM. The CIM penetrated deeply into China; its missionaries wore native clothing and spoke native dialects. The society received enormous publicity in 1885 when the "Cambridge Seven," a group of noted athletes from Cambridge University, volunteered to serve in China.

Long ago the "father of Protestant Christian missions," England's own William Carey, had astounded the English with the enormity of the unsaved heathen population in the world: 557 million souls! Thousands of missionaries went forth to India, China, and Africa. Still, the number of unsaved souls in the world grew even larger. Now it was Hudson Taylor who cried from the rooftops: The total was a staggering 865 million. Even more heartbreaking was the fact that, every day, fifty thousand of these souls died unsaved. Fifty thousand every day!

Amy was there at the 1887 meetings in Belfast with her mother and aunts to hear it all. Her aunts were outspoken and invited Robert Wilson, the coal tycoon and one of the first organizers of the Keswick meetings, to come to their house for a visit. Wilson obliged and seemed intensely moved by the joy in the Carmichael home. Wilson was a huge, bearded man, making his gentleness and taciturn speech all the more noticeable. A Quaker, he simply retreated into silence if pressed into an unpleasant exchange. Amy respected his silence. His blue eyes and pinkish face seemed as innocent as a child's.

Early in 1888, Mother announced during one of their evening get-togethers that their funds were almost gone. Amy felt no sorrow at all. God's Word prevented any self-pity. Jesus Himself said it in the book of Matthew. "Seek ye first the kingdom of God." What could be clearer than that?

Amy learned that Robert Wilson had lost his only daughter, Rachel, a young lady about Amy's age. Perhaps that was why he looked at Amy in such a fatherly way. She was certainly struck by the fact that Robert Wilson was very nearly the age of her own departed father! When he left the Carmichael home, Amy felt very strongly in her heart that she would see Robert Wilson again. Months later, she received a letter from him, inviting her to the 1888 Keswick meeting.

In Keswick, Amy confirmed all she had heard. All doctrinal distractions were to be avoided. The object of Keswick was sanctity. The self must be subdued. Conquer the smallest sin. Put away all bitterness and rancor. Abide every hour in Christ. Call on divine power to strengthen every weakness. Robert Wilson and his friends could scarcely rub elbows with a firebrand like Hudson Taylor and not feel an obligation to save the heathen. When the Keswick Society decided to start the funding necessary to send forth missionaries sometime in the future, Amy found herself strangely excited.

Do I dare think of myself as a candidate for such an honor? she wondered.

Yet Amy became more agitated, too. Didn't the call to evangelize the unsaved heathen interfere with what she was doing in Belfast? It seemed so. In the flyleaf of her Bible this time she wrote from Paul's second letter to the Corinthians, "And he said unto me, My grace is sufficient for thee: for my strength is made perfect in weakness. Most gladly therefore will I rather glory in my infirmities, that the power of Christ may rest upon me." When she wrote the words, she repeated "of Christ," revealing her confusion and troubled thoughts. And she added part of a verse from Psalm 121: "from this time forth, and even for evermore." She had omitted the first half of the verse: "The Lord shall preserve thy going out and thy coming in." *Why?* she wondered later. Could she not put to paper the thought of "going out"? Was such a thing too much of a commitment? Did she love her work in Belfast too much?

If the Lord calls me to go forth, am I unwilling? she asked herself.

FOUR

Shawlies came to Amy's meetings in such great numbers that they could no longer be accommodated by the church that let her use its facilities. In the church magazine, *The Christian*, Amy read of a large hall, prefabricated from sheet metal, that could be erected for five hundred English pounds.

She urged her girls to pray "unto Him that is able to keep you from falling." But she also recalled an experience from her past. She had been staying with Grandmother Filson in Portaberry. Amy, virtually a native of that village, went out to collect for the poor. She knew of one man who would surely give her some money. He had just built himself a fine house. But no! With a scowl, he shooed her away. He couldn't love God. The implications were enormous.

And so Amy prayed now that those who loved God would give her money for her mission hall. Almost miraculously Amy was invited to lunch with Kate Mitchell, an older and very wealthy matron. The butler served them lunch in a sunny room. To Amy, the older lady was a "white violet" in the sunshine. Amy explained, bolstered by the hope Christ can give, that the mill girls would certainly like to meet in their own hall. All they needed were the land and five hundred English pounds to build such a hall of sheet steel.

Yet, within days, Amy received a letter from Kate Mitchell. "Build your hall," she wrote. But Amy still needed property on which to build. She rushed to the office of a wealthy mill owner. "Can you not encourage the moral strengthening of the mill girls?" she argued. Had he known Amy's father? Or was he overcome by Christ? He virtually donated the property for the hall. Soon construction was begun on the grounds at Cambria Street. Some dubbed the hall the "tin tabernacle," but Amy named it "Welcome Hall." The grand opening was set for January 2, 1889, which she announced in printed cards with the simple invitation:

Come one, Come all,
To the Welcome Hall,
And come in your working clothes.[1]

Amy had secured an affiliation with the Young Women's Christian Association, known as the YWCA. For the opening of Welcome Hall, she hung a banner above the speakers' platform to the glory of the Lord: THAT IN ALL THINGS HE MIGHT HAVE THE PREEMINENCE. They were the apostle Paul's words in his letter to the Colossians. Of course, Amy, the "Nobody," was not on the speakers' platform. She sat inconspicuously in the midst of her shawlies. But when the real work began, once again she was front and center.

The first Wednesday of every month was their gospel meeting. Every Sunday they had Bible class, followed by a meeting of the Sunbeam Band. Monday was choir practice, Tuesday was night school, Wednesday was girls' meeting, and so on throughout the week. Not one day lacked activity. With more than five hundred girls involved in the activities, Amy needed to enlist many helpers. And more money was needed. So the mill girls held bazaars in which they sold their own handiwork. Amy's work was truly blessed. Amy's Welcome Hall was now becoming known to Christians all over the British Isles. Letters came, too. One in particular was startling.

"Mr. Jacob MacGill of Manchester has invited me to come there to begin another 'Welcome Hall' for their mill girls," Amy told her mother. "He wants you to come to superintend a rescue mission for women."

So in 1889, the same year Amy opened her first Welcome Hall, she traveled to Manchester, a great factory city in the west of England, to open another. The Welcome Hall in Belfast was left in the very deserving and capable hands of Kate Mitchell.

In *Scraps*, Amy's brothers reported that she candidly predicted she would never be a wife. She was twenty-two years old, and it wasn't that she did not love men, but her love for men was agape, the Greek word for true Christian love, not physical love. In fact, Amy loved all people, men and women, with agape. Her agape was tested in Manchester, where she lived in the slums. Nighttime was the worst. Toughs fought in the streets. Women were molested. Hiding away in a room at night was no haven, either, because the rooms crawled with loathsome creatures of the night: roaches, ticks, bedbugs, rats.

Once Amy walked late at night through the slum to the train station. She intended to take a train to Cheshire, where her mother had a cottage. Suddenly, she was surrounded by young men, loud and smelling of rum. She was calm, fending them off as a gentle lady would. But the hooligans goaded each other on in their evil intentions. It was soon apparent that Amy might suffer the same fate as many other shawlies.

"Stop!" A door suddenly opened, and a woman hurled herself into the mob. She grabbed Amy's hand, and somehow the two muscled their way through the throng of young men. The woman shoved Amy inside her house and turned to face the mob. Amy heard the woman deliver a tongue-lashing; the words were indistinguishable, but the force was as violent as a storm. Whatever the brave woman said to the mob worked, and the hooligans were soon gone. Amy continued on to the train station in a daze. It was as if she had been rescued by one of Lot's mighty angels. And who could say the fierce woman was not an angel? In either case, the Lord was faithful.

As her mystical experiences increased, so did her humility. Why did she deserve such grace? Robert Wilson often invited Amy and her sisters and younger brothers to Broughton Grange, his majestic estate near Cockermouth, in Cumberland, above the River Derwent. No more than ten miles to the west, Solway Firth yawned into the Irish Sea. To the east ranged the Cumbrian Mountains. About twelve miles upriver, hugging the high lakes, was Keswick. The area reeked of history. William Wordsworth and Samuel Taylor Coleridge both had lived and had written poetry in this lake country. But as much as Amy loved poetry, she was more impressed by church history.

Amy went once again to the Keswick meetings as a guest of Robert Wilson, whom all the Carmichaels now referred to as "the D.O.M.," for "Dear Old Man." Never had he seemed more fatherly to her. Amy still wrestled with her thoughts of "going forth." In the flyleaf of her Bible, she recorded for "Keswick 1889":

> *How great is His Goodness,*
> *and how great is His Beauty!*
> *Jesus I am resting resting,*
> *in the joy of what Thou art*
> *I am finding out the greatness*
> *of Thy loving heart.*[2]

Amy had taken Zechariah 9:17, "For how great is his goodness, and how great is his beauty!" and added her deepest belief that while she was resting, she was fathoming the Lord's greatness. Unsaid was her conviction that all this was in preparation for some future endeavor.

When she returned to Manchester, she became ill. Others—like her very good friends Ella Crossley and Mary Hatch—blamed her poor eating habits. As often as not, Amy made a meal of an orange or a tomato, while her eyes were locked on the pages of a book. There weren't enough hours in the day to do everything she wanted to do. And now she was sick. She did not regard her body as some regarded their bodies, as either a terrible prison of the soul or a thing of glory. No, Amy agreed with the saintly Francis of Assisi. Her body was like a donkey! Often it was sturdy and forbearing and lovable. But on the other hand, so often it was lazy and stubborn and exasperating!

Then came a development that stunned her.

AMY CARMICHAEL

In 1890, Robert Wilson asked Mrs. Carmichael if Amy could come to live with him at Broughton Grange. He would take her in as his own daughter. He had not only lost his only daughter, but he had also lost his wife. Broughton Grange was a lonely, unlovely place without the companionship and refinement of a lady. Mrs. Carmichael agreed.

Mr. Wilson had been born a Quaker, and the Friends' Meeting House was nearby. Built in 1653, it was not quite as old as the nearby Baptist Chapel. Wilson and his two bachelor sons, William and George, were quite active in both churches. Once, after reading the Bible intensely, Robert Wilson had determined that baptism was a righteous thing. And although Quakers did not baptize, he had himself baptized.

"We must drop labels," he said to Amy. "If our precious Lord came tomorrow, what use would we have of such labels?"

Amy had already begun to think similar thoughts. She had known Presbyterian ways from babyhood, but she had learned in Harrogate to appreciate the pious yearnings of Methodism. She had also learned to value the beautiful ritual of the Church of England. Now she would learn to enjoy the quietness of the Quakers and the earnest beliefs of the Baptists. Surely these were all good things, all meant to honor the Lord.

Robert Wilson instructed her like a father. "Be a deep well, daughter," he told Amy.

He had become chairman of the Keswick Convention. Though he spoke with many people, he had learned never to divulge privileged conversations or repeat gossip. Amy was now privy to many of these same confidential talks. She, too, had to be a deep well who knew much but said little. Robert Wilson demonstrated a gentleman's sensitivity for everyone. Many times he plucked a flower for Amy. He bought her a spirited pony to ride. He surprised her with a pup. She named the frisky black and tan terrier Scamp.

But Amy was hardly a coquette or an idler. She had to be busy for the Lord. She was active in the Children's Special Service Mission in Broughton Grange. Tuesday nights at the mission hall belonged to the children. Amy appeared as a quiet force and soon ran the meetings. Although George and William Wilson participated, it was often Amy who delivered the talks. And more and more children flocked in to listen. She was so successful and the children were so demanding that Bible classes were added on Saturdays.

In 1890, Amy attended the Keswick meeting again, this time recording in the flyleaf of her Bible:

Thou hast put goodness in my heart.
   Thou wilt perfect that which concerneth me.
Lord, let the glow of Thy great love
   Through my whole being shine.[3]

Amy often combined her own compositions almost seamlessly with verses from the Bible. Her own "Thou hast put goodness in my heart" she followed with "Thou wilt perfect that which concerneth me," from Psalm 138, inserting her own thought once again of being prepared for some future mission.

Her heart told her that this time at the Grange was a preparation for her "going forth." She was never idle. She reinforced her spiritual reading. She had a stable of favorite authors whom she studied. Some were lesser known, like Brother Lawrence and Samuel Rutherford. To Amy, Rutherford, the seventeenth-century Scottish nonconformist, was very wise, very deep, a spiritual forerunner of her D.O.M. Others she read were widely known, like Thomas à Kempis and John Bunyan. Reading Bunyan's *The Pilgrim's Progress* was like reading the Bible. Amy was fascinated by Bunyan's *Grace Abounding*, too. In his autobiography Bunyan detailed how God had revealed Himself. Once. Twice. Yet, for a long time, Bunyan refused to believe the "miraculous."

In fact, many of Amy's favorites had one thing in common: God had revealed Himself to the writer. It was no surprise that she was attracted to the writings of the "English Mystics"—a medieval group that included Raymond Lully, Lady Julian of Norwich, and Richard Rolle. How passionate was Rolle's love for God. Amy also passionately desired His love, His revelation!

Could Amy herself write with such passion? Her friendship with the Faith Mission brought an invitation to write an article for their magazine, *Bright Words*, but she was reluctant. Amy was startled to hear the words, "I will hold thy right hand!"[4] Had she actually heard God speak? Was she going to be a doubter many times over like John Bunyan? She recognized the allusion to Isaiah 41: "For I the Lord thy God will hold thy right hand, saying unto thee, Fear not; I will help thee." So Amy began writing what she knew about: the shawlies. Her article, which she titled "Fightin' Sall," chronicled the conversion of a shawlie at the Welcome Hall in Belfast.

But as contemplative and creative as Amy became, she remained very active in religious life, too. In 1891, she went with Hannah Govan of Faith Mission to evangelize along the Clyde River in Scotland. Amy's talks were well received. This approval among the Scots—who were known to be so taciturn that even John Wesley had thrown his hands up in despair—was surely a good sign. And she recorded in the flyleaf of her Bible, on September 23, 1891—a hymn-singing Wednesday to be precise—one of the very special reminders:

And God is able to make all grace abound toward you; that ye, always having all sufficiency in all things, may abound to every good work.

Once again, Amy was strongly affected by John Bunyan, because the verse she records—2 Corinthians 9:8—offered both theme and title for his autobiography, *Grace Abounding*. And it was clear she intended to abound in good work, just as soon as God revealed His plan for her. Still, at Keswick that year she prayed for release from this constant inner tension about going forth to the heathen. Could not God give her some peace? Was it wrong for her to want to remain with Robert Wilson to comfort him? And could she have not only peace, God, but gladness also? Joy?

By January 1892, Amy had been at Broughton Grange nearly two years. Her piety had finally conquered the Wilson sons, George and William. At first resentful that this strange young woman had entered their lives, they now treated her like a younger sister. Amy had regarded their coolness as a trial for her. Though she seemed almost at peace now, it was true that joy was not there yet. But she was patient.

FIVE

The morning of January 14, 1892, a very shaken Amy wrote to her mother:

My precious Mother,

Have you given your child unreservedly to the Lord for whatever He wills? . . . Oh, may He strengthen you to say "Yes" to Him if He asks something which costs.

Darling Mother, for a long time, as you know, the thought of those dying in the dark—fifty thousand of them every day, while we at home live in the midst of blazing light—has been very present with me, and the longing to go to them, and tell them of Jesus, has been strong upon me. Everything, everything, seemed to be saying "Go," through all sounds the cry seemed to rise, "Come over and help us." Every bit of pleasure or work which has come to me, has had underlying it the thought of these people who have never, never heard of Jesus. . . .

But home claims seemed to say "Stay," and I thought it was His Will; it was, perhaps, until yesterday. I can't explain it, but lately the need seems to have come closer, and I wrote down a few days ago, just to have it in black and white, why I am not going.

1. Your need of me, my Mother.

2. The great loneliness it would mean to my dear second father.

3. The thought that by staying I might make it easier for the others to go if He called.

4. My not being strong.

But. . .yesterday. . .I went to my room and just asked the Lord what it all meant, what did He wish me to do, and, Mother, as clearly as I ever heard you speak, I heard Him say, "GO YE"[1]

So there it was.

How the devil had planted good reasons for her not to obey! Several days later Amy received her mother's answer:

Darling, when He asks you now to go away from within my reach, can I say nay? No, no, Amy; He is yours—you are His—to take you where He pleases and to use you as He pleases. I can trust you to Him, and I do.[2]

Some people around the Broughton Grange bluntly called Amy a selfish ingrate. But the D.O.M., Robert Wilson, the one person other than her mother who should have been hurt most by Amy's departure, wrote to Mrs. Carmichael:

> *It hardly seems a case for anything but bowing the head in thankful acquiescence, when the Lord speaks thus decidedly to one so dear. . . . She has been and is more than I can tell you to me, but not too sweet or too loving to present to Him Who gave Himself for us.*[3]

By the same post Amy admitted to her mother she didn't really know *where* she was going forth. Ceylon? China? Africa? Robert Wilson began to make discreet inquiries to various mission societies. It was hardly a surprise that China came into focus. After all, Hudson Taylor was a personal friend of Robert Wilson's. And Amy had actually met the great missionary to China. By May 1892, the D.O.M. had arranged for Amy to meet the Robert Stewarts in Bedford. The Stewarts were on leave from their mission in China. Ironically, the Stewarts were not missionaries of Taylor's China Inland Mission Society but of the Church of England's Church Missionary Society. Amy would represent a distaff society called the Zenana Mission Society. Again Amy was thrilled by the history of her surroundings; John Bunyan had written *The Pilgrim's Progress* in Bedford. Everything seemed most congenial with the Stewarts. They would return to their mission in the seacoast province of Fukien in the autumn. Amy would be a welcome addition.

But July brought a disappointing letter to Amy back in Broughton Grange. "Oh no. The Stewarts are not going directly to China. They are being detoured to Australia."

Suddenly, Amy was the topic of discussion at the annual Keswick meeting. For several years they had saved funds to sponsor a missionary. Now Robert Wilson, who happened to be the chairman of the mission committee, pushed hard to make that first missionary none other than Amy Carmichael. Amy wrote in the flyleaf of her Bible: "Keswick, Tuesday, July 26, 1892: Day the Mission Committee met,"[4] then the telling passage from Psalm 47: "He shall choose our inheritance for us."

Robert Wilson's motion carried.

Present at the meeting was Hudson Taylor. So Amy was not surprised to find herself traveling in September to the China Inland Mission offices in

London. The D.O.M. escorted her. Their hostess was Henrietta Soltau, who took charge of all women candidates for missionary work. To honor Robert Wilson, Amy signed the papers "Amy Wilson Carmichael." After the D.O.M. left for Broughton Grange, Henrietta helped Amy settle into her room at one of their residences on Pyrland Road.

How at peace Amy now felt with her own future.

But then her peace was shattered.

"The doctor has not approved you for China," Henrietta Soltau told her.

Amy felt the world had fallen on her. Was her "going forth" destined to be like that of the great missionary pioneer, William Carey? Carey had been on his ship, waiting for the crew to draw anchor and cast off for India. Instead, he and his son were cast off the ship. Then he went through weeks of agony, sheepishly shrugging his bewilderment, wondering if he would ever go to India. Oh, the pain and shame for Christ. Would Amy prepare to leave and then return sheepishly to her loved ones again and again?

Yet Amy was restless in the extreme. This setback simply would not do. She would never rest until she went forth. God had commanded her. On January 13, 1893, precisely one year from her commission to go forth, she was struck by the thought that her destination was Japan. So the D.O.M. wrote Reverend Barclay Buxton, who ran a mission on the west coast of Japan. Buxton was a missionary for the Church Missionary Society. However, he had in his organization missionaries of other less substantial societies, one of which was called the Japanese Evangelistic Band. When Wilson heard through Hudson Taylor that three missionary women of the China Inland Mission were sailing for Shanghai, Amy jumped at the opportunity to have travel companions. She was going to wait for Buxton's reply, not in Broughton Grange but in Shanghai!

On March 3, 1893, Amy sailed aboard the middling steamer SS *Valetta*. She did not have funds to travel the luxurious Peninsula & Oriental line, even in second class. She was drained. First, she had endured a tearful farewell in Manchester with her mother and brothers and sisters. Then she had withstood an elaborate but emotional farewell in London with Hudson Taylor and other officials. Then at the port of Tilbury she had weathered another heartbreaking parting with Robert Wilson. To her dismay, as the ship cast off, Robert Wilson was able to stroll along the dock for half a mile, all the while reciting scriptures that tore at her heart. They exchanged soul-wrenching hymns until Amy's throat was raw from tension.

She felt broken. But not too broken to record the date in her flyleaf and the phrase "He Goeth Before," alluding to John 10:4: "And when he putteth forth his own sheep, he goeth before them, and the sheep follow him: for they know his voice." She was compelled to make herself useful. She offered her services to the captain. He humored her by asking for a fresh Bible verse every day. She cheerfully obliged. But soon Amy was part of a Bible class with the other missionaries and a few passengers. One passenger she actually seemed to pull to Christ. Surely one soul was worth a thousand such trips, although she remembered not to credit the conversion to her one "hammer blow."

In the Mediterranean Sea, the ship was battered by a vicious storm. It seemed almost a test from God. Some of her fellow passengers were trembling in terror.

She was at total peace! The freedom from fear made it seem a very fruitful voyage. Besides, there were few things Amy liked better than the companionship of other devout Christians. She marveled at that one-hundred-mile wonder, the Suez Canal. In April, the SS *Valetta* sailed into the Indian Ocean toward Ceylon. Nearly all voyages to the Far East stopped at this British colony.

"Land ho!" yelled one of the crewmen.

The distant horizon sprouted a dark bluish halo, which gradually transformed into a cap of green that grew into a lush landscape. They anchored in the harbor at Colombo, the capital city of the island of Ceylon. The English, who ruled that part of the world, talked as if there was no difference between Ceylon and its giant neighbor, India. But Amy was sure they were quite distinct. The people of Ceylon were predominantly Buddhists. The Indians were Hindus and to a lesser degree Muslims.

Tall, swaying palms flagged the sky everywhere above a city that seemed a great garden. The air was hot and humid and heavy. The pungent odors of spices and sweat flooded Amy's nose. Shouting merchants, dinging bells, buzzing flies, and hammering shoemakers assaulted her ears. Movement was everywhere: people, pastries, sacks of grain. And such a kaleidoscope of colors: dark skins, ivory teeth, glittering jewelry, enameled boxes, combs, silks, brocades, merchants wrapped in various bright colors. Many of the men were half naked with only their waists covered. The missionaries were whisked off in rickshaws pulled by men in harness, like draft animals. They rode to a mission where they were served breakfast.

Everyone at the mission made much of Keswick, and it seemed that many knew of the Keswick meetings. Amy was known as the "Keswick missionary." She was so emboldened, she played the organ and led the others in one of her favorite Keswick hymns. Inspired by the words of dying Samuel Rutherford, "Glory, glory dwelleth in Immanuel's land," the hymn was called "The Sands of Time Are Sinking."

Amy next played another Keswick favorite, Frances Havergal's "Like a River Glorious" and its promise of Isaiah's "perfect peace." How relaxed Amy was. Yes, a life of trusting Christ did give perfect peace. The Lieschings, correspondents with the Carmichael family, were there in Colombo, too, to express the hope Amy would join their Heneratgoda Village Mission in Ceylon.

Somewhat startled by their interest, which seemed eerily prophetic, she boarded the *Sutlej*, a ship far inferior to the *Valetta*. Because Amy was not going on to India, Britain's "crown jewel," she had to change ships. The squalor aboard the *Sutlej* was no worse than the conditions she had suffered in Manchester. She conquered the insufferable smallness of her compartment by sleeping on deck. In the minute cabin, she hung a piece of paper on which she had written Paul's "In every thing give thanks." As usual Amy offered her services to the captain. He was a troubled man, and to Amy's amazement, her conversations with him restored his faith and brought him to Christ.

Again Amy reminded herself not to take credit for the one "hammer blow." Still, she instructed the captain and arrived in Shanghai with her heart singing. How many people were waiting for a witness? She urged the captain not to backslide and left with the other missionaries to go to the China Inland Mission. Awaiting her there was a letter from Barclay Buxton. He was ecstatic that she was joining him and his wife. They had recently lost several workers, and in their province they had to evangelize more than one thousand villages! Mr. Buxton assured Amy that he cared nothing about denominational differences, even quoting the Keswick motto: "All one in Christ Jesus."

The morning of April 25, 1893, on the steamer *Yokohama Maru*, Amy arrived in Shimonoseki, Japan. The Sea of Japan was known for its calmness, yet the steamer was caught in a storm in the Tsushima Strait and could not anchor in the harbor. Amy had to be lowered into a heaving tug to make it to shore. There a missionary from the Japanese Evangelical Band was supposed to pick her up. But all she encountered were gesticulating, chattering Japanese. What were they supposed to do with this young woman, so frail and pale? Amy could not help but laugh at the absurdity of her circumstances. Finally, an American was attracted to the frantic situation. He surmised that her contact had been waylaid by the storm and had a rickshaw take her to a local mission.

It was at the mission that Amy had an experience reminiscent of the great David Livingstone's when he first arrived at a mission in Africa: The various missionary societies were bickering with each other, and the missionaries squabbled among themselves. "All one in Christ" seemed a foreign concept to them.

Shimonoseki was the westernmost town on the island of Honshu, by far the largest island of Japan. Shimonoseki had more than one hundred thousand people. Nearby was the giant city of Hiroshima. Much of the island was mountainous, so the inhabitants crowded along the lowlands bordering the Sea of Japan. A seemingly endless series of small towns hugged the northern coast of Honshu, which stretched for 150 miles to Matsuye. One never seemed really away from a town, and in that way Japan seemed like southern England. The people cultivated rice and vegetables to eat with the bream and mackerel they netted from the sea.

Christianity had been introduced to Japan as early as 1549 by the Jesuit missionary Francis Xavier. At first, the Japanese feudal warlords—the shoguns—were receptive, allowing several hundred thousand Japanese to be converted from their peculiarly lifeless mix of Buddhism and Shintoism. But the shoguns soon became alarmed at the rapid conversions. By 1612, they looked the other way as Christians were massacred. By 1624, foreigners were not permitted to remain in Japan at all.

"By the second half of the nineteenth century," one missionary explained, "the pendulum had swung back the other way, and now Japan madly embraces Western traditions."

Feudalism had been replaced by a powerful emperor. Education, industry, the military, politics, and every other aspect of Japanese life seemed to be in the process of being Westernized. In 1872, primary education was mandated. By 1879, the university system was started for higher education. Christianity was allowed, but the tolerance was not easy to understand. Shintoism was the state religion, which emphasized worship of the divine emperor and the racial superiority of the Japanese.

The current political system, with its Western-style cabinet, a prime minister, and a privy council, was an invention of the emperor and his advisers. The new constitution, based on extensive research in Europe and America, was initiated in 1889. Any resemblance to a democracy or a republic was an illusion. The emperor and his advisers were in complete control.

But all this speculation scarcely affected an English missionary or the average Japanese. And at the moment Amy had to learn the language. Long ago the Chinese taught the Japanese their method of writing by characters, or ideograms. Each Chinese character represented one particular word. Eventually, the Japanese began using Chinese characters as phonetic symbols, each representing one syllable.

The sounds of the Japanese language had only five vowels and nineteen consonants. Some sounds had no English equivalents. Their *r* was a result of flapping the tip of the tongue far forward in the mouth. Their *f*, produced with the lips not touching each other, was to Amy almost indistinguishable from their *h*. Some syllables were emphasized in Japanese by differing the pitch or tone, but the language was not a highly complex tonal language like Chinese.

But the more Amy learned of the Japanese language, the more confounded she was by its complexity. Japanese vocabulary was very imprecise regarding the "visual." For example, the word *aoi* meant either "blue," "green," or "pale." On the other hand, Japanese was much more precise regarding sensations of hearing and touching. It seemed every circumstance had its own unique word.

And then came the worst of all: Japanese grammar. The usual order of words in a sentence was subject, object, and verb. Modifiers usually preceded the words they modified. Nouns had neither gender nor number. No articles or prepositions, as known in the English language, were used. The verb had no number, no person, and no tense as understood by the British. Still, the use of the verb had to indicate whether the action was completed.

"It sounds so difficult," admitted Amy. "But surely, after I have a chance to practice, it will get easier."

SIX

Amy arrived in Matsuye on May 1, 1893. The town of about one hundred thousand people was buffered from the sea by a lagoon and an outer peninsula, although the gentle Sea of Japan was almost tideless anyway. Barclay Buxton and his family, though well intentioned, were unimpressed by Hudson Taylor's philosophy of missionary work and chose to live like colonialists. They resided in one of the town's largest houses, fully staffed by servants. The children had an English governess. They dressed in British clothing, and they ate potted meat and bread. They drank tea, but certainly not the weak Japanese variety.

When Amy first arrived and took up residence in the Buxtons' home, she, too, wore a proper English wardrobe. When the summer temperatures climbed into the nineties, she wore her cotton dresses. As fall approached and the air cooled, she wore warmer clothing like her blue serge dress. When the winter air had a bite in it, she added a light coat. And if January was especially bitter, her tweed coat and fur gloves were available.

Buxton had converted a Shinto temple into his Christian church. In spite of its promotion by the imperial government, Shintoism was not popular among the common Japanese. Buddhism was. But except for honoring the tradition of removing shoes, Buxton's church was undefiled by "foreignizing elements." Nevertheless, the charm of the Japanese way enthralled Amy. Their homes were all wood and paper with large sliding doors. Visible from all over the interior of the house was a spacious backyard, replete with dwarf trees, sparkling pools, and elaborate rock work. Cultivated all around Matsuye were mulberry, cypress, yew, box, holly, myrtle, peach, pear, and orange trees. Above the town was a remnant of old feudal days: a walled castle of pagoda design in blues, greens, purples, and browns. The hills were forested with beeches, willows, chestnuts, and conifers. Matsuye was so beautiful, one was tempted to lead a life of contemplation.

Amy moved into another part of Matsuye to live with two other missionaries and began to venture out among the Japanese. She loved the Buxtons and regarded Barclay Buxton as a man of Christ, but she could not agree with his aloofness from the Japanese. She was enchanted by Japan. From the very first day, she wrote page after page of dialogue on thin rice paper for her family, occasionally intended for the newsletter they still called *Scraps*. Her letters were often adorned with exquisite drawings. Once Amy sketched a kimonoed geisha girl strumming a stringed instrument like a guitar. The girl played only two notes but so gracefully it was mesmerizing. In many ways, Japanese customs proved the adage that less is more.

"But not so the elaborate complexity of their language," admitted Amy. "It so stumps my 'won't-work' brain, I must resort to hiring an interpreter!"

The young woman Misaki San became her interpreter. Misaki was a Christian and very affectionate, but this use of an interpreter seemed a real defeat for Amy. She had been inspired by stories about how the great, irrepressible Dr. Livingstone had run off to isolate himself with the Africans until he was fluent in Bechuana. But, for some reason, hiring an interpreter seemed to Amy what God wanted her to do. One of the most difficult features of the Japanese vocabulary was the enormous number of respectful words— "honorifics"—indicating status. Their proper use was absolutely necessary. Misaki San guided Amy through the endless maze of honorifics.

That summer her determination was tested. A man near her residence was said to be possessed by six "fox spirits." Amy had Misaki San take her to the man. The family resisted. They were strict Buddhists. They had no need of this Englishwoman's foreign superstition. Amy persisted. What was the harm? After all, the whole neighborhood had heard that the man was nearly dead. The man's wife agonized, then shrugged. She led Amy up a ladder to an attic room, where an old man was bound with cords to the crossbeams. Little mounds of powder smoldered on his chest, designed to drive off the spirits. Several had burned him badly. The Lord's words came to Amy, "In my name shall they cast out devils." The words could have been etched in stone. Amy felt enormous power.

She had Misaki San translate, "In the name of the Lord Jesus we will cast out the fox spirits!"

With that announcement, the man writhed and began to rage. He cursed and screamed and struggled to get loose. This disturbed the man's wife and the other Japanese so much that they quickly ushered Amy and her interpreter downstairs. Amy was mortified. What had she done? Had she humiliated her Savior? But suddenly she was seized by courage.

Calmly she asked Misaki San to translate to the man's wife, "We are returning to our house to pray to our Lord Jesus, the living God. Our God will conquer. Please let us know when the fox spirits are gone."

And pray Amy did.

One hour later, a man arrived at the house. With a smile that seemed a mile wide, Misaki San said, "He says the old man is well. The fox spirits are gone."

Hallelujah!

When Amy and Misaki San visited the house, the old man was tranquil. In complete control again, he presented Amy with a branch of pomegranate in flower. Did the old man know this orange-red was the hue of the fox? Perhaps not, but Japan seemed to flower for Amy now. Japan was a bouquet: blossoms of cherry, plum, azalea, peony, lotus, and yet to come were the chrysanthemums.

Because Amy had a substantial history with mill girls back in Ireland, she decided to approach the factory girls of Matsuye. *Will the girls come?* wondered Amy. They toiled from five o'clock in the morning until six at night, with one day off every ten. To her astonishment, she drew eighty girls to a meeting! They were hungry for something different; she gave them Christ.

In August, Amy went up into the mountains. The missionaries were holding a consecration meeting at Mount Arima. Amy needed such a meeting. She had met a young Christian man who did not disguise his matrimonial interests in her. It was not the first time for Amy. After all, she was literate and perky and not homely at all. A few serious men had eyed her as a wife. But somehow she did not feel the need for a husband. She consoled herself with words of Thomas à Kempis: "True peace of heart can be found only by resisting the passions, not by yielding to them." At Arima she slipped inside a cave to pray for many hours. Years later she recalled:

> *The devil kept on whispering, "It's all right now, but what about afterwards? You are going to be very lonely." And he painted pictures of loneliness—I can see them still. And I turned to my God in a kind of desperation and said, "Lord, what can I do? How can I go on to the end?" And He said, "None of them that trust in Me shall be desolate."*[1]

Newly consecrated, Amy returned to Matsuye determined to evangelize. She was more and more uncomfortable remaining so English. She began to eat more of the Japanese food. At first it was repugnant to her. Much of what they ate was raw fish; various, unidentified eggs; seaweed; sea slugs; and a very challenging-to-the-palate paste of fish. Nevertheless, Amy persisted. It was not all alien. Rice and chicken seemed dear old friends after eating a slurry that reeked of too-ripe fish.

Her English clothing began to bother her, too. One late fall day dawned unseasonably cold, and Amy wore her tweed coat and fur gloves. That morning, through her translator, Misaki San, Amy explained the gospel to an old woman who was very ill:

So I spoke and Misaki San translated, and our hearts prayed most earnestly. "Lord Jesus, help her. O help her to understand and open her heart to Thee now."

She seemed to be just about to turn to Him in faith when she suddenly noticed my hands. . . . "What are these?" she asked, stretching out her hand and touching mine.

She was old and ill and easily distracted. . . . I went home, took off my English clothes, put on my Japanese kimono, and never again, I trust, risked so very much for the sake of so little.[2]

The color of Amy's kimono was blue. The elegant dress was trimmed in green, and down the left lapel she sewed in Japanese symbols "God is Love."

In November, the month of the chrysanthemums, she and Misaki San visited from house to house, a venture that steeled the nerves. One could never be sure of a warm reception. Once she and Misaki San virtually barged in on a man who was in his Buddhist devotions. Yet he was polite. After all, this honorable young woman was dressed as a Japanese. She was said to eat raw fish and sea slugs, too. But he was cautious.

"If what you say is true," he said to Amy after she presented the Good News, "then you are an angel from heaven to us. But that is all preaching. Can you show us you live in Christ?"

So there was the challenge for evangelizing: Could the evangelist show that she was living in Christ? She became less and less privileged, more and more like the common Japanese. She traveled in third class. She stayed in their hotels, sleeping on the floor in their communal bedrooms under blankets. This lifestyle obligated her to a great loss of privacy. Emboldened by her submission to their ways, many people on the street stared at her. They would even try to touch her. It was innocent enough.

Each time before she left Matsuye, Amy prayed fervently for the Lord to guide her. In November, she decided to visit the village of Hirose up in the nearby hills. On her first venture, a young woman was converted, a silk weaver. By this time, Amy had learned that converts in Japan were not ostracized as they were in some other countries. If a young woman was converted, she could still remain with her family. In December, two more were saved in Hirose. Two weeks later, four were saved, the last on Amy's twenty-sixth birthday, December 16, 1893.

In January 1894, eight others were converted on a trip to Hirose. By this time, all the missionaries in Matsuye were praying with Amy. It had escaped no one's attention that, on each trip, the number of converts doubled. But the miraculous expansion soon ended. Perhaps the missionaries assumed too much. Or perhaps it was Amy's health. By January, she was suffering agonizing headaches. In fact, during the conversion of the eight, she wrote her mother, she could scarcely think from the pain. After she returned to Matsuye, she was in bed for a week. Sometimes her eyes refused to see!

" 'Japanese head,' " pronounced Mr. Buxton.

"What is 'Japanese head'?" asked Amy in alarm.

"I don't think anyone really knows," he said in a puzzled voice, then added brightly, "but it's not permanent. That is, if you leave Japan."

"Leave Japan!"

"Don't be upset, Miss Carmichael. Perhaps it will go away on its own," he said unconvincingly.

Amy was depressed. She had given up on the Japanese language. She recorded with exasperation in her notes that the translation for the English expression "I like fine weather better than wet" was constructed in Japanese as "rain of coming down bad honorable weather than even good honorable weather of days of side good is."[3] How could she ever learn it? And now she had "Japanese head," a malady untreatable except by flight!

In May, Barclay Buxton suggested sending Amy to a China Inland Mission doctor in Shanghai. Perhaps the doctor there could help Amy. But Amy resisted. She had been in Japan only one year. A worried Mr. Buxton left Amy to her own devices when he departed Japan to take his family on leave. Almost immediately, Amy heard that the missionary in Imaichi was ill and needed assistance. She rushed to help. Imaichi was a village north of Tokyo on the other side of the great island of Honshu. Perhaps the different climate would improve her health. Amy decided to travel by ship. She finally arrived in Imaichi but in worse shape than the missionary she had come to replace.

When she was well enough again to travel, she returned to Matsuye, aware that now she must go to China. She had the joy of attending the baptism of some of her converts before she left. She lamented her outcome in Japan:

> The crossed endeavour, earnest purpose foiled,
>> The strange bewilderment of good work spoiled,
> The clinging weariness, the inward strain,
>> Will not the End explain?[4]

In July, Amy bought a round-trip ticket and sailed for Shanghai. The parting was painful. Everyone pretended she would be back in six weeks. But who believed it? Amy felt as tragically temporary as a butterfly. On board, she opened a note from Misaki San. "I know you will miss me," Misaki San wrote bluntly, "but Christ is sitting by you now, so please talk with Him to forget me."[5] It was a brave note, but Amy knew that Misaki loved her like a sister and never wanted her to forget her.

The doctor in Shanghai recommended that Amy go to Chefoo in northeast China. His reason was that Chefoo was not only cooler but had a dry winter. But suitable accommodations at Chefoo didn't materialize. Meanwhile, Amy had an overwhelming desire to go to Ceylon! Was such a detour possible? She prayed that this was not God's will. People would think her erratic wanderings those of a madwoman. She went to the senior missionary in Shanghai, William Cooper. He did not discourage her at all but prayed with her. But her doubts remained.

Amy wrote to a very young missionary friend at the mission the Lieschings ran in Ceylon. In the meantime, she discovered that passage to Ceylon was actually cheaper than traveling to Chefoo. That startling fact was a great relief to her. At least the trip didn't seem so crazy. Psalm 77:19 expressed her feeling so perfectly that she wrote it in the flyleaf of her Bible: "Thy way is in the sea, and thy path in the great waters, and thy footsteps are not known." She wouldn't wait for a response. On July 28, she was aboard ship and on her way to Ceylon.

Amy's health was still shaky. Battling a fever, she arrived in Colombo on August 17. Her young friend was there to meet her. Amy found to her utter amazement that the Lieschings had both succumbed to malaria. They were dead! The three rudderless young women remaining in the mission prayed fervently for help. The date they had beseeched God for a leader was July 14.

Amy gasped, "Why, I had my overpowering urge to go to Ceylon just after that!"

Though as a green missionary she scarcely regarded herself as a leader, Amy went happily to the mission, pushing aside the worry that she was not likely to recover her health in a malarial jungle. Ceylon was ancient like Japan but less populated. Although local cultivation had driven elephants and tigers back into the deeper jungle, leopards had a nasty habit of adapting to civilization. Snakes, too, stubbornly abounded. Amy chose to see the rose among the thorns:

> *There, in the bright sunshine like a bit of blue flame among white flowers, the tiny chirping thing [a hummingbird] flitted to and fro. Now poising itself on a spray of shining blossom, diving its curved beak deep into each fragrant flower, never marring a petal, now fluttering in and*

out of the bush on which they grow, its clear electric tinting showing well against the green, and now for a moment motionless, half hidden in the whiteness, a little living jewel in a snowdrift of white flowers.[6]

The Ceylonese people near the mission practiced Buddhism and spoke Sinhalese. The three young missionary women were of a mixed descent called "Burgher." Their ancestors were both Dutch and Ceylonese. Of course, the young women were perfectly fluent in Sinhalese. The tenor of their lives was revealed to Amy one day when a man barged into the mission house. He was the husband of a woman who had recently been converted. He waved a murderous-looking machete. Two of the young women knelt on the floor, closed their eyes, and prayed. Amy followed suit. What faith! At last she could not resist. She had to steal a glance. There he still stood—with the machete overhead!

She squeezed her eyes closed and implored *God, Be merciful unto me, O God, be merciful unto me: for my soul trusteth in Thee: yea, in the shadow of Thy wings will I make my refuge until these calamities be overpast."*

When Amy next looked up, the man was gone!

Letters from outside unsettled Amy. First, there were letters from Misaki San, whose courage had broken down. How she missed Amy! Then there was a letter from Barclay Buxton. Imagine his shock to hear that Amy had left Japan while he was on leave! "What a void you left!" he lamented. Mr. Buxton's consternation paled in comparison to the sentiments expressed in a letter she received from Robert Wilson. He was much disturbed by Amy's detour to Ceylon. After all, she was a missionary of the Keswick Mission Committee. He warned her not to officially join any mission house. This upset Amy more than anything. And she wrote him and her mother again that this effort in Ceylon was of God. She had only followed His calling.

In all the muddle of activity—some upsetting, some uplifting—Amy had scarcely noticed how much her health had improved. But hadn't she been "Sent of the King" as she recorded in the flyleaf of her Bible? She saw a doctor. He warned her that under no circumstances should she try to return to Japan. She had just about resolved to write Matsuye to request that the rest of her belongings be sent to Heneratgoda, although it broke her heart to think of how Misaki San would receive the news. Perhaps the D.O.M. didn't want her to officially attach herself with this mission, but Amy was quite pleased with Ceylon. Even the Sinhalese language was coming to her. Surely the Lord wanted her there.

So the letter that she received November 27, 1894, hit her very hard.

SEVEN

Robert Wilson had suffered a stroke!

Within an hour of receiving the news, Amy had explained to her friends at the mission what had happened and had departed for Colombo. On December 15, 1894, the day before her twenty-seventh birthday, Amy was met by her mother in London. By December 21, she was at Broughton Grange comforting the D.O.M., who by now was almost seventy years old. Already he was recovering, but Amy had no regrets about her hasty return. She would stay with him at Broughton Grange.

"You must write about your experiences," urged the D.O.M.

"Oh, but I have. I've written letters home, some in the form of the newsletter *Scraps*. I've written letters to the Keswick magazine, too."

But soon she was synthesizing it all into a book. She even had her own line drawings for it. Robert Wilson's son William added some appropriate sketches of his own. After several months it was accepted for publication by the Marshall Brothers of London. The title would be *From Sunrise Land*, the intent a prayer for the heathen of Japan. Amy did little else that winter, except attend to Robert Wilson and ponder her future. In Japan she had failed as a missionary on two fronts. Her health was too fragile, and her facility for the language was lacking. But her stay in Ceylon had given her new hope. Perhaps there were places she could stay without being sickly. Perhaps there were languages she could master.

A letter from a friend in Bangalore, India, intrigued her—especially because the friend was a sister at the Church of England's Zenana Hospital and knew medicine. Amy noted:

> She said the climate was healthy, delightful, in fact; it might be possible to live there even if China and Japan and the tropics were taboo. . . .[1]

It pleased her mother, Robert Wilson, and all the other Carmichaels and Wilsons, too, for they had sensed that Amy was determined to "go forth" again. At least the locale in India appeared to be a congenial place. The British maintained a huge presence in India. And the climate seemed the kind that would not destroy Amy's health. So Amy agreed, although this time she received no specific "call" from the Lord. Bangalore was simply a convenient place to go.

For the first time in a very long time, Amy remembered that the dear Reverend Mr. Beatty of Millisle had a brother who had been a missionary to India. During one of the missionary's furloughs, he and his wife lived near the Carmichaels in Millisle. On Sunday afternoons, the wife regaled neighborhood children with stories of India. Amy—a young child at the time—was so fired by them that she didn't want to leave the woman's side. She didn't want the stories to end. But her childhood was so rich that the stories had become lost in her great treasury of stories.

As usual, Robert Wilson, the D.O.M., could facilitate almost anything. In May, Amy was given an interview in London with the Church of England's Zenana Mission Society. By July 26, they had notified the Keswick Mission Committee that Amy was accepted for duty in Bangalore. At a meeting the next day in the large tent at Keswick, Amy expressed her gratitude and said her farewells. Her departure was yet several months off. In the meantime, whether she liked it or not, she was instructed in the ways of India.

Because it was Britain's crown jewel, it seemed everyone had an opinion of India, even though its immensity defied generalities. In size, it was twenty times greater than the British Isles. The land teemed with mountains, jungles, plateaus, yawning rivers, and arid deserts. India's population—an estimated three hundred million inhabitants—was ten times greater than Great Britain's. The subcontinent was home to many languages and religions. The suffering in India was overwhelming. Several men sought to explain Indian politics to Amy. Britain, the great world power, had controlled India since the 1600s, over the centuries steadily increasing their influence. But in 1885, educated Hindus organized a nationalist movement, embodied in the Indian National Congress. Intrigue increased. Even now, the British were encouraging the formation of a Muslim League. This, reasoned the devious British, would split the native effort into bickering between Hindus and Muslims.

Then dreadful news swept the Keswick community. The Robert Stewarts, whom Amy was going to accompany to the province of Fukien back in 1892, had all been murdered in that very province! That saddened everyone and reminded most of all her mother and Robert Wilson just how dangerous Amy's missionary work was. But on October 11, 1895, she once again endured the heartbreaking good-byes and sailed for the East, aboard a mediocre steamer in second class.

Her destination was Madras, a port on the southeast coast of India. From there she would travel about 150 miles west into the highlands to reach Bangalore. Bangalore rested on the Mysore Plateau at an elevation of three thousand feet. The great city of more than one million inhabitants was known for its mild, dry climate. To grasp the enormity of India, Amy had only to remember that Bangalore was more than nine hundred miles from Calcutta to the northeast and nearly twelve hundred miles from Delhi to the north. On November 8, the ship anchored at Madras, and she disembarked. Naked poverty raged. Families were living on the streets, the better-off ones lying on mats made of palm leaves instead of the bare dirt. Virtually naked, many of these natives nevertheless wore bracelets and anklets with rings dangling from their noses and ears.

Madras had once been the focus of British power. Enormous Italianate buildings displayed massive columns and arches near the harbor. Although British power had shifted mainly to Calcutta, Bombay, and Delhi, Madras was still very important for the administration of southern India. Amy discovered that much of India had been annexed by the British outright. Although her destination, Bangalore, was in one of the native states, the entire eastern half of southern India was ruled by the British through subdivisions called "districts."

Amy soon learned that all European men were called *sahibs* and all European women were *memsahibs*. In every instance, native Indians deferred to a sahib or a memsahib. If a sahib or memsahib wanted something at a shop, the shopkeeper would abandon a native customer without hesitation. "Memsahib!" he would say, giving the palms-together salute of respect. Even on a crowded street, a native had better not brush against a sahib or memsahib. European travelers were whisked to a hotel and offered curried chicken and rice. Not so with an Indian. A native Indian was insane to think he might ever dine in English clubs or ride a horse on their polo greens.

From Madras, Amy should have taken a train west to Bangalore. But the Church Mission Society official in Madras, Mr. Arden, asked if Amy would stay with his daughter Mary while he visited an outstation at Ootacamund—which they all called "Ooty"—with his other daughter, Maud. Of course, Amy agreed.

November was the rainiest month of the year in Madras, with many drenching downpours. Still, she was assured, the temperature reached only about eighty-five degrees in the afternoon, compared to one hundred degrees in the summer; and in December, the monsoon rain abruptly tapered off. In the week or so before Mr. Arden and Maud left, Amy learned much more about India.

"Don't you know the apostle Thomas came to India right after the Resurrection?" chirped the daughters. "He may have gone to China, too, but he returned to India before he died. He was martyred at Malabar. He is buried at

Mylapore just outside Madras."

The daughters pointed out the very spot south of the Aydras River. The thought of one of the Lord's disciples—even his cast-off shell—being so nearby was stunning. India was so rich in history. The daughters were not ignorant about later Christianity in India. "Christians arrived at Kerala from Syria in the sixth century. At Kerala the Christians even retain a Syriac order of service. Of course, in 1542, Francis Xavier, the Jesuit from Portugal, arrived at Goa. Protestants quickly followed suit. Both the Dutch and English established themselves in the Bengal area by the early 1600s. Of course you know all about the Baptist missionary William Carey, who worked near Calcutta and translated the Bible tirelessly into every language of India."

The daughters also breezily discussed the religion of the Hindus. "Their behavior is far simpler than their beliefs," said one. "They don't eat meat, especially their sacred cows, although they do eat eggs and fish. And they marry within their own caste. Probably few of them actually understand the complexities of their religion."

"Their caste system is very old," volunteered the other. "Originally there were four main castes—with another group of people excluded completely: the 'Untouchables.'"

"They believe in being reincarnated as another life form. The catch is that one can be reborn into a higher caste only if one stays strictly within that caste in this life. So you see it is very hard to get a Hindu to 'break' a caste. They are gambling with their souls."

"Yet there seems no hope for the Untouchables."

Except the hope of Christ, thought Amy.

Finally, one of the daughters said reproachfully, "You have been here for a week, and you haven't said one word about the Lord Jesus Christ."[2]

Amy was flooded with shame. Later she wrote:

It was true I had not said one word. The girls were like butterflies, pretty and dressy, and I had been shy of them both. I had no idea they cared for the things of Christ and had thought I should wait until I knew them better before speaking of these things. . . . The friend who had led them to Christ had said I would be coming by the next boat and that I would help them. So all the time I had been thinking of them as pretty butterflies they were really hungry lambs. . .[oh,] the shame of that hour. But we have a forgiving Lord. He gave us a wonderful time together. We rode together, read together, prayed together. We became fast friends.[3]

The first week in December, Amy was aboard a train rumbling west into the highlands. Rice paddies were replaced by fields of millet carved into tropical forests. Usually the countryside was peopled only in rough huts or drab mud-brick buildings. But Hindu temples of all sizes were a frequent sight. Muslim mosques, flagged by their distinctive Byzantine minarets, could be seen less often. Rarest of all was the sight of an enormous palace, so Italian she could have been in Rome.

At Bangalore Amy's train was met by the friend who had written her about the healthful climate. Almost immediately Amy was confined to bed with a raging fever.

"Oh, my bones ache so," she told the doctor at the mission hospital.

"That's Madras for you," he said sourly. "You've picked up dengue fever."

No! Dengue fever was also known as "breakbone" fever. Amy now knew why. She ached everywhere. The only good thing about dengue fever was that the severe pain ran its course in one week. However, several weeks were required to fully recover. It was during this recovery period that Amy had her twenty-eighth birthday. She was lying in a lounge chair by an open window. No one knew it was her birthday, yet suddenly a garland of flowers flew through the window to land on her lap.

"Why did you do that?" she called out the window.

"I don't know," answered the puzzled thrower.

Amy was quickly discovering that these Bangalore missionaries were the "verandah" type that the great Dr. Livingstone had held in such low regard. They spent a great deal of time enjoying the status of being British colonials. They hired natives—usually Muslims—to teach in their schools instead of mastering the languages and delivering the Good News themselves. They sat about, prattling and complaining and speculating.

In Japan, Amy had mulled over the question of whether Mr. Buxton of Matsuye was too much in love with British ways to be a good missionary, but Barclay Buxton was far superior to these missionaries in Bangalore. At least he had mastered Japanese so he could deliver the Good News.

The missionaries in Bangalore often gossiped about a missionary named Thomas Walker. He was a bit of a renegade, working far to the south, down in the hot lowlands of Tinnevelly.

Yet the missionaries quoted Mr. Walker so often that Amy concluded that they really respected him. Amy tried to fathom this Thomas Walker. He sounded like a scholarly but very opinionated old person, who was cranky besides.

One of the other young women at the Bangalore mission came to Amy because she had heard that Amy wrote articles for mission magazines. The young woman said, "I sent a story to our mission magazine in England about a young Muslim girl who very much wanted to convert, but her parents prevented it. They wrote back that the ending was too discouraging. Should I invent a happy ending?"

"Heavens no, you mustn't change the truth to please anyone!"

This righteous attitude did not endear Amy to some of the other missionaries. And they let her know it. But Amy accepted the hostility as whittling away at herself, a process she welcomed. And no complacency among others was going to keep her from serving Christ. As much as Amy had loved Misaki San, this time she was determined to remove the language barrier between herself and the local people. This zeal found her a vocation; she would be the one missionary at the hospital who spoke Tamil, one of two common languages in the province of Mysore. *Tamil will prove more valuable*, thought Amy, *because the other language, Cannarese, is more provincial.*

Tamil was some kind of ancient, classical language for southern India, similar to the way that Latin formed the foundation for the European Romance languages. If Amy could master Tamil, she reasoned, she could make herself understood throughout southern India, even northernmost Ceylon. Perhaps it would also ease the learning of other southern Indian languages. She tried to ignore the raised eyebrows of other missionaries when Tamil was mentioned; apparently it was *the* most difficult language on the Indian subcontinent!

Still, Amy began to study Tamil six hours a day. The hospital even provided her regular lessons with a native language teacher, called a *moonshee*. It was a comfort when she first realized Tamil's symbols—in fact, all the languages of India—were written horizontally from left to right, like English. Words were separated from each other by a space, too.

But the alphabet!

"It is rather different from what I'm used to seeing," she volunteered lamely to her moonshee.

"Ah! You see Tamil was originally incised into palm leaves with a stylus." He noticed her blank look. "In contrast to the northern languages of India that are written on paper with ink."

"Well, actually, I meant it is different from the English alphabet. How many vowels are there?"

"Only twelve."

"So many?"

"You see the Tamil alphabet is phonetic. Long and short sounds then must have their symbols. Yes, you have more letters to learn, but once you master the sounds of the alphabet, you master the sound of any word in Tamil." He added wryly, "Unlike English."

"How many consonants are there?" she went on doggedly.

"Consonants and vowel-consonant combinations," he corrected. "Only thirty-two."

"So I must learn forty-eight symbols in all?"

"Well, there are some sounds of the alphabet that require more than one symbol."

So Amy attacked Tamil. Some variations in Tamil were obvious, even pleasing. For example, the long and short *a*'s differed only by an added squiggle, as did the two *o*'s. But the two *i*'s were completely different. And symbols for some sounds were exasperating. *Kau* required three symbols. And learning the alphabet was only the first step. She knew no vocabulary, no grammar. Still, she had once experienced something mystical with the Sinhalese spoken in Ceylon. She had prayed fervently for help, and the Sinhalese symbols that looked like so many worm tracks within a very short time became an alphabet.

"Oh, Lord, please help me with this Tamil language," she prayed. "With Your help I can do anything."

Such a severe regimen demanded a release of tension. Even though Bangalore had a rather peculiar two seasons of rain, in summer and fall, the rainfall was much less than along the coast, and the temperatures were much milder. There were only a few days when outdoor activity was marred by the weather.

The attitude of some missionaries that they were in India to protect British interests disturbed Amy very much. But she had to admit she herself did not feel very British. She never had. She didn't feel particularly Irish, either. Not even Scottish. She was, in the haunting words of Moses, "a stranger in a strange land," no matter where she went. Her only true home was sometime in the future: with God. As she learned more and more of the British rule of India, she became certain the British also had a caste system. It was impossible to miss. At the highest level were the government officials—and their wives, of course. At the next level were the professional army officers. Below them were the businessmen. And at the lowest rung were the common soldiers. And where were the missionaries?

"We are the 'Untouchables,' " confided one not-very-discreet missionary. "Most British don't want us here. We interfere too much with their very pleasant lives."

Not enough, thought Amy.

A letter from Keswick cautioned her not to "cool." "Look to Him to keep you burning and shining."[4] Her old friend from Manchester, Ella Crossley, visited her early in 1896 and gushed over how well Amy spoke Tamil. But Amy was unhappy with her comfort—yes, even her wild pony rides—in Bangalore. The atmosphere was far too congenial. Once again she had spurned a marriage proposal. And the sad truth was that the large staff of missionaries was converting almost no one! When she got a chance to go out to Ooty for a meeting of people from the field missions, she jumped at it.

It was there she finally met Thomas Walker of Tinnevelly. His wife was there, too, a very pleasant woman.

EIGHT

Thomas Walker was not much older than thirty-five, with jet black hair. He was so fiercely concentrated and humorless he seemed tedious to Amy. He was going to speak at the meeting, and she was glad she had brought her Tamil language books with her. His talk would probably be insufferably dull. But it wasn't. She thanked him afterward.

"I see you're studying Tamil," he said, glaring at the books in her hands.

"Yes," she cried enthusiastically, "and I long for the chance to live among the natives—in a mud hut preferably—and to learn the language directly from their lips."

"That method won't work at all," he said brusquely.

"I suppose you know a better way?" she asked, trying to smile.

"Yes, I do, young lady. You must come out to Tinnevelly, where Tamil is the first language of the natives, but not to live in a hut! I will personally instruct you."

She didn't answer. Confused, she went off by herself and sat under a great tree. She mustn't waste time brooding. For a long time she had been practicing the simple mysticism of Brother Lawrence as revealed in his tiny classic, *The Practice of the Presence of God. If one tried always to please God, one would know God's will*, she reminded herself.

Amy opened her Tamil grammar book. Suddenly, she felt a Presence, a Listener. It was He. Amy realized she was to listen *with* Him. *"The voice of thy brother's blood crieth unto me from the ground"* was what came into Amy's mind as she listened. The book of Hebrews had expanded on that ancient cry from Genesis: "And to Jesus the mediator of the new covenant, and to the blood of sprinkling, that speaketh better things than that of Abel. See that ye refuse not him that speaketh." Time seemed to stop for Amy. Yet when she finally arose, she realized she had been sitting under the tree for hours.

"Here in Ooty I'm not in the real India at all," she murmured.

Every Indian in Ooty served a European. The truth was that Ooty itself was very British. One would never have known that in India the British were outnumbered one thousand to one by the native Indians or even that the sacred cows numbered tens of millions. With Simla, Darjeeling, Muree, and Naini Tal, Ooty was one of the acceptable "hot weather" retreats. Every place she had been, in fact, was insufferably British. Ooty was so British that "the right sort of people" assembled regularly to "ride to the hounds." Yes, they even maintained a pack of the very finest foxhounds, imported from England. Their quarry was a jackal, which served well enough as a substitute for a fox.

Bangalore was little better than Ooty. So on November 30, 1896, Amy, now almost twenty-nine, left Bangalore for Tinnevelly. She left the highlands, too. She traveled by train first to Madras, then south to the port of Trichendur, then nearly forty miles up the muddy Tambaravarni River to Tinnevelly. This low country would be much hotter and much more humid than Bangalore—more like Madras. It seemed a plain of silver with all its rice paddies. Palms stuck up here and there and were an important source of matting and the food starch sago. Tinnevelly was not as remote as Amy had imagined. The rail service went even beyond the town, farther into the interior. Tinnevelly and Palamcottah, its neighbor across the river, probably totaled fifty thousand natives. Myriad tiny villages added many thousands more.

Hindus outnumbered Muslims ten to one in southern India, so generally the missionaries encountered Hindus. Tinnevelly was very old with a long history—one thousand years at least—of strife between Hindus and Christians. The town not only had a very Anglican church, but a Catholic church with a bishop. Thomas Walker had been there eleven years. Just as Amy got to Tinnevelly, Thomas Walker did what everyone back in Bangalore had been gossiping about.

"I've resigned from the Church Mission Society," he told Amy as she arrived.

"But I've never belonged to it," she said. "I'm a Keswick missionary."

"Then we had best get on with your study of Tamil."

Thomas started her on not only basic grammar and vocabulary but Tamil classics. "Isn't this a waste of time," she asked, "when I could be studying the gospel and learning how to preach to them?"

"One must learn first to think like them."

"I'll do it then—against all logic!"

With a great deal of effort, one could read Tamil, even write it. Then eventually one's ear became tuned to understand it when spoken. But to speak it so that the natives could understand it was difficult. Tamil was a rich language, almost without equal. There was a special word for every shade of meaning. And besides the enormous vocabulary to master, there was an equally enormous reservoir of idioms to learn.

Amy learned that Thomas was under enormous pressure. His independence was much resented by other missionaries. In fact, she soon saw him come out of his study, white as a ghost, yet his eyes burning. He had just read a petition mounted against him—based on lies and jealousy—addressed to none other than the head of the Church of England, the archbishop of Canterbury!

So was it any wonder Thomas was occasionally cranky? He was by no means humorless. Once he wrote Amy a poem of which one stanza said:

Who plays the part of kinsman stern,
And makes my soul with anger burn?
It is that cold and taciturn
Annachie.[1]

Annachie was Tamil for "big brother." Yes, Walker was her bossy big brother. And Amy was the pesky little sister who would fight back!

Amy lived with the Walkers in a bungalow. Bungalows of a standard type had been built by the thousands all over India by the British, so the word *bungalow* had a very specific connotation. And, if one was European, one lived in a bungalow. First of all, the bungalow was within a nice-sized compound with walls and well set back from any dusty road. A verandah ran around the bungalow. The interior rooms were large, high ceilinged, and whitewashed. The plan was U-shaped, with bedrooms in the wings. The main part of the house had the living room facing the front, with the dining room behind. Behind the house were quarters for the servants. Also removed from the house was the kitchen, which generated odors and heat and attracted flies. About the only variation in the design of bungalows from one region of India to another was the type of roof: steep pitched in rainy country, flatter pitched in dry country. Furnishings were standard, too, with much rattan furniture on the verandahs, especially the ubiquitous lounge chairs. Flower beds were rarely cultivated. All decorative plants were in huge pots.

"Even you live in a bungalow and employ servants," Amy once said bluntly to Mr. Walker.

"The Indians expect us to live in a bungalow and give them jobs. You mustn't vary from the norm too much, Amy, or they will shun you completely."

As Amy continued to venture out, she discovered that Thomas Walker was quite right in crushing her desire to live among the Indians. Many of their customs appalled her. For latrines, the Hindus used nearby fields, gutters, alleys, even the floors of their own huts. The waste festered until an Untouchable carried it off. The injustice to Untouchables was staggering. These pariahs—one of every four Hindus—survived by being the sole caretakers of all waste and all death. The sole exception was the waste of the sacred cows. This the devout eagerly gathered.

Walker's resignation freed him and his wife to move. Pannaivilai was also on the Tambaravarni River, closer to the coast, but more in need of the gospel than Tinnevelly. The town was already pastored by the Reverend Isaac Abraham, a Christian native, but he needed help. The Walkers would rent a bungalow there.

In July 1897, the Walkers and Amy moved into a bungalow in Pannaivilai. Amy, who was always independent, began forming a "women's evangelical band." By 1898, at the age of thirty, she had gathered three very devout sisters. Leyal was the pastor's daughter; Sellamuthel, or Pearl, was a young woman with one arm; Ponnammal was a young widowed mother, the daughter-in-law of a convert.

Amy had adopted the native dress of the Hindus. The Hindu women wore one very long rectangle of coarse cotton cloth, a *sari*. The sari was wrapped securely around the waist twice, then brought up across the chest and over the left shoulder. The remainder hung down the back or was brought up to cover the head. The cotton cloth for the sari usually had one decorated border. Amy's sari was plain white at first. She did not oil her hair as the Indian women did. She tried it once, but the smell offended her. And she wore her bun higher on the back of her head than the Indian women did. In camp, she did not yet cover her head with the sari.

The few wealthy Indians wore silks and brocaded clothes, and the poor Indians dressed in simple cotton cloth; but the two main religious cultures could easily be distinguished. The Hindus' garments were "draped"; the Muslims wore "tailored" clothing. In contrast to the sari of Hindu women, the Muslim women wore tailored cotton tops called *choli* and bottoms that were loosely fitted but gathered tight at the ankles. They often added a cloth to cover the head, as well as to give the clothing a more draped appearance. And, of course, the face was covered by a veil.

Muslim men also wore tailored clothing, while Hindu men had a draped appearance. The Hindu man wore a *dhoti*, a rectangle of cotton cloth wrapped around the waist and securely tucked. He was often uncovered above the waist. Both Hindu and Muslim men usually wore turbans. All Indians wore sandals. Most wore a great deal of jewelry on their fingers, toes, noses, necks, wrists, and ankles. Wealthy men and women of southern India dripped jewelry of gold and precious stones, including lockets hanging from a heavy chain around their necks and an even heavier girdle around the waist. The women added much more adornment, featuring a lavish ornament on the forehead and a lesser bauble in the side of the nose. If they were married, the jewelry was to show how well the husband provided for them. If not, the jewelry was to show what a splendid dowry their father would provide. Even poor women were expected to be adorned with a minimum of two good-sized earrings, ten finger rings, ten toe rings, two necklaces, a dozen wrist bangles, and a dozen anklets—if not gold, silver; if not silver, good brass; if not brass, copper or steel; if not copper or steel, glass.

Amy tried to learn as many of the customs of the Hindus and Muslims as she could. Of the Hindu rites, it seemed that three were observed by all castes. Twelve days after birth, a Hindu baby was placed in a swinging cot above twelve candles, and the priest announced the baby's name. A second rite was marriage. The first marriage for a man was almost always arranged. But if he later became wealthy, he could add wives of his own choice—as many as he could afford. Of course, no woman could have two husbands! The third rite was at death. The Hindus believed the soul, trapped in the skull, could be released only by sacred fire. So they burned their dead, making sure the skull was burned up or broken open. Three days later, they scattered the ashes into a river.

Amy was surprised at how many rites the Muslims had taken from the Jews. It seemed the only things the Muslims couldn't eat were blood and pork. Muslim boys also were circumcised, although not before the age of seven. Seven days after birth, a baby was named in a ceremony called *aqiqah*. A Muslim man could have as many as four wives if he treated them as equals. For the dead, a service was given before burial. In the grave, the face of the corpse faced their holy city of Mecca. Two main sects of Muslims had evolved: Sunnites and Shiites. The Sunnites were more pious, more accommodating. The Shiites were mystics yet often quite violent.

Of course, Amy tried to comprehend their religious beliefs. The Muslims' faith she found rather Jewish but stripped of all the wonder, all the miraculous. It seemed a bare-boned desert religion. Hinduism she found too encompassing, too tolerant. The Hindus were all too ready to embrace Christ, but only to set Him beside their other one thousand gods. Their tolerances seemed as abominable as their intolerances. She knew that some of their horrible practices, such as burning widows and sacrificing baby girls, had been banned by the British. But she had heard rumors of some current temple practices that she prayed were not true.

Amy and her band were energetic. The locals already called Amy the "*Musal.*" Musal was Tamil for "rabbit." Amy was always moving, always busy. The natives called the entire band the "Starry Cluster." Amy and her band were admired. The natives honored people who adhered to religious vows. In the one-hundred-degree days of hot weather, the Starry Cluster evangelized around Pannaivilai. When the weather was cooler—except for June and October, when the monsoons brought the rain in buckets—they hired a driver to haul them farther afield in a wagon pulled by oxen. It was commonly called a bullock cart and was covered by folded-over mats. The women would camp in clearings, usually by a river, and venture forth from there to the surrounding villages.

It was not unpleasant to wait for the curious. Strains of Indian music teased Amy's ears. Sometimes it was classical music, called in southern India *karnatak*, which was considered less contaminated by Muslim influences than northern music. Typically it was performed by a drummer delivering the rhythm, a guitarist droning with a four-stringed *tanpura*, and for the melody either the peculiar stringed instrument called the *vina*, or the Western violin, or the flute. Often a vocalist joined the three instrumentalists. Amy never felt more in India than when she bathed in their exotic music.

Camp life was congenial, too, if one watched out for scorpions and cobras and one kind of white ant that bit viciously. The women slept on cots with mosquito netting inside a large square tent, twelve feet to a side. The driver and cook slept in a smaller tent. If Thomas Walker was along, he slept in a tiny pup tent. The tent life for evangelism had been pioneered long before by Ragland. Camping itself had been refined and perfected by the British in their many foreign conquests. Very sophisticated and portable equipment was available. The larger equipment all folded up, even bathtubs. Airtight boxes protected valuables. Every utensil was protected by a special cover. Within a short time at a campsite, all gear was unfolded and set up. Experienced helpers could have dinner on the table—with tablecloth and all—in very short order. This art of civilized camping was so old with the British that Amy thought very little about it.

Amy tried to be fair by paying the Starry Cluster when they first ventured forth from Pannaivilai. The sisters refused the stipend. And once in Pannaivilai they astonished Amy.

They had removed all their jewelry. Amy never would have asked them to surrender their jewelry. The sacrifice seemed beyond belief. What holy women He had selected for Amy's work! And what was the reaction of the Hindus? The fathers who had bought the finery were furious, but many other Hindus respected the women even more because the Hindus honored holiness. The word soon spread to thieves that the Starry Cluster women possessed nothing. It really seemed like the hand of God to Amy.

"Refuge! Refuge!" cried a girl's voice outside the bungalow in Pannaivilai one morning in early 1898.

A girl of sixteen, never seen before by the Walkers or Amy, was calling at the gate. She had gone to a mission school in nearby Perungulam and, by reading the Bible, had become a believer. In India, in contrast to Japan, one could not be a believer and remain at home. Nevertheless, her relatives besieged the bungalow, demanding that the girl be returned. The Walkers and Amy refused to give her up. They offered her sanctuary. Next, Thomas Walker went about securing legal sanctuary for the girl by seeing the proper authorities.

Fortunately, the young refugee was of age, so her independence was entirely legal. Krishna Pillai, a Christian and a poet, dubbed the girl "Jewel of Victory." There was nothing Jewel of Victory's relatives could do legally to get her back. But there were illegal means. Kidnapping was common. But in this case, the relatives chose to punish the perpetrators.

"They've burned the mission school in Perungulam," Mr. Walker told Amy one morning.

Another girl sought sanctuary that same year. Again the Walkers and Amy withstood the storm of protest from relatives. Fortunately, she, too, was of age. Krishna Pillai dubbed this girl "Jewel of Life."

Each summer, the Walkers went to Ooty in the highlands. There they stayed with Mrs. Hopwood at her great house called "Farley." She ran it as a haven for missionaries. Amy did not want to go, but the Walkers explained that by escaping the blistering plains in the summer, a missionary could put off much longer a furlough to England. So in the summer of 1898, Amy went to Ooty with the Walkers but brought her two recent refugees with her. Mrs. Hopwood, who was wealthy but devoid of any notions of British superiority, accepted the young girls wholeheartedly. Mrs. Hopwood and her daughter were much like Amy: blurs of constant activity. But Ooty never seemed so refreshing as when Amy thundered across the greens on a pony. Her hair was flying. No head covering could survive such a charge.

After a few weeks of recuperation on soft feather beds, and English breakfasts of bacon, eggs, toast, and marmalade, they returned to the sizzling plains. By early 1899, several converts, including men and boys, were baptized in Perungulam. Most of the girls were sent on to a Church of England Zenana school for converts in Palamcottah. The twenty-mile distance seemed a sufficient barrier to retaliation by relatives.

Amy, compelled to write, had recorded all these events in a manuscript. By late 1898, she had sent it off to a mission society that seemed interested. They quickly returned it. It was far too pessimistic, they said. Couldn't she eliminate the failures and accentuate the successes? They obviously did not know Amy Carmichael. Bosh! She put the manuscript aside.

Then came a real test.

"You are how old?" Amy asked a young girl who had come for sanctuary.

The girl was radiant in a crimson and orange sari. Bangles reflected light off her like facets of a diamond. Her eyes were large and warm.

"Eleven," replied the child.

"We cannot keep you here, but you can come here for instruction if you like."

The girl, named Arulai, did come for instruction. Amy soon learned that her father had enormous pressure on him to stop her from coming. But he was a tolerant man. When the girl became ill and Amy visited the house to nurse her, the father became even more tolerant. His tolerance was impressive in view of the fact that Arulai's cousin was tied up in an attic and tortured for trying to do the same thing Arulai had done.

One day the father came to the bungalow. He seemed dejected. He said Arulai could no longer come to the bungalow.

When her father reached to take her, his arm fell lifelessly at his side. This phenomenon happened several times.

"What is this?" he finally exclaimed. "It is as if my arm is paralyzed."

"It is the one Lord God of heaven," Amy told him. "He has marked this child as His."

Miraculously, the father relented. Arulai begged to have her younger sister, Mimosa, brought to Christ, too, but the father would not even bring her to the bungalow. Still, Arulai was allowed to remain and live with Amy.

NINE

For five years, Amy had been receiving letters from Robert Wilson. They tore at her heart because he pleaded with her to return. But her return to England was more impossible now than ever before. Now she had in her trust not only the Starry Cluster but Arulai. Arulai's going back into her Hindu family was unthinkable.

So Amy prayed again and again, "Oh, please, God, ease Robert Wilson's heart." And on July 4, 1900, she received a letter from the D.O.M.:

> *The Master's Word was brought to me this morning early: "He that loveth son or daughter more than me is not worthy of me." "Bind the sacrifice with cords, even unto the horns of the altar." No drawing back. Amen. May it be so in the strength He gives. It is well to have some gift of value to present to Him Who gave His all for our redemption. Praise Him.*[1]

Thomas Walker was asked to help at a seminary for boys in Dohnavur, a village in the lowlands remote from the railroad and main roads. So the Walkers moved there. And so did Amy and her Starry Cluster, as well as Arulai. Dohnavur—"woe-raw-poor" went its rhyme—had grown up around a Christian church built there in 1824. It was a small enclave of Christian natives, mostly of the palm-climbing caste. From Dohnavur Amy and her Starry Cluster could evangelize thousands scattered in many tiny villages, most within a two-hour walk!

About this time—late 1900—Amy was visited again by Ella Crossley of Manchester. This time Mary Hatch was with her. The two visitors traveled on the evangelistic sojourns with Amy and the Starry Cluster. Ella put her hobby of photography to good use. During their stay the two visitors harangued Amy about her idle manuscript. No, she did not need to embellish it, they assured her, just update it. "We will take it back to England, and with Ella's photographs we will find a publisher!"

Meanwhile, the entire world of missionaries was stunned by news from China. China had been seething with resentment against foreigners ever since the Japanese thrashed them in the Sino-Japanese war, which ended in 1895. The resentment spawned a secret society of Chinese known to Westerners as "Boxers." They were little more than thugs. The dowager empress Tz'u-hsi officially denounced them but knew the Boxers might defuse a lot of bitterness against her own incompetence. In 1900, the empress let the Boxers loose. The rampage was called the Boxer Rebellion. The easiest targets were missionaries, both Protestants and Catholics. By the hundreds they were rounded up, then slaughtered. Hudson Taylor's venerable China Inland Mission lost half its missionaries. In the province of Shansi alone, the CIM lost more than one hundred, including children. *"Sha! Sha! Sha!"* chanted the Boxers. "Kill! Kill! Kill!"

Amy was saddened to learn that William Cooper, who had given her wise counsel in Shanghai in 1894, was murdered in the uprising. Naturally the missionaries in India speculated whether such a thing could happen there. Most concluded that although there was resentment against the British presence, it was not enough to confront British weapons.

Early in 1901 at Dohnavur, five boys from the Pannaivilai area were baptized. One was Supu, one of Arulai's many cousins. Within one week all five boys became deathly sick. Two of the boys died, including Supu. The fact that the malady struck only the five converts seemed a case of poisoning. But in India, where cholera was so common and acted so rapidly, with death in a few hours, one could never be sure. And so Amy could only grieve for the boys.

Cholera was not the only widespread disease. The natives suffered also from malaria, leprosy, tuberculosis, and various parasitic worms. Hookworm was the most common parasite, producing severe fatigue. The most hideous manifestation of a parasite was elephantiasis, gross swellings of certain body parts. Good hygiene offered some protection against diseases, especially cholera. But in the back of Amy's mind grew the need to offer Indians modern medical treatments. What a boon that would be. All the diseases could be treated to some degree. Even the dread leprosy was treatable with chaulmoogra oil. But how would a tiny insignificant mission like Dohnavur ever attract a doctor? In the meantime, the missionaries had to treat the human soul.

In March 1901, Amy and the Walkers visited Pannaivilai after nearly a year's absence. One morning a village woman, a Christian convert, appeared with a small girl in tow. Amy was sitting down drinking tea. The girl gawked so rudely that Amy knew she knew nothing at all about white-faced foreigners with frizzy brown hair. But why was the girl there?

"Preena came to me last night—out of sheer desperation," explained the convert. "She is only seven. She escaped the Hindu temple in Perungulam. Preena is to be a *devadasis*, a 'woman of the temple.' First they teach her to sing and dance for the temple gods. But eventually she will entertain Hindu men who patronize the temple."

A temple prostitute. What an abomination!

"Come up here with me," said Amy in Tamil and lifted the girl onto her lap. "Why, your tiny hands are scarred!"

"From burns," said the convert. "She has been punished for an earlier escape."

"What a brave little soul you have, Preena." Amy hugged and kissed her. The girl melted.

"How desperately she wants that affection from her own mother," said the convert. "But the first time Preena escaped from the temple and ran to her mother—her *amma*—she was pushed away, right into the arms of her pursuers."

"Amma, I want to stay with you always," sobbed Preena.

Amma! Amy had become the girl's amma, her mother, her protector. "Patience, dear," soothed Amy.

Amy knew how cautious Thomas Walker was. He might want to do a hundred things to placate the Hindus. Besides, this girl was not of age. No district collector would support Amy's sanctuary for her. But when the pursuers arrived—the older devadasis women of the temple—and a crowd gathered, it was Preena who suddenly stepped forward.

"I won't go with them!"[2] she screamed.

Miraculously the crowd dissipated. Amy had made an important discovery: The Hindus were so anxious to conceal their evil, they might not appeal to authorities. When Amy and the Walkers returned to Dohnavur, Preena—the "Temple Child"—went with them. Before they left Pannaivilai, however, Arulai was baptized with Arul Dasan, her cousin who had once been bound in the attic. He, too, went to Dohnavur.

Back in Dohnavur, Amy was startled at the affection she and Preena had for each other. Preena was too young to go out evangelizing with the Starry Cluster, and each time Amy returned to Dohnavur, the child glowed with happiness. March 7, 1901, marked a great event in Amy's ministry. Preena told Amy and the Walkers about evils they had never suspected. Was there any abomination in India worse than using young girls as temple prostitutes? Once widows had been burned with their deceased husbands, a vile custom called *sati*. But thanks to protests by missionaries like William Carey, the British had stopped that evil. Once girl babies were sacrificed to the gods, in reality abandoned to be eaten by wolves or crocodiles. But that horrendous evil had also been stopped by the British, thanks to proof offered by Carey. So, in her heart, Amy knew using girls for temple prostitutes was about the most evil custom remaining in India. It must be exposed and abolished. Until then she would save as many girls as possible. She would offer sanctuary to "temple girls" and to those likely to become temple girls.

This traffic in temple girls—though true—was well hidden. It was so secretive that many missionaries believed temple prostitution was not true. Even Walker felt that way. But he was alarmed enough by Preena to seek information from the seamier elements of Hindu life. Slowly over the next several years he convinced himself of the truth. Girls were indeed sold to the temples, and it was worse than that. Infant boys were bought by temples, too, to be used to satisfy temple patrons or to be resold later to itinerant acting troupes. Was there no form of perversion not offered by temple priests?

Once Amy and her Starry Cluster were far south of Dohnavur, sleeping in a stable. Through the walls they overheard a transaction. A priest was negotiating with a father for his daughter. Amy sought help from a missionary doctor in Neyyoor, Howard Somervell. Somervell had the courage of a lion. They rescued the girl. But rescuing children already being defiled in temples seemed virtually impossible because they were so well guarded. Yet orphan girls began to come to Amy. By June 1901, Preena—nicknamed Elf—had been joined by four scamps nicknamed Imp, Pickles, Brownie, and Tangles. They all called Amy "Amma."

The rest of Amy's retinue was growing, too. She had five convert girls. The Starry Cluster had grown by two more. Marial was a small sturdy woman, very independent. Another was Blessing, who had a habit that drove Amy wild. She was very slow and deliberate.

Amy was ever Musal, the rabbit. She never idled. She never even walked. She scurried! As more and more children were brought to Amy, she traveled less and less. She would have to decide if Dohnavur was a good place for an orphanage, for it now seemed her calling. At age thirty-three, Amy certainly was grown-up. It was time to build a lovely place, to deliver little girls from a life of shame. Near the old whitewashed Christian church, the Walkers and Amy had found a run-down mud-brick bungalow, approached through an avenue of delicate acacia-like tamarinds. The trees seemed like giant ferns with their delicate leaves. Goats nibbled scruffy grass that grew on the rust-colored grounds. A gang of beady-eyed macaque monkeys studied these gentle newcomers. Four tiny cottages were also part of the compound. A few miles southwest was an alpine-spiked peak of the Western Ghats called the Holy Washerwoman.

Ella Crossley and Mary Hatch, her friends from Manchester, visited again in 1903. They traveled with Amy on one of her last such ventures. Once near the temple village of Kalakadu, they stopped to look over a wall at a pond full of beautiful white lotus blossoms. "Let us gather some," suggested someone. "They belong to the temple!" someone in the Starry Cluster shot back. Suddenly, Amy had a vision. The smallest—the lotus buds—were lifting their innocent faces to the light. Words from Ezekiel boomed into her mind: "Behold, all souls are mine!" Yes, how could she accept the contention that the lotus buds—the innocents—belonged to the temple? They belonged to the Lord. After that, Amy often thought of the temple children as "lotus buds."

In late 1903, Thomas Walker's wife was so ill he had to take her back to England. Amy's friends also returned to England. With the Walkers and her friends gone, she began to brood. On December 16 she turned thirty-six. In her heart she had consecrated herself to saving temple children. But where were they? Was her new calling mere folly? She prayed fervently for lotus buds. On March 1, 1904, a pastor from the northern part of the Tinnevelly district arrived at Dohnavur. He carried a baby girl, a wispy thirteen days old and so tiny. *Another orphan?* thought Amy.

"I saw a group of temple women in the night," said the pastor. "They were ushering several of their small victims to the temple. I prayed, and God commanded me to barge in among them. The Lord delivered this baby to me."

The Starry Cluster now numbered seven. Ponnammal was Amy's greatest help with the children. Pearl was nearly her equal. But a new member, Devai, was without equal at ferreting out children in peril. She was an older woman, shuffling but driven. It seemed she was always on the trail of some child. Did she ever sleep? More often than not she failed. But how she persevered. It was Devai who brought most of the new children in. By June 1904 Amy had seventeen children at Dohnavur.

In November 1904, Thomas Walker returned, without his wife, who needed more time in England, but with Amy's mother! Mrs. Carmichael was just in time. Amy not only needed her motherly comfort but her motherly advice. Caring for the children—especially the babies—was overwhelming. And Amy had neither nurse nor doctor to help her. Indian women—even Christians—refused to wet-nurse. What was she to do with the babies she had? They tried goat milk. They mixed in other ingredients to make their own "formula." Amy worked ceaselessly. Often she was awake half the night hovering over a sick child in the nursery. But several of the babies worsened and soon died. A third baby, Sapphire, or "Indraneela" in Tamil, also became sick. She was older, and her baby antics had endeared her to everyone. Indraneela was often in Mrs. Carmichael's lap. She called her "Ahta" for grandmother. When Indraneela died January 6, 1905, Amy consoled herself with the fact that Indraneela was with the Lord; then she wrote a poem:

> *Dear little feet, so eager to be walking*
> *But never walked in any grieving way,*

Dear little mouth, so eager to be talking
  But never hurt with words it learned to say,
Dear little hands, outstretched in eager welcome,
  Dear little head that close against me lay—
Father to Thee I give my Indraneela,
  Thou wilt take care of her until That Day.[3]

Amy resolved to keep the sixth day of the month as a day of prayer for imperiled children, for not only had Indraneela gone over to God on that day, but Preena had escaped the temple on the sixth day of March. In unguarded moments, Amy was stung by the accusation that the deaths of the babies were the fault of well-intentioned but bungling do-gooders! Surely that was Satan attacking. Amy armored herself with the words of her Lord: "Fear not, little flock; for it is your Father's good pleasure to give you the kingdom." And in her heart she knew God wanted her to continue.

On June 19, 1905, Robert Wilson also went to join the Lord. The abandonment of her D.O.M. weighed heavily on Amy. It was another of those burdens missionaries carry. Few earnest missionaries escaped being accused of neglecting their loved ones. At least during her grief over Robert Wilson and the three babies, Amy had the comfort of her mother. Mrs. Carmichael stayed until March 1906, making it a very full fifteen-month stay in India.

By 1906, Amy knew that the tragic deaths of the babies had been caused by a mysterious epidemic. No babies had died since. Still, the family needed medical help, and they had outgrown their facilities at Dohnavur. Children were being rescued at the rate of one a month. The family totaled more than fifty now. Sometimes Amy laughed as she remembered her naive expectations. Never had she envisioned that instead of evangelizing, her mission would be to trim thousands of tiny toenails and fingernails!

The youngest wore simple pullover dresses—blue, of course. Her older girls all wore saris, usually white. Unlike poor Tamil women who wore nothing underneath the sari, they wore petticoats and a blouse—usually yellow—with sleeves past the elbow. Amy also wore a sari, hers creamy yellow, white, or lavender, with a blouse of coordinating color. And no clothing of Dohnavur was other than opaque.

Their overcrowded nurseries were simple enough, little more than mud-brick walls with thatched roofs and dirt floors. Furnishings were grass-mat beds and plain cupboards for the few belongings. She began earnest prayer for more land and buildings that would house a new nursery or two, a schoolroom, and quarters for the workers. *Fired-brick walls, too, Lord.* And red-tiled floors that busy little hands could chalk. None of that had materialized yet; the purchase of a typewriter had been a major item. So they set about remedying not only overcrowding but lack of professional medical care.

A bungalow became available at Neyyoor to the south, near Somervell's London Missionary Society hospital. So Amy had her most trusted helper, Ponnammal, go there with the most vulnerable children. The family continued to grow. Between Dohnavur and Neyyoor, it now numbered seventy.

By Easter of 1907, after six of the children had been baptized, Thomas Walker insisted that Amy depart for Ooty before the hot weather set in.

At Ooty, Amy bolstered herself with words from *The Spiritual Letters of Pere Didon*: "This sacred work demands not lukewarm, selfish, slack souls, but hearts more finely tempered than steel, wills purer and harder than diamond."[4]

Of course, Amy did not agree with Catholicism in its obedience to a pope and its plethora of sacraments, but she never hesitated to gain inspiration from Catholics who lived in Christ. Why should she not be inspired by Thomas à Kempis and Brother Lawrence and the great Augustine? To accept less was to deny what some worthies had done for Christ.

Meanwhile, she finished writing another manuscript about her own work for the Lord and sent it off to England. It would be titled *Overweights of Joy*. Without being dishonest, she tried to make it more joyous than her first book. Reception to *Things as They Are* had been mixed. Negative criticism claimed she had painted much too dismal a picture; Indian paganism couldn't be that bad. But the book sold well, and in the second printing the publishers added testimonies by experienced missionaries from India affirming that Amy had in fact painted a very real picture.

The year 1907 was a blessed year. Amy learned that a woman—in the same vein as Kate Mitchell of Belfast—wanted to make a large donation, which would enable them to build. . .more nurseries! Soon bricks were being laid. Ponnammal and all her charges could be brought back from Neyyoor, because now Amy also had her first real medical practitioner, Mabel Wade, a nurse from Yorkshire. Amy was thrilled when Mabel exclaimed, "Have I been here only a few hours? I feel like I am really at home."

Occasionally, Dohnavur had a real teacher volunteer for a short stint, but as yet they had no regular teaching staff. But the Indian helpers were growing in number. Several were offspring of those already supporting Dohnavur. Ponnammal's daughter, Purripu, appeared to be as industrious as her mother. Another was Pappammal, granddaughter of Krishna Pallai, the Christian poet in the Pannaivilai area. Volunteering must not have been Pappammal's idea, however, because she slouched in, expecting to be overwhelmed by the gloom.

"Instead," she gasped, "Dohnavur overwhelms me with love and joy!"

In the meantime, they fought for the souls of the children. On March 10, 1909, a woman bedecked in gold jewelry that obviously established her wealth breathlessly entered the compound with Muttammal, her very undersized twelve-year-old daughter. The mother was living in sin, so she could not keep her. The girl's father had died, making her heir to a substantial amount of land. Muttammal's uncle wanted control of her. Her life was in great danger. People in India died so easily; treachery might be suspected but could seldom be proved.

"I've heard of Dohnavur since I was only eight," Muttammal said boldly to Amy. "I want to grow up good. Won't you protect me?"

"I may not be able to," answered Amy honestly. "This may be a legal matter."

"But I've always heard your God answers prayers!"

"Stay here, then," said Amy. "We will pray."

TEN

Weeks of bantering began between Muttammal's uncle and the Christians at Dohnavur. Meanwhile, the uncle coerced the mother to change sides. Now she demanded that the girl live with her uncle. Amy, who rarely had a moment to spare, was absorbed with the problem. Her writing was the activity that had to be put aside. She sought the help of the highest British official in the district, the collector. He expressed his sympathy but insisted that the uncle had every legal right to take custody of the girl. Amy traveled to several towns trying to enlist a powerful lawyer. All shunned the case. The uncle had every right to the girl! Finally, she tried a lawyer who had just returned from England. He was both Tamil and Christian. Amy begged him to save the girl.

Miraculously the lawyer accepted the case and negotiated a settlement. Muttammal could remain at Dohnavur, but she must not break caste or be baptized before she came of age. Amy was delighted, even though not breaking caste meant the girl had to have her own food prepared, a very real inconvenience to Dohnavur. Her denial of baptism was inconvenient, too. Yet there was hope.

Muttammal gloried in Dohnavur. Discipline was hard, but she enjoyed the wonderful games the children enjoyed, as well as adopting one of the pesky macaque monkeys for her own. Tumbie was his name.

Despite the intervention by the Christian lawyer, Muttammal's uncle continued his efforts to gain custody of her. Besides fending off constant legal assaults, Amy had to make sure Muttammal was watched at all times. At last, the uncle found a willing judge. On March 27, 1911, the judge decreed that Amy must not only return Muttammal to the uncle within one week but pay all court costs as well. All previous agreements were void.

That very night, Muttammal disappeared.

The authorities were furious, especially the superintendent of police. Police and their spies watched Amy and Thomas Walker night and day. Thomas was especially suspect when he had to take his wife to England again. Finally, they started watching Mabel Beath, a woman from England who was visiting her missionary sister, too. After she returned to London, an Indian showed up at her house in a very transparent attempt to find Muttammal. Of course, Muttammal wasn't there. Mabel had merely taken the first step of many in the actual escape plan. Amy had anticipated what great wealth could do in tracking

Muttammal. So Mabel had disguised Muttammal as a Muslim boy and spirited her to a waiting wagon. From there Muttammal passed from willing hands to willing hands. Eventually, she ended up in Ceylon! But even that was not the end of the escape plan. Amy had approached a missionary named Handley Bird. She scarcely knew him, but she told him everything.

"Won't you help Muttammal take the next steps?"

"But what are they?"

"Pray that God will tell you."

Handley Bird sighed. "Well, then, I'm off to Ceylon."

It would be many years before Amy learned Muttammal's fate. She would always think of Handley Bird as the magnificent "Greatheart" of Bunyan's *The Pilgrim's Progress*. For it was Greatheart who guided the pilgrims on the Way to the Celestial City. No charges were pressed against Amy for the disappearance of Muttammal, though not for lack of effort on the uncle's part. There was no evidence. His lawyers advised him he could just as easily be accused of being the kidnapper as Amy. But Amy nevertheless was responsible for court costs, which were sizable. She had no funds for the debt. Then one day the exact amount of the court costs showed up in the mail in a check from a publisher. The publisher insisted he knew nothing of her legal problems, although he had had an overwhelming compulsion to send her the money!

In August 1912, a five-year-old child named Lulla was dying in the nursery. Her labored breathing, growing worse every second, disturbed Amy so much she could not bear to watch. She went outside into the night and prayed for the Lord to take the child.

"Amy, come into the nursery, quick," whispered Mabel Wade into the darkness.

Amy entered to see the child smiling and holding her arms out to someone no one else could see. The child clapped her hands in glee! Then she passed away. Amy was stunned. She had witnessed a Christian passing into the Lord's glory! That miracle helped Amy cope with the rest of that tragic August.

First, Mrs. Hopwood of Ooty died. Amy had often thought that Mrs. Hopwood's counterpart in *The Pilgrim's Progress* was "Discretion," of the House Beautiful atop the Hill of Difficulty. For surely Mrs. Hopwood had been a saint to all tired travelers on the Way to Salvation.

But Amy had no such consoling thoughts on August 24, when she read a telegram from the village of Masulipatam. It just wasn't possible! "Thomas Walker is dead!"

Thomas was only about fifty years old when he died. Unfair! What had happened? It was so incredibly swift. Snakebite? Food poisoning? But what did it matter? He was dead. And Amy fought using her own grief as a form of self-pity. Yes, it would be very difficult to continue on in Dohnavur without the wisdom and strength of Thomas Walker holding her up. And Ponnammal would be heartbroken. She had been so close to Mr. Walker that she had virtually considered him her father. He was Ponnammal's D.O.M. Mrs. Walker was still back in England. She would be the most devastated of all. Amy forced herself to be strong. Even though her own heart was breaking, she would have to comfort these grieving souls, assuring them again and again that Thomas was in the lap of the Lord.

Learning that Thomas Walker had died of food poisoning helped her not at all. She didn't indulge in the hapless "if only he had not done this or if only he had done that" lament. A person of faith could not do that. God was the Master of history.

Over the next few weeks, aided by an exchange of letters with Mrs. Walker, Amy emerged stronger. She was, just as Mrs. Walker wrote, driven closer to God. Every man falls and every woman falls—"as grass: as a flower of the field"—but God is always. And other missionaries of southern India rallied around her. Mr. Carr came from Palamcottah and played the organ every evening. Amy's grief was salved by joyous hymns sung by her little songbirds. Agnes and Edith Naish, two teaching missionaries, arrived almost immediately to take over the teaching for Amy. It was the first time the children really had professional tutors. Arul Dasan arrived to help with the management of Dohnavur. It was no small operation, now nourishing in body and spirit well over one hundred Christians.

The year 1913 held no relief for Amy. Ponnammal became very sick and had to be taken to the Salvation Army Hospital in the large city of Nagercoil near Neyyoor. The diagnosis was a virtual death sentence: cancer. There was a chance the cancer might be surgically removed. So Ponnammal endured surgery, then after that attempt had to suffer it a second time. Meanwhile, Amy got the shocking news that on July 14 her mother had died. Her mother had traveled to Canada to visit Amy's brother Alfred and had only recently written encouragement to Amy that Ponnammal would recover in "God's mighty protecting Arms of love and care."[1] Amy forced herself to recite her mother's favorite verse, "The Lord is good, a stronghold in the day of trouble."

Mother had comforted Amy with it when her father died in 1885. Amy could also take comfort in what her mother had done. Mrs. Carmichael had been far more to Amy than simply a loving mother. She had served Amy as her main representative in England, which entailed some publicizing of the good work in Dohnavur. By October, Mrs. Irene Streeter, wife of Canon Streeter of Oxford, became Amy's main representative in England. Mrs. Streeter had visited Dohnavur twice. Poems of comfort often just came to Amy. She could be suffering a midnight headache or bumping along in a stuffy bullock cart. Once she scribbled a poem on the brown wrapper of a medicine bottle she was bringing from Nagercoil:

> *I have no word,*
> > *But neither hath the bird,*
> *And it is heard;*
> > *My heart is singing, singing all day long,*
> *In quiet joy to Thee Who art my song.*
> > *For as Thy majesty*
> *So is Thy mercy,*
> > *So is Thy mercy.*
> *My Lord and my God.*[2]

Life rushed on for Amy. The next episode in her life involved the beautiful curly-headed child called Kohila. Kohila arrived at Dohnavur in December 1913. Her first day became her "Coming Day." This day would be celebrated every year like a birthday. An arrival's actual birthday was rarely known. On the Sunday preceding the Coming Day, the child's room was festooned with flowers. She was given a special card with a small gift, such as scented soap. At the evening hymn singing, the child was garlanded with flowers.

But Kohila's peace was short-lived. Like Muttammal's relatives, her family members threatened to bring a lawsuit against Amy if the child was not returned. And once again Amy had to find her Greatheart. This time it was Arul Dasan who spirited the child away. For weeks, Amy wondered whether she would be arrested for her defiance. When Arul returned, she was even more apprehensive. But nothing happened. In August 1914, all attention was diverted by the beginning of a colossal war in Europe. Some British missionaries said the war began as a local skirmish between Austria-Hungary and Serbia. But convoluted alliances mushroomed the skirmish first into a European war, then into a world war, the first in humankind's bloody history.

Both Hindus and Muslims rallied to the British cause. The native drive toward nationalism had been dormant, especially since the Muslims had founded the Muslim League and thus fragmented the native effort. If the Indian National Congress and the Muslim League ever united, who knew what might happen to the British in India?

"There's a Hindu lawyer up in Bombay who might emerge as the real leader of India someday," said one missionary in Madras. "I heard him speak here not long ago. He made quite an impact in South Africa—especially advancing the lot of the Tamil-speaking Indians working there. He's pushing *swaraji*, or 'India for the Indians.' He was educated in London, yet wears nothing but a dhoti. He endorses a simple native diet and cottage industries. He is honest. Many Indians already regard him as holy."

"Who is he?"

"Mohandas Gandhi."

Amy had her own struggles. Ponnammal was dying of cancer and was in agony. The wasting away of Amy's dear friend was doubly painful because of Ponnammal's constant regret that she was deserting Amy. "You must bear the burden alone," lamented Ponnammal. Once when she seemed in unendurable pain, she told Amy, "If the pain does not get any greater than this, I can stay and help you." Such devotion ripped at Amy's heart. Finally, the pain was so bad, Ponnammal was virtually comatose from doses of morphine. Yet she lingered on. She had suffered for more than two years. The shadow of the valley of death took on new meaning for Amy. It was so much longer, so much denser, a thousand times more dreadful than she had known. *Why, God, why? But Your will be done.* On August 26, 1915, the Lord took Ponnammal.

It had been eighteen years since Ponnammal joined Amy's Starry Cluster. What a great foundation she had been. The first and the brightest. Pure gold. Amy had to wonder at herself. She was forty-seven years old now, and any thoughts of marriage—other than to Christ—were long gone. Moreover, she was "Amma," the mother of dozens of girls and boys.

Arulai returned from Ooty with Bright's disease, or nephritis. The sweet child had already survived typhoid and a mild attack of tuberculosis. Now this. By December Arulai was "at the Gates." She heard celestial music just as Ponnammal had. She even saw Thomas Walker and Ponnammal waiting to greet her. Amy wired friends of Arulai that she was dying.

A friend from Palamcottah rumbled his wagon over the rough roads all night to reach Dohnavur. His only wish was to see the love in Arulai's warm brown eyes just one more time. He feared he would only see her buried. But on the morning of December 7, he witnessed a miracle. Arulai had improved.

It was such a blessing when things turned out well. Another blessing soon followed. Kohila appeared, hoping that, after many months of exile, she had been forgotten by her relatives.

Arulai had long prayed that not only would Muttammal return one day but marry her cousin Arul Dasan! Amazingly, Amy later dreamed the same thing, specifically that Muttammal and Arul Dasan would marry in a church in Ceylon. By this time, Amy knew that Handley Bird had taken Muttammal to China. Back in 1911, her "Greatheart" had gone all the way to Nanning in the province of Kwangsi. There he left Muttammal with Dr. Lechmere Clift and his wife. So Muttammal had been safe with a good Christian family all those years.

Now in 1915 Arulai and Amy talked to Arul Dasan. He agreed to let them arrange a marriage!

Who knew how Muttammal might feel about it? Or the Clifts? But Amy soon knew her dream had come from above. Muttammal and the Clifts were in complete agreement. But when and how? Letters flew back and forth.

By 1916 Amy had received her finished life of Thomas Walker, titled simply *Walker of Tinnevelly*. The story seemed almost petty, the cover blurb by Eugene Stock gratuitous, when hundreds of thousands of soldiers were being slaughtered in the soggy trenches of Europe. And Walker would not have approved of a book about himself at all. Yes, destroy the self. Realize one's own littleness. God's mightiness. Amy felt enormous shame on seeing the finished book. Had she done no more than glorify herself?

Eleanor McDougall, principal of the Women's Christian College in Madras, became a spiritual partner. When Amy first met her, she visualized Eleanor as the embodiment of a Tamil proverb: "Better to plow deep than plow wide." Eleanor plowed deep. She knew many of the mystical writers Amy knew. Together they spent many hours in prayer and discussion of the great mystics. But Eleanor, spiritually helpful as she was, could visit Amy only occasionally. So on March 18, 1916, Amy started a group of spiritual sisters. She was inspired by *The Imitation of Christ*, the small classic of holy life. Thomas à Kempis drew much of his inspiration from the other holy brothers in his own order, a lay group with no vows. The brothers strived to imitate the lives of Christ and the apostles and lived in a community that shared food and shelter. They were not to live apart from the world like monks. They worked as common men during the day, consequently their name: Brothers of the Common Life.

"Thus today we launch the 'Sisters of the Common Life,'" Amy explained to the seven women she had invited.

The sisters included Arulai and Preena. All, like Amy, had decided they wanted to live in Christ without the distraction of marriage. Every Saturday they met in a wooded area to discuss God and holiness. Amy indulged this meeting in English. It was justified because that way she could share her favorite writers with the sisters without the exhaustion of trying to translate every word. Only the Bible and *The Pilgrim's Progress* were available in Tamil.

Energy would be conserved and spent in God's glory. She shared her favorite passages from Thomas à Kempis, of course, but also other ancient worthies like Brother Lawrence, Richard Rolle, Raymond Lully, and Julian of Norwich. Samuel Rutherford and the inexhaustible John Bunyan were very dear to her, too. Her more modern favorites included the missionaries Josephine Butler of India and Bishop Moule of China.

They had a creed of sorts:

My Vow:
Whatsoever Thou sayest unto me, by Thy grace I will do it.

My Constraint:
Thy love, O Christ, my Lord.

My Confidence:
Thou art able to keep that which I have committed unto Thee.

My Joy:
To do Thy will, O God.

My Discipline:
That which I would not choose, but which Thy love appoints.

My Prayer:
Conform my will to Thine.

My Motto:
Love to live; live to love.

My Portion:
The Lord is the portion of mine inheritance.[3]

Prayer was essential. And it was deep, practiced prayer. For many years Amy could feel the presence of a distraction in group prayer. Time had not dulled her sensitivity. She would stop the prayer and demand that love be restored. Service was essential, too. The sisters took on jobs no one else wanted to do. But they did it with joy. Joy was vital. After all, joy was one of the fruits of the Holy Spirit. If it was lacking, it signaled a spiritual lack, perhaps a lack of desire to do the Lord's will. Sometimes when Amy was alone, she reflected on Walker, Ponnammal, and her mother. If she had feelings of sadness, she became very upset with herself.

"I must remind myself to live in the joy of those gone, not grovel in the sense of my loss."

She angrily scribbled that into her diary October 10, 1916. For although the outside world and even those close by Amy perceived her as a busy, busy woman, Amy was constantly seeking holiness. Even so, occasionally she was prey to attacks that no one can prevent.

ELEVEN

Nightmares.

Amy began having dreams that frightened her very much. *Oh God*, she prayed, *don't let this dream be a premonition that I might someday be disabled, even an invalid. Is the devil trying to trick me?*

But Amy's anxieties were usually on behalf of others. Perhaps it was not apparent to those who saw her quick decisions, but, oh, how she lamented the girls who lost their way. Then she remembered a gift to Dohnavur perhaps not handled properly. The memory of Ponnammal's agony haunted her, too. And Dohnavur now wrestled with emergencies in twelve nurseries!

Discipline on the children was strict. They were not allowed to be slackers. A few were rebellious, reminding Amy of herself as a child. Dohnavur harbored many endearing stories of the antics of children now. Every parent has a hundred stories. Amy had a thousand. She gave every child a good-night kiss, and she would continue to do so until there were not enough minutes in the evening to do it. Love was their blanket.

One game the children played was acting out a poem as Amy recited it:

> *Our mother was a butterfly,*
> > *We are her little eggs,*
> *Inside us caterpillars lie,*
> > *Young things with many legs.*
> *I am a little caterpillar,*
> > *Very soft and fat,*
> *I'll change into a chrysalis,*
> > *What do you think of that?*
> *I am a little chrysalis,*
> > *And very still I lie;*
> *For folded up inside me*
> > *Is a little butterfly.*
> *I am the little butterfly,*
> > *I want to fly about;*
> *I'm so tired of being here,*
> > *Oh, now I'm out! I'm out!*
> *O kind wind, come and fan my wings,*
> > *O sunshine, make them dry,*

AMY CARMICHAEL

O flower, I come to you! Away,
Away, away I fly.[1]

Many of the children adopted their own special monkey among the band
that cavorted around Dohnavur. Also allowed as pets were squirrels, dogs, and
exotic animals like the loris that Amy's people back in England could only
wonder about. Amy loved animals and birds. In fact, her weakness for birds
was becoming legend. Occasionally in the open market she would be overcome after seeing "little living jewels" in tiny rickety cages. On those occasions
she would come back to the compound with as many cages as she could carry!
There the birds settled into larger cages or aviaries.

In 1917, Muttammal—now twenty years old—finally consented to marry
Arul Dasan. Dr. Clift was due to go to France as a medical officer. Mrs. Clift
was going to America to wait out the war. But first they would all convene in
Colombo, Ceylon, for a wedding. It was just as Amy had dreamed it, down to
the last detail! In May, Arul Dasan and Muttammal returned to Dohnavur. It
was a great blessing to Amy. Not only was she joyous over seeing Muttammal,
now called Kunmunnie to hide her identity, but she needed Arul's help.

Summer retreats were no longer spent in Ooty, because Thomas Walker
had always been part of Ooty, too. And Amy's family was so large now, they
overwhelmed the accommodations at Farley. In 1915, after Amy had inquired
about nearby highland forests, the forest department let her use an empty
bungalow located at Sengelteri, a mere eight miles northwest of Dohnavur.
Cool air and a waterfall were most refreshing. What a peaceful kaleidoscope—
the children dressed in blues and yellows flickering through green and brown
forest glades!

The forest was more real than any forest in Rudyard Kipling's *The Jungle
Book*. Real panthers lurked instead of Bagheera, and genuine tigers, not Shere
Khan, were to be feared. The bears were real as well, unlike Baloo. Once, Amy,
who by now was almost fifty, exercised her wild Irish humor. When she and
three girls spotted Pearl and the rest of the group coming back from the river,
they hid behind a tree and growled like bears. Their victims flew into a panic.
Led by rail-thin Pearl, they danced about and waved flimsy sticks in defense
against the forest phantoms.

"Whatever is the matter?" yelled Amy, stepping out from the tree.

"Bears! Bears!" screamed Pearl and the others.

There was no need to explain the hoax after the small girl with Amy fell
to the ground in a fit of giggles. How could the family ever stop going to the
forest?

But soon the facility at Sengelteri grew too small. What were they going to do? The forest was such a delight. In the summer of 1917, Amy and others from Dohnavur began looking around for a forested property they might buy for themselves. Amy prayed their wish was not frivolous. Surely the family needed such a retreat. Eventually, an old Hindu Brahmin led them to an area called the "Gray Jungle," which lay on the flank of a mountain, below the great forests of teak and sal. Within a thick growth of evergreen oak and chestnut was a river and a waterfall, and the forest opened into a beautiful glade, as if inviting Amy to build a cottage there. The Gray Jungle could be entered only by climbing up a scary cliff. It was perfect.

"The Brahmin tells me you are interested in buying land," said a Muslim who appeared out of nowhere.

"Yes, I might be interested," said Amy, disguising her amazement.

"I am the owner," he said matter-of-factly. "For one hundred English pounds you can own thirty-seven acres of this paradise."

So much! And yet so little.

"Sisters," said Amy, "let us pray: 'Lord, if it be Your will, may You send us a sign.'"

It was as if she had thrown out a fleece. That same night, they returned to Dohnavur. In the mail from a lawyer in Ireland was an inheritance bequeathed to Amy by an old friend. The sum was one hundred pounds!

On September 17, 1917, the Gray Jungle became the family's legal property. Building in the highlands was difficult, though. It was hard to get laborers up the cliff. And the caste system drove Amy wild. The men who cut down a tree were allowed to do nothing else, and the men whose caste allowed them to saw the tree into planks were not there that day. Then, when the boards were ready, the carpenters were not there. If it rained, none of the men showed up, and the family had to hurriedly cover all the mud walls with mats to keep them from disintegrating. Much of the work had to be done by the family. They made amateur mistakes, with walls collapsing and roofs leaking. But what a wonderful sanctuary the forest house was when the summer sun blistered the plains below.

Near the forest house, the pool swirled out of the ancient core rock of the mountain. The pool was a special place where every child was taught to swim, just as Amy had been taught as a child in the mill pond. Once they were blessed when two carpenters—captivated by Christ in their meetings—asked to be baptized in the pool. An ordained friend of Amy's was happy to come to the Gray Jungle and oblige:

The Pool looked its very loveliest. A rock runs into the heart of it, and on it we can stand. This rock was colored a sort of dull gold that day because of the way the light caught it. On either side the water was jade green, till it reached the rocks which are gray, splashed and veined with crimson, brown and yellow, and their colors were brokenly reflected in the water. A little waterfall tinkled at the other end. This is a pool of many joyful swimming hours. . . . But never was it so happy a pool as that day when those two men confessed Christ crucified. The toil of the house was nothing then.[2]

Construction of a forest house in no way slowed the expansion of Dohnavur. In fact, it seemed to explode. Amy's conscience had been troubling her for some time—at least eight years—about taking only girls. One day in the forest house, God reminded her to take boys. She was stunned. How was this to come about?

Then in January 1918 another baby—this one more than one year old but bundled—was delivered into her arms at the gate of the compound. The baby smiled wearily and held out wanting hands. Amy remembered thinking, *What a brainy little head! If only this baby were a boy.* She handed the precocious infant to Mabel.

"It's a boy!" screamed Mabel from the nursery five minutes later.

And thus began their haven for boys. In 1919, Irene Streeter visited to break the ground on yet another nursery, the third of a new series. And she stayed long enough to break the ground on a fourth. Nurseries now numbered more than twenty! But 1919 marked the beginning of great upheaval in India. After the Great War ended in 1918, the little lawyer from Bombay, Mohandas K. Gandhi, who had supported Britain during the war, wanted justice for the Indians. British authorities brushed him aside like a pesky fly. But Gandhi persisted. To his credit, he advocated peaceful resistance. This pleased the British very much. But something happened that no one in India—not even Gandhi—expected. If Gandhi showed up somewhere to file a protest, as he did for sharecroppers in Champaran, within hours there was a sea of peasants by his side. Thousands upon thousands. Only Gandhi could control their anger. Occasionally even he could not restrain his single-minded followers. Riots ended in bloodshed. But the most savage atrocities were committed by the British against the Indians. In 1919, Amy became acceptable to that very British establishment. It would be hard to imagine a greater shock than receiving the news from Lord Pentland, governor of Madras, that she was now included on the Royal Birthday Honors List. It didn't seem that long ago that the district collector and the superintendent of police gladly would have paid her passage back to England or anywhere else!

Then Amy was informed she was the recipient of the Kaiser-i-Hinds Medal for her services to India. She fired a letter to Lord Pentland:

> *Would it be unpardonably rude to ask to be allowed not to have it? . . . I have done nothing to make it fitting, and cannot understand it at all. It troubles me to have an experience so different from His Who was despised and rejected.*[3]

But friends convinced her it was unpardonably rude to refuse it. It might even hinder her efforts in Dohnavur. So she relented. But she refused to go to Madras to accept the medal. She wanted no glory.

One day Arulai's long-lost sister, Mimosa, turned up at the gate of the compound. With her were three of her four sons, one a baby. Mimosa's husband had not allowed the teenage son, Rajappan, to come. Mimosa wanted to leave her four-year-old and her seven-year-old. Amy welcomed them, stunned by Mimosa's haggard appearance. She was two years younger than Arulai but looked much older. Her story was the most heartbreaking story Amy had ever heard. Poor Mimosa had wanted to come to Dohnavur back in 1899, but her father refused. But in the briefest of interludes when Arulai had counseled her, Mimosa had been smitten by the love of Christ. After Arulai had left, Mimosa existed among the Hindus like an illiterate Abraham, knowing only that she must love the one true God.

She refused to indulge Hindu customs. And she had been a pariah all these years. Her own brothers treated her with the disrespect normally reserved only for Untouchables. Naturally such a woman, who was not practicing Hinduism and getting poorer every year, could find only a lazy scoundrel for a husband. Her life had been ten thousand times harder than Arulai's. Yet she had her one God—whom she worshipped in a primitive but pure way—and she had her four sons.

Years before, Arulai had heard of her plight and written to her. It was the only letter Mimosa had received in her entire life. A cousin condescended to read it to her. She kept it like it was treasure. At long last she had come to Dohnavur to give her sons a chance. If only she, too, could learn to read, she said, so she could savor God's Word. But she had to go back to her husband to try to save the oldest son, Rajappan. Amy's heart ached that Mimosa had to return to that very hard life. Had there ever been such a poor, ordinary, illiterate girl who was so tenacious for Christ? Amy resolved to someday write the story of Mimosa.

Amy continued to write. Writing was like breathing to her. As if she did not have enough to do, she began to write letters to individuals within the compound, too. Of course, she had always written down day-to-day requirements and fired them off to workers; but now she wanted to do something more spiritual, more loving. She also continued to write for the public. It was very important for many reasons that the story of their ministry be told outside India. By 1918, she had added two more books, including one loving tribute to Ponnammal. Now she was writing about their experiences in the Gray Jungle. Poetry still expressed her thoughts best:

> Dim green forest
>   Of a thousand secrets,
> When you were planted
>   Did the angels sing?
> Many things I wonder,
>   Are they all your secrets,
> Won't you ever tell me anything?

> Great white waterfall
>   Breaking through the forest,
> Where do you come from,
>   Where do you go?
> Had you a beginning,
>   Will you go on forever?
> For ever and for ever will you flow?

> Great black, glistening wall
>   Veiled in shining glory,
> Piled among the waters
>   Rock upon rock,
> O to have stood and seen
>   Hands at work upon you,
> Shivering you and shattering shock upon shock.

> Deep, dark, silent pool
>   Hollowed in the water's foot,
> What do you think of
>   All the long day?

Do you hear the thunder
   Of tremendous waters?
Do you hear the laughter of the spray?[24]

Tranquil thoughts.

But when Amy first encountered Jambulingam, her life was scarcely tranquil. Jambulingam was a notorious robber. He called himself the Red Wolf. The English newspapers labeled him Robin Hood. Amy rather liked that name herself. Just like Robin Hood, he gave rise to stories that were far-fetched. He robbed from the rich to give to the poor. He leaped across wide streams in a single bound. He was a crack shot. No handcuffs could shackle him. No jail could hold him. Like everyone else, Amy was enchanted with the stories. Amy was not shy about asking God for favors, either. So she prayed that she could meet this Robin Hood. On October 12, 1921, when Amy was returning from the Gray Jungle, a man stepped out in front of her.

"I am Jambulingam," he said.

"Whatever do you want with me?"

"I felt a compulsion to meet you."

Thus Amy learned firsthand about this Robin Hood. He claimed he had been falsely accused of a crime many years before. He panicked and ran. By not clearing his name right away, he gave his accusers the opportunity to soil his reputation even more. He then made another poor choice and turned to crime. Yes, he gave money to the poor, but only to ease his conscience. He was nothing like a "merry" Robin Hood. He was intensely unhappy. While he was running from the law, his wife had died and left his three children to the cruelties of India. It was when Amy learned of the children that she knew the reason God had forced them together.

"I will take your children in at Dohnavur," she offered. "But I urge you to surrender to the police and get this meaningless life behind you."

He refused to surrender, but he did deliver his children to Dohnavur. Five days later, he was captured and savagely beaten. Could Amy doubt that God had brought them together in the most unlikely of meetings to save his three children? She was allowed to visit him in the prison hospital. He was a broken man. She counseled him in the Lord. She gave him a Bible to study and visited him often. She prayed for his soul. Then she dreamed she went to Jambulingam in prison to ask him if he wished to be baptized. He said yes. So she visited Jambulingam in prison and asked him if he wished to be baptized. And he became a Christian just as she had dreamed it.

One day a sister rushed to her. "Jambulingam has escaped!"

No! Why had she considered him safe? Why had she not prayed for him fervently? Why did she not know he could not resist the temptation to escape? Amy was very worried. Yes, he was popular with the people, even with a lot of the British. She prayed that he would give himself up. Yet new robberies were attributed to him. Amy was certain the crimes were done by others and conveniently blamed on Jambulingam. Efforts of hers to arrange a secret meeting with the fugitive were unsuccessful for many months. She even saw an official who reported to the collector. The official said if Jambulingam would vow that he had committed no more crimes, the officials would believe him. Jambulingam would not be prosecuted for them. Finally, she did secretly meet with Jambulingam. He had given up hope. He had made the British officials look foolish. He didn't believe what the official had told Amy. He would be killed in prison for sure. "Just promise me you won't die with blood on your hands," said Amy sadly.

He promised.

Amy tried to put aside her worry. Worrying wasn't Christian. Christ's words were plain enough: "Take therefore no thought for the morrow: for the morrow shall take thought for the things of itself. Sufficient unto the day is the evil thereof." And a wonderful thing happened. Arulai's sister Mimosa was rescued at long last. She had come to live at Dohnavur. And the oldest son, Rajappan, was with her. Mimosa had rescued a niece, too, a neglected toddler. What a life Mimosa had led for Christ!

Yes, today had its own troubles. But Amy's problems were now the problems of prosperity and expansion. For her recent acceptance by the Crown caused donations to flood into Dohnavur. Nurseries were under construction constantly. By 1923, they were building the thirtieth! Whereas once they had virtually no boy babies, there were now dozens. Amy had twenty-seven helpers, of whom thirteen were from Britain and Ireland. Chief among the helpers were Pearl, Arulai, and Mabel Wade. And new living quarters had been built for her helpers. The new quarters offered the one luxury enjoyed by these older individuals: privacy. Each had ample water to bathe, as well as a chamber pot.

Dohnavur now even boasted an automobile, which greatly speeded up trips to Palamcottah and Neyyoor. All this she reported in her newsletter, renamed the *Dohnavur Letter* because *Scraps* suggested to some readers the trivial. Readers also became acquainted with a certain nomenclature in Tamil that had arisen for the Dohnavur family. Older girls were "Sitties." Those older sisters in authority were "Accals." The equivalent "big brothers" were "Annachies."

TWELVE

On September 20, 1923, Jambulingam had been trapped by the authorities in the village of Caruniapuram. Some stories that circulated about the event broke her heart, for they said the police had subdued him, beaten him in their rage, and then shot him through the head. Edith Naish had been in the village when it happened but knew only that Jambulingam was indeed dead.

Remembering his pledge not to die with blood on his hands, Amy had to ask her, "Did he die clean?"

"Yes. He could have surely used his gun to kill, but he did not."

Over the next weeks, Amy was very troubled by Jambulingam's death. She hoped the police would clear his name. Instead, they insisted it was good riddance to an evil man. One police official sneered that Amy would be very disappointed if she expected to see Jambulingam in heaven. Even after she had written the story of Jambulingam in the book *Raj, Brigand Chief* and learned that many Indians were inspired to come to Christ because of the conversion of Jambulingam, she felt little better. She was haunted by the police official's claim that Jambulingam had not been saved. Then on December 15, the evening before her fifty-sixth birthday, she was resting in her room and enjoying the words of a hymn sung by others in the dining room. Suddenly, she was flooded in waves of light. Her spirit soared. The Lord had washed away her darkness, her doubt.

Workers from Ireland and the British Isles continued to arrive. One family—the Neills—was so gifted, it seemed too good to be true. Husband and wife were both doctors. They came about the same time as another doctor, May Powell. At long last, Dohnavur had real doctors. The Neills's son Stephen had been at Cambridge studying for the clergy. He had not been ordained, but he was thoroughly steeped in the doctrine of the Church of England. Amy, influenced by Robert Wilson, claimed no denomination. Besides her love of Christ, she expressed her beliefs as three principles. First was the divine inspiration of scripture. Second was the power of prayer to enlist God's help against the enemy. Third was the necessity of the faithful to love one another. In the spirit of Keswick, Amy cared nothing for doctrinal hairsplitting. The church service that had evolved from Amy's beliefs was partly Anglican, partly Quaker, partly other churches, if one had to use labels. Amy did not. But Stephen Neill did. He labeled Amy one of the "Plymouth Brethren." Stephen's mother asked, "Since Amy often has services led by those not ordained, why shouldn't Stephen—by far the most qualified—take over the services?" Slowly but surely, maintained the mother, Stephen would steer the wayward services back to the purity of Church of England ritual.

What had seemed so providential became chaos from Amy's standpoint. Stephen Neill—prodded by his mother—was virtually aspiring to be the "bishop" of Dohnavur. The father and mother were trying to get Amy to agree to have all medical facilities at a separate locale—under their supervision, of course. Besides that, the father was spending far too much time with the girls at Dohnavur. This kind of relationship was anathema to the Hindus. It could stain Dohnavur. The Neills were truly brilliant people, and they expected their brilliance to be given free rein. But Amy had cautiously built Dohnavur into an oasis island of Christianity in a vast ocean of Hindus and Muslims.

When she opposed all the Neills's programs, which she felt were undermining the security of Dohnavur, the Neills were stung by her "fear," her "insecurity." She was a myth, they whispered, trying to keep control of something that had grown far beyond her competence. But Amy persisted against the Neills. They dug in. They were not quitters. Brilliance would triumph. But Amy knew this competition for power could not continue. After six months of turmoil, she informed the Neills they must leave Dohnavur. And so they did, much of the conflict remaining secret and untold, the wounds never healing.

The conflict ushered in a new era for Dohnavur.

Amy officially severed all ties with missionary societies. After all, she always declared the society was not responsible for any debts she might incur. But after the Neills tried to wrestle Dohnavur away from her, she knew that stronger, more legalistic measures were required to protect her work. The Zenana Missionary Society had become more and more intrusive, too, demanding written reports as to what she planned to do, as to what she planned to spend, and answers to dozens of other questions.

Over the next two years, Amy crafted the Dohnavur Fellowship, whose prime allegiance was always to the cross. Her motto was "The Cross is the attraction," but devotion to it had to have a human purpose, too:

To save children in moral danger; to train them to serve others; to succour the desolate and the suffering; to do anything that may be shown to be the will of our Heavenly Father, in order to make His love known, especially to the people of India.[1]

And who led the Fellowship, who made its plans?

The Leader with the help of the Council shall direct the conduct of the
Fellowship according to the plans that God shall reveal. It is agreed that
the supreme authority is vested in the Unseen Leader, the Lord Jesus
Christ, while the human leader seeks, in cooperation with the other mem-
bers, to carry out the mind and will of the Divine.[2]

The council consisted of eight of the best-qualified helpers. Of course
Arulai was one. As far as qualifications to help at Dohnavur, Amy had only
a list of about twenty-five questions she liked to ask volunteers. They were
thoughtful questions with no right answers. Her hope was that the persons,
in answering the questions, would be able to decide themselves whether they
were fit for service or not. Some of the questions were:

Samuel Rutherford said that there are some who would have Christ
cheap, Christ "without the Cross. But the price will not come down." Will
you pay the price to live a crucified life?

Are you warmed or repelled by the thought of a hard life?

Do you know the Dohnavur Fellowship is a family, not an institu-
tion? Are you willing to do whatever job helps the family the most?

Besides the Bible, which three or four books have helped you the
most?

Besides reading books, what activity refreshes you best when tired?

These questions were designed to ferret out any doubts that the volunteer
might have. Not the least troubling was the very real possibility of spending as
long as two years learning Tamil, for this necessity could not be shirked. Nor
could the necessity to do whatever work was required, no matter how menial
or tedious or perhaps even revolting. Hopefully she would not get people with
their own ideas of what needed to be done. The Dohnavur Fellowship had to
become a legal entity, too. The mission society took the news like a lamb. They
donated all property to the Dohnavur Fellowship. Buildings and land were being acquired all the time. In July 1925, Amy had purchased sixty acres of rocky
hillside halfway between Dohnavur and Neyyoor. She called the spot "Three
Pavilions," because legend said three ancient kings had conferred there. Also
in 1925, she launched a project she had cherished for a long time: a house of
prayer. It would be Indian in architecture, pagoda-like with tiles and multiple
eaves, certainly not the foreign-looking Church of England style with stained-
glass windows that so offended Indians. Amy had an aversion to images of the
Lord anyway, so few were ever found in Dohnavur. The cross was the image

of Christ she wanted to see. The only other symbol in the House of Prayer was a large brass-rimmed wagon wheel. To Amy the wheel symbolized the Fellowship, an instrument to perform good hard work. The polished brass rim represented the bond of love that held the Fellowship together.

By 1926, there were seventy boys at Dohnavur. It was obvious they needed a strong leader. Arul Dasan was willing but lacked education. For that matter, new leadership for the entire Dohnavur Fellowship would have to come eventually. Amy was now fifty-nine. And there was the hospital she so desired. Few things attracted natives better than medical facilities. She had put the main thrust for a hospital aside until her House of Prayer was finished. But where were the doctors going to come from? Praise God, Dr. May Powell had remained, even though she was often bogged down in her study of Tamil. But even when Dr. Powell hit her stride, Dohnavur needed a male doctor for male patients. Indians would accept nothing else. Women doctors must examine girls. Men doctors must examine boys. All these things Amy now prayed for.

Dr. Godfrey Webb-Peploe had visited in 1925, but he had moved on to fulfill his commitments in China. Then in January 1926, his mother and his brother Murray, also a doctor, visited Dohnavur. Murray was the extrovert, Godfrey quiet and withdrawn. Both were steady and dedicated physicians.

Amy found in Murray a soul mate. He was just as spontaneous as she was. If she heard the call to go somewhere, Murray was always ready to go with her. Off they would rumble in the Fellowship automobile! Murray was devout, too. He carried a well-worn New Testament in Greek and liked nothing better than to savor the Word.

After Murray departed with his mother for China in May 1926, Amy was torn. "My heart turns to him as Thy chosen leader for the hospital," she admitted to God in her diary. "I see in him and in Godfrey my very heart's desire." But guilt overwhelmed her. "Let me not covet my neighbor's goods—nor his manservants. Murray and Godfrey are China's manservants. Lord, help and forgive me."[3]

Still, Amy plunged ahead with her plans for the boys' compound. In September, she made a down payment on the land. Amy was in turmoil over the lack of a leader for the boys, writing in her diary the very next day, "It is as if the evil one were seeking to undermine what he failed to overthrow by open assault, our perfect unity."[4] But one week later she received a cable that was like a monsoon of joy. Godfrey and his mother were returning to Dohnavur! Godfrey had a touch of lung trouble and had been ordered to leave China until he felt better. Once again, Amy had to scold herself. She must not take joy in China's loss. But how could she stop her own hopes for India? And when

Godfrey told her he had resigned his post in China, her heart soared.

Godfrey soon set her straight. "Don't count on me for Dohnavur," he said morosely.

Lord, how could she have been so selfish? So foolish? So presumptuous? Did Godfrey see Dohnavur as nothing more than a pleasant diversion while he was recuperating? Yet when Godfrey returned to Dohnavur, Amy felt sure God had been telling her that sober, steady Godfrey was her future leader for the boys, her future doctor for the hospital. How could she have been so wrong?

On December 15, 1926, the evening before her fifty-ninth birthday, she got the best present she could possibly get. A note from Godfrey asked Amy for fellowship in Dohnavur. And his note revealed what had been troubling him. He had doubted he was worthy of what she expected of him. Yes, he was a doctor, but could he lead the boys? At last he had decided he must try. Amy had that effect on people. She made Godfrey want very much to be what she thought he was.

Godfrey tackled Tamil and was so adept at it that he had a working knowledge of it by the time his health was back to normal. Then he assumed all the duties Amy had bestowed upon him. To make the Webb-Peploe saga even more miraculous, Murray's station at Hangchow was overrun in 1927 by the Chinese civil war. Murray had to flee to Dohnavur. But he assured Amy he had every intention of returning to China when the shooting was over. Again, Amy had a call from God to proceed boldly. In January 1928, she bought the land for the hospital.

It seemed hopeless to defy Amy's plans, which were responses to God's call. By July 1928, Murray, too, had pledged to the Dohnavur Fellowship. With Godfrey in charge of the boys' compound, it was left to Murray to ramrod the construction of the new hospital. It would require the most funds they had ever committed. Even the children worked to raise funds. Southern India was not a hot spot for the politics that were sweeping northern India. But Amy followed what was happening. Mohandas Gandhi was in and out of jail. His nationalist movement, embodied in peaceful resistance to British rule, was now called *satyagraha*, or "force of truth." Often Gandhi would appear to be doing nothing, then suddenly surface in a cauldron of unrest.

The last few years had been fruitful for Dohnavur. The House of Prayer was finished. Development of the boys' compound was under way. The hospital was started. Although it would take many years to complete the hospital, in 1929 Murray performed what Amy called his "first big spectacular operation"![5] Eventually, there would be a prayer room above the operating theater.

But during that first surgery, Amy had the entire family in the House of Prayer petitioning God for success. For two hours they prayed and sang—two minutes it seemed to Amy—before a messenger came to tell them the result of the operation.

"Praise God for that success!"

The leadership Amy had prayed for was now in place. In January 1931, she gathered together many of her helpers to confide in them. Amy was now sure God wanted May Powell to lead the girls. No one disagreed.

The Fellowship branched out beyond Dohnavur. This was not itinerant evangelizing but a serious effort to establish permanent facilities, initiated by medical dispensaries. Four miles to the northwest they were taking root in Kalakadu, a stronghold of Hindus. Two miles south they entered Eruvadi, a Muslim stronghold.

On Saturday morning October 24, 1931, Amy prayed, "Do anything, Lord, that will fit me to serve Thee and help my beloveds."[6]

In Kalakadu, her helpers had secured a house that was supposedly haunted. It would carry Christ's cross. Two of the Fellowship would be stationed there, led by May Parker. Amy had visited it on October 9, noting work being done on the bathing shed. This Saturday, she went once again to Eruvadi. Even though it was late in the afternoon, she decided to go with two Sitties to visit Kalakadu again. So the driver chugged the automobile over to Kalakadu. Amy left the car and approached the house in dimming twilight. Off to the side was the shed that would shelter their outdoor toilet. Had they dug the pit yet? Perhaps she should check.

Then Amy tumbled into the center of the earth!

THIRTEEN

She was at the bottom of a pit, which had been dug where she hadn't expected it. Her hands clutched the sandy soil to fight the pain in her ankle. It was severely sprained, perhaps broken. But where was help? She clawed up the walls of her pit to get upright, taking care to keep weight off the injured ankle. Upright, she felt joy. Praise God she had not broken her neck. Hands suddenly lifted her from the pit and gently stretched her out.

"The demon struck you down, memsahib," said a man in awe.

Why argue? Maybe it was true. She spotted her driver among the faces. "Please get word to Dohnavur I've had an accident," she groaned.

The pain grew. Two hours later, May Powell arrived in a truck. Now Amy understood as never before what the appearance of medical help meant to these Indians. Medical people seemed absolutely angelic. And how the Lord must love these willing workers. By now her ankle felt like a great melon, the skin about to burst.

After a few minutes of examination, May Powell said, "We must take you to Neyyoor. The ankle must be X-rayed at the London Mission Society Hospital."

So off into the black night they rumbled the forty-six miles to Neyyoor on a "road" built up between rice paddies. Ronald Proctor drove the truck. May Powell and Mary Mills, a nurse, comforted Amy during the bumpy ride. Rain was making the road even more treacherous. It was Sunday evening by the time the ankle was X-rayed in Neyyoor. Amy learned her leg was broken above the ankle. She needed surgery.

"How long before I'm walking about again?" asked Amy.

Doctor Somervell said, "The ankle must be in splints for eight weeks. Let us pray: 'Oh Lord, make this ankle strong enough to bear burdens again.'"

Amy prayed, too. Psalm 6 expressed her concern perfectly: "Have mercy upon me, O Lord; for I am weak: O Lord, heal me; for my bones are vexed." But wait. Had the good doctor evaded her question? He hadn't actually said she would be walking, had he?

The next day, Amy groaned involuntarily as the pain-numbing morphine wore off. "If only I could take your pain from you," sighed Mary Mills.

Amy blurted, "Your joy no man taketh from you."

God's words from scripture had just come to her, as they so often did. With Mary's help, the passage was found in the sixteenth chapter of the book of John:

A woman when she is in travail hath sorrow, because her hour is come: but as soon as she is delivered of the child, she remembereth no more the anguish, for joy that a man is born into the world. And ye now therefore have sorrow: but I will see you again, and your heart shall rejoice, and your joy no man taketh from you.

So there it was. This agony was the birth of some joy.

Back in Dohnavur, on November 3, the pain subsided, which allowed her doctors to wean Amy off the morphine. Too much use was habit-forming. But then the pain returned. And it grew in intensity. The ache remained day after day. Then week after week. The pain robbed her of her sleep. Amy spent her sixty-fourth birthday in her room, quite unable to do anything but lie in bed and try to read, though her mind was befuddled and exhausted from lack of sleep. Her visitors were allowed a mere fifteen seconds to wish her well. The others began to sense that the injuries were much worse than voiced by the doctors.

On Christmas Day, carols were sung outside Amy's room. On January 4, 1932, the council requested three solid hours of prayer by the Fellowship. Amy actually did seem to improve. She was well enough to be transported about in the automobile to survey various projects. When Dr. Somervell visited in February, he seemed satisfied with her progress. But sometimes she felt she was not mending well at all.

But usually Amy was as convinced as everyone else that she was on the mend. Every advance was noted. Six steps one day. Ten steps another day. Went for a drive in the automobile. Walked out on the verandah. Walked down the steps to the prayer room. This great accomplishment was just before her sixty-fifth birthday. She certainly didn't waste her time, even though she had not one night of real sleep since the accident. For a long time, friends had urged her to write a history of Dohnavur. Besides being an artist with words, only Amy had the knowledge to readily synthesize such an enormous amount of activity.

As if Amy didn't have enough to do, she now pecked out on the typewriter the *Daily Manna* for distribution within the Fellowship. The creation of this daily spiritual aid was of course spurred by the fact that she could not circulate to mother her flock as she had done for so many years. An example of her spiritual buffering in the *Daily Manna* read:

Have we any prayer like "use me, O Lord" in the Bible? . . . [No] I could not find any such prayer. . . [I] find every other verb occurring in prayer—teach me, lead me, bless me, and so on—but not this verb which we would naturally expect. . . . The Captain will use the soldier if he be prepared for use; words of beseeching on the soldier's part are not required.[1]

The next day in the *Daily Manna* she expanded her thoughts:

I have three pens, one for ordinary writing, one a little finer, and one for fine work like corrections. . . . The pens are always ready for use, "very usable." Even so, just as a fountain pen is all the better for being sometimes left under water, so our souls do often need to be bathed afresh in the love of God. . . . And we are given one day in seven for something of this sort.[2]

The year 1932 also saw the Indian struggle against British domination continue. Gandhi—now called the Mahatma, or "great soul"—and thirty-five thousand others of the National Congress were imprisoned. Confusing nearly everyone, Gandhi protested the British announcement that they would allow the Untouchable caste to hold their own separate elections so that they could have representatives in the provincial legislatures. Gandhi said if this were done, he would starve himself to death in prison!

One could never be sure what Gandhi would do next. He seemed utterly original. In his unpredictable way, he said he didn't care a whit for what he had said twenty years before; he cared only for truth. He knew the Sermon on the Mount by heart. He would startle onlookers by leading them in his favorite Christian hymn, "Lead Kindly Light." He anguished that Hindus were so hidebound they would prevent someone from killing a rabid dog. Yet Gandhi, himself of the Vaisya caste, defended much of Hinduism. He fathomed the complexities of Hindu society, and he didn't want India to collapse into chaos. Most Indians knew little of his actual politics. The only thing everyone knew about him was that when he was free, he drew immense crowds. Tens of thousands. Indians believed he was the one authority who cared if they lived or died.

Although Amy's pain and sleepless nights continued, she seemed to improve. She even took trips to the Gray Jungle. She felt so invigorated on one trip that she tried to run on the verandah of the Forest House. But then she began to get worse. Her left hand numbed into a useless thing. The sight in one eye deteriorated. Arthritis stung her with every breath, especially in her back. Oh, how she thought she would die in harness. But no, her fate seemed the worst possible.

"Do not, I beseech Thee, let me be disabled by pain or inability and live on as a burden to others," she had written after a nightmare many years previous.

Now the nightmare was all true. She began to hate her spacious room, which had a sign over one door that said ROOM OF PEACE. It was originally intended to be a room where several of the Fellowship might sleep. It was never intended to be the sumptuous room of the pampered queen bee. It even had a teakwood partition, deemed important now that she was almost an invalid. When visitors entered the room through blue curtains, they saw no bed, only the partition on the right and bookcases on the left. Straight ahead were large windows onto the wide verandah. On the best of days blue kingfishers could be seen knifing down into huge vessels full of minnows.

There was a desk there, too, with a wicker-backed chair. Amy had her reminders posted. Most prominent was "God hath not given us the spirit of fear." The bookcases were filled with all of her favorites. Besides writing the *Gold Cord*, the history of Dohnavur, at the desk and her normal correspondence, Amy was also writing about her illness. Many letters were to other invalids, a group eventually deemed the "Dohnavur Invalids' League." Some letters were cranky; all were seeking the why of sickness. Amy became more pensive, more meditative than ever. Her Bible study led her to resolve to enter into this torture heart and soul. Yet she was reluctant to admit illness made prayer easier. Still, one night "after neuritis had taken possession" of her "from shoulder blade to fingertips," a "prayer, so simple, so easy for a tired heart, had a delivering power."[3] She thought much about prayer. She noted "the gates of access into the Father's presence are open continually. There is no need to push—perhaps 'trying to pray' is sometimes a sort of pushing."[4] She was startled by the thought that at times she might be working more in the Lord's will as an invalid than she did as Amy the Musal. And she wrote:

> *Is it not worth our while to call a halt and ask the question? Are we so busy with our multiform labours of philanthropy and love that we have no time to stop and think? India can show a missionary army of hardworking men and women. Go where you will throughout this land, you will find the Christian workers incessantly busy at their work. . . . No charge of idleness can be made against us, as a whole. But how is it that so much of our busy energy appears to be expended in vain? Holy scripture, personal experience, the voice of conscience, all these alike suggest one answer—we have neglected largely the means which God Himself has ordained for anointing from on High.[5]*

Prayer!

Amy was certain that the weakness of their prayers was the reason heathenism still enslaved the Indians. How could missionaries neglect the greatest source of help from God? The Lord certainly had not neglected prayer in the Gospels. So Amy formulated discourses on prayer, noting that it all meant nothing unless put into practice:

1. Don't get into bondage about place, or position of the body. . .sometimes, at least, [our Lord] went into the open air to a hillside; to a garden. . . . I have known some who could kneel hours by a chair. . .walking up and down. . . Some go into their rooms and shut the door. . . . Let the leaning of your mind lead you; a God-directed mind leans to what helps the spirit most. . . .

2. Don't be discouraged if at first you seem to get nowhere. . .no command in the Bible [is] so difficult to obey and so penetrating in power. . .[as] "Be still and know that I am God."

3. Don't feel it is necessary to pray all the time; listen. . . . And read the Words of Life. Let them enter into you.

4. Don't forget there is one other person interested in you—extremely interested. . .there is no truer word than the old couplet "Satan trembles when he sees/the weakest saint upon his knees."

5. Don't give up in despair if no thoughts and no words come, but only distractions and inward confusions. Often it helps to use the words of others. . .Psalm, hymn, song—use what helps most.

6. Don't worry if you fall to sleep. "He giveth unto His beloved in sleep."

7. And if the day ends in what seems failure, don't fret. Tell Him you're sorry. Even so, don't be discouraged. All discouragement is of the devil.[6]

Another time she noted three more things about prayer:

1. We don't need to explain to our Father things that are known to Him.

2. We don't need to press Him, as if we had to deal with an unwilling God.

3. We don't need to suggest to Him what to do, for He Himself knows what to do.[7]

Of a group prayer meeting in her room at the Forest House in October

1933, Amy said, "There are many in our family who come to prayer meetings because it is the custom to do so, but who are not urged by a great desire. It is the lack of prayer-hunger that often makes a big united meeting difficult."[8] Soon after she expressed the opinion her pain became so great she could no longer be present in group prayer meetings. Her unrelieved agony was too great a distraction for the others.

FOURTEEN

A few months later in Dohnavur, one thoughtful council member suggested that they routinely assemble in Amy's Room of Peace before their general meeting to pray with her.

"That quarter of an hour was like one long drink of cold water on a hot day!"[1] Amy gasped in appreciation.

Amy's surroundings were improved by the addition of a spacious bird habitat, more an aviary than a cage, on the verandah. But to her nurse's consternation, she often allowed some of the birds into her room. Her Room of Peace now also displayed Doctor Somervell's oil painting of Nanga Parbat, the most treacherous peak in the Himalayas. No one had ever managed to reach the summit. Many had died trying. Somervell was a climber of renown himself. Nanga Parbat was an old foe. But to Amy, Somervell would never reach greater heights than he had in rescuing a child from temple prostitution thirty years before. She continued to write—had she ever been more productive than when she was an invalid? In 1934, she told her publisher—which since 1928 had been the Society for the Promotion of Christian Knowledge—about her latest book, *Ploughed Under*, "A book is a child. . .I want the book thin. I don't like podgy books. . .don't let my little lover come out fat."[2]

Godfrey had written the *Dohnavur Letter* for a couple of years. But in 1933, Amy added a second newsletter called *Dust of Gold*. It was in that new creation that she wrote:

> *Pray that every book, booklet, letter, that goes out from this Fellowship*
> *may have blood and iron in it. Pray that we may never degenerate to the*
> *merely interesting, the pretty.*[3]

The return, in June 1935, of Murray from his furlough in Australia—he came back with wife, Oda, and two new twin boys—did not bolster Amy's spirits as she had anticipated. By this time she began to suspect the worst: She was not going to recover. Was the Musal dead? She had rested for more than three years and was in more pain now than when she fell into the pit.

That Amy was looking forward to release from the constraints of her earthly body was clear in July 1934, when upon hearing one of the doctors say she probably had only five years left of her earthly existence, she dropped him a note the next day:

I wonder if ever before you made anyone so happy with just a few words. . . . I know He might even now ask for longer than that five years, but that there is even a natural hope of that little while being enough, is purest joy. Last night I lay awake too happy to sleep. . . . Only pray that He will "take from me all slothfulness that I may fill up the crevices of my time," and truly finish all He wants me to do.[4]

And yet at other times—her Gethsemanes—she longed to recover and had to write, "O Lord, forgive. . . Canst Thou not deliver me from the strivings of my longings to be well and with my Family again? But a thousand, thousand thanks to Thee for their longsuffering love, for everything."[5]

Godfrey's duties finally became so crushing and Amy was doing so well with *Dust of Gold* that the *Dohnavur Letter* was discontinued. But Amy's health was not improving. From 1931 to 1935, she had been carried up to her precious Gray Jungle every September. But after 1935, this trip was deemed too strenuous for her. So, in hot weather, Amy would now have to suffer the sizzling summer heat.

Amy battled self-pity. In spite of her productive writing, she was isolated. And pain never left her. Again and again she caught herself yearning to be mobile again. When she heard children were being taken on their first trip up into the Gray Jungle, she wrote, "I was longing to see their pleasure as they see it for the first time. . .when suddenly I remembered that I shall see them when for the first time they look at the loveliness *There* (heaven). I shall be *There* to show them everything."[6]

Amy's earlier petition to spare her from "slothfulness" was not an empty plea. For many months, her strength and desire ebbed. Amy realized a real need to record the development of the Dohnavur Fellowship since *Gold Cord*, published in 1932. So she had started this needed work, which she titled *Windows*, but the strength to pull all the information together just wasn't there. Such a compilation was much more taxing than a poignant story like *Mimosa*. *Mimosa* had been a sensation. Since 1924 it had appeared in nine languages besides English. Letters of appreciation came to Amy from all over the world. And even after her accident, she had written *Ploughed Under*, the story of Arulai. No, a compilation like *Windows* was hard to do. So she set it aside. She soothed her regret over it by reminding herself that God knew when things had to be done. Suddenly, one morning in July 1936, for the first time in eight months, power came to her. She worked on *Windows* thirteen hours a day for three days!

Amy's strength fired up again in late 1936. Another story, as poignant as *Mimosa* or *Ploughed Under*, had to be told. This one she would call *Kohila*, for the beautiful curly-headed child who first came to Dohnavur in 1913, then had to be exiled for a while. Kohila was darling but had a spitfire temper. Once she had refused to share her room, clinging to it like a tiger. But once in Christ, no one shared more or worked harder. Maturity of several more years brought Kohila real passion:

> *Give me a passionate passion for souls,*
> *Give me a pity that yearns,*
> *Give me the love that loves unto death,*
> *Give me the fire that burns,*
> *Give me, O Lord, to be fervent in prayer,*
> *Pouring out all for the lost;*
> *Give me to pray in the Conqueror's Name,*
> *Spirit of Pentecost.*[7]

Kohila grew into a woman of great commitment to Christ. Few worked harder. She had become a head nurse at the Place of Healing. One of her best friends was soon to have a Coming Day. Up in the Gray Jungle, Kohila knew of gorgeous purple flowers, extra precious because they grew on a high rocky slope and were difficult to get. As she climbed after them, she slipped and fell, and at the age of twenty-eight, Kohila was dead.

Yes, Amy had to write this story called *Kohila*. In it she also wrote more extensively than she ever had before of spiritual training. But necessity taken care of, Amy's strength would wane again. And worse, her pain would increase. On November 9, 1937—her special anniversary day of coming to India back in 1895—she was too much in pain to see anyone. Still, she gave God thanks when Mary Mills, her "perfect nurse," said everyone in the Fellowship prayed for Amy in the House of Prayer. It was a time like that when she worried most about her successors. Oh yes, the Webb-Peploe brothers and May Powell were in place. But the three were physicians—and Europeans. Amy firmly believed Europeans should be behind the scenes, never in front. "India can be best reached by Indians,"[8] she had always maintained. But where was the Indian leadership?

There should have been little concern in her mind. After Ponnammal passed away, Arulai was the natural choice for Indian leadership. In *Ploughed Under*, published in 1934, Amy declared of Arulai, "She has shared in every part of the work from the beginning. . . . To me no word so perfectly describes her as the great word *loyal*. Her faithful heart has never swerved."[9]

For many years, Amy was certain that Arulai was to be the eventual leader of the women's side of the work at Dohnavur. Her Tamil was good. Her English was good. She read the New Testament and the Septuagint version of the Old Testament in Greek. She was very discerning of the qualities of Sitties and Accals. And she had compassion. The only question was her health, and it had begun to fail in 1935. Though Arulai seemed to bounce back, Amy was worried. And before the year 1938 was out, Arulai's valiant younger sister, Mimosa, died.

Then in the early days of 1939, Arulai's health failed again. It was not languor, nor weakness, but a precipitous decline. Soon she, too, was an invalid. Amy and Arulai sent letters back and forth. Ironically, the doctors advised against either one visiting the other because of their fragile health. When Arulai became gravely ill, Amy asked of her nurse, "Tell her that after I see His Face the first face I shall want to see will be hers, and for ever and for ever we shall be together again."[10]

On May 24, 1939, word came to Amy that Arulai was with Christ. Amy called all of Arulai's friends to her room and hugged them one by one. Tears were streaming down her face, but she assured them they were tears of joy. Because Amy was too feeble to attend Arulai's funeral in God's Garden, Arulai's nephew, Rajappan, stayed in Amy's room to comfort her. Together they read the book of Revelation and the magnificent portion of *The Pilgrim's Progress* where Christian enters the Celestial City.

It was no surprise that Amy wished fervently for her own "perfection."

FIFTEEN

In October 1938, Amy had said of a dream, "Is it imagination, Lord, or Thine own word to me, that I shall come to Thee in sleep—no rending good-byes—no distress to anyone? . . . However it be, I ask that it may be the easiest way for my beloveds."[1] Her pampered queen bee existence gave her guilt. One month later she prayed, "Lord Jesus, Thou hast made my prison so beautiful and my bonds so light that I greatly fear I do not 'suffer with' Thee."[2]

To remind herself how fortunate she was, Amy had only to remember faithful Irene Streeter, who had recently died in a plane crash. In 1939, Amy wrote to Olive Gibson, Irene's replacement as representative of the Fellowship in England:

> Go gently. Don't do as I know I did, for truly I had to do it. Don't work each day till you are unable to do one minute more. Don't. Leave a margin. It doesn't matter that I did it, for there are all these [the Webb-Peploe brothers and May Powell] ready to take over. . .[but] there is no one as yet preparing to [replace you].[3]

The sprawling Dohnavur grounds had long been inaccessible to Amy by walking. Only in her memory could she walk off her verandah to the nearby guest cottages, then beyond to the buildings that housed the weaving shed, the girls' dormitories, the medical dispensary, the girls' school, the milk kitchen, the many nurseries, the workrooms, and the House of Prayer. Certainly she would never make it to the hospital, the swimming pool, the playing fields, or the various boys' compounds. From north to south the complex stretched six hundred yards, from east to west even farther, because the Place of Heavenly Healing was across the irrigation channel. The buildings must have covered one hundred acres.

Since the accident in 1931, Amy claimed to have had only eight nights of real sleep. Right after the accident she hardly slept at all and often read. For the first time she had tried a novel, something she previously dismissed as far too trivial. To her delight she found a novelist in harmony with her own thoughts: John Buchan. Buchan was a contemporary, a Scot. A novel so true to real life, she decided, was not a waste of time but akin to reading poetry.

The events of late 1939 threatened even that tiny indulgence. Europe seemed headed toward another great war—not drifting but wildly careening. India's turmoil continued, too. Gandhi, who had hoped to "retire" into his spiritual pursuits, was forced into the fray again. He fasted in protest over a British agreement with the maharajah of Rajkot. The British acquiesced, proving the old man still had more influence than any native leader in India. But this squabble soon paled next to world events. Germany—led by a dictator so demonic he seemed the Antichrist—began conquering Europe. Gandhi and the National Congress demanded that Britain state its war aims to the Indians. When Britain ignored the demand, the Hindu leaders insisted that this was one war in which Indians would not participate. But to further divide India, the Muslims declared their support for the British war effort.

Britain plunged headlong into war against Germany. Three young men of the Fellowship went into the British army. Several of the Tamil youths went into the Indian armed forces. Murray suggested a Spiritual Civic Guard on the home front. Amy had mixed emotions:

> *Can you even begin to imagine what it means to me that while I lie here like a slug on a cabbage leaf. . .you are strong and doing exploits? . . . You have the glorious double message to give—the certainty of the triumph of righteousness, whatever the sacrifice be, and the fact that all this turmoil is perhaps the last herald of the Coming of the King. . .[but] I mustn't get too hot over Spiritual Civics—it's just the heritage of my Scottish–Northern Irish blood.*[4]

In 1940, a pact among Germany, Italy, and Japan caused more fear in Asia. Japan, so near India, was very powerful militarily. On December 7, 1941, Japanese dive-bombers devastated the American naval fleet in the Pacific Ocean. This would keep Americans from helping any victims in Asia for a long while. The Japanese began aggression in earnest. They struck the Chinese in force. Later they attacked Burma, too, pushing the British out. Burma was India's neighbor.

On April 6, 1942, the Japanese bombed Madras!

Dohnavur sensed the immediacy of the war. Evacuation plans were developed. If the Japanese invaded, everyone in the Fellowship under the age of thirty-five, now numbering more than three hundred, would proceed immediately to the Gray Jungle. But the Japanese attack on Madras was only a probe. The first great manifestation of the war was a famine in the area around Calcutta. The immense paddy lands of the Bengal had not failed the Indians in recent memory. Hundreds of thousands of fields were scattered along immense rivers. The rice was delivered to the millions in the cities in thousands of boats. But now country people flocked into Calcutta, carrying everything they owned in one basket or a box. "Where is the rice?" they cried.

Soon the tragedy was known. All boats had been requisitioned by the British for the war effort. The catastrophe of 1943 seemed to prove that the British didn't care if Indians lived or died. Everywhere in Bengal people starved. Mothers' milk dried up. Babies died. The numbers of dead mounted. Ten thousand. One hundred thousand. Finally, one million. Two million! More. Mountains of smoke plumed into the air as Hindu dead were burned in pyres along the rivers. Gandhi was imprisoned, silenced. No one spoke for the Indians. It was some consolation to Amy to learn a recent estimate placed the number of Christian Indians at seven million, an increase of four million in the last thirty years.

Amy labored the only way she could. She continued to counsel, inform, scold, shepherd, and perform a dozen other duties by writing. By 1943, she had once again updated the history of the Dohnavur Fellowship, this time in a book titled *Though the Mountains Shake*. So this book, *Things as They Are*, *Gold Cord*, and *Windows* chronicled the more than forty years of the Dohnavur effort. *Though the Mountains Shake* also included the wrenching account of Arulai's death.

The disaster in India worsened on December 5, 1943. Explosions shattered the silence in Calcutta. Yet the bombing of Calcutta was just another probe by the Japanese, followed by nothing. After that bombing raid, life actually began to improve for the Indians. Britain was more sensitive to their needs. Although the boats were needed in the war effort, they nevertheless delivered rice again. One of the greatest famines in the history of the world ended, seemingly no more than a footnote in the worst war in the history of the world.

SIXTEEN

Some Indians were so bitter they joined Japanese armies in Burma. Japan sensed that 1944 was the right time to conquer India. In March they bombed airfields in the Naga Hills six hundred miles northeast of Calcutta. That same month, they surged across the Chindwin River into India. Most Indians realized that the Japanese were no liberators. Between the monsoons and the savage resistance of Indian troops, the Japanese invaders were battered. By summer they were out of India, leaving behind thirty thousand dead. The war that had looked so hopeless early in 1944 had completely reversed. The Japanese were being pummeled everywhere in the Pacific, just as Hitler's forces were being driven back in Europe. The defeat of both evils was imminent.

Gandhi was also finally out of prison.

The turnabouts defied belief. It seemed the war had drained Britain. In September 1944, newspapers carried reports that Gandhi and the leader of the Muslims were negotiating the nature of the independent state or states that would result from British withdrawal. The negotiations, as miraculous as they sounded, were not simple. Gandhi wanted a united India. But the Muslims wanted their own state, because they were afraid they would be overwhelmed by the more numerous Hindus.

In May 1945, the terrible war ended. But Amy's work was not yet finished. Nor was India's. Before 1945 ended, Britain announced it would give independence to India. Month after month, Hindu leaders and Muslim leaders bickered. Speculation began. Some began to hoard food. Some began to starve. Riots broke out. Muslims killed Hindus. Hindus killed Muslims. Amy was amazed at the insanity of it all.

Her own situation at times seemed insane, too. At one point in 1946, Amy realized she had not seen the sky in ten years! And yet the turmoil in India overshadowed all individual complaints. Hindus and Muslims squabbled and fought, but no one was prepared for what happened in Calcutta on August 16, 1946. Muslims had gathered for a rally in the great park called the Maiden. Hindus agitated the Muslims. Scuffles broke out. Fighting spread like wildfire. Blood poured out of lives all over the streets of Calcutta. The killing was not by guns, but by the butchery of *lathis* and knives and hatchets. Deaths were silent, except for screams of pain. Thousands died.

In August 1947, two countries were born: India for the Hindus and Pakistan for the Muslims. Satan continued his work. Hindus began to coerce Muslims remaining in India to convert to their faith. Likewise, Muslims began to force Hindus left in Pakistan to convert to their faith. Again, killing erupted. Hindus overpowered the Muslims left in India and slaughtered them. Muslims slaughtered the Hindus left in Pakistan. Refugees by the millions fled to safety.

In February 1947, Amy was stunned to learn that Murray's wife, Oda, insisted on an English education for the boys but refused to dump them in a boarding school. Amy remembered the pain of her own experience. Murray would either have to go to England or endure separation from his family. He decided to go to England. Amy did not take it well. Death would hardly have disappointed her more.

She still had enough strength at the age of eighty to get fired up. Upon reading that she wrote popular books, she stormed, "Popular? Lord, is that what these books written out of the heat of battle are? Popular? O Lord, burn the paper to ashes if that is true."[1] Sometimes she was so tired that she fell into self-pity. "For years, patiently the prayer meeting went on praying for me," she recorded. "It does not seem to do so now. I was feeling the need of prayer very much, but to ask for it would be selfish."[2]

At times now, Amy's strength failed her. On one morning in 1948, she wrote that she "woke feeling like ashes—as dull, as gray, in spirit—and all one ache in body."[3]

Would she have the strength to cooperate with Bishop Frank Houghton? Houghton was an old "China hand" from the China Inland Mission. He had been commissioned to write her biography. Amy felt just as George MacDonald had; the denial of self required that her personality be brought forth only so far as needed to advance good works. Anything more was intolerable. Still, if she had to trust someone to do her life, Frank Houghton was a good choice. She had corresponded with him many years. He and his wife had visited Dohnavur three times from 1943 to 1947. He had his hands full to be sure. He was awash in material. He arranged with Amy to send his product to her chapter by chapter for her critique. With God's help—and the assistance of Mary Mills and Neela—she would oblige him.

But on the evening of June 23, she slipped and fell in her room.

SEVENTEEN

Neela immediately sent for the doctors. Amy's injuries turned out to be a broken arm, a fractured thighbone, and an injury of undetermined severity to her hip. Amy hardly had the chance to feel sorry for herself. Godfrey Webb-Peploe was in worse shape than she was. His activity was now sharply curtailed because of failing health. Were all successors going to fall before she did? Ponnammal, Arulai, Murray. Now Godfrey?

December brought numbing news. Godfrey had a clot in his right leg. He had to have complete rest. The clot must not move. On February 19, 1949, Mary Mills came to Amy's side and said simply, "Godfrey is in heaven."[1]

Amy seemed to weaken within seconds. What was going to happen to their wonderful enterprise for Christ? Where was the leadership? She was now eighty-one and very weak. On top of everything else, the new Indian government was making new rules and regulations all the time. The Fellowship now had to send out students to other schools just so they could get certification to teach and train the children at Dohnavur. But something wonderful happened.

Ponnammal's daughter, Purripu, began to emerge as a real leader. And so did Mimosa's son, Rajappan. Why had Amy doubted God? Did she think she personally had done all this? Praise God for His grace. All her old axioms came flooding back: "If the day ends in what seems failure, don't fret. Tell Him you're sorry. Even so, don't be discouraged. All discouragement is of the devil." "We don't need to press Him, as if we had to deal with an unwilling God." "We don't need to suggest to Him what to do, for He Himself knows what to do." It seemed that in her fatigue Amy had forgotten all her own advice. But it all would end for the good. God was the Master.

By the time Amy turned eighty-three, she was truly immobile. She thought of little but her glorious homecoming. Oh, praise God for the joy of the moment! Think who she would see: her mother, her father, the D.O.M., Thomas Walker, Ponnammal, Kohila, Mimosa, Arulai, Godfrey. The moment surpassed all her capacity to even imagine such joy. Once in a while she was brought back to the present. Had she heard someone speak of a headstone? She had told them emphatically that under no circumstances was she to have a headstone in God's Garden.

"And no coffin, just a wooden slab," she reminded her surprised nurse.

Amy heard whispers wishing she would tell them that she heard celestial music and saw Bunyan's marvelous Shining Ones and so forth. Hadn't she told the Fellowship, poor souls, that—except for flowers and songs of joy—she wished to go quietly? Had they forgotten that the Lord had told her in a dream, "I shall come to thee in sleep—no rending good-byes—no distress to anyone"?

On January 18, 1951, He quietly kept His promise.

NOTES

Chapter 1

1. Houghton, Frank, *Amy Carmichael* (Fort Washington, PA: Christian Literature Crusade, 1953), 2. Copyright © 1953 by Dohnavur Fellowship. Used by permission.

Chapter 2

1. For further reading on this and other classic hymns, see Kenneth Osbeck, *Amazing Grace: 366 Hymn Stories for Personal Devotions* (Grand Rapids: Kregel, 1990), 73.

2. Houghton, Frank, *Amy Carmichael* (Fort Washington, PA: Christian Literature Crusade, 1953), 115.

Chapter 3

1. Kenneth Osbeck, *Amazing Grace: 366 Hymn Stories for Personal Devotions* (Grand Rapids: Kregel, 1990), 284.

2. Elisabeth Elliot, *A Chance to Die* (Grand Rapids: Revell, 1987), 39. Copyright 1987 by Fleming H. Revell. Used by permission.

Chapter 4

1. Elisabeth Elliot, *A Chance to Die* (Grand Rapids: Revell, 1987), 44.

2. Ibid., 36.

3. Ibid.

4. Houghton, Frank, *Amy Carmichael* (Fort Washington, PA: Christian Literature Crusade, 1953), 40.

Chapter 5

1. Houghton, Frank, *Amy Carmichael* (Fort Washington, PA: Christian Literature Crusade, 1953), 44.

2. Ibid., 46.

3. Ibid., 47–48.

4. Elisabeth Elliot, *A Chance to Die* (Grand Rapids: Revell, 1987), 36.

Chapter 6

1. Houghton, Frank, *Amy Carmichael* (Fort Washington, PA: Christian Literature Crusade, 1953), 62.

2. Ibid., 59.

3. Elisabeth Elliot, *A Chance to Die* (Grand Rapids: Revell, 1987), 82.

4. Houghton, *Amy Carmichael*, 72.

5. Elliot, *A Chance to Die*, 98.

6. Ibid., 104.

Chapter 7

1. Houghton, Frank, *Amy Carmichael* (Fort Washington, PA: Christian Literature Crusade, 1953), 83.

2. Ibid., 84–85.

3. Ibid., 89.

Chapter 8

1. Houghton, Frank, *Amy Carmichael* (Fort Washington, PA: Christian Literature Crusade, 1953), 97.

Chapter 9

1. Houghton, Frank, *Amy Carmichael* (Fort Washington, PA: Christian Literature Crusade, 1953), 109.

2. Ibid., 115.

3. Ibid., 134.

4. Ibid., 154.

Chapter 10

1. Houghton, Frank, *Amy Carmichael* (Fort Washington, PA: Christian Literature Crusade, 1953), 177.

2. Ibid., 172.

3. Amy Carmichael, *Gold Cord* (Fort Washington, PA: Christian Literature Crusade, 1932), 178. Copyright © 1932 by Dohnavur Fellowship. Used by permission.

Chapter 11

1. Houghton, Frank, *Amy Carmichael* (Fort Washington, PA: Christian Literature Crusade, 1953), 239.

2. Ibid., 201.

3. Ibid., 195.

4. Ibid., 196.

Chapter 12

1. Houghton, Frank, *Amy Carmichael* (Fort Washington, PA: Christian Literature Crusade, 1953), 255.

2. Ibid.

3. Ibid., 265.

4. Ibid.

5. Ibid., 323.

6. Ibid., 284.

Chapter 13

1. Houghton, Frank, *Amy Carmichael* (Fort Washington, PA: Christian Literature Crusade, 1953), 335.

2. Ibid., 336.

3. Amy Carmichael, *Rose from Brier* (Fort Washington, PA: Christian Literature Crusade, 1933), 53. Copyright 1933 by Dohnavur Fellowship. Used by permission.

4. Houghton, *Amy Carmichael*, 318.

5. Amy Carmichael, *This One Thing* (Fort Washington, PA: Christian Literature Crusade, 1950), 79–83. Copyright © 1950 by Dohnavur Fellowship. Used by permission.

6. Amy Carmichael, *Edges of His Ways* (Fort Washington, PA: Christian Literature Crusade, 1955), 194–197. Copyright © 1955 by Dohnavur Fellowship. Used by permission.

7. Houghton, *Amy Carmichael*, 322.

8. Ibid., 322.

Chapter 14

1. Houghton, Frank, *Amy Carmichael* (Fort Washington, PA: Christian Literature Crusade, 1953), 326.

2. Ibid., 332.

3. Ibid., 329.

4. Ibid., 309.

5. Ibid., 307.

6. Ibid., 318.

7. Amy Carmichael, *Kohila* (Fort Washington, PA: Christian Literature Crusade, 1939). Copyright © 1939 by Dohnavur Fellowship. Used by permission.

8. Houghton, *Amy Carmichael*, 344.

9. Ibid., 355.

10. Ibid., 358.

Chapter 15

1. Houghton, Frank, *Amy Carmichael* (Fort Washington, PA: Christian

Literature Crusade, 1953), 311.
    2. Ibid.
    3. Ibid., 340.
    4. Ibid., 304.

Chapter 16
    1. Houghton, Frank, *Amy Carmichael* (Fort Washington, PA: Christian Literature Crusade, 1953), 329.
    2. Ibid., 324.
    3. Ibid., 312.

Chapter 17
    1. Houghton, Frank, *Amy Carmichael* (Fort Washington, PA: Christian Literature Crusade, 1953), 363.

CORRIE TEN BOOM

FAITH AMIDST FEAR

SAM WELLMAN

ONE

The vaporizer on the small alcohol stove spewed a fog of camphor and water into the air of the dark bedroom. The vapor settled over Corrie ten Boom, who clutched a blanket over herself on a bed. Aches shadowed every movement of her body.

Corrie ten Boom felt her years. It seemed as if until today she had never stopped long enough in all her fifty-two years to let age catch up with her. But more than age caught up with her today. Her prayer was a plea for many things to pass. Jesus had been in her heart for a very long time, and she hoped her fear was just momentary, just another unpleasant symptom of the flu.

It seemed everyone in Holland must know the ten Booms were hiding fugitives in their house. After all, it was 1944. Holland had been infested by German soldiers for four years. The worst of all the Germans were the slithery Gestapo, the secret police of the Nazis. The ten Booms had been hiding Jews and Dutch boys in their house for two years. They never had fewer than seven fugitives living with them these desperate days. How much longer could their secret last before the dreaded Gestapo bashed on their door? The Gestapo struck at night like vipers. Their victims were groggy, unprepared—like Corrie felt now.

She had slept in this very same bedroom in this very same house as long as she could remember. Her home was precious to her. The past was so wonderful that thinking about it softened her pain. Her thoughts drifted back. . . .

As far back as Corrie could remember, her home was *gezellig*, close and warm and cozy—smelling of soup and fresh bread, and sounding of soft laughter and the rustles of Mama and three aunts in long dresses. A five-year-old like Corrie could have a wonderful party with her doll Casperina under the dining room table. She could even creep down the steps into Papa's workroom behind his shop that faced Barteljorisstraat. Silently she sat and smelled his cigar and listened to clocks ticking and tocking like hundreds of heartbeats. She watched bearded Papa bent over his bench. Each time he placed some tiny thing in a watch, he would pause and say, "Thank You, Lord," as gently as if he were talking to Corrie or Mama. That was Papa. God must have been right there with him.

Still, as gezellig as the home was, there were limits on the quantities of sound and activity that were correct and proper for a Dutch home in 1897. And to be allowed to explode beyond those limits, five-year-old Corrie had to play outside in the narrow alley. Her aunts with their tight-bunned hair seemed very happy when she asked for permission to play outside before she dashed into the alley. But Mama was not so happy.

Except on her sick days, Mama's great wide blue eyes would appear in the dining room window again and again to check on her. Aunt Bep called Corrie the "baby" of the family. Corrie heard her say that while she was playing with Casperina under the table one day. Corrie didn't like to be called a baby. If another baby would just arrive, she wouldn't be the baby anymore.

Out in the alley, Corrie was not a baby. She was just one of many children who played there. Except for the town square and streets, which were bricked solid and overrun with grown-ups, there was little other open space in downtown Haarlem. The alleys were not much more than sun-starved slits among tall buildings, but they did have precious space. And they weren't dangerous like the streets. It was rare for a wagon or a rider to intrude into the alley.

Corrie skipped rope by herself on her sturdy legs or joined the other children to play bowl-the-hoop or a game with a ball and stones called *bikkelen*. Even blue-skinned Sammy was out there almost every day, bundled up and slumped in a wheelchair. It was hard to include him in much more than an occasional game of tag, when he was home base. Sammy's moment came when Corrie's sister Nollie—the *moedertje*, the "little mother"—came home from school. She would start to play with the other children, but in no time at all, she was pushing Sammy's wheelchair, mothering him.

Nollie's return expanded Corrie's world.

While Sammy slumped even more in his wheelchair and began grumbling about potholes rattling his bones, Nollie would go inside to get permission to go to the square with Corrie. The two sisters would hold hands and hurry down the alley. On Barteljorisstraat horses pulled trolley cars, clanging toward the town square only half a block distant. From the square itself, rich bells bonged and pealed. They would whisk down the narrow sidewalk past tall, dark brick buildings until Corrie saw the gothic spire of Saint Bavo's towering over the square. The girls would find a bench and watch grown-ups strolling through the square or hurrying to their trolley.

The square was crowded with tailors' businesses and shops of housewares and other specialties of all kinds. Many people bustled in and out of the shops. Nestled against St. Bavo's was the fish market. Across a tiny street was the butcher's hall. On one side of the square was the town hall. Three times a week the area was choked with farmers walking in wooden *klompen*, selling fruit and vegetables to the women of Haarlem, who wore long black dresses and black bonnets.

When the square was too crowded with farmers, the sisters would find cousin Dot, who lived next to Saint Bavo's, and sneak inside the great cathedral. Uncle Arnold was an usher of the church. Inside was a colossal golden organ that sounded as heavenly as it looked. The cathedral always made Corrie think of heaven.

Sometimes they ventured a short way down Damstraat to the Spaarne River. It was a bouquet of colorful boats. Their pilots bragged they could take Corrie anyplace in Holland on a boat. It was no surprise to her. She couldn't go more than a few blocks from home in any direction without coming to a canal or the river. And of course if she walked west of Haarlem with Papa, in not much more than an hour's time, she faced the mighty North Sea.

But the two sisters didn't always leave the alley to go to the town square. Sometimes while they played, Corrie would hear a commotion from the direction away from Barteljorisstraat and plead, "Oh, please, Nollie, let's go see!"

Nollie didn't ask permission. "We'll only look."

Nollie would take her cautiously down the alley to Smedestraat. There they might see the bad-smelling man called Crazy Thys, whirling in confusion, teased on all sides by children. But lately it was Corrie, not seven-year-old Nollie, who scolded the children for their cruelty. Or they might see police scooping up drunkards in front of saloons and dragging them off to the station house. The saloons on Smedestraat always made Corrie think of hell.

Their home seemed balanced between a world tainted with sights and sounds of hell on one side and a world blessed with sights and sounds of heaven on the other side. But heaven and hell were real places. She knew this because Papa read the Bible aloud to them every day at exactly eight thirty in the morning and nine forty-five at night. In the Bible, Jesus spoke of heaven and He spoke of hell. It wasn't that long ago that on one of their walks she and Nollie were bowled over by a nasty man on a bicycle. Spattered with mud, they ran inside the house. Everyone came running to the squalling Nollie. While they wiped the mud off Nollie and hugged away her hurts, timid Corrie stood aside in a corner, silent and trembling, her hurts unnoticed. But that was before Jesus came into her heart.

And not long before that she and Nollie had gone with Mama when she took fresh bread to Mrs. Hoog one block away. Right in the midst of several unusually quiet grown-ups in a room was a crib with a baby in it. The smooth white face with delicate lashes over the closed eyes looked sweeter than any doll. Nollie gently touched the cheek. So Corrie touched the tiny hand. It was ice cold!

"Baby is dead!" gasped Corrie.

That night in bed she clutched Nollie's nightgown tighter than ever.

Death. A baby. If an innocent baby that looked sweeter than any doll could die, then why couldn't anyone die at any time? Even Mama. Even Papa. Even Corrie herself! If Papa didn't talk to her about Jesus every night, would she ever be able to sleep again? Would she ever let go of Nollie's nightgown?

And yet one day not long ago, as Corrie played under the dining room table, Mama had suggested she invite Jesus into her heart. After that she no longer clutched Nollie's nightgown at night. Jesus was not just in the Bible. He was real. He was alive inside her heart. She was as sure of that as anything in her world. Mama said Jesus would never let her down. Unless, of course, Corrie forgot He was there.

TWO

Corrie was six when one morning came that she dreaded. Summer was over, and more than that was over. Betsie, her oldest sister, who seemed almost grown-up because she had something called anemia and had to sit around knitting, was in the bedroom with her and Nollie.

Now was the perfect time for Corrie to explain her plan to her sisters. "I've decided," rattled Corrie, "it would really be best if I stayed home to help Aunt Anna. Why start school at all?"

In a tired voice, Betsie said, "Let me help you lace your shoes, Corrie." And she used a buttonhook on Corrie's high-topped shoes.

Corrie said, "Did you hear me? I've decided—"

Nollie interrupted her, "Don't forget your hat, Corrie."

Corrie looked at the gray hat Nollie had worn to school last year. "You don't understand. I've decided..." She stopped. Her sisters had already left the bedroom to go downstairs to breakfast.

They wouldn't listen. She had never been to school one day in her life, and she didn't intend to start today. She saw the clock on the dresser. It was ten after eight! She grabbed the floppy gray hat, even though she had no use for it, and ran down two flights of stairs. In the dining room she slapped it on a peg on the wall next to Nollie's pillbox hat and hopped into her chair.

Papa was at the table. Mama and Aunt Anna were serving. Brother Peter, eleven and always hungry, impatiently cracked his knuckles and eyed the pot of yellow cheese and a platter with a large, round loaf of fresh bread. Everyone was at breakfast but Aunt Jans. Corrie could tell Papa and Mama now of her wonderful plan....

But Mama spoke first. "Aunt Jans is making a tonic in the kitchen." Corrie listened with deaf ears as Mama explained why Aunt Jans didn't feel well. There was always some reason.

There was so much commotion and breakfast tasted so delicious, Corrie forgot something. Then she remembered! Now she would announce her wonderful plan....

The door to the alley opened. "The workers are here," said Peter impatiently.

Corrie joined the others at the table in exchanging a friendly "*Goedemorgen*" with the clock man and the errand boy who worked in the shop for Papa.

"Sit down, friends." Papa put on his rimless glasses and opened the Bible.

He read a psalm in his slow, deep voice.

The instant Papa gently closed the Bible, Peter jumped from the table, snatched his cap from a peg, leaped down the five steps of the stairway, and bolted out the door into the alley. Nollie was right behind him.

As Betsie gracefully followed them down the stairs, Mama's eyes widened at Corrie. "Nollie forgot to take Corrie with her."

Thank God Nollie forgot, thought Corrie. *It's not too late to explain.* Corrie said, "I've decided that it would really be best if I stayed home to help Aunt Anna. Why start school at all?"

Papa rose from the table. "Corrie doesn't want to go alone on her first day to school." He took her hand in one hand and the gray hat from the peg with the other.

It was only long after Papa had firmly removed the hand she tried to anchor to the railing on the stairs and had tugged her to school that she remembered Jesus. He was in her heart. She asked Him for courage. Almost at that moment she saw her cousin Dot in the classroom. They were already good friends. For years they would go to school together. Corrie would not be alone.

School was not without peril. One terrible recess, Corrie stepped on a blue ceramic tile that the headmaster had warned all the students not to touch. Out of nowhere, a ham of a hand popped her in the face. She had never even been spanked before. The headmaster's slap was the most humiliating moment of her life. The horror burned into her memory like a photograph: a girl in a red dress and white apron stood in front of her, and there was a green gate—then the vicious slap, a punishment a thousand times worse than her "sin."

By the time Corrie was ten, she had the nickname Kees. It was a boy's name because she was a tomboy. Betsie was a tall, delicate, sloe-eyed seventeen-year-old with thick chestnut hair. Nollie was twelve, solid and blond, with a square face and nose so perfect they belonged on a princess. Both sisters turned the heads of boys like magnets. But then there was Corrie. The pretty little girl lengthened and strengthened in all the wrong places. She became pigeon-toed and high-hipped. Her lips were wide and so thin they were a cartoon. Her jaw got stubborn and never softened. Her eyes, turned down on the corners, would have seemed perpetually sorrowful if she hadn't smiled so much. Such slight differences between beautiful and homely!

But realizing she was not attractive to boys seemed to make Corrie ornery. She and Dot had some very good times—before and after school. Once Dot found a dime broken into two pieces. They carefully pieced it back together on the countertop at the sweet shop to pay for ten pieces of candy. They were running out of the shop as the dime disintegrated in the owner's fingers. Another time they snowballed top hats off stuffy gentlemen on the sidewalk. What a great trick it was to play the sweet little angels and retrieve the top hats from the street. As she and Dot conscientiously brushed the snow off the splendid hats, they acted as indignant as the gentlemen as their outraged eyes searched the streets for the villains.

But she and Dot had the most fun in Saint Bavo's Cathedral. For as long as Corrie could remember, she had gone there every Sunday morning for the service. She put on her Christmas dress and trudged behind Papa and the ladies. Some said the organ in the cathedral had five thousand pipes, but who could count them? High above the pews hung tiny bells in the form of ships. The cavernous cathedral, which was always cool during the summer and in winter bone-chilling, seemed warm when she played there with Dot after school.

Dot actually lived in a little house for the usher nestled into the side of the cathedral. Dot and Corrie could play inside the vast interior everywhere but the pulpit. They played tag around the massive pillars. They hid in closets during hide-and-seek. They slipped through the swinging half doors on the pews and defended themselves against Napoleon. They opened closed doors and climbed the Matterhorn on winding staircases. They clomped up the very steps Mozart climbed into the organ loft, and they pretended to play the colossal organ with its sixty-eight stops. The great stone-and-brick interior echoed with their screams of delight. Once in a while Uncle Arnold would shush them for a moment with, "Please, children, there are graves of saints below you." But that didn't slow them down for long.

Corrie loved to scheme and make plans. It was a trait of everyone in her family, but it amazed her girlfriends who did not know that.

But Corrie might have been better off if she had not carried out some of her plans. Once at school she wanted to show off her watch. She was the only one of sixty in her class who had one. She hatched a plan. She urged her classmates to smuggle their caps and hats into the room and hide them under their desks. She would signal at precisely two o'clock, and they would all pop their caps and hats on their heads to astonish the teacher. The teacher wouldn't punish the whole class. But at two o'clock, when Corrie waved her hand, popped her blue and white sailor hat on her head, and looked around triumphantly, the other students just gazed at her with cow's eyes. She realized the joke was on her as the teacher angrily sent her away to the headmaster.

That night Nollie was aghast. "Papa would be so ashamed that you used your watch that way."

"That's not all," admitted Corrie. "I didn't go to the headmaster. I hid in a coat closet until school got out."

She had never seen Nollie so upset. "Do you remember the line that is repeated over and over in Psalm 107, Corrie? 'Then they cried out to the Lord in their trouble, and he saved them from their distress.' You had better do just that!"

So that's what Corrie did the rest of the evening. She cried out to the Lord in her trouble. She prayed and prayed. The next day she almost crawled to the headmaster. He didn't punish her at all for her "sin."

Corrie kept telling herself she didn't care how she looked. And so what if she did act like a boy once in a while? Once she skipped home from school smashing big black flies against a wooden fence. She smashed more than one. Then she heard the deep voice behind her, "What a joy to meet my youngest daughter here on the street." It was Papa. There wasn't the slightest reprimand in his voice, and at that moment she was embarrassed. She felt dirty. When they walked through the door from the alley, he said, "I know you will want to wash your hands before you see your mother."

The love in her home finally seemed to put out the fire of Corrie's rebellion.

THREE

Corrie began to care about her manners. She didn't want to be a tomboy. She knew she would never be beautiful, and she would never have the desire or flair for elegant clothes that Betsie and Nollie had. But she did want to be a young lady. No one could long resist the love of a family so grounded in Christ.

The outside world made Corrie cherish home life more. Nothing unfair happened at home. Even Aunt Bep's sour outlook on life was only a mild irritation. Mama made her understand that much of Aunt Bep's unhappiness was only talk. Bitter talk was certainly a sin, warned about in the Proverbs, and in the book by James. But it need only be a small sin if smothered by love so it would not spread. Corrie understood Aunt Bep was to be tolerated, even loved.

On the other hand, the peculiar ways of Aunt Jans were amusing. She was imperious and demanding but also generous. Once she came into some money, and her first act was to go out and buy presents for everyone in the family. Aunt Jans would never hoard the money for herself. Her husband, Hendrick Wildeboer, who had died young, had been a minister. Aunt Jans still ministered in her own way. She was well known around Haarlem for the fiery tracts she wrote. Then there was wise Aunt Anna. Corrie's prospects were so poor when she was born prematurely that Mama wrote later: "Nearly dead, she looked bluish white, and I never saw anything so pitiful. Nobody thought she would live." It was Aunt Anna who took Corrie—who had come too soon from Mama's womb—and carried her wrapped in her apron snug against the warmth of her plump belly, as if she still were in the womb. Aunt Anna was the one who kept the house spotless and the soup on the stove. Aunt Anna was the one Papa paid one guilder a week, only to have to ask for its return before the week was out. Aunt Anna was the one who added a sash or ribbon to Corrie's Christmas dress so it would look a little different on every Sunday and every special occasion as she wore it for the obligatory year.

Corrie's sisters and brother were the best of friends. Willem was witty but too often lapsed into seriousness, even gloom. Nollie was the strong sister. Of all the children, she was the most "normal," rarely ill or in trouble. Betsie was a sleepy-eyed beauty but had resolved never to marry because she had anemia. Marriage would destroy her. One had to look no further than Mama to see how bearing children could break a frail woman down.

Not that Mama ever seemed to regret it. Although barely forty years old, she lived in white-knuckled pain from gallstones. For several years, when the pain became too intense, she resorted to surgery. But after she had a minor stroke, the doctor gave her bad news: The surgery was too dangerous now; she just had to bear the pain of the gallstones. She never acted the martyr, but always the peacemaker. It was Mama who understood what was in someone's mind in a flash and smoothed things over before anyone else even realized what was happening. It was Mama who knitted baby clothes or wrote cheery messages for shut-ins—often from her invalid's bed!

And then there was Papa, so well known as the best watchmaker in Holland that young men came from all over Europe to ask to be his apprentices. Papa always tried to accommodate them. But he was much more than a superb watchmaker. How he loved the Jews, God's chosen people. He came from a long line of ten Booms who were never afraid to take God's side as revealed in the Bible. Papa's grandfather Gerrit lost his job as a gardener because he spoke up against the dictator Napoleon. Papa's father Willem, the original watchmaker at Barteljorisstraat, started a Society for Israel—a fellowship to pray for the Jews—in 1844 when it was unpopular to befriend the Jews.

Papa's love for the Jews matured in his first years as a watchmaker in the poor Jewish section of Amsterdam. He read the Old Testament—their Talmud—with them and even celebrated their Sabbath and holy days. He lived fifteen fruitful years in Amsterdam. He met Mama there. All the ten Boom children were born there. Aunt Anna and Aunt Bep were already living with him in Amsterdam.

Soon Papa returned to Haarlem. His father, Willem, died, and his mother needed help with the shop.

Papa accepted God's love, and he loved everyone. Like Jesus, he told parables on many occasions. One time she told Papa she was not only afraid of dying, but she was afraid someone in the family would die. After all, Mama and Jans both were sick a lot. How could she bear such pain?

Papa asked her, "When we take the train to Amsterdam, when do I give you the ticket?"

"Just before we get on the train."

"And so God will give you the courage to carry the pain when the time comes for someone to die. Until then you should not carry the pain. God does not want you to."

Before and *after* every meal Papa would ask God to bless the queen. He ended grace with, "Let soon come the day that Jesus, Your beloved Son, comes on the clouds of heaven. Amen." He never stopped reminding everyone that Christ was going to return.

Papa made sure the ten Booms didn't neglect what Haarlem had to offer. Right in the town hall hung paintings by Holland's masters of light, Vermeer, Rembrandt, and Haarlem's own Frans Hals. The masters reminded Corrie of the "Golden Age" of Holland and the terrible price they paid for it.

It was the sensitive Betsie who helped Corrie understand the groups of burgher guards and Haarlem corporations painted by Frans Hals. Each individual was bathed in light, caught in a fleeting moment hundreds of years before, somehow more real than the gawkers in the town hall. Every time there was a concert, all the ten Booms but Mama would traipse to the concert hall, not to go inside, but to gather in the alley outside the hall with other music lovers too poor to buy tickets. The glorious music came billowing right out the stage door to those willing to stand for hours in the chilly night.

It seemed that every evening at home blossomed with activity. The family gathered on the second floor, in Aunt Jans's rooms, crammed with huge furniture she brought with her after her Hendrick died. A favorite pastime was reading aloud wonderful books by writers like Charles Dickens or Louisa May Alcott. Once Corrie was so inspired she secretly labored over her own masterpiece. It was a magnificent tale of the adventures of Corrie, Dot, their friends, and no parents. She learned the hard way not to flaunt her manuscript. Betsie was brutally frank about its flaws. Corrie angrily hid the manuscript in the attic, and by the time she thought of it again, it had been critiqued into shreds by mice.

Often the family would sing. They learned to sing everything from hymns to the Bach chorale "Seid froh die Weil." Willem sang tenor, Nollie soprano, and Corrie alto. Another favorite was Bible study combined with language study. That was one of the ways Corrie learned to read English and German almost as well as her native Dutch. Mama would read a passage in Dutch. Willem would read the same passage in Hebrew or Greek. Papa or Betsie would read it in German. Nollie would read it in French. And Corrie would read the same passage in English.

Every time the family was blessed in some way, Mama would put a penny for the missionaries in a small metal box in the dining room. This was her way of showing thanks to God. Guests would bring flutes and violins and all kinds of instruments to play in Aunt Jans's front room, where she had an upright piano. Aunt Jans even began inviting soldiers she saw loitering in the streets. One soldier was such a talented musician she talked him into giving Nollie and Corrie lessons on her pump organ.

It seemed every member of the family was a natural organizer. Soon Aunt Jans organized a soldiers' center and raised funds for a building of their own.

She went there herself to give Bible lessons and sing hymns. Corrie sang there, too. Even solos.

Aunt Anna was an organizer, as well. She organized a club for servant girls. The poor innocents needed encouragement. They were often alone and preyed upon. Every Wednesday she would meet with her girls for Bible study and hymns. And if one of her girls got in "trouble," Aunt Anna couldn't have been more heartbroken if the girl were her own daughter. Papa organized, too. He published a little magazine for watchmakers. He was always involved in civic events such as the annual parade for the queen's birthday. And every week when he visited the houses of rich Haarlemites to wind their clocks, he would adjourn afterward with the servants for Bible lessons. One just couldn't live in Christ without wanting to help one and all. And sometimes it was necessary to organize to get started.

By the time Corrie was fourteen, she had a perspective on life that never changed. She had Jesus in her heart. She was a lady. She loved Holland and the queen. She knew a good family was a wonderful blessing not to be neglected, yet she still had to cope outside the family. The world outside could not be avoided, but she knew that success or failure outside in the world must not interfere with the family.

FOUR

Corrie was fourteen years old when she met Karel. Willem brought him home from college for one of Mama's celebrations. All she remembered from that occasion was tall, blond Karel. A young man of nineteen like Willem, he smoked a cigar like Papa. Karel was polite, but his deep brown eyes remained aloof.

It was not unusual for Corrie to be struck by love. She had loved every boy in her class at one time or another. Of course, none of them knew it. She was too shy and much too sure of her homeliness. But this love for Karel was different. Here he was—right in their home. That familiarity made him special, as if he, like her family, cared nothing about how she looked but cared only about what was in her heart.

Thus began a time in her life when Corrie was glad to be female. How she liked romance stories now. It seemed she was in the public library every day checking out romantic novels. Two years later, Nollie and Corrie decided to visit Willem at his university. Leiden was no more than a short train ride south along the dunes. Corrie tried to calm herself as the train rumbled along. She must not expect too much. Karel probably wouldn't even be there. Besides, how many times before had she mooned over a boy only to discover in the light of day that the boy was truly a monster? She must be more like Nollie— just be nonchalant and let things happen. But how could she be calm when her heart was beating like the North Sea crashing against the dikes?

Willem greeted them on the fourth floor of a private home where he roomed. It seemed like only moments until Karel and three other men appeared in Willem's room.

It was in that moment that Karel won Corrie's heart. Somewhere in the exchange of pleasant introductions, he said, "Why, of course. We already know each other."

Was he looking at Nollie? No, he seemed to be looking at Corrie! Her romance novels failed her. She could not think of a single word to reply.

Corrie sat there, paralyzed.

When Karel looked right at her and asked her if she was going to normal school next year, Corrie blurted, "No, I'm staying home with Mama and Aunt Anna."

Later as they returned home on the train, her answer lingered with her, childishly weak. Yet she was needed at home more than ever. Aunt Bep had tuberculosis. The poor woman lay in her room most of the time now and coughed. Faithful sweet Aunt Anna alone tended to her so that no others would be exposed to the germs. Mama was not strong either. And Aunt Jans was just Aunt Jans. Aunt Anna did need help, but Corrie really wasn't sure if she wanted to stay at home. She finished secondary school and began working at home. She was not happy. She felt hot and weak. Surely it was her indecision. Once when the doctor made his regular call on Aunt Bep, Mama asked him, "Can you examine Corrie? She seems feverish to me."

In far too short a time, the doctor said, "Corrie does have a fever. She has tuberculosis." Her future was yanked away from her as cruelly as a fish suddenly hooked and yanked from the North Sea!

The doctor ordered bed rest immediately. Bed rest was a stunning blow. Corrie's life seemed barely started. At least Aunt Bep had gone out into the world for thirty-five years. How could God do this to her? How could this be happening?

She hid her bitterness. In a house of the chronically sick, such as Aunt Bep, Aunt Jans, and Mama, how could she complain? She didn't want to be sour like Aunt Bep, but tuberculosis for people with little money was a death sentence. Only an expensive sanitarium and special care could save a victim of this dreaded lung disease.

Who counseled her? Was it Papa? Or was it in her own feverish hysteria that she quoted Paul's litany of miseries from 2 Corinthians?

It was definitely Corrie who responded testily, "What is the point?"

"The point, dearest Corrie," answered a voice, "is that it is an honor to suffer for Christ."

Willem came by to sit with her. His exams were coming up. He had her drill him on theology, and he left some books with her. She passed the time reading books about church history. She studied her Bible. She read of Paul and his never-ending trials. She found strength in the Gospels.

She began to sense the living Christ. She prayed more and more. Soon she was praying for hours every day, but she had to keep telling herself she was not losing hope, because deep in her heart she felt doomed. And as if she did not have enough to worry about, she developed a pain in her stomach.

She had been in bed five months when the doctor paid one of his regular visits to his patients in the ten Boom house. "How are you doing, Corrie?" he asked routinely. Corrie pressed the right side of her abdomen. "I have a pain here, doctor."

He poked and watched her wince. "You have appendicitis."

After the operation, her fever vanished. Corrie was perfectly healthy. She had never had tuberculosis at all!

The time in bed had solidified Corrie's flabby plans about getting out into the world. She began normal school and eagerly sought things to do outside the home. Her friend Mina talked her into telling Bible stories in Mina's class in a Christian school for children. Unsure of herself, Corrie asked Betsie's advice. Betsie had a perfect solution. Corrie would polish her technique in Betsie's Sunday school class first.

What a revelation. Her first time in front of children Corrie exhausted the story of Jesus feeding the five thousand in five minutes! Without a moment's hesitation, as if it had been planned, Betsie took up the story. She made the story come alive. Where were people sitting? Where had they come from? Did Jesus speak to them from the bottom of the hill or the top? What did the Sea of Galilee look like? What were the people thinking before the miracle? What did they think after the miracle?

After that Corrie realized Betsie really did know how to tell a story. It was as if she painted a wonderful detailed picture, like one of the old masters. So Corrie perfected her technique in Betsie's class, then began to tell Bible stories in Mina's class, always remembering Betsie's flair for telling a story so it came alive. Corrie continued her studies in normal school and became more confident outside the home. Now she definitely wanted to leave home, but she felt guilty. They needed her so much.

She asked her own Bible teacher Mrs. van Lennep, "Am I wrong to want to leave home when they can use my help?"

"To want to leave home is natural. Actually, to leave may be wrong or right. Perhaps you will never have a chance to leave, Corrie. If something definite comes up, then decide."

Something definite did come up. A wealthy family named Bruin needed a governess for their little girl. Corrie had diplomas in child care, needlework, and other domestic skills from normal school. Her moment had finally come.

She told Mama and Papa about the opportunity.

Mama saw immediately what was bothering her. "Don't feel you have to stay at home. We did not ask your brother Willem or your sisters to stay at home."

"Everyone expects the son to leave home. And Nollie and Betsie are still here at home," argued Corrie.

"Nollie teaches school. She doesn't really stay at home."

"But Betsie really stays at home," argued Corrie.

Mama said, "Betsie stays by her own wish."

"But she helps Papa in the shop. You and Aunt Anna need help in the house."

Papa said, "You go take that job. If God thinks it's a bad idea, you'll know."

So Corrie left for Zandvoort, a sunny town by the North Sea, only five miles southwest of Haarlem. Zandvoort had wide sandy beaches and bright sprawling mansions. The Bruins lived in a mansion. The little girl was a difficult charge, but Corrie knew how to hold a child's interest with a good story. Although she soon won the little girl's respect and trust, the Bruin family was very alien to Corrie. They were selfish and cynical. They gloated over their social superiority. They talked of nothing but money and possessions. Corrie was miserable. She didn't want to stay. How could she remain in such a sinful place? But she didn't want to quit either. Perhaps she could sow the seed of the gospel in the little girl. Who would save this little girl if she left?

One day Willem appeared at the mansion. "Aunt Bep is dead. At last her suffering is over. You must come home, Corrie. Aunt Anna is exhausted from caring for her. Mama is getting sicker every day. Betsie must work in the shop. Nollie has a permanent job as a schoolteacher. And you know Aunt Jans is just Aunt Jans."

The logic escaped Corrie. "Why does Aunt Bep's death change anything? She was no help anyway. It seems as if Aunt Anna would be free to do more housework now."

"Corrie, I have seen the state of the house. Help is needed. None of them would ever complain; you know that."

So the decision to leave was made for her. When she left the mansion, she was sad for the little girl. But Corrie knew when the family found out that she had been teaching her about the Bible they would have forced Corrie to go anyway. The great sandy beach was a novelty for Willem, so they strolled its vastness for a while before they returned to Haarlem. Slowly, joy grew in her heart. God knew best. But she couldn't bring herself to approve of Willem singing Bach at the top of his lungs.

"How can you sing when Aunt Bep just died?" she asked.

"A true Christian rejoices when a loved one goes to heaven to be with the Lord. Grief is an indulgence for ourselves."

Couldn't the reason for joy be mistaken for something else? Or was worrying about what other people thought an indulgence, too? Corrie would have to think about it a lot more before she could bring herself to sing. Besides, her grand venture into the world was over, and she felt she had failed.

FIVE

Once again Corrie was home. Now Corrie was the housekeeper of the home. She didn't get comfort from the acts of cleaning house and cooking like Mama and Aunt Anna did. Her goal every day was simply to finish the work faster than she did the day before.

Mama bluntly told her, "Housework is not fulfilling for you, Corrie."

Papa said, "Yes, Corrie. You need more. What about the new Bible school that just opened in Haarlem?"

So once again Corrie attended school, attacking what seemed to be their entire curriculum at once: ethics, dogmatics, church history, Old Testament, New Testament, Old Testament history, and New Testament history. She studied very hard in her moments outside of housework.

Other activities began to occupy her outside the home, too. Jan Willem Gunning was organizing groups in Holland for foreign missions. All four young ten Booms became active: Corrie, Willem, Nollie, and Betsie. The purpose was to have the Dutch meet real missionaries from around the world and be inspired to support mission work.

Corrie went to one conference alone. She heard the testimony of a young missionary named Sadhu Sundar Singh. He told the conference, "As a boy in India, I learned to hate Jesus. I burned a Bible. I threw mud at missionaries. But it was out of frustration, not hate." He prayed that if God really existed, He would reveal Himself. He longed to know if there was life after death and if there was paradise. He decided the only way to know for sure was to die, so he was going to throw himself in front of a train. Suddenly, in a blaze of light, he saw a man. The Sadhu heard a voice from the light ask him how long he would deny Him who died for him. Then the Sadhu saw the man's pierced hands.

Corrie was in awe. The Sadhu had had an experience like Paul's on the road to Damascus! How Corrie longed for such an experience. Why was her life so never-endingly drab? Wasn't she, too, a child of God? Didn't she let Jesus come into her heart? And then a very strange thing happened to her. Strolling alone in the heather, she met the Sadhu out walking alone, too. Somehow she never imagined him being alone.

She couldn't contain herself. "Why haven't I had such an experience? I received Jesus as my Savior. I believe in Him with all my heart."

"Then your experience is more miraculous than mine. In chapter 20 of the book of John, Jesus told Thomas: 'Because you have seen me, you have believed; blessed are those who have not seen and yet have believed.' I had to see Jesus to believe. You believe in Him without seeing Him."

Corrie was stunned. Of course the Sadhu was right. Why was she such a doubter, asking for miracles like the Pharisees?

Soon Corrie wondered what she would do after she passed Bible school. She had been studying for two years. Soon she would take the final exams. The first part of the examination at Bible school was to give lessons to students and answer their questions. This she did with ease. After all, she had been giving Bible lessons for several years now anyway. She was very able with students.

The second part of the exam was in Saint Bavo's. It was held in a conference room off one of the pillared corridors. Several ministers sat at a massive oak table. This room in the cathedral was like a tomb. It really seemed God had deserted her.

They began with ethics.

"You studied only the teachings of Mr. Johnson?" asked one of the ministers, not hiding his displeasure.

"He's one of the instructors," she answered lamely. Corrie knew she was in trouble. Her brain began to curdle. Too late, she realized that God had not deserted her but she had deserted God. Why hadn't she asked for His help sooner? Was she so proud of her learning? The subjects rose one by one. All seven. At the end of the day, she had a perfect record: She had not passed one subject. She had failed utterly and completely!

At home Betsie said, "You must take the exam again right away."

But Corrie did not do that. The defeat was too stinging. Maybe she had attempted too much. After all, she could still serve the church by teaching catechism to children. She could still prepare people for confirmation. And she could teach Bible lessons in the public schools. She knew she was a good teacher, even a gifted teacher, thanks to all her practice and Betsie. But she was in no hurry to be humiliated again by the ministers—after all her hard work!

Haarlem was not stagnant. A new Frans Hals Museum opened in the very home for the elderly where Hals had died in 1666. The city's collection of masters was moved there from the town hall. The masterpieces were better lit and more accessible. And the town hall was rebuilding its wonderful gothic tower that was torn down in the 1700s.

But the times were full of bad news, too. Europe rippled with rumors of war. Rumors threatened to poison the prayer group that Corrie, Betsie, and Papa met with every week. They took the trolley south to the village of Heemstede every Saturday night. Papa continued to pray for the queen and Holland, but some in the meeting objected now. Christians should not support governments. Papa countered with what Paul said in chapter 2 of 1 Timothy:

> *I exhort therefore, that, first of all, supplications, prayers, intercessions, and giving of thanks, be made for all men; for kings, and for all that are in authority; that we may lead a quiet and peaceable life in all godliness and honesty. For this is good and acceptable in the sight of God our Saviour.*

The message seemed clear to Corrie. Holland even managed to stay neutral in the war that exploded across Europe in 1914. It was called the "Great War," whose awful trenches threatened to grind up all the young men in France, Germany, and England. But the prayer group disintegrated anyway. Bad news flooded their home, too. Mama was sicker than ever. And a new doctor, Jan van Veen, diagnosed Aunt Jans with diabetes, as sure a death sentence as tuberculosis! Aunt Jans had always been preoccupied with death. Now the end was inevitable.

Every week Aunt Jans had to have her blood tested for sugar content, which reflected the progress of the disease. Dr. van Veen decided it would save everyone a lot of time and money if Corrie would do the test at home, so he taught Corrie how to do the test and left vials of chemicals and measuring spoons. Corrie dreaded doing that test every Friday. First she fretted over doing the test correctly on their old coal-burning stove. Then she had to give Aunt Jans the results. God forbid that the final liquid in the beaker would ever be black, which meant death was near. The news was not all bad in the house. Once Dr. van Veen's nurse—and sister—Tine, visited Aunt Jans. Willem was home. He was just months away from being ordained a minister. The moment was electric for the two. He and Tine scheduled their marriage for two months after his ordination. Long overdue cheer entered the home. The ten Booms would have their first wedding. Corrie knew it was much more. Karel would be there.

Corrie was now twenty-one, and Karel was twenty-six. They were no longer girl and man, but woman and man. Corrie was as attractive as she would ever be. Betsie spent an hour on Corrie's dark blond hair that morning. Corrie wore a very elegant silk dress that Betsie had made. Karel came to her like a moth to a flame.

He was attentive. He flattered her. Could anyone doubt his intentions? Corrie could hardly remember Willem and Tine's wedding, she was so shaken. She thought her heart would explode.

But as surely as she soared into the clouds with that event, another event brought her plummeting down. One Friday morning when she tested her aunt's blood, the liquid in the beaker turned black! How could she tell her? It was Papa who handled it. First, he politely asked Corrie if she was sure she did the test right. Then he asked her to take the beaker to Dr. van Veen. Soon Corrie was back. The doctor said the test was valid. Aunt Jans had three weeks of life left at the most.

"All right," said Papa. "We'll all go up to see her."

Aunt Jans was writing at her table. Her slight exasperation at the interruption become wonder as she realized she had five visitors: Papa, Mama, Aunt Anna, Betsie, and Corrie. It was Corrie her eyes froze on.

"Today is Friday!" she cried. "Black. . ." Aunt Jans swept the papers aside. "All is vanity!" She crumpled and sobbed. But abruptly she looked up, tears streaming down her face. "Dear Jesus, I thank You that we must come to You with empty hands. I thank You that You have done everything for us on the cross, and that all we need in life or death is to be sure of this." After her many years of worry about death, she triumphed in a twinkling. It was just as Papa had told Corrie all her life. When the time comes, God provides for the faithful.

Four months after Aunt Jans's funeral, Willem gave his first sermon. After serving as assistant pastor for almost one year in Uithuizen, a village about as far north as one can go in Holland without walking into the North Sea, Willem was given a church as full pastor in the even smaller village of Made, which was at the southern end of Holland.

No family would miss a minister's first sermon. The ten Booms and Aunt Anna arrived in Made on the train. Three days later, Corrie's wish came true. Karel arrived. He was an assistant pastor himself. He was as free now to marry as Willem had been, a fact that was emblazoned in Corrie's mind.

Karel wasted no time. Soon he and Corrie were walking farther from Willem's rectory each day. The talk was suited to Corrie's fondest dreams. They spoke of what they would do to decorate a rectory, what furniture they would have, a hundred other things.

Their tastes were very much the same. Any differences were trivial. Karel wanted four children; Corrie wanted six. They never actually spoke of marriage, but who could doubt that matrimony was in the offing?

Willem doubted, and he let Corrie know it. "I went to school with him for many years, Corrie. I know how he thinks. I know how his family thinks. He must marry well. Even my sister is not good enough for him."

Gloomy old hard-nosed Willem, fumed Corrie to herself. How she resented his pessimism sometimes. How she wanted not to listen to him. So she refused to believe. A veteran of hundreds of romance stories, Corrie would never quit now. Karel's stuffy family was a mere obstacle in the plot that just made the resolution—their happy marriage—more satisfying.

And as if to prove how wrong Willem was, Karel and Corrie wrote each other letters. Corrie never relented in her happy barrage of letters, but Karel's output declined. He had a good reason, of course. He had become the full pastor at his church. He surely would have written more if he had not taken on so much more responsibility. Visits with parishioners were time-consuming.

One November day Corrie answered a knock on the door to the alley.

"Karel!" she cried.

"Hello, Corrie. I came to introduce my fiancée."

SIX

Beside Karel's shoulder was a radiant face above an elegant ermine coat collar. Karel was going to marry well. Karel stayed only a short time to proudly introduce his fiancée to the rest of the family. After they left, Corrie slipped away to her bedroom.

Papa followed her. "Love is the strongest force in the world," he said. "And when it is blocked, there is great pain."

"It's excruciating."

"We can kill the love to make it stop hurting. Or we can direct the love to another route."

"I will never love another man. I know that for sure."

"Give your love to God."

After Papa left her, Corrie prayed that her love would go to God. She was only twenty-three years old. Her unmarried status was hardly glaring. Betsie was thirty and unmarried, and Nollie was twenty-five and still single. Corrie had had two aunts who never married at all. She could not feel sorry for herself very long.

She began studying her Bible school subjects again and tried to fine-tune her housework like a virtuoso. After all, housework seemed to be her life's calling. She still gave Bible lessons at the public school. And she used her earnings to improve the home. It was Corrie who paid for two toilets that actually flushed the waste into the sewer system. Before that, city workers had to come and empty the waste. It was Corrie who bought a bathtub for the home. Before that, they sponged themselves out of small washbasins.

Good news or bad, nothing remained the same very long in the ten Boom house. Mama had a stroke so severe she went into a coma. For two months around the clock they watched her in shifts: Corrie, Betsie, Anna, Papa, and Nollie. And one morning Mama woke up!

They moved her bed into Aunt Jans's front room so Mama could watch the Haarlemites she loved so much walk on Barteljorisstraat. She recovered enough to walk again, but only with help. She could not use her hands to write or knit. She spoke only three words: "Corrie," "yes," and "no." Corrie believed her name was one of the words only because she was with Mama in the kitchen when she had her stroke.

To understand Mama's wishes, they played a guessing game. Mama would answer "yes" or "no" to question after question until the answer she wanted finally came. It was just one more example of the love and patience in the ten Boom home.

The Great War ended. Much of Europe was devastated. Papa was not interested in assigning guilt. He knew many children were destitute. As chairman of the international watchmakers, he urged his membership to take children who had been victims of the war into their homes. The ten Boom house itself had little money but much love.

It wasn't long before the ten Booms welcomed Willy and Katy, urchins from the streets of Germany. Soon they were joined by Ruth and Martha, sisters from Germany. So there were four children ranging in age from four to ten in the home. The children adapted well. Even Mama was up and about, fussing over the newcomers.

The next months were blessed for the ten Booms. The four foster children became so healthy again that they returned to relatives in Germany. Corrie took the exam at the Bible school and passed. And Nollie met another teacher named Flip van Woerden and they were married. At the end of the wedding ceremony, they sang Mama's favorite hymn: "Fairest Lord Jesus."

Within a month Mama passed away. Corrie wrestled with the injustice of Mama's suffering. Why did such a warm, loving woman have to suffer as she had? Why? Finally, Corrie decided that she had learned from Mama that love could transcend all human affliction. Her whole life, Mama had shown her love by doing things for people, but in the end, with her normal expressions of love paralyzed, Mama's love still radiated, whole and complete. Nothing can defeat love.

Christmastime that year was a great turning point for Corrie. She was twenty-eight years old. The change started innocently enough. Betsie got the flu, so Corrie helped Papa in the shop. She greeted customers and worked with the bills and correspondence. As Betsie got better, she began picking up Corrie's duties in the house. Sensitive, artistic Betsie was much better at housework than Corrie. She had a special touch, like Aunt Anna. It was painfully obvious to Corrie.

But the reverse was true, too. Corrie was much better at working in the shop than Betsie had been. God surely arranged this insight. And to make it a source of joy and not consternation, they each loved their new role. Without a moment's hesitation, they exchanged duties.

Corrie was amazed at Papa. He had trained under Howu, recognized as one of the great clockmakers. He published a newspaper for watchmakers. He was chairman of the international watchmakers. He was known far and wide as the best watchmaker in Holland.

But he was so inept at sound business principles she was flabbergasted. He had no bookkeeping system. He forgot to make out bills. He did not price his watches low enough to sell. He closed his shop just as people began to stroll the street and window-shop after they got off work. He didn't even light up his windows in the evening. He shuttered them!

The truth was Papa cared nothing for money.

Keeping the books and welcoming customers was not enough for Corrie. As soon as she established a system she was happy with, she asked Papa if she could work on watches.

"You're the only one of the children who ever asked me that," he answered in surprise. "But if you had been the fourth, I still would say, 'Yes, of course you may.' I will teach you."

So Corrie was trained by the best watchmaker in Holland. Papa even sent her to Switzerland to work in a watch factory for a while, but soon she was back. With Papa's help, she became the first woman watchmaker licensed in Holland. Her specialty was the new rage: wristwatches. Even that was not enough for Corrie. She gave Bible lessons to children as always, but now she had a special class for the retarded. She was sure Jesus revealed himself to these children.

Encouraged by a wealthy ladies' club concerned about lack of activities for teenage girls in Haarlem, Corrie and Betsie started taking a few girls for walks before church on Sunday. They ran a blunt ad in the newspaper:

DO YOU LIKE TO GO ON WALKS? IF YOU WANT TO MEET
OTHER GIRLS AND HAVE FUN, COME TO THE TEN BOOM
SHOP AT BARTELJORISSTRAAT 19.

It seemed like a small thing. But soon they and the girls were meeting on Wednesdays to walk to gardens in the wealthy suburb of Bloemendaal near the seashore. Estate owners were happy to encourage exercise for young girls. When the weather got cold, Corrie and Betsie began meeting with the girls in large rooms in wealthy homes in the same suburbs. The meat of such endeavors—the gospel—was always sandwiched in the middle of fun things to do.

Corrie's club work grew into something she never imagined in the beginning. Early in the effort, she and Betsie had to recruit other young ladies to help. Soon they had forty ladies, each with a troop of eight girls. Their three hundred girls became quite a presence in Haarlem. Once a year, they rented the concert hall to show a thousand friends and relatives the skills they were learning in the clubs. Corrie was a fearless public speaker by now. Always, right in the middle of the show, she offered the gospel in talks with catchy titles, such as "God's telephone is never busy" and "Do you have your radio tuned to the right station?" Her organization officially became the Haarlem Girls' Clubs. Soon they were welcomed into the Christian Union of the Lady Friends of the Young Girl, with headquarters in Switzerland. The ladies and the girls now wore uniforms!

Another death struck the family. Faithful Aunt Anna died. All four Luitingh sisters were now dead. Every one of them had died in the ten Boom house within a span of one decade. It was as if they were a certain kind of fine clock all wound by God at the same time about seventy years before.

Papa's house had once resounded with nine people living in seven bedrooms. Now only Papa, Betsie, and Corrie remained. Papa was not one to waste empty bedrooms. The ten Booms had bedrooms to share. And plenty of love.

Papa said, "Do you remember what Mama said about missionaries?"

Betsie added, "I remember Mama saying if we did anything to help the missionary effort, we should help the children of missionaries."

"When do we begin?" asked Corrie.

They began to take in children left in Holland by missionaries. This was no small undertaking. These were children to be raised to adulthood. And even though they were the offspring of missionaries and usually eager to please, many were at a difficult age.

The first ones to arrive were eleven- and twelve-year-old sisters Puck and Hans, and their brother, Hardy, fourteen. Soon a girl named Lessie arrived. And not long after that Miep and another girl came to live with the ten Booms. The new children named the house "Beje," pronounced *bay-yay*, the initials of Bartel Joris, for whom Barteljorisstraat was named. Betsie and Corrie became their "aunts." Papa became *Opa*, Dutch for grandpa.

A watch company sent Papa complimentary red caps, and soon Corrie was exercising the six children on long walks. People in Haarlem joked abut Corrie's "Red Cap Club." They shook their heads in amazement. Corrie was really devoted to young people. God's love gave her love to give.

A sense of humor helped, too. Her club girls had a gymnasium section. At one of the meetings they voted on a slogan. Corrie always knew she was high-hipped with pigeon toes, but now shorts revealed another flaw: knock-knees. One girl looking at Corrie's legs suggested the slogan "We make straight what is crooked!" Corrie did not mind. She loved to be teased. To her, teasing was a form of friendship. She was not too proud to take a joke, even though young people often pushed her to the limit.

Summers became a time for camping out. The first rule of camp was not to gossip. Instead, the highlight of each day was the telling of inspiring stories around the campfire. Eventually, Corrie got the use of a cabin that would hold sixty girls. On the last evening of their campout, she would sneak from the cabin after lights-out and sing a warm good-bye song. But one year her song was drowned out by a horrible din. She was sure she battled the devil himself. She didn't stop singing. She fought the good fight. The next day her girls insisted that she had never sung more beautifully and that they didn't hear any noise at all.

Separate clubs were formed for individual activities, too. Corrie's favorite was her Catechism club. This was the one in which girls studied to enter the Dutch Reformed Church. But Corrie taught the gospel in small potent doses in all groups. One girl who accepted Jesus was Pietje, a small hunchback. One day Corrie was told to rush to the hospital.

Little Pietje was dying, her face twisted in pain. Corrie said, "It's such a comfort to know Jesus is our judge. How He loves you, Pietje!"

Pietje's face relaxed. Corrie stroked her forehead and prayed aloud for the Good Shepherd to take His lamb into His arms and carry her through the valley of the shadow of death to His Father's house with many mansions. As Corrie said, "Amen," Pietje opened her eyes and smiled. Then she died.

After many years of blessed health in the Beje, Papa ten Boom was struck down by hepatitis. It was 1930. He was within days of reaching his three score and ten years of life. His beard turned white as snow as he clung to life in small inconspicuous Saint Elizabeth's hospital.

Corrie prayed that God's will would be done.

SEVEN

Papa ten Boom recovered.

Papa's illness was a wake-up call for Corrie. He was seventy years old. They had already hired a bookkeeper for the shop, a surly woman named Toos, who seemed to like no one in the world except Papa. But, unfriendly as she was, Toos really helped Corrie more than she helped Papa. It was time to get Papa some help.

One day, in walked a shabby man who introduced himself as Christoffels. "I am looking for work," he added.

After only a moment or two, Papa hired him. Papa was excited later. "Don't judge him by his ragged clothing. He's the old-style clock man, the kind who roams the country fixing any kind of watch or clock you can name. He will be invaluable to us."

Corrie's girls' club evolved into the Girl Guides, another international organization. This relieved her of many duties. But Corrie became unhappy with the Girl Guides. They seemed to pander more and more to short-sighted squawkers in the organization who tried to squelch the teaching of Christianity. So she left it—with all her girls.

Her group of girls became local again: the Triangle Club. The triangle represented social, intellectual, and physical skills. But the triangle was inside a circle. This meant being in the right relationship with God. Their four club rules were:

1. *Seek your strength through prayer.*
2. *Be open and trustworthy.*
3. *Bear your difficulties cheerfully.*
4. *Develop the gifts that God gave you.*

In 1937, the watch shop celebrated its first one hundred years. Christoffels and Toos were there even earlier that morning. Nollie was to come later with her husband Flip and their six children. Willem and Tine would be there with their four. And the ten Booms expected many visitors that day. Papa was seventy-seven now, the opa for many in Haarlem.

It was a golden age for the three ten Booms at Beje. Troubles seemed in the distant past. Such peace, such prosperity, such health worried Corrie a little. And there was that evil that appeared on the eastern horizon. Since 1927,

315

when Willem studied in Germany for his doctorate, he had railed about what was happening in Germany. The thing growing in Germany was a socialism of the most heartless kind. It called itself the National Socialist German Workers and became known as the Nazi Party. The poor, the old, the feebleminded, and the handicapped were enemies of progress. Soon Jews were included as enemies, too, then Communists.

The Nazi outrage was engineered by a man named Hitler. He appeared laughable at first—comical, then maddening. But soon there was nothing amusing about him at all. Holland would stay neutral no matter what happened, reasoned Corrie. And surely gloomy Willem was exaggerating about the Nazis. The day of the hundredth anniversary, people rapped on the door to the alley constantly. Flowers, flowers, and more flowers arrived. And Christoffels, of all people, decorous in coat and tie as he had never been before, was greeting well-wishers and formally escorting them into the shop like a butler at a mansion. Everyone seemed almost saintly today. It was going to be a great day for Papa.

The Beje was soon milling with visitors. One of Corrie's favorites was Herman Sluring, a man the ten Boom sisters had dubbed "Pickwick" many years before. To them he looked just like the Charles Dickens character. He was grossly overweight, and his wide-set eyes darted different directions like a chameleon's. Both he and Papa were always engulfed in children. Papa attracted them with the pockets of his suit coat, which buzzed and ticked and whirred because he carried dozens of watches. Pickwick lured them with tricks, such as balancing a cup of coffee on his mountainous belly.

All day long, guests flowed in and out of the Beje. Papa had hundreds of friends. Willem's family was there, and finally Willem himself came in the late afternoon. In Hilversum, some twenty-five miles east of Haarlem, he ran the Dutch Reformed Church's outreach program for Jews. He even opened a home for destitute Jews, so his Jewish companion should have been no surprise. But he was a surprise. His face was red and raw.

In a bitter voice, Willem explained, "He's from Germany. Hooligans in the street set his beard on fire."

But as the months passed, Corrie began to understand. They had two radios in the Beje now. The table model was in Aunt Jans's big room, and they had a small portable radio on the kitchen table, a present from Pickwick. Almost all the time the speakers carried blissful concerts carefully managed by Betsie from radio schedules, but once in a while as the dial searched for a station the speaker erupted with fiery screams from Germany. They seemed straight from hell. This man Hitler sounded like the devil himself.

Papa's young apprentice, a German named Otto, brought the message home to the Beje loud and clear. One day he attacked Christoffels. His reason was that Christoffels was old, decrepit, and worthless. Papa fired Otto immediately. In 1938, the radio told them that Germany was meeting with Italy, France, and Britain in Munich to discuss Hitler's demand for an area of Czechoslovakia called the Sudetenland. After the meeting Hitler's Germany possessed the Sudetenland.

Six months later Hitler's army walked into Czechoslovakia and took over the entire country. The radio said the American president Franklin Roosevelt wanted an assurance from Hitler that he would not start a fight with certain countries. Roosevelt listed twenty-nine countries.

But the radio crackled two weeks later with Hitler's answer. It was a long speech, not in the usual screaming style—but humorous, all the while mocking Roosevelt, ridiculing him. Corrie shivered. This man Hitler was afraid of no one. And he was not a raving lunatic. He was diabolically shrewd. Thank God Holland was a neutral country.

Later, in 1939, Germany signed a pact with Russia.

One week later, Germany invaded Poland. This conflict was not like the one in Czechoslovakia. The Poles fought hard. But the news on the radio was heartbreaking. Hitler's tanks crushed horses of the Polish cavalry. The Germans split Poland with Russia. The Americans declared their neutrality. The French and British declared war on Germany. Which was worse? To fight or to be neutral? Who could know?

Nothing more happened for weeks. The Russians invaded Finland, but that hardly concerned Holland. Perhaps Hitler was satisfied. Only the French and British opposed Hitler. The British had a new prime minister, a belligerent man named Churchill. The British were already fighting the Germans at sea. The German battleships *Graf Spee* and *Deutschland* were the rage of the sea. They sank ship after British ship. The battleships were invincible, bragged the Nazis.

But finally the British navy trapped the German battleships in a bay in Argentina. The battleships were destroyed. Corrie felt her heart soar. Then she realized she was caught up in war fever. In late December of 1939, Hitler said the Jewish-capitalist countries would not survive the twentieth century. Was he only indulging his flaming rhetoric again? Wasn't Holland a capitalist country? Thank God Holland was neutral. Surely Papa was wrong. Hitler's armies were doing nothing on the European continent now.

But suddenly, in April of 1940, Hitler invaded Norway and Denmark. He said he was protecting them from the French and British who had designs on them. In early May the prime minister of Holland came on the radio to reassure the Dutch: Holland was neutral.

Papa snapped off the volume.

"I'm sorry for all the Dutch who don't know God. Because we will be attacked by the Germans, and we will be defeated."

War!

It was the worst shock of Corrie's life. She seemed plunged into hell. In the hours that followed, she and Betsie prayed for Holland. Betsie even prayed for the Germans. What sisters Corrie had! Nollie could not tell a lie, and Betsie prayed for everyone, including their enemies.

While praying, Corrie had a vision. Surely she couldn't have dreamed it. Who could have slept at such a time? In the town square she saw four enormous black horses pulling a farm wagon. In the wagon was Corrie herself! And Papa. And Betsie. She realized the wagon was crowded. There was Pickwick and Toos—and Willem and Nollie! Even young nephew Peter. None of them could get off the wagon. They were being taken somewhere. What could the vision mean?

The bombing stopped.

Once again they listened to the radio, joined by Papa, finally looking all of his eighty years. The radio said Germans were bombing airports all over Holland. Germans had parachuted into Rotterdam, Dordrecht, and Moerdijk.

Papa said, "The Germans want to capture the bridges in those three places, so their tanks can move freely back and forth from northern Holland to southern Holland." Dear Papa, seemingly so naive in business, was so wise in the affairs of men. But how could one read the Bible like he did and not know every nuance of men and their flawed ambitions?

There were damaged hearts in Haarlem, especially among the Jews. Fear was written on their faces. This was a bad time for them. They knew what Hitler had been saying about Jews. All anyone could do was wait. The queen fled to Britain on May 13. The Dutch army collapsed into a small area from Amsterdam to Rotterdam they called "Fortress Holland," as if it were impregnable against the Nazis. Within two days the Dutch army surrendered.

Days later German soldiers arrived. They were the Eighteenth Army of German Army Group B under General Fedor von Bock. There was no resistance. The Germans marched on parade, goose-stepping in crisp gray and black uniforms. They had tanks and cannons, trucks and half-tracks, and hundreds of huge red flags, each with a black swastika inside a white circle. It was ironic that the flags reminded Corrie of her Triangle Club, except the swastika was completely at odds with God, swirling and ripping and tearing like blades of the devil.

The Germans assured the Dutch that they had come to defend them against the French and British, but the news on the radio of how they ruthlessly bombed Rotterdam while that Dutch city tried to negotiate its terms of surrender exposed the lie. It seemed to Corrie that the German soldiers were embarrassed to have killed their friends and neighbors, the Dutch. Or was that only her wishful thinking?

The occupation began. The government was now under the control of Reichs Commissioner Artur von Seyss-Inquart. Holland was now part of the glorious Third Reich, which was to be the third great empire, after the Roman Empire and Charlemagne's Empire.

At first, the occupation did not seem so evil to Corrie. The German soldiers had money. They bought things at the shop. They even bought all of Papa's *winkeldochters*—"shop daughters"—clocks and watches that had been in the shop for years without being sold. There were a few inconveniences, such as that the Dutch could not be in the street after ten o'clock at night. Each Dutch citizen had to carry an identity card in a pouch hanging from a "necklace." Food and merchandise had to be purchased with coupons from ration books. The Germans were very well organized. The Dutch could have no telephones, but heaven knows people listened to too much gossip on phones anyway. The newspapers no longer carried any real news. The news was depressing anyway. All of Europe was falling into the Third Reich, even France.

When the Dutch were ordered to turn in their radios, they were upset. Radios were still novel. They loved to listen to their concerts. Willem insisted the Dutch would also soon be hopelessly lost in a world of never-ending lies and deceit. Even Nollie's sixteen-year-old son Peter knew it. So Corrie was convinced to turn in the portable radio and lie to the German officer about not owning another one. She felt bad about lying. She told herself she was only being as wise and shrewd as a snake but innocent as a dove, as Jesus advised one to be against a world of evil. But she didn't seek the opinion of Betsie or Papa.

Betsie said, "Oh, did the Nazis let us keep our other radio?"

The Dutch were not pleased about losing their bicycles either. Everyone rode bicycles, even Corrie. It started with German soldiers stopping riders and confiscating the tires. The tires were shipped back to Germany. Rubber was precious. The practical Dutch could understand that, even if they didn't like it. They quickly learned to wrap the rims with cloth and ride the bicycles anyway. But soon the soldiers were confiscating the bicycles. So the Nazis had more in mind. They didn't want the Dutch moving around. Soon the Dutch hid thousands of bicycles inside their homes.

Corrie had to surrender her work with her girls' clubs. The Nazis were not about to allow any well-organized network of over three hundred Dutch to exist in one town—even teenage girls and their leaders. Who knew how such people might be used by an underground of traitors to the Third Reich? Gradually, the ten o'clock curfew was moved earlier and earlier. It wasn't long into the Nazi occupation until being out after dark was forbidden. Nighttime was just too convenient for Dutch troublemakers to move around.

"The nighttime is good for us now," said Kik, Willem's oldest son. And his sentiments were echoed by Peter. Corrie noticed that young men and older boys seemed very active at night.

To Corrie, the Nazis were no more than a dreadful nuisance, almost like parents who were far too strict. So a letter from the ten Booms' foster child, Hans, shocked her.

EIGHT

Hans lived in Rotterdam with her husband and two small children. The German soldiers there bragged that the terrible bombing of Rotterdam was a brilliant tactic of war called *schrecklichkeit*. The deaths of eight hundred Dutchmen were not necessary to capture Rotterdam; the deaths were designed to fill the Dutch with such fear that their resistance would permanently vanish. Hans and her family now lived in a cellar in constant fear. Hans was pregnant again, too.

Never was Corrie torn by so much doubt. Who could love Nazis? They were such snakes. They even turned on the Russians in June of 1941 and were mangling Russian troops on a battlefront east of Germany. The Nazis seemed invincible. Their occupation of Western Europe displayed more evil every day. Signs appeared in Dutch shops: NO JEWS SERVED HERE. Surely those were just a few misguided anti-Semites, said Papa. But then a sign appeared in a public park: NO JEWS ALLOWED. Soon Jews were made to wear a large yellow star of David with *Jood*, the Dutch word for Jew, sewed inside.

Papa was dismayed. "The Jews are the apples of God's eye. The Germans cannot go further than this. I pity them."

One night in the summer, the sky over Haarlem not only roared and whined with the noise of engines but flickered with light. The fiery traces were not the paths of shooting stars but bullets! There was a battle above Haarlem. The ten Booms huddled in the dining room until the night sky was silent.

Later Corrie found a hunk of metal on her bed. "Betsie! If I had been in bed it would have struck me right in the head."

Betsie smiled patiently. "In God's world there are no 'ifs.' No place is any safer than any other place. Our only safety is in the center of God's will. Let us pray that we know His will."

For a year and a half, the three ten Booms had tried to live their normal lives. One November morning in 1941 changed that. Corrie was on the sidewalk folding back the shutters on the watch shop when four German soldiers with rifles rushed into the furrier's shop across the street from the Beje. Moments later a soldier prodded the owner, Mr. Weil, into the street with a rifle muzzle.

Corrie ran inside the Beje. She and Betsie watched through their shop window in horror as the soldiers smashed up Mr. Weil's shop and stole his furs. One soldier opened a second-story window. Clothing cascaded to the sidewalk. Mr. Weil stood on the sidewalk in a daze.

"We must help Mr. Weil," cried Corrie.

She and Betsie ran out to help him gather his clothing off the sidewalk, then quickly they ushered him down the alley and up into their dining room.

"I must warn my wife," worried Mr. Weil. "She's visiting relatives in Amsterdam. She must not come home."

Corrie felt herself pulled into the battle. "Willem will know what to do." And almost as if in a dream she found herself walking north on Kruisstraat to the railway station, then riding the train through Amsterdam all the way to Hilversum. She got off the train at midday.

Tine was at Willem's nursing home with her grown son Kik. They listened to Corrie. Kik said, "Have Mr. Weil ready to go as soon as it gets dark. And what is the Amsterdam address where Mrs. Weil is visiting?" He sighed, as if reluctant to draw his fifty-year-old Aunt Corrie into the fray.

Once again Corrie rode the train between Hilversum and Haarlem. That night Kik came for Mr. Weil and they disappeared into the dark alley.

When Corrie saw him two weeks later, she whispered, "How are the Weils?"

"If you are going to work in the underground, you must not ask questions. The less you know the less the Gestapo can torture out of you." Kik was smiling apologetically, but Corrie shivered. Everyone in Holland now feared the Gestapo.

The significance of Kik's words slowly sank in. Her nephew Kik was involved with the underground. And surely so was her brother, Willem.

Some of the Dutch openly defied the Nazis, and once again it hit home at the Beje. This time it was Peter, Nollie's son. He played the organ at the church in Velsen, north of Haarlem. Occasionally Corrie went to their service with Papa and Betsie so they could hear him play. On May 12, 1942, after the sermon and hymns and the final prayer, the organ began blasting nothing other than "Wilhelmus"!

The Nazis had banned the Dutch national anthem, "Wilhelmus." And as Corrie and her family went to Nollie's house in south Haarlem for lunch, the magnitude of Peter's indiscretion mounted for Corrie. Nollie and Flip were sheltering two Jews: a young blond woman named Annaliese, who looked very Dutch and went about freely, and Katrien, an older woman who posed as their maid. What would happen to this house if the Gestapo came after Peter? Wednesday morning it happened. The Gestapo arrested Peter. They were myopic. They overlooked the two Jewish women. It was not until Saturday that Nollie and Flip heard Peter was in a federal prison in Amsterdam.

It seemed to Corrie that the ten Booms and their whole extended family were irretrievably committed to defying the Nazis. Would word of their defiance spread? It was not two weeks later that Corrie heard a desperate knock on the alley door.

Corrie didn't hesitate a moment when she saw the fear in the woman's eyes. "Come inside!" She rushed the woman up to the dining room.

"I'm Mrs. Kleermacher. I'm a Jew," said the woman.

"God's people are always welcome in this house," said Papa.

"Thank God," she said. "I heard you ten Booms helped Mr. Weil."

The Gestapo had ordered her to close her family clothing store. Her husband had already been arrested. What choice did she have now but to hide? And what choice did the three ten Booms have but to hide her?

Two nights later, an elderly Jewish couple joined Mrs. Kleermacher in hiding. Corrie knew the situation was explosive. Jews were fleeing to the Beje. It could be nothing more than a rest stop. The Jews had to move on to safer places. But where did they go? Once again she traveled to Hilversum on the train.

This time Willem was there. He said, "Most Jews work on farms. But that's getting more and more difficult. Even the farms must account for their food now. We can find places on farms if they bring food ration books with them. Otherwise—"

"But Jews aren't issued ration books!" cried Corrie.

"They can't be counterfeited either. The Nazis change the design too often. We must steal the ration books." And he sighed as he noticed Corrie waiting expectantly. "I can't do it, Corrie. They watch me now every moment."

She fretted about it all the way home on the train. There was a girl who had come to her Sunday school class for the retarded for twenty years. Her father worked at the Food Office. Could Corrie prevail on this man for help? She had sought help from people for years for her many projects, but never was so much at stake as now. What would the Gestapo do to this man if he were caught? What if he were a Nazi sympathizer? What would happen to her and Betsie and Papa? Never had the world seemed so evil.

She rode her bicycle to the man's house that very night. He listened to her impassively. There was no anger, no sympathy. Perhaps she saw some fear.

He sighed. "The ration books must be accounted for a dozen ways. There is only one way to get any books for your purposes. We must be robbed. It happens more and more these days with Dutch people so desperate for food. They wouldn't necessarily suspect me. How many books do you want?"

Three? No, she argued with herself, there would be other Jews fleeing.

Five? How many should she ask for? He was going to be robbed. He would be grilled by the Gestapo. That sacrifice should not come cheap. "I need one hundred ration books," she said stoutly, hardly believing her own ears.

A week later she visited the man again. The food ration books were in an envelope. His face was hamburger. His friends had done it to him. He paid a heavy price for the books. Yet she knew the Gestapo probably would not have believed anything less than a bloody thrashing.

The glory of it was that the staged robbery did not have to be repeated. The last coupon in the book was presented to the Food Office for the next month's ration book. So Corrie had one hundred permanent food rations to dispense. One hundred lives saved!

But it was much too dangerous for Corrie to come to the Food Office. Sometimes the shrewdest of the Gestapo were lurking there. Her brave helper preferred to bring them to the Beje. He was once a meter man for the electric company, and soon they worked out a plan where he would come every month in his meter man's uniform to check their meter. The quick precious exchange would take place then.

One night Kik surprised Corrie and took her out into the darkness of the night to Aerdenhout, a wealthy suburb of Haarlem. Inside a mansion milled many people. And there was an old family friend.

"Pickwick!" she exclaimed.

Waddling up to her, Pickwick confided, "We are the link between the Free Dutch and the British. We also get crews from downed British planes back to England. There's a lot of sympathy here for your work, too." And suddenly he introduced her to the group. "Miss Corrie Smit is the head of an operation rescuing Jews here in Haarlem."

In a daze she whispered, "Me? The head of an operation? And I'm certainly not Corrie Smit."

"We have no other last names in the underground, Corrie Smit," said Pickwick soberly. He smiled. "Peter is going to be released. Cheer up."

How did Pickwick know ahead of time that Peter was going to be released? He must have been powerful indeed, thought Corrie.

It was just a few days later that a frail man with a goatee came to the Beje. Corrie had been told about him at the underground meeting. Of course, he was named Smit.

Mr. Smit was soon exploring the house. "This structure is a dream come true," he said. "Never have I seen such a hodgepodge of rooms."

"We prefer to think of it as unique," said Corrie, not the least bothered by his remark.

She wasn't happy when he seemed to focus on her small bedroom on the third floor. He said, "This is perfect. It's high. It gives people time to get up here and hide as the Gestapo sweep through the lower part of the house."

"But this is my bedroom. And it's so small."

One week later, Corrie's bedroom was even smaller. The man and his helpers had built a fake brick wall. There was now a small room between the fake wall and the real, outer brick wall. The room was two and a half feet wide by about eight feet long. The new brick wall had been painted yet looked a hundred years old. The paint was peeling and water stained. The original molding was put back. In front of the wall was a dilapidated wooden-backed bookcase. Under the lowest shelf was a sliding door.

"Keep a mattress in your secret room, along with water, hardtack, and vitamins," said Mr. Smit, and he left.

Corrie felt very cold. Would the Gestapo ever be in her room scratching the walls, sniffing about like great stinking rats? She must have faith in God. The Gestapo would never find the secret room. It was guarded by God's angels. She would now call it the angels' crib!

The Gestapo was not the only ugly arm of the Nazis. With so many of their own men in uniform fighting the British in Africa, fighting the Russians in the east, and occupying unfriendly countries all over Europe, the Germans desperately needed workers for their war factories. So in 1942 German soldiers began to raid Dutch homes.

At any moment in any neighborhood, German soldiers might appear in force to scour every house for Dutch men between the ages of sixteen and thirty. Then with rifles and threats they nudged their captives into waiting trucks. The trucks took the men straight to Germany. Such a raid occurred when Corrie, Betsie, and Papa were at Nollie's home to celebrate Flip's birthday. Nollie was still out shopping with her two oldest girls, Aty and Elske.

Suddenly, Nollie's sons, Peter and Bob, raced into the kitchen. "Soldiers are coming! It's a *razzia*!"

They immediately moved the kitchen table aside and yanked a rug away to expose a trapdoor. It was no more than a potato cellar. They opened the trapdoor and dived below.

Those above had barely replaced the rug and table before soldiers burst into the house.

The German soldier demanded, "Do you have brothers?"

"Yes." Nollie's youngest daughter, Cocky, answered.

"How old?"

"Twenty-one, nineteen, eighteen."

"Excellent." The soldier actually smiled. "Now be a good girl and tell me where they are."

"My oldest brother Fred is at theological school."

"And where are the other two?" he asked impatiently.

Corrie held her breath. How long could Cocky have evaded that horrible ultimate question? Corrie felt sick. Nollie couldn't tell a lie, and Cocky was just like her. But surely Cocky wouldn't give up her dear brothers to the Nazis—and to a death sentence in the war factories in Germany!

Cocky sighed. "They are under the table."

The soldier yanked away the tablecloth and peeked under the table, rifle ready. He blinked at empty space. "Don't think we are fools!" he snapped angrily.

Within moments the soldiers were gone, terrorizing the next house. The van Woerdens and ten Booms had more than Flip's birthday to celebrate that afternoon. They celebrated the narrow escape, but during the party Corrie argued with Nollie about telling lies. Nollie insisted a godly person must tell the truth. Corrie didn't agree. How terribly evil the Nazis were to force people into such moral dilemmas. They were demons.

Flip wouldn't take sides. He was thankful, but his face was as white as bleached celery with worry. "We were very lucky they were such young soldiers. They never even questioned Katrien."

Corrie knew he was right. Katrien would not fool anyone for very long. She was much older than Annaliese. She looked Semitic. And she knew nothing about actual maid work. She did not even have false papers. The Gestapo would see through Katrien in a flash.

Living with Nazis among them was a never-ending nightmare. Corrie remembered the first motto of her girls' clubs: Seek your strength through prayer. She could find the strength from God. And she needed it. The Beje was as dangerous as Nollie's house. They were hiding Jews at the Beje all the time, too.

Good news crackled over the radio from Britain in January of 1943. The hearts of the Dutch soared. The Russians had stopped the German advance eastward and were even thought to be turning them back! The new year really seemed a turning point in the devil Hitler's fortunes. The British and Americans had routed the Germans from North Africa. At long last the sleeping giant America was fighting. If Hitler expected any help from his Japanese allies, he would not get it. They were being pummeled by the Americans in the Pacific. Glory to God, there was hope for Holland at last.

As if to remind Corrie that a few battles won against the devil did not mean the war was over, that winter in Holland was long and severe. Poor old

Christoffels froze to death in his bed in a rooming house, the water in his wash basin frozen solid as rock. Food and fuel were in short supply all winter. And so were safe havens for Jews while the underground sought farms for them. And even the few havens like the Beje were not so safe.

NINE

The operation at Beje expanded. More and more, Corrie became the command center, and more and more Dutch joined Corrie. It seemed that she always needed more messengers and more people with special skills. A fugitive would sicken and die, so Corrie needed a burial. A pregnant Jewish woman's water would break, so Corrie needed a doctor immediately! She needed transportation for fugitives, identification papers for fugitives, food ration books for fugitives. Soon she had eighty people working directly in her operation.

A distribution center for fleeing Jews and Dutch men got special treatment from the Dutch underground. The Beje's phone connection was restored. A buzzer was installed that sounded at the top of the house to warn their fugitives to get to the secret room at once. Buttons that triggered the buzzer were scattered through the lower part of the house, all hidden. But those conveniences came with a heavy price.

More and more people knew about the Beje. More and more Nazi edicts were violated by Corrie and her cohorts. More and more fugitives became difficult to distribute. Some of their Jews simply could not be moved to farms. They looked too Jewish. The farmers would not jeopardize themselves, their families, and their other fugitives to hide such obvious Jews. The rejection wasn't always because of the way a Jew looked; it might be because of something else that made the fugitive too conspicuous: a rattling cough, a pregnancy.

The first of the Beje's new permanent residents was Meyer Mossel. He was their first "watch with a face that needs repair," their underground code for a fugitive too Semitic-looking. He not only looked Semitic but was uncompromisingly orthodox with long sideburns. The farmer who was hiding Meyer's son and wife would not take him.

He and Papa were immediate friends. Meyer was a godsend to Papa. He had been a cantor in the synagogue. The Old Testament was heavenly when Meyer read it. And he knew scripture backward and forward like Papa did. He also had a wonderful sense of humor about himself. In that way he was like Corrie. Jews like Meyer kept Corrie from feeling like a martyr. He was a joy to have in the Beje. It was no great sacrifice to hide such a charming man.

Fugitives were coming to the Beje all the time to stay a short time. And they were slipped away in the night to go to some farm. A number could not be placed. So the permanent residents grew to seven. The most dangerous was seventy-six-year-old Mary. Her asthma made her wheeze and cough uncontrollably.

After rising in the morning, all who were in hiding had to drag their bedding, nightclothes, and toilet articles up to the angels' crib. These were exchanged for their day things. Just before bed they exchanged their day things for their night things. This was routine.

They began to drill for the unexpected. It was no game. If only one were caught by the Gestapo, they were all caught. So they drilled. The underground had warned Corrie the Gestapo liked to strike at mealtimes and in the middle of the night. The villains especially looked for wastebaskets and ash trays. At night the Gestapo felt every mattress for warmth. The Beje drilled for a raid at mealtime. The buzzer sounded unexpectedly. All those in hiding grabbed their dishes and huffed up the stairs. The first time it took them four minutes to disappear into the secret room. A man experienced in the underground acted the part of the Gestapo. He searched the Beje. On the kitchen table were two unexplained spoons, on the stairs was a carrot, and in one of the bedrooms were ashes from Meyer's pipe. The man scowled. It was fatally obvious they were hiding people. They would have to do much better.

So they practiced and practiced until they cut the time to two minutes and left nothing incriminating behind. Then they practiced more. Their goal was one minute. The task was not made any easier by having constant additions to the household. That was why they could never stop practicing. Slowly they brought the time down: ninety seconds, eighty seconds, seventy seconds.

Papa, Toos, and Corrie polished techniques to stall the Gestapo as they swept through the watch shop. They prayed it wouldn't be hard to stumble apologetically in front of some eager Nazi underling or to cause some grim Nazi searcher to hesitate with a well-chosen ambiguous remark about a high official in the Gestapo. Betsie practiced the same techniques on the side door to the alley. They must do everything they could to slow down the Gestapo.

Mealtime drills were just half of the drills. The other drills were for night raids. Corrie hated that drill most of all because they did it after she was asleep. She knew those in hiding jumped up, turned their mattresses over so they were cold to the touch, then hustled their night things upstairs to the angels' crib.

The part she despised was her part. They would shake her awake. "Where are you hiding the Jews?" they would scream in her face.

Corrie was a very heavy sleeper. Time and again she blurted something incriminating. It was a long time before she passed her part. How she dreaded the thought of a real raid in the night!

But life in the Beje was not all stress. At night they gathered in Aunt Jans's rooms. It was like old times. They sang. They studied the Bible. They played the pipe organ, the violin, and the piano. They performed plays. They gave each other language lessons. But after a while the people of Haarlem only had electricity a short time each night. Candles were too precious to use for fun, so the revelers would retreat into the kitchen where Corrie's bicycle was propped up on a stand. A volunteer would pedal wildly to generate electricity for her headlight. In its beam one of them would read a play or a novel to the others. These were the ways they clung to their sanity in such mad times.

One day Corrie looked out the dining room window. Cowering in the alley was a woman, confusion and terror written all over her.

"Katrien, of all people!" Corrie rushed down and pulled her inside.

Katrien was babbling. "Your sister has gone crazy."

"Crazy? Nollie?"

"The Gestapo came to the house. And Nollie told them right out that Annaliese is a Jew. I ran out the back door."

It was preposterous. But Corrie knew it was true. If the Gestapo asked Nollie a question, she would tell them the truth. It was daylight, a very dangerous time to be riding a bicycle. But Corrie careened frantically across the town square, over the canal on the Grote Haut bridge, and along the Wagenweg. Within ten minutes she leaned her bicycle on a lamppost on Bos en Hoven Straat and waited.

It was true! Out of Nollie's house came Nollie escorted by a strange man in a suit. Behind them with a second strange man was Annaliese, almost limp.

It was not long before the ten Booms learned Nollie was only a short distance away in the jail on Smedestraat. By all reports she was in high spirits, singing hymns. Poor Annaliese was in the old Jewish theater in Amsterdam, awaiting transport to Germany. Were there really death camps there in Germany? That's what people were saying now. It was monstrous, disgraceful, outrageous, intolerable, shameful, scandalous, intolerable—in short, impossible. Yet for anyone who had suffered under Nazis, it did not seem impossible at all.

How could Nollie have betrayed sweet Annaliese?

Six days later Pickwick phoned Corrie and in code urged her to rush to his house in the suburb of Aerdenhout. There he told her, "We freed forty Jews from the old Jewish theater in Amsterdam last night. One of them was very anxious that Nollie know about it."

Annaliese was free! So the only harm done was to Nollie. Corrie felt terrible now for berating Nollie. And the news got worse. Nollie was transferred to federal prison in Amsterdam. Poor, sweet Nollie. But Corrie knew no prison could defeat Nollie's spirit. She was much too near God. Oh, how

Nollie would frustrate her captors. How her sweet soprano would fill their cold-barred world with hymns.

But Corrie wasn't going to sit on her hands.

Following Pickwick's advice, she visited the doctor in charge of the prison hospital. The Beje residents had been reading Dale Carnegie's *How to Win Friends and Influence People*. There were few times in Corrie's life when she wanted to influence anyone more than she did now. And when she saw Doberman pinschers in the waiting room, she knew which strategy from Dale Carnegie's book she would use.

"How smart of you, doctor!" she said brightly in German. "You brought those lovely dogs with you to keep you company here in Holland."

"Do you like dogs?" He was suspicious, but what dog lover can resist talking about his incomparable dogs?

Corrie was almost breathless as she rattled on about dogs and sought the doctor's good advice on dogs. Corrie became spellbound by the many excellent qualities of the Dobermans. But the doctor finally tired of bragging and asked, "Why are you here?"

"My sister, Nollie van Woerden, is here." Corrie suddenly decided to be as recklessly honest as Nollie. "She's here for hiding a Jew. My sister has six children."

The doctor stood up. "You must go now."

Corrie went back to the Beje. Had she succeeded in anything at all? She told herself to be patient. If the doctor was an ally to their cause, she must not jeopardize such a valuable man by hanging around asking favors. What if the Beje operation was discovered by the Gestapo? Wouldn't they backtrack Corrie looking for others? But finally her patience ran out. She returned to the doctor. He grimaced, but then he quickly enthused about dogs again, mentioning a breed that is particularly stubborn. Still smiling, talking about how that breed is not popular these days, he ushered her to the door and said softly, "For heaven's sake, don't come back here again. I must have time for my work."

The ten Booms got an early Christmas present. Nollie was released from prison. Apparently the prison doctor thought her blood pressure was dangerously low. Nollie shrugged. She never doubted God would take care of her.

In December the Beje started to celebrate not Christmas but Hanukkah. Betsie found a Hanukkah candlestand, and each night they performed the rituals. With Meyer's help their celebration was very authentic. And joyous. And loud. Corrie was chilled when the wife of the optician who lived next door asked discreetly if they could sing with a little less volume. So their neighbors knew! Who else knew? Who walking by in the street might hear their Jewish festivities? How close was the Beje to discovery?

In January of 1944, Corrie was jolted. She received a message to come to the police station on Smedestraat. She was baffled. That was not the way the Gestapo operated. But what was she to think? Nollie's captivity had not gone to waste. Corrie first packed a prison bag. In it went a Bible, a pencil, needle and thread, soap, toothbrush, and comb. She took a leisurely bath, then dressed in several sets of underwear and her warmest clothing topped by two sweaters. Then she trudged—no innocent—to the police station.

The chief of police himself wanted to talk to her. After she entered his office, he closed the door. The two were alone. He was a brusque man. He didn't waste any time. He turned the volume up on a radio and leaned forward, barely talking loud enough for her to hear him only inches away.

"I know all about you and your other work," he mouthed.

"My work with retarded children?" she asked evasively.

"No," he said. "Never mind. I'm not trying to force you to admit it, but I do know you're working in the underground with the Free Dutch. I have someone I need silenced—permanently. Can you give me the name of someone in the underground who can take care of my problem?"

The chief was Dutch, a native of Haarlem. But had he been corrupted by the Gestapo? What should she do? Why would such a man, who knew the name of every roach in Haarlem that crawled under a rock, need her help? Surely it was a trap.

She said, "My role is to free lips, not silence them. I can't help you. But I will pray with you that this problem is removed from your life. And I will pray that no one has to be silenced."

The chief prayed with her. He was much too taciturn for her to know if he was trying to trick her or not. She returned to the Beje, not confident at all. The activity at the Beje was becoming too obvious. If the chief really had a spy in his office, how long would the Beje's secret last? And many people now just came to her off the street, always asking for help. Could she hide a Jewish woman and her baby? Could she find a place for a Dutch boy to hide? Could she give them guilders to bribe a policeman? Could she get a message to someone in jail? And who was to know if the plea was coming from a spy for the Gestapo? And could she ever refuse to help someone?

Each day now seemed more treacherous than the last. And to compound the agony, Corrie came down with the flu. She lay under her vaporizer, aching with every breath. Oh, how she longed to hear the radio exultantly announce that the British and Americans were storming the shores of France! It was February of 1944. The Nazis had infested Holland for almost four years! How much longer could the amateurs in the Dutch underground hold out against ruthless snakes of the Third Reich? How horrible Corrie felt.

What was that sound? Thumping feet? Was she dreaming, or was this real? Were those frantic whispers she heard? Had she heard the buzzer? She struggled to rise.

TEN

B odies were scrambling under her bookcase!

How many had entered the angels' crib? Then Mary appeared, slumped in the doorway, gasping for air. She had to be the last one.

Corrie jumped from the bed, her head booming pain with every heartbeat. She rudely shoved Mary under the bookcase. A man she had never seen before scrambled in after Mary. So Mary wasn't the last one. Corrie slammed the sliding door shut. She arose on wobbly legs and toppled back into bed.

Voices came from below: harsh, demanding. In German. *"Schnell!"* Thumps. *"Passen sie auf!"* Nasty even for a German soldier. *"Wo sind die Juden?"* No, these weren't soldiers. The Gestapo!

In between the shrill barks below came a sound from the secret room: wheezing! It was Mary, breathing like a freight train.

"Oh please, Jesus, heal Mary. Now! I know You can do it," cried Corrie.

"Was is das?" A man rushed into the bedroom. "Who are you talking to?" he barked in Dutch.

"No one you would know," mumbled Corrie as she clutched the covers around her.

"What did you say?" he growled.

"Why are you here?" asked Corrie, clutching the covers tighter.

"I ask the questions here!" The man wore a blue suit. He was tall but portly, with a pasty face. "What is your name?"

"Cornelia ten Boom."

"Prove it."

She opened the pouch she wore around her neck. She pulled out her identification folder. "Here."

He yanked it from her hand and checked a notebook. "So it is you!" He threw the folder back in her face.

"Why are you here?" She coughed at him with all her might.

"Cover your mouth! Have some decency." He backed up. "What is that smell? Menthol? Camphor? Get up at once and get out of here." He backed up through the door. "Your room smells like a sewer. You really are sick, aren't you?" His pasty face sagged with revulsion. "Come downstairs at once. And no funny business." He held a handkerchief over his nose and mouth. Corrie lurched to her feet. "Let me dress, please."

"Hurry up!"

She wanted to get out of the room as fast as possible herself. Mary might start wheezing any moment. She tugged clothes over her pajamas. She struggled to put on two sweaters.

"I said no funny business!" he barked.

"I have the chills," she said. She grabbed her winter coat. Where was her precious prison bag?

Her prison bag was by the sliding door!

How could she have been so careless? She couldn't draw attention to it now. What if Mary coughed or wheezed just then? Corrie had to keep coughing herself. The man might not notice an extra cough or wheeze. But how could she draw attention to the door? Yet how could she leave her precious bag? Prison would be hell without it. But she couldn't take the chance. She had to get out of her bedroom as soon as possible. The man was repelled by her room, yet now he seemed torn. He inched closer, as if he should really stay and poke around for a while. And what if Mary coughed? Corrie lurched out of the room and stumbled down the stairs.

A soldier stood in front of Aunt Jans's rooms. Hadn't there been a prayer meeting there earlier? It was Willem's meeting. It was for real. It gave Willem an excuse to keep coming to Haarlem. Even Nollie and Peter were in his prayer meetings. Oh, surely they were gone by now. What time was it? How long had she slept? What day was it?

In the dining room, a man in a brown suit sat at the table. Corrie cried, "Papa. Betsie. Toos." They were sitting on chairs against the wall. Beside them were three workers from the underground. Corrie could see daylight out the dining room window.

The pasty-faced man in the blue suit said in German, "I've got Cornelia ten Boom here." He paused for effect. "The ringleader," he sneered.

"Ringleader?" answered the man at the table in German. He looked up. He had been counting silver coins hidden under the staircase with the radio. "That old frump?" He shrugged. "Take her downstairs and find out where the Jews are hidden." He shivered and glanced toward the barren coal hearth. It rarely had a fire these days. "You people live like barbarians. I'm surprised you have chairs." He began counting again.

The man in the blue suit prodded Corrie through the workroom into the front showroom. He slapped her hard. "Attention now!"

She held her stinging face. "What do you want?"

"Where are you hiding the Jews?"

"We have none."

He slapped her again. "Where are the stolen ration books?"

335

"We don't have any—"

He slapped her again. "Where are you hiding the Jews?"

"Oh, please, Jesus, stop him." She was coughing. She tasted blood in her mouth.

He lowered his arm and backed up. "What do you have? It's not tuberculosis, is it? What a dirty business this is." He scowled at his notebook again. "Which one is Elizabeth?"

Soon Corrie sat in Betsie's chair in the dining room and Betsie was in the showroom taking the blows from the man in the blue suit.

But soon she was back, slender and limp, lips trembling and swollen. Corrie rose and helped sit her down. Betsie whispered, "I feel sorry for that man."

A woman blundered in the alley door. "They arrested Herman Sluring!"

"Quiet!" screamed Corrie.

"You be quiet!" The man in the blue suit struck Corrie.

The man at the table glared at her. "We might have learned something from that silly fool," he said to the other man in German. "Bring her up here."

But the woman froze. Now she knew she was in the hands of the Gestapo. Corrie was depressed. So they had arrested Pickwick, too. And there was Papa. *Please, Lord Jesus, don't let them hurt Papa.* She heard noises of splintering wood above them. Had they found the room? But there were no screams. No cries of triumph. Perhaps not.

So far the Gestapo had found the hidden silver that was supposed to have been surrendered to the Nazis long ago. They found the radio, the telephone, even the alarm system. Only a fool would have failed to realize that the ten Booms were in very deep trouble. There would be no evading Nazi injustice for these violations.

A man blundered in the alley door. He was arrested. Then another man. Finally, the traffic stopped. The word was out. The Beje had been raided.

The man at the table stood up. "I guess we can leave now," he said in Dutch. He smiled evilly at Corrie. "Aren't you happy? Your Jewish roaches are safe, aren't they? Well, when you are rotting in prison, reflect on this. We will surround your house for as long as it takes. The Jewish roaches in your secret room will turn into mummies. It will be a very long, very painful death!"

But Corrie was happy. The Gestapo had not found the secret room. There was still hope for the people in the angels' crib. The Gestapo had failed!

Suddenly, captives began filing out of Aunt Jans's room, past the dining room, and down the stairs. There was Nollie! And Peter! And Willem! Every ten Boom. Thank God Mama had not lived to see this awful day.

And yet all the way down the alley and the half block up Smedestraat to the police station Corrie thanked Jesus for helping them. Mary had not made any noise in all that time. Their fugitives were still safe.

Inside the station, not police but soldiers herded them down a corridor into a gymnasium. Thirty-five people had been arrested at the Beje. The men of the Gestapo looked very proud. This was quite a roundup for them—so large, they would probably brag, that they needed a gymnasium to hold all the criminals. In the gymnasium, the captives could talk among themselves. They even used the toilets off the gymnasium to flush papers that should not be discovered. So the Gestapo was not so smart after all. Just active and evil.

The next morning they were marched out of the police station. In the street waited a long green bus. Some soldiers were already inside it. Suddenly, Herman Sluring was swept past Corrie. She hadn't even known Pickwick was in the police station. He was hatless. His bald head and face were mottled with angry red welts. Corrie squeezed onto one double seat with Papa and Betsie. As the driver ground the gears and the bus labored away, Corrie saw Willem's wife Tine in the crowd of stunned gawkers along the sidewalk.

The green bus rumbled across the town square. In the bus were Corrie, Papa, and Betsie. Farther back were Nollie, Willem, and Peter, Pickwick and Toos. Each one of them wanted to get off but couldn't.

It was a bright winter day. The bus headed not east to Amsterdam but south along the dunes that held back the North Sea. In two hours, the bus was rumbling through the streets of The Hague.

In Dutch, Willem said, "The Hague has the headquarters of the Gestapo for all of Holland."

Inside the headquarters was not terror but grinding bureaucracy. The men in suits were now clerks for the Gestapo, behind a high counter, asking questions and typing answers onto papers. One answer was never enough. Every question had to be asked a dozen times—not as a shrewd tool of interrogation but the result of an overreaching fumbling bureaucracy. If Corrie had not been so sick with the flu, she probably would have laughed. How could anyone respect such fools?

Many hours later soldiers prodded them into the back of a canvas-topped army truck. They bounced and rattled on a long ride. But more than soon enough, massive gates clanged behind them. Where were they? Corrie could see nothing.

In a loud voice, Willem said, "We are at the federal prison in Scheveningen."

They scrambled down out of the truck to stand dazed in a courtyard surrounded by high brick walls. Soldiers prodded them inside a long low building. They lined up facing a wall inches from their noses.

"Women prisoners, follow me!" screamed a woman's voice.

Corrie turned, blinking into the bright ceiling lights. There was Papa not far away, sitting very erect in a high-backed chair.

"Good-bye, Papa. God be with you," cried Corrie.

"God be with you, Papa," echoed Betsie.

"And God goes with you, my daughters," Papa said in a voice that was clear but thin with exhaustion.

Corrie looked desperately for Willem and Peter. Where were they? A soldier approached with a rifle. She must keep moving. She held Betsie's hand and rushed ahead with the flow of prisoners. Then she saw Nollie just ahead.

A door banged behind them. Coconut-palm matting ran down the center of the hallway. It sponged under her tired legs. The prisoners were urged along by women guards, armed with billy clubs.

"Follow the matron—but keep off the mat!" barked a guard. "Prisoners never walk on the mats."

The flow stopped. They waited their turn to once again give their names to a woman at a desk in the hallway. But this time they were ordered to surrender anything of value. Corrie gave up her Alpina wristwatch, a gold ring, and a few Dutch guilders. Her belongings disappeared into a large envelope.

Now they marched down the cold hallway scarred by narrow metal doors, stopping only for the matron to unlock a door and a guard to roughly shove one of the women inside. Betsie was the first sister to go into a cell. Nollie went in a cell two doors beyond Betsie's cell. If only Corrie were next. She would at least be close to her dear sisters.

But they went on and on, turned a corner, turned another corner, and then another, until Corrie was hopelessly disoriented. Finally, a guard shoved her stumbling inside a cell. Four women were imprisoned in the cell with one cot. Three thin mats were on the floor.

The matron snapped, "Give this prisoner the cot."

Corrie began coughing.

"Don't put a sick woman in with us," whined one of the inmates.

But they were not all so rude and selfish. Corrie was even comforted by one of the cellmates after she collapsed on the cot, clutching her coat around her aching body against the clammy air.

It didn't take long to learn prison routine. Once a day they got hot food, usually gruel. Once a day they got a piece of dark bread. Once a day they passed out the bucket they had to use for a toilet. It was returned empty. Once a day they passed out the washbasin full of gray water. It was returned with clean water.

All day long one of the women walked the length of the narrow cell. Six steps from end to end. One naked lightbulb burned overhead. There were no windows.

In spite of her illness, Corrie tried to talk to the women. They were curt. They guarded their pasts. Their universe now was prison. It was only painful to speak of the outside. Would Corrie get that way?

A noise rattled in the hall. Feet padded in the hall, too. "That's a trusty with the medical cart. Someone is sick," said one woman.

A door opened. There were footsteps.

"That's the matron," said the same woman. "I'll bet she found someone with an extra blanket."

A door opened and closed somewhere in the hall. There were footsteps.

"That's someone in 316 being lead away by a guard. Toward the interior. For a hearing," said the same woman.

"How can you know all that?" asked Corrie, unbelieving.

"We get four kinds of visitors," said the same woman in a resigned voice. "Trusties are not too bad. Guards are usually bad. The matron almost always brings bad news. And a soldier puts your heart in your mouth."

"But how can you know so much?" asked Corrie.

"She's been here three years," snarled one of the other cellmates bitterly.

One of these women had been here three years! Corrie found that fact so depressing she shut up. A hunted animal didn't have senses finer tuned than the woman who had been here three years. She knew every sound. How the woman must have longed for freedom. Or had she given up? It seemed useless to ask.

Corrie thought about Papa. What a miserable place this was. How would her dear Papa survive this? He was eighty-four. She always felt he lived on because he was buoyed up by love and friendship in the Beje. How would he do now?

She wasn't getting her health back. As often as not she was limp as a rag on the cot, coughing and aching.

One day in her second week of imprisonment the matron unlocked the door. "Get your hat and coat, ten Boom!"

"Something unusual is up!" blurted the inmate who had been there three years. Her mouth was gaping.

"Good or bad?" asked Corrie.

"Shut up, prisoner!" growled the matron. "Come with me."

ELEVEN

Oh God, if freedom is Your will, please let it be true. How Corrie hated the cell. And using the bucket in front of the others was so degrading. It was awful. Why couldn't she be free? Nollie had been freed from a federal prison after admitting she hid a Jew. Of course it was true. Oh, it was wonderful to be out of the cell. She refused to think about the worst possibility.

"Stay off the mat!" barked the matron.

Corrie almost felt good as she stepped out into the courtyard with the high brick walls. She gazed at the marvelous blue sky.

"Get your nose out of the clouds!" snapped the matron. "Get in the automobile."

The matron shoved Corrie in the backseat of a black automobile next to a soldier and woman who looked sick. In the front seat was the driver and a man who was also sick, his head lolling back like his neck was a rag. The massive gates swung open and the automobile sped through.

They drove into The Hague. Dutch people were actually strolling the sidewalks. How precious. Were they thankful? Soon they stopped at a building. The sign said it was a medical clinic. They were being taken to a doctor. The soldier watched them. When Corrie asked him for permission to use the bathroom, he had a nurse take her.

Inside the bathroom, the nurse whispered, "Can I get you anything?"

"I need most of all a Bible. And also a. . .a needle and thread. And soap. And a toothbrush."

"I must go. Hurry up or the soldier will be hammering in the door."

After the doctor had taken her temperature and listened to her chest with his stethoscope, he diagnosed pleurisy. The nurse returned her to the soldier, pressing something into her hand. It was wrapped in paper. Corrie shoved it into her coat pocket. It seemed miraculous. But the miracle faded as she realized she was being returned to prison.

"It is you. You're back!" exclaimed the woman whose hearing had been acutely tuned for three years. "Where did you go?"

"A medical clinic." Corrie waited to hear the door lock and footsteps retreat down the hallway. Then she pulled out the bundle. "I have something." She unwrapped it. "Soap!" She held up two bars. "Who wants to wash first?" The soap was snatched out of her hand. She held up a packet. "Look, safety pins."

"What treasure," said one of the inmates.

"Finally, the best of all," said Corrie. "The Gospels." She held up four tiny books.

The others drew back. "Are you crazy? If you're caught with a Bible, the Nazis double your sentence!"

That punishment took Corrie's breath away. "How the Nazis fear the Bible!"

Just two days later the matron entered again. "Get your hat and coat, ten Boom!"

"Something's up again," said the astonished inmate who had been there three years.

"Stay off the mat!" snapped the matron in the hallway.

Had a cellmate squealed on Corrie? Surely there was no reason to call her out of the cell again. And sure enough she was not heading for the courtyard and freedom. She was walking deeper into the prison. The matron finally stopped and unlocked the door of a cell.

"Get inside."

Corrie entered an empty cell. The door slammed behind her. The cot smelled foul. The stench seemed to trigger something, because she became very sick, even feverish. She was so sick she collapsed on the stinking cot and couldn't even get up to get her food when later it came through the slot in the door.

A medical trusty visited her. He gave her a dose of medicine that tasted as foul as it looked then took her temperature. All of the menial work was done by trusties. She asked the trusty about Papa, but the trusty would not talk to her. They were not about to jeopardize their privileged positions, whatever that got them. Corrie was sure she would never be a trusty.

For a while the medical trusty came every day. Finally, he stopped coming. Corrie did begin to feel better. She knew now she was in an outside cell. It was much colder than the other cell. There was a barred window high above her, open to the outside. Oh, what if Papa had been locked in such a cell? March had been bitterly cold. It was now April. She had been in prison one month.

As the weather improved, the window became an ally. For one hour a day, a ray of sunshine swept the lower reaches of the cell. Corrie bathed in it. It made her feel healthy again. But health brought memories back. Worry over Papa crushed her. And the collapse of her Beje underground was a terrible worry. What had happened to all her cohorts? And what about the fugitives in the angels' crib?

She had neglected her precious Gospels. But she had no choice. Her eyes had been so bad. Praise God, Papa had encouraged her to memorize verses.

That satisfied her hunger for the Bible. Now she was well enough to read again. She read constantly. The Gospels rejuvenated her more than the sunshine. What seemed like failure could be a colossal success. Her spirits rose.

Her birthday came and passed, observed by no one. But she did get a treat two days later on April 17: her first shower in six weeks. Other prisoners were showering, too. What a joy it was to see and hear other women. She had been in solitary for one month. She resolved to bring three of her Gospels with her when she took her next shower and give them away. How could she hoard such a treasure for herself?

Life seemed to spring from God's grace now. An ant scurried out of a crack in the floor. It was a major event. Corrie felt honored. It had seemed for a while no life was low enough to visit such a cell as hers. But now she had an ant visiting, a forerunner of better things. Then she received a package! Nothing was written on it but Corrie's name and the address of the prison, but Corrie knew it was from Nollie's family, the van Woerdens. In it were sandwiches, a brown cake, and a pan of porridge. And there was much more: a needle and thread, two bottles of vitamins, and a brilliant red towel! How Nollie's family understood prisons now.

She wrote a letter thanking the van Woerdens for the package, assuring them she was recovering from pleurisy, and putting her solitary confinement in a positive light: Gregarious, nonstop Corrie was forced to stop and see deep inside herself, to see her sin. Praise God. The evening of April 20 was very unusual. For seven weeks the prison had been like a tomb. Usually she had to strain to hear anything more than padding feet and squeaking cart wheels. But this evening she heard shouts. Yes, actual shouts. What was it? She was very lucky. The food shelf in her door had been left open. She pressed her ear against the opening.

"What is it?" shouted someone. "Where are the guards? Are we being rescued? Are the British and Americans here at last?"

"You might as well hope for a visit from the queen," answered a voice choked with bitterness. "It's Hitler's birthday. The guards are celebrating with the other miserable Nazis."

"Don't waste this time complaining," urged another voice. "We can exchange information."

What happened next was miraculous to Corrie. Somehow these poor lost souls organized and disciplined themselves to spread news all around the prison.

"I'm Corrie ten Boom in cell 384," yelled Corrie. "Where are the ten Booms: Betsie and Casper and Willem? Where are the van Woerdens: Nollie and Peter?"

And so the messages flew back and forth. It was a glorious time. Especially when news cycled back: Nollie was released! Oh, Nollie. Wouldn't you know it? Nollie always landed on her feet like a cat! Young Peter was released. Praise God for that. Willem was released. Praise the Lord. Herman Sluring was released. Even Pickwick! And Toos! The news stunned Corrie. Had they all been released? Please God, let it be true. Then she heard Betsie was still in cell 312.

That evening soothed much of the ache in Corrie's heart. But there still was no news of Papa. One week later another package was thrown into her cell. It was addressed by Nollie! Corrie could tell her handwriting. Inside was Nollie's favorite sweater: pale blue with flowers embroidered over the pocket. How wonderful. And more vitamins. And cookies. Rewrapping her treasures, Corrie noticed something odd about Nollie's handwriting. It seemed slanted toward the stamp. Quickly she worked the stamp loose with water. Yes! There was a message under the stamp!

Corrie whispered the words to herself, "All the watches in your closet are safe."

So the fugitives in the angels' crib in the Beje had escaped! Praise God. Corrie should not have worried about them after being processed by the Gestapo in The Hague. Such bunglers could not sustain a watch around the Beje week after week. Constant vigil was nothing but an empty threat by the Gestapo, hoping she would panic and talk.

She had only one worry now: Papa. Where was he?

One day Corrie was pulling thread from the red towel to embroider colorful figures on her pajamas. Her food shelf opened and something drifted in like a beautiful snowflake. Her very first letter. It was from Nollie! It read:

My dear Corrie,

How happy we were with your letter and that the Lord has heard our prayers and you are at peace and happy. When I heard you were alone, I was so upset. Darling, now I have to tell you something very sad. Be strong.

On the tenth of March, our dear Papa went to heaven. He survived only nine days. He passed away in Loosduinen. Yesterday I fetched his belongings from Scheveningen. I know the Lord will help you bear this. It was pneumonia. Betsie knows it already and wrote us about it. She already had premonitions about this, years ago.

So Betsie knew about Papa. Betsie had a real gift, almost a gift of prophecy.

And why not? Did Corrie know anyone more in Christ than Betsie? How she wanted to talk to Betsie now. Poor Papa. No, Corrie mustn't grieve in the wrong way. Not with pity or sorrow. She must be sorry only because she missed his wonderful presence. Papa said he would gladly die for the Jews. And he did.

Corrie gathered her thoughts for a letter. She mustn't waste precious opportunities to write.

> *Dear Nollie and all the other loved ones,*
> *On May 3rd I received your letter. First I was sad, but now I am comforted completely. Father can now sing:*
>
> > *I cannot do without You,*
> > *You, Jesus, my Lord,*
> > *Thanks, praise, adoration,*
> > *Never will I be without You again.*
>
> *How beautiful his voice will sound. I am so happy for him. When I think of those nine days I quickly switch to the present and concentrate on how happy he is now, for he sees the answer to everything.*

The days dragged on. Corrie thought of many things. But she tried not to think how, of all thirty-five people arrested in February, only she and Betsie were still in prison. But she did think about it. Why was it? Was it because she and Betsie were such notorious members of the Dutch underground? She had to laugh. She didn't have one-tenth the influence that Pickwick had. So why were she and Betsie still in prison? Poor sweet Betsie. She had only helped like the others. She wasn't in the center of the storm like Corrie. Maybe Corrie did belong in prison in this insane world of the Nazis. But not Betsie, not even among Nazis.

Not long after Corrie was allowed to exercise in an open area inside the prison. Other prisoners walked there, too. Corrie could smell the North Sea beyond the wall. Her rubbery legs walked a rectangular path around a lawn. Shrubs by the path flowered red. Primroses were in bloom. The sun was warm. The sky was blue. Was this so bad? Surely she could endure this. Did monsters keep such gardens as this?

But then she saw a freshly dug trench. No. She must not even think her suspicions. But it spoiled her reverie. She noticed now the high walls were topped with broken glass. There was a burning smell in the air, too. It smelled like nothing she had ever smelled before. Her soul wanted to cry out. Another inmate walked by her and whispered the smell was from burning flesh. The prison has a crematorium. *No! That is too preposterous,* thought Corrie. *Not even Nazis are that evil.* Suddenly, her ears were pounded by noises beyond the walls. Is that a jackhammer? She was afraid to look at the other inmate.

"That was a machine gun," whispered the inmate, "I know. I was at Rotterdam."

Corrie welcomed her gray cell. *Oh Lord, let me out only when I can walk with children of the light.* It was only days later that Corrie listened to rain fall outside her window. It was a gray, gloomy day when one wanted nothing to happen. What good could happen on such a gloomy day? She chided herself. Now she was letting the weather be her ouija board. She heard the footsteps of a guard. *Just keep right on walking,* prayed Corrie.

She heard a key in the lock. The door opened and a female guard stepped inside. "Come with me, ten Boom."

Corrie asked, "Do I need my coat and hat?"

"No!" The guard raised her billy club. "Do as I say! Come with me. Stay off the mat!"

TWELVE

The guard led Corrie into a courtyard somewhere in the midst of the prison. In the courtyard were four small huts. The guard knocked on the door of one hut. Corrie stood beside her, rain dripping down her face.

After a voice inside answered, the guard pushed Corrie inside. A tall, thin man in a crisp gray and black uniform of the Nazis stood by a small potbellied stove. "I'm Lieutenant Rahm," he said in Dutch. "Sit down. It's chilly in here," he added, more to himself than Corrie.

Corrie sat. The chair had a back and arms. She felt so privileged. She watched the lieutenant scoop coal into the stove. He was in no hurry. She enjoyed every minute of the experience. Did he know that? Was that why he dawdled, stirring the coals around with a poker? How could she credit a Nazi with such feelings of compassion? But soon he had a cozy fire started. She smelled and felt the warmth. What luxury.

He sat down. "If I'm going to help you, you must tell me everything."

So that was it. The snake was just getting her to relax. "What would you like to know?" she asked dully.

Lieutenant Rahm discretely probed. His face was chiseled with sharp features, a face easy to interpret as evil. Yet the face had something soft and haunting, too. Corrie had seen that look before. But she must not jump to conclusions with a Nazi. After many questions Corrie figured out what he was after. He had a list of people and addresses the Gestapo must have found at the Beje. It was a very real list of Dutch people active in the underground. But the lieutenant seemed to think the Beje might have been a center for planning raids on food offices and stealing food ration books. He seemed unable to make sense of the list. No one could ever make sense of the list from the Beje in regard to raids on food offices. Corrie relaxed, blissful in her ignorance. She could betray no one in any operations that raided food offices.

"I don't know what you mean," she kept repeating.

All the while she enumerated her many activities before the occupation. Yes, she took teenaged girls hiking and camping. Yes, she helped raise children left in Holland by missionaries. Yes, she gave Sunday school lessons to retarded children.

"Retarded children?" It was the first time his face looked hard like the Nazi he was. "What a terrible waste."

"God values a retarded child as much as a watchmaker like me."

346

"And just how do you know what God thinks?" he asked. His eyes were sorrowful.

"He gave us the Bible so we would know what He thinks."

The lieutenant sighed. "I believe we have talked enough." He rose and opened the door. "Guard, take the prisoner back to her cell."

Next day Corrie was back. This time the lieutenant held their conference in the courtyard. They sat by a wall. "You need sun," he said. During a long pause, Corrie closed her eyes and honored the sun. Finally, he said, "I couldn't sleep last night. I kept thinking about the work I do. And I kept thinking about the work you used to do before we came here to Holland."

"Are you worried?"

"My wife and children are in Bremen. Bremen is being bombed. The war is going very badly."

This time she was sure about the look in his face. Corrie had not counseled hundreds of young people out of their despair without knowing all the symptoms of someone truly crying out for God. "You are in darkness, lieutenant."

"A good person like you cannot know darkness like mine."

"Jesus is the light of the world. Whoever follows Jesus will never walk in darkness." Did this man know the words of Jesus in the book of John? No, the lieutenant showed no trace of recognition.

She had four hearings with the lieutenant. She learned a little about her own situation. Her solitary confinement was not punishment. She was isolated because of her contagious illness. She was in prison, specifically charged with helping Jews. But for how long she could not discover.

It was the first week in June when she was escorted to the lieutenant's office again. Inside was Nollie! And Betsie! And Willem! Tine and Flip!

"We are being released!" cried Corrie and wildly hugged them.

"No," said Betsie, hanging tight to Corrie. "It's the reading of Papa's will."

The lieutenant excused himself. He looked haggard and haunted as he walked outside. When the door closed, Willem said, "Everyone thinks the invasion is coming! Pray to God that the British and Americans are soon headed this way. The Russians are already rolling over the Germans from the other direction. Praise God, the Nazis are almost finished."

They discussed what they knew about Papa's death, which was nothing more than that he had died in the corridor of a hospital waiting for treatment. He could have suffered far more. While they talked, Nollie pressed a pouch in Corrie's hand. It contained a complete Bible! Corrie quickly put the string of the pouch over her head and slipped the treasure down inside her dress. Willem believed they might get Corrie transferred to a sanitarium because of her illness. The paperwork was being done.

Suddenly, the lieutenant returned to read the will. He had left them alone as long as he could. The will surprised no one. There was no money, only the Beje. And Papa left it to shelter Corrie and Betsie as long as they wished.

The prison erupted a few days after that. After the morning meal, guards were screaming everywhere. "Inmates must throw their belongings into pillow slips and stand at attention in the hallways!" they yelled.

After a tiresome wait in the hallway, Corrie heard the guards scream, "March this way!" They didn't even bother to mention the precious mats.

In the courtyard next to the outside gate were buses! Corrie searched desperately for Betsie. Maybe they could get together at last. But Betsie was nowhere to be seen in the milling prisoners. *Oh please, Jesus, let us be together again,* prayed Corrie, as the buses spewed black smoke and churned across the countryside.

When the buses unloaded them at the railway station, they stood at attention once again until their legs were shaky. Suddenly, they were streaming onto railroad cars. Corrie hung back. Where was Betsie? As she was jostled along toward a railroad car, she saw Betsie behind her. Her prayer was answered! She waited and threw her arms around her. They were giddy as they found seats together on the car. How she had missed Betsie. The sisters talked for hours, loud at first like everyone else, but finally in hushed whispers. Corrie was stunned to hear that Betsie had prayed with Lieutenant Rahm, too. So sweet Betsie had something to do with his remorse, too. Corrie should have known.

"Thank the Lord we Dutch do not have an evil government," said Betsie. "You know, Corrie, many Germans are victims of the Nazi madness, too." And they both prayed for the lieutenant and his family.

"Praise to God that we are not going east to Germany," whispered Betsie. "A while ago I thought I saw in the distance the cathedral in Delft."

"If you're right, we're going south." Corrie was so happy to be with Betsie she had not worried where they were headed. Betsie didn't really worry at all. Betsie was certain every action was planned by God, no matter how hard it was for a human mind to understand. But Corrie wasn't at all sure of that. Now she was worried. Before she went to prison she really did not believe the terrible stories about death camps in Germany. But how could she doubt them now?

Corrie pressed her face against the glass. "If only the clouds would part for a moment." If only she could see the stars. She sat on the left side of the train. If she saw the golden warmth of the star Arcturus, they were headed north, deeper into Holland. If she saw that icy blue diamond Vega, they were headed south toward Belgium. But if she saw the north star—God forbid—they were headed east into hell: Germany. For just a moment Corrie thought she saw Vega! They were headed south! The wheels changed pitch. The train was zipping across a trestle. But the trestle went on and on. Only one bridge was that wide. The bridge at Moerdijk. They were headed south!

Sometime in the night they stopped. They were rudely prodded off the train. Soldiers brandishing rifles bordered a rough path through the woods. The prisoners stumbled through the night. They slogged through puddles where it had rained. *Oh, how malleable people are,* thought Corrie. *We prisoners have no idea how long this nightmare will continue, yet we labor on obediently, almost complacent, no reward except that we avoid as much abuse as possible. We are still alive.*

They learned during the next day that they were in Holland on the perimeter of a prison camp near the village of Vught. This was not a Dutch prison. It was a concentration camp built by the Nazis for political prisoners. That fact was enough to alert everyone that this camp might not be an improvement over Scheveningen. For days the newcomers were idle as they were being processed into the camp.

But one day Corrie and Betsie were prodded into a long line. The news filtered back down the line: Twenty women at a time were being herded into a shower. Finally, as the two sisters neared the head of the line, they heard a guard shout, "Undress!" His voice was nasty, but there was more in it. Soon they could see the men guards relishing their power, laughing as they enjoyed the sight of naked women wiggling under the icy water. The women had to shower right out in the open!

Oh, please, God, don't make us do this, prayed Corrie as she and Betsie waited in a long line of women. *Poor, sweet, innocent Betsie. Don't let this happen to her, Lord.*

Moments before their group was to undress, a guard yelled, "We are out of uniforms. Send the cows back later." His voice was bored. When the women's camp received a new supply of uniforms, the men guards had returned to the men's camp. Corrie and Betsie showered under the sneering eyes of women guards. It was degrading but still a small miracle.

In their barracks lived 150 women. And small children! It seemed so strange to be around children again. If a new prisoner was pregnant, she had her child in the camp, and there the child remained. The inmates slept on real beds with two blankets. The ten Boom sisters must have looked warmhearted. Corrie knew Betsie did; she radiated love. A young Jewish girl walked right up to her like a baby chick. "I'm so scared." And Betsie pulled her into her arms.

There was an undercurrent of joy in most prisoners. Camp life really was better than prison life. The British and Americans were coming. It was inevitable now. The Nazis were short of soldiers. Work was largely in the hands of prisoners. An *oberkapo*, or boss, a prisoner himself, examined the newcomers, as icy-veined as any Nazi. How power corrupts! Frail Betsie did not fool the oberkapo. He contemptuously shunted her aside into a group of the infirm who sewed prison uniforms. Corrie was marched to the "Phillips factory," which was no more than additional barracks situated between the women's camp and the men's camp. Hundreds of men and women prisoners sat on benches hunched over radio parts on long tables. Guards rarely strolled the aisles. The work was supervised by another oberkapo, a very soft-spoken, very shrewd Dutchman named Moorman.

With Corrie's energy and background, she was soon assembling radios instead of sorting parts as they arrived. The real art was to assemble the radio in such a way that it was hopelessly defective but not obviously defective. The radios were installed in German fighter planes. The undermanned Nazis did reward the workers for their twelve-hour workday. Here at Vught they ate three times a day. And the food was better than the food at Scheveningen. After lunch the workers even had an hour off to rest. It was summer, so Corrie would stretch out on the ground for a nap. There was plenty of time for chatter while they worked—if no guards were strolling the aisles.

One day a voice woke her. "Corrie?"

Corrie blinked the sleep out of her eyes. "Mien? What joy!"

Mien van Dantzig also worked in the Phillips factory—the very sister of Hennie who had worked in the watch shop in the Beje. Mien was a thin young woman and very sly. Corrie soon learned she was a "scrounger." She helped the nurse in the camp. If a prisoner needed medicine, Mien might be able to get it for them.

Betsie greeted Corrie every evening at the barracks. She would say warm things to Corrie, such as, "I prayed with a woman from Hilversum today who knows Willem," or chilling things, such as, "A Belgian woman just got here who said the British and Americans are trapped at Cherbourg," or cheering things, such as, "The Russians are in Poland already!"

Their talk transcended gossip. To survive, one listened to information, judged its credibility, and shared it with others. She and Betsie even found out the name of their betrayer! He was a Dutchman from Ermelo. How Corrie hated him. And how she hated herself for hating him. Jesus commanded her to forgive enemies. But how could she ever forgive the wretch who caused Papa to die? And to think what suffering she and Betsie had been through! Betsie was weaker every day. And Willem had looked very unhealthy when she saw him in Lieutenant Rahm's office.

Corrie forced herself to pray for him. She knew from years of trying to live in Christ that a righteous act, no matter how reluctantly performed, often captured the heart. But she doubted it would work in the case of this dreadful traitor. But praying did do something for her. For the first time since she learned the man's identity, Corrie slept without bitterness and anger.

The prison routine rarely varied. Stiff and sore, Corrie stumbled out for first roll call at five o'clock. She ate black bread and drank blacker coffee at five-thirty. She hiked to the Phillips factory where she worked until six o'clock in the evening. She trudged back to spend precious free time with Betsie. She kept telling herself that a Christian can never really be imprisoned.

They were allowed to exchange letters again with Nollie's family and Willem's family. Nollie's first letter to Corrie got them very excited.

THIRTEEN

Nollie's letter to Corrie read:

After we were together in Scheveningen, the notary and a few others went to see the gentlemen who are now in charge of your case, and the result was that the house and the shop were released. We went there immediately and cleaned the whole house. The shop is open and everything is waiting for you both. We have been absolutely assured that the letter for your release was sent some time ago. . . . Mr. Rahm phoned again to say that the letter, which will set you free, has been sent.

Was it possible? Corrie and Betsie were breathless as they motioned a gnarled veteran named Floor to meet them in the latrine. All important business took place in the latrine. The male guards, as brutal as they were, never went there. A lookout was posted to watch out for the female guards.

In the latrine the veteran Floor told the sisters, "If you helped Jews, that gets you locked up for six months."

"Are you sure?" asked Corrie.

"You know the Germans. If that is what it says in their little Nazi rule book, that is what it is. You'd have to get that crackpot Hitler to change one of his own rules."

"Six months?" cried Corrie. "Let me see. We started our sentence the last day of February. March, April, May, June, July, August. We'll be free by September 1st!"

Corrie and Betsie rejoiced. Less than two months to go! They could serve that time easily. They gave Bible lessons to the others. They sang hymns. They held evening devotions. As more time passed, they began to give sermons. Several dozen inmates, putting their bitterness on hold, listened to the ten Boom sisters deliver the gospel.

Corrie had gained twenty pounds in the camp! She could almost have become complacent if she wasn't so worried about Betsie. Poor Betsie weighed less than one hundred pounds. Her glasses were always broken, always askew. She had to pin her overall straps closer together to keep her modesty. Even packages from Nollie crammed with sausages and fudge couldn't seem to keep Betsie from wasting away. And Corrie discovered the sewing brigade wasn't such a wonderful thing. Many times the brigade had to braid rope, and at the end of the day, Betsie's long, delicate hands were raw and bleeding. Corrie knew that if there was one thing an anemic person couldn't withstand very long, it was bleeding.

To squelch the last crumb of complacency Corrie might have harbored, there was the men's camp next to the women's camp. Every rifle shot ringing from the men's camp brought suspicions of an execution. At first she and Betsie refused to believe executions were so routine. It was too monstrous. But Corrie worked at the Phillips factory with men from the camp next to them. And many of the women had husbands in the camp.

How Corrie longed for September 1 and freedom!

And then came the best rumor yet: The British and Americans had taken Paris back! Their ground forces were knifing through France. They would soon cut Hitler's throat! Could it be true? Soon they saw proof with their own eyes. Almost daily by the end of August hundreds of silvery planes glimmered overhead, all headed east into Germany. One afternoon after the great silvery armada passed overhead, the women heard what must have been a tremendous battle in the sky just east of them. They laughed like fools as projectiles nicked trees around them and pinged into the barracks. Corrie later learned five women were in the hospital, injured by shrapnel.

Days later, explosions rocked the area.

Floor turned their blood to ice. "They're blowing up the bridges here. These Nazis are going to pull out and blow up every bridge between here and Germany. The question is: What are they going to do with us? Take us with them? Or leave us here? And if they do leave us here, is it with a song of freedom on our lips—or rotting in a mass grave? Which do you think Nazis will do?" She sounded very bitter.

"Surely they won't execute the whole camp?" said Betsie in horror.

"Maybe not us. They don't respect us. They think we are weaklings. But I'm not so sure about the men."

Corrie was stunned. For a hundred reasons. She could only say, "But our time is almost up."

Floor laughed sourly. "Do you think they're going to process anyone for release now?" And she continued as if speaking just to herself, "Winter is a very bad time in the camps. And this winter will be the worst yet. No fuel. Little food. The weak ones will never. . ." She seemed to notice Betsie. "Never mind. Enough of this doomsday talk."

As the magic date approached, conditions worsened in the camps. Executions in the men's camp were more frequent. Guards were extremely edgy in the women's camp. Finally, the day arrived: September 1!

It was a Friday. Corrie could hardly wait through morning roll call to hear the list of prisoners to be released. But there was no list that day. She stumbled off to the Phillips factory, as depressed as she had been at any time since she arrived in the camp. How she had waited for this day! She forced herself to be more alert. She prayed to Jesus for courage. Where else would she get it? She had to have it. This was a dangerous time. Prisoners who gave up hope seemed to have terrible accidents.

That night Betsie consoled her, "The notice of our release may be a day or two late. The Nazis seem to be distracted now."

Sweet Betsie. Who was more vulnerable than she was? And yet she had to console Corrie. Corrie was ashamed. But she did have a feeling of dread. They had to get their freedom now. If they didn't, two terrible choices awaited them: execution here or winter in Germany.

Rumors oozed through the camps now: The British and Americans had captured Brussels. Belgium was almost free again. Holland would soon be free! No. Brussels was still in the clutches of the Nazis. No, the British and Americans had Brussels, but they were going to bypass Holland and thrust straight to the black heart of Germany. No, the British and Americans were going to free Holland first.

They would take each rumor and extrapolate. The latrine was crowded with orators. If Holland was bypassed, their life would not change that much. No, in that case the guards would take it out on the prisoners. If Holland was attacked, they would be executed; the Nazis had no time for prisoners. No, they would be evacuated to Germany; Hitler was a madman bent on revenge. No, they would be freed. The Nazis wanted leniency after they lost the war. On and on went the arguments.

If there was one thing Corrie knew it was that their captors knew as little as their captives. Every one in Holland knew something about how Nazis suppressed the truth and advanced their lies—even to their own stooges.

One morning there was no roll call.

A guard burst into the barracks long after they were usually up. "Get your things together!" she screamed. The guard was frightened.

The women heard the dreaded *pop-pop-pop* of rifles from the men's camp. Were the men being executed? What was happening? Were the Americans and British attacking? Perhaps they parachuted during the night! The women were marched into a field. There, unbelievably, a German soldier stood in the bed of an army truck passing out blankets. A thousand women filed past and took a blanket. But hadn't they just left blankets in the camp?

They marched out of the camp in their usual five abreast. As they passed through the gates, Corrie saw the same rough wooded path they had walked three months ago. They marched to the same railroad tracks. Soldiers lined them up along the track three deep. They waited, clutching their blankets and pillowcases stuffed with belongings.

Far down the track were male prisoners. Maybe there were no executions. Who could know for sure? Some women were saying 180 had been shot. Some were saying 700. Some were saying none. Who could know the truth in the Nazi madness?

On top of the freight cars were German soldiers with machine guns. More soldiers were walking alongside the train, stopping at each car, throwing the bolt lock, then sliding the door open. After they opened the door to the car nearest Corrie, a red-faced soldier yelled, *"Schnell! Gehen sie weg!"*

The women were being forced inside the freight cars! The soldiers helped them climb up though the door, soon breathless from laughing and grabbing handfuls of unwilling flesh as the women scrambled awkwardly into the freight car. Corrie flailed at their steely groping fingers. She swatted their filthy hands off Betsie. The prettier the woman the more outrageously they pinched and groped her. But the worst treatment went to a Dutch woman with a red circle patched on the back of her overalls. That patch meant she had tried to escape from the camp. This woman had no protection at all. They slapped her to the ground and kicked her senseless before they picked her up and threw her in the boxcar. Somehow she still clutched her pillowcase and blanket.

The car stank of mildewed grain. The women were all standing up on the rough wooden floor of the car. But the soldiers kept adding women until they stood so close together Corrie had to wonder how they would ever rest. Suddenly, they were plunged into blackness. The bolt slammed shut on the door. They were locked in!

Somehow in the darkness they found rest. They sat like members of a bobsled team, their legs wrapped around the hips of the woman in front of them. Buffered by blankets, it was almost tolerable. Those on the side were attacking the walls. They had to have air. With anything they could find they gouged tiny holes until sunlight appeared.

The train lurched ahead—its destination unknown to the inmates. When Corrie got her turn at an air hole, she saw the night sky. She was on the right side of the train. There was Antares in the southern sky. They were traveling east—into Germany. The air in the car was very foul. If there were buckets for waste in her part of the car, they knew nothing about them. Somewhere in the car bread was stored, because it was being passed around. But the smell in the car was nauseating. It would be a long time before Corrie could eat her piece of bread in that stench. And she was very thirsty.

Each day the car got hotter and hotter.

Corrie prayed the ride was a nightmare few people would ever have to endure. They were numb with heat and thirst and the stench of soiled clothing. The sun was blinding when the door opened somewhere and a guard ordered them out.

They were too stiff to stand up and walk.

They crawled to the light and fell out the opening like blind crabs, clutching their blanket and pillowcase. They sprawled like fish on a bank gasping for air, praying for water. Yes, someone had a pail. There was a lake nearby, someone said. The stronger ones began to crawl toward the lake. Corrie stayed with Betsie. She made sure Betsie got water when pails of water finally worked their way back to the weak ones still sprawled by the tracks.

Corrie began to look around. Their guards were young boys in baggy uniforms, standing far off, repelled by the stinking women.

Corrie looked at Betsie. Yes, she was pitying the boys. That was Betsie. She was merely seeing more victims of the Nazis. If Betsie had been strong enough, she probably would have been on her feet organizing a prayer meeting among the boys. But she looked very old today, far older than her fifty-nine years. More white showed under her pupils than ever before. Her sunken chest was heaving. She had scarcely moved since Corrie tried to soften her fall from the freight car.

The boys marched them along the shore of the lake, then up a hill. The men prisoners were nowhere to be seen. They passed a few farmers and their families on the way. The country folk were red-cheeked, dressed in feathered caps and lederhosen. Could such people live their wonderfully pure lives these days? It seemed impossible. It was Betsie who reminded Corrie their good fortune was an illusion. That family had probably lost a brother, an uncle, a son somewhere in the mud of Russia.

When the women reached the crest of the hill, they saw down in the next valley their new camp. It was not a scar in the woods like Vught. This camp was a cancer, the trees having been cleared far back from the enclosure, which was not wire fences, but concrete walls with strands of wire at the top. Inside the walls stretched dozens and dozens of cold gray barracks. A tall stack fouled the blue sky with smoke.

As they got closer, Corrie could see the strands strung along the top of the concrete walls were not barbed wire. ELECTRIFIED WIRE warned the signs in German. Guard towers were spaced along the wall.

Corrie called to Floor, "What is this place?"

"Hell on earth." The blood seemed to have drained completely from Floor's face. "I think this must be Ravensbrück."

FOURTEEN

Any woman imprisoned in Holland by the Nazis had heard of Ravensbrück. Especially those women who had worked in the underground. Ravensbrück was not just a camp for women, but a camp for women who were considered incorrigible by the Nazis. It was a work camp. But the rumor was that the inmates were worked to death. There was no way out. Ever.

Once inside the massive gates, dozens of guards drove the one thousand newcomers to a large tent. And there they waited day after day, often pointlessly standing at attention until their knees trembled. Ones who collapsed were taken away and not seen again. They were no longer under the tent but beside it in the open air. No one complained. They were veterans of Nazi inhumanity. It took the Nazis days and days to process prisoners. Besides, waiting must be better than working in this place. And anything was better than the hell of the freight cars.

Lice at Ravensbrück were not a new problem. It was their abundance that was the problem. The ground swarmed with lice. The women had no choice. Their hair had to go. It was not the guards who insisted on it. The women did it themselves.

"Oh, Betsie, your beautiful chestnut hair," cried Corrie as she sheared the wavy locks off her sister. And it was more than that. Betsie looked so inconsequential with her tired shorn head wobbling on a thin goose neck. Never had she looked so frail, so wispy, so marginally alive.

Betsie was silent as her hands snipped Corrie's hair. As the locks fell to the ground, Corrie realized why. What could Betsie say? Corrie's thick, dark blond hair was now streaked white!

They surrendered their names. Betsie was now Number 66729. Corrie was Number 66730. More of the reality of Ravensbrück soon hit them. They were asked to surrender all their belongings.

The one thousand women lined up. The guards were shuttling fifty at a time into the shower room. Before they went into the shower room, they dumped their possessions into a pile. No one seemed to be recording anything. It seemed painfully obvious nothing was going to be returned.

Farther on in the line the women stripped and dumped their clothing into a second pile. They then walked naked past several deadly serious guards into the shower. These guards were not leering. They were tired of this place, of these emaciated licey women. They hated it. When the women reappeared from the shower room, each one wore a threadbare prison dress and leather shoes.

Before her group reached the first pile of abandoned possessions, Corrie clutched the bottle of vitamins in her hand. Then she and Betsie dropped their blankets and pillowcases into the pile. How it hurt to surrender their nice blankets, combs, needles, thread, all the things they had so painstakingly collected over six months. But they still had their most precious possessions: vitamins, Betsie's sweater, and the Bible.

Oh, please, Jesus, prayed Corrie, *please allow us to keep Your precious Word.*

Suddenly, Betsie doubled over, seized by a severe cramp.

"Please, sir," Corrie implored the guard in German, "she has diarrhea."

The guard scowled in disgust. "Well, don't let her do it here! Get her in there." He jabbed his finger at the shower room.

Corrie rushed Betsie into the shower room. No one was there. It was empty! They were between groups. Corrie quickly took the sweater from Betsie, wrapped the Bible and bottle of vitamins in the sweater, and hid the bundle behind a wooden bench crawling with roaches. Stacked in the other end of the shower room were the dresses and shoes they were to wear.

They returned to the line, shed their Vught overalls, and Corrie imagined to herself no one saw them as they walked past the guards. Inside the shower room, after the short icy blast, they dressed in their new camp garb—plus one sweater, one bottle of vitamins, and one Bible. But their problems were not over. The Bible in the pouch hanging from Corrie's neck on a string was not well concealed under the flimsy dress. She had no choice but to pray again. *Oh, please, Jesus, protect me. Surround me with your angels.*

They marched slowly past guards who made no effort to hide their disgust as they searched every woman from head to toe with groping hands. Rough hands covered the woman in front of Corrie. Rough hands covered Betsie behind Corrie. No hands touched Corrie. It was as if she were invisible. It seemed that the worse things became for Corrie and Betsie, the more God intervened to protect them.

The one thousand newcomers spent day after day in Barracks 8, which was a quarantine compound. It was deliberately placed next to the barracks where women were punished. During the day the newcomers spent hours outside standing at attention. All day and all night they heard screams of agony. They heard whacks and thuds that caused the agony. Soon Corrie even flinched at silence. Silence meant the victim had either passed into pain so excruciating it was paralyzing or had died. It was heartrending to listen. Each day Corrie felt closer and closer to Jesus. How else could one endure such pain? She could never be defeated in Jesus.

All the newcomers encouraged each other. Their permanent barracks would be better. They would have nice blankets again. They would get real medical attention when they needed it instead of degrading inspections every Friday in which they stripped naked to have their teeth examined. In their permanent barracks, they wouldn't have to sleep five to a bed with one blanket. Gripers were shouted down in a hurry. No one was allowed to mention the obvious: Each night was colder.

Finally, the guards marched them into the main camp and prodded them ten abreast past the permanent barracks. The small army would stop while several numbers were called, thinning their ranks, then continue. Corrie and Betsie stopped at Barracks 28. A not-very-happy guard briskly led them and several other newcomers, including Mien, straight into the dormitory.

"What a smell!" blurted Betsie.

"Ignore it, you cow," growled the guard. "There are worse things than that in here."

Perhaps one could learn to ignore the smell of rotting straw. Could one ignore the smell of vomit and human waste? But there were things that were worse. Their five to a bed seemed a wonderful luxury now. This dormitory was jammed with square platforms covered by straw and stacked three deep. The platforms were shoved together so that one aisle had to serve many platforms. Corrie and Betsie would have to crawl across three platforms to reach their own platform. What Corrie and Betsie did not know yet was how many women shared each platform square.

The guard quickly took the newcomers to a central room. About two hundred women were seated around tables knitting army socks from gray wool. "Get to work," said the guard, who no longer seemed to be in a hurry. Half a dozen other guards moved listlessly around the room.

Corrie and Betsie sat down. Corrie whispered in German to a woman next to her, "Is this a knitting barracks?"

"No. The others are out working."

"How many live here?"

"Fourteen hundred. The barracks are supposed to hold four hundred."

Corrie learned prisoners were from all over Europe. At first the camp had been full of Poles, Finns, and Russians. Now women flooded in from everywhere as the Nazis were being pushed back on all fronts. The barracks had Dutch, French, Belgians, Danes, Norwegians, and even some poor mysterious women no one in the barracks could communicate with at all.

"And how many are in the camp?" asked Corrie of the woman.

"They say thirty-five thousand," she answered lifelessly.

The others returned at six o'clock from their work. But the last thing they wanted to talk about was work. And Corrie found little conversation from anyone but Betsie as they drank a tasteless broth with shreds of cabbage floating in it. After supper, once again they went outside to stand at roll call.

That night they learned more stark truths. Their half of the dormitory had eight toilets for seven hundred women. They shared the platform with seven other women, who were not happy about their arrival. A crash nearby and screams and curses informed them the slats under the straw were very unstable.

The next morning, Corrie was awakened by a whistle. Choking dust filled the air as women scrambled off the platforms for black bread and coffee in the knitting room. Slowpokes found little left.

"What time is it?" asked Corrie, chewing the tough bread. "Didn't we just fall asleep?"

"Four o'clock. Same time it was at this time yesterday," grumbled someone.

At four thirty, fourteen hundred women stood outside Barracks 28 under streetlights for roll call. To Corrie it represented a further decline of their fortunes. At Vught they had roll call at five o'clock. Since February 29, 1944, it always seemed to Corrie that life could not get worse. But under the Nazis, she learned life always did get worse.

Amazingly, Corrie and Betsie marched with several thousand other women right out of the massive gates of the camp, across the barren area, and into the woods!

"We're going to the Siemens factory," grunted a woman to Corrie's obvious question.

The work at the Siemens factory was backbreaking. It was one of the great iron and steel works of Germany. Corrie and Betsie had to push a handcart to a door at the factory where German civilians loaded it with heavy metal plates. The civilians refused to look at the prisoners. Then Corrie and Betsie threw their weak middle-aged bodies into the loaded cart to push it along a dock where they finally stopped it by a boxcar. They tried to get their breath as they helped load the plates into the boxcar.

At lunch each prisoner feasted on one boiled potato and a cup of broth. "Praise the Lord," said Betsie weakly. "I heard in the camp they get nothing for lunch."

Betsie could hardly walk the mile and a half back to camp, not that any prisoner wanted to return to camp, but guards were quick to lash out at stragglers. The guards were particularly brutal on the way back to camp. They wanted their day to end as quickly as possible.

After a dinner of turnip soup, Betsie recovered enough for the most important moments of the day. They found a lightbulb in the dormitory and read from the Bible. The first night those who had come with them from Vught joined them, along with a few of the curious.

Corrie was worried. Wouldn't it attract a guard? But strangely, guards were almost never to be seen in the dormitory of Barracks 28. And stranger still, Betsie got stronger and stronger as they read. As the days passed, the reading seemed to be enough to get her through the next workday as she weakened every minute during work and then strengthened every minute at night.

The nightly readings attracted more and more listeners. It was no longer enough to read the Bible in Dutch. Corrie would translate the passage into German. Another woman would repeat it in Russian. Another in Danish. Another in French. And on and on went God's true Word in the world's stumbling tongues.

One night Corrie asked a woman, "Why do the guards never come in the dormitory?"

"They are repelled by the fleas."

"Praise the Lord for the fleas."

Another miraculous thing that happened to them was the miracle of the vitamin bottle. It never seemed to run out of drops of liquid. Corrie was just certain it had to be exhausted. But it wasn't. She fretted about it all the time. Betsie depended on the vitamins to fight her anemia. And to worry Corrie even more, Betsie shared the bottle with everyone who asked.

Betsie just shrugged. "Don't you remember in First Kings the story of Elijah and the widow of Zarephath of Sidon?"

Corrie blinked. "The widow who had the jar of flour and the jug of oil? And they both seemed almost empty yet never ran out." But Corrie worried anyway. If only she had Betsie's faith. Nollie was like Betsie. Why was Corrie such a doubter? She remembered the man's cry for faith in chapter 9 of Mark: "I do believe; help me overcome my unbelief!" That was her. *Oh God, help me believe,* she prayed.

One day Mien found Corrie. "Tonight you can relax," said Mien. She pressed something into Corrie's hand. It was a new bottle of vitamins! Once again wonderful little Mien had somehow attached herself to a nurse and was scrounging things for the inmates.

And that very night the old bottle of vitamins ran out of drops. It was bone dry.

Did God's miracles never cease? "Oh God, I do believe," said Corrie.

In November they were issued coats. And no more work details went to

361

the Siemens factory. Why the work there stopped was a mystery. But bombs were dropping in the vicinity every night, and the great iron and steel works was probably a prime target. And Ravensbrück was not that far from the most prime target of all: Berlin, the heart of the Third Reich—if such a monstrosity had a heart.

In the camp, Corrie and Betsie were put to work leveling rough ground close to the concrete wall. Shoveling dirt was grueling on the best of days. But this day was after a rain, and Corrie felt as if she were shoveling lead instead of water-soaked soil. Betsie's health was failing. She could hardly lift her shovel. Corrie eyed the guard. Would the guard notice how little Betsie was doing?

FIFTEEN

W hy are you not working harder?" screamed the guard at Betsie. "That's nothing but a spoonful of dirt on your shovel."

"I'm sorry," Betsie answered good-naturedly, "but even spoonfuls add up."

If the other prisoners hadn't laughed, Betsie probably would have been all right. But no one swollen with pride can stand laughter. The guard struck Betsie with a leather crop. Betsie was bleeding. Her precious blood, of which she had so little, was streaming into the void. Corrie wanted to kill the guard. Betsie grabbed her hand. She saw the hatred in Corrie's face.

Rain and cold worsened Betsie's health. She now coughed blood. Again and again Corrie supported Betsie while she escorted her to the infirmary. Again and again the effort was in vain. Only a fever of 104 degrees got medical attention. Sick call itself was unhealthy, even dangerous. The women stood in line outside in the elements for hours before they were examined.

One day Betsie reached the threshold. Even though she was finally admitted to the infirmary, Corrie couldn't be happy. A temperature of 104 degrees was too close to fatal. Yet Betsie had to get medicine and rest. Betsie disappeared within the infirmary. Corrie was alone. How she wanted to be at Betsie's bedside.

Betsie returned to Barracks 28 three days later. No doctor had ever seen her. No medicine had ever been given to her. She still had a fever. But the visit was not in vain. She was rested. And somehow she had been transferred to the knitting room. Had Mien done something? The scrounger was everywhere. Her experience in the underground served her well. She kept her secrets to herself.

The general health of the women was so poor now the knitting brigade overflowed into the dormitories. The dormitory was paradise for Betsie. She was a very fast knitter and finished her quota of socks by noon. And because a guard rarely ventured into the dormitory, she could move among the knitting brigade with the gospel. What bliss for frail Betsie.

Miraculously, one day Corrie joined her. She had intentionally not joined a work crew that would have taken her away from Ravensbrück. She simply walked into the central room like she belonged there, grabbed a skein of gray wool, and joined the knitting brigade in the dormitory.

Betsie began to speak of a mission after the war. They would help poor people who were warped by the war find Jesus. There would be plenty of them.

363

She and Corrie would live with them. But not at the Beje. It wasn't big enough for Betsie's vision. She had envisioned a mansion in Haarlem. She could even describe the inlaid wood of the golden floors and the manicured gardens that surrounded it. There was a gallery around a central hall. Bas-relief statues adorned the walls. There were tall leaded windows, a gabled roof. Corrie was stunned by how vivid Betsie's vision was. It seemed Betsie was standing right there in Haarlem looking at it. Once again, she seemed prophetic. Betsie really seemed to be living in Christ.

Corrie was trying to get there. She seemed terribly flawed to herself. But wasn't that the first step to redemption and living in Christ? She hoped and prayed that it was. Because every day revealed a flaw. What was happening to her? The closer Betsie got to God, the more Corrie drifted away!

At least she knew she was straying. *Oh Jesus, help me. I'm sinking.*

One December day a passage from Paul's second letter to the Corinthians fairly exploded in her face:

And lest I should be exalted above measure through the abundance of the revelations, there was given to me a thorn in the flesh, the messenger of Satan to buffet me, lest I should be exalted above measure. For this thing I besought the Lord thrice, that it might depart from me. And he said unto me, My grace is sufficient for thee: for my strength is made perfect in weakness. Most gladly therefore will I rather glory in my infirmities, that the power of Christ may rest upon me. Therefore I take pleasure in infirmities, in reproaches, in necessities, in persecutions, in distresses for Christ's sake: for when I am weak, then am I strong.

Corrie's mistake was in thinking she was in power. Jesus was in power. And the weaker she became the stronger Christ became. She could see it so plainly in Betsie's case. And now her own case, too.

One morning as Corrie read the Bible to a group of knitters, she noticed the group seemed frozen. Someone was behind her. It must have been a woman guard. Corrie could feel the hammering hearts of the other inmates. But Corrie's new strength, which was from Christ and not from herself, compelled her to forge ahead. When she put down the Bible and started singing a hymn, the other inmates were really frightened. Now they had to make a choice. How could they deny to the guard their willingness to celebrate the gospel if they sang now? But Christ's strength was in them, too. And they did sing.

After they finished the hymn, Corrie waited for the leather crop to slice agony across her back. But a voice behind her pleaded, "Sing another one—like that one."

Later Corrie found that guard alone, so she could tell her about Jesus. Corrie knew now that even the guards still had a tiny trace of decency left. Even the guards could be salvaged if they could find Christ. Hadn't Paul held the coats of the villains who stoned Stephen? She and Betsie got bolder and bolder in Christ.

As blessed as Betsie's life was in the dormitory, she could not escape the dreaded roll calls twice a day. In December the air iced their bones, and all too frequently they were kept at roll call until prisoners started keeling over. Dear wonderful Mien brought them newspapers to insulate themselves, but Betsie was getting weaker. December 9 came and passed. They still hoped to be released.

One week before Christmas, Betsie could not move off the platform for morning roll call. Another prisoner helped Corrie carry Betsie to roll call. Betsie had to go there before she could go to sick call. But blocking the door to the outside was a ruthless woman guard called Snake. It was not many days before this morning that Snake had whipped a retarded girl mercilessly for soiling herself.

Snake looked at them. "Get her back inside."

They carried Betsie back to the platform. Then miraculously, orderlies appeared in a few minutes with a stretcher. Snake even stood by as Betsie was carried away to the infirmary. It was as if God had intervened to put His hand on Snake. Betsie had suffered enough.

Maybe this time Betsie would get the medicine she needed. Corrie wasn't going to rush to the infirmary. It might botch things. It seemed now that Betsie had friends, even among the very worst Nazi guards. But one dreary day at noon, Corrie could wait no longer. She didn't even know if Christmas had come yet or not. She slipped away from her work detail and crept around the infirmary until she found the window looking in on Betsie's ward. There was her dear Betsie on a cot. Corrie tapped on the pane.

Betsie opened her eyes, looking very tired, probably sedated. She tried to smile. She nodded "Yes" after Corrie mouthed, "Are you all right?"

Praise the Lord, Betsie was resting, out of the cold. She was fifty-nine years old, but she had never been strong. She had a miraculously productive life for someone who was virtually an invalid. But why was Corrie thinking such final thoughts? Betsie would recover. They would be freed. They would open their mission. She just knew it. After all, Betsie had a vision. And God didn't make mistakes.

The next day she sneaked back. Where was Betsie? On a cot was the corpse of an old woman, completely naked. She was pitifully thin. Yellow skin stretched over bone. Hair was matted. It was so sad. But where was Betsie? Was Betsie up and about all already? It seemed too much to ask. What was that by the cot? Nollie's sweater?

And the truth hammered her. The dead woman was Betsie!

She stumbled from the window and wandered in a daze. Betsie! Dead! How was it possible? Her dear, sweet older sister whom she had seen almost every day of her life for fifty-two years. And now she was dead. She had just weakened second by second, day after day, week after week, month after month, and slipped away to Jesus. If only they had been released September 1! Or even December 9, sweet Betsie would have lived. But what had Betsie told her when the terrible occupation began? *There are no "ifs" in God's world.* It was Betsie's vision that troubled Corrie. Betsie was gone. To paradise, yes. But why had she told Corrie her vision so many times? Because it dawned on Corrie that she was not going to survive either. How many roll calls in icy wind could her aging body withstand? She had long ago lost the weight she gained at Vught. She was a bag of bones. How much punishment could one undernourished, bony body take?

January would be even worse. Corrie felt like her blood was frozen slush now. The strong ones stomped their feet during roll call to keep from freezing. But eventually one became too weak—like sweet Betsie—to do that. Corrie saw how swollen her own legs and feet had become. Her shoes were ridiculous flaps of leather. It took only one small cold to become a bad cold with drainage, to become raging pneumonia, to become a woman's last rattling breath.

"Jesus, help me," she prayed. "I must not give up hope." She must never think Betsie suffered such a long time in vain. Sweet Betsie had changed the lives of so many inmates. But what if none of the prisoners survived? What was the point? The point was, she reminded herself, to save them in Jesus and get them to heaven. Corrie must not lose sight of Betsie's great victory—which was really the victory of Jesus.

One morning at roll call the guard called out, "Corrie ten Boom. Fall out!"

Not Number 66730! But Corrie ten Boom. What did it mean? She was no fool. Some of the older women did not die. They simply disappeared. It was a horror no one talked about. And inmates talked about almost everything. But not that smokestack. There was never the sound of gunshots. One wouldn't need a bullet to kill an inmate of Ravensbrück. They were so weak a sharp blow to the head would do it. So after all the waiting and hoping, it was no comfort to Corrie to have her name called at morning roll call. And it was no comfort to remain behind like Corrie did as the others went on their work details. It was no comfort to get release papers like Corrie got later that day.

The Nazis were such devils.

She smelled a trap when she was taken for a medical examination. A doctor who appeared not much older than a teenager said, "You have edema. You must be treated before you can leave here."

She couldn't deny her feet and ankles were horribly swollen. But she had never been more suspicious. She was taken to a ward with very unhealthy inmates. They too had been "released." This delay was no comfort. The Nazis were slow, bungling, ugly—but as certain as a great cancer. This ward might be no more than a holding area until the Nazis could work through their backlog of undesirables at the furnace.

The timing of her release—if it was that—nagged at her, too. Betsie had not been dead one week. Why couldn't she have lived? Never had Corrie's trust in God been tested more. This *was* God's plan for her and Betsie, she kept telling herself. And no one would have insisted that was true more emphatically than Betsie herself.

So she must not give up hope. She gave her Bible to an inmate she hoped would continue Betsie's good work. She could get another Bible in Holland. Holland! Could her release be true? Or was this a trick? She waited for her release, wondering if Holland was free yet. Her swelling had gone down considerably now that she no longer stood at roll calls. Why were they keeping her? And she had a horrifying thought. If she were released just as the Russians arrived, would she ever get back to Holland anyway? She would be behind the Russian army. But she must not think that way. There are no "ifs" in God's world.

Her heart was in her mouth the morning they marched her and several other older inmates away from the infirmary to a shed near the outskirts of the camp.

A guard sneered. "Step inside the dressing shed."

SIXTEEN

Dressing shed?" asked Corrie. Her heart was in her mouth. Was this another Nazi trick?

Once again she put her trust in God and stepped into the unknown. Inside the shed a guard actually issued Corrie some underwear, a wool skirt, a silk blouse, and shoes, none of it new, but to her it looked too nice to wear. She was given papers to sign that she agreed she had never been mistreated at Ravensbrück. So that was it. Some Nazis were already thinking about the consequences of the war. And this was "proof" of their innocence. She signed the paper anyway. Freedom was too close—if this was not a diabolical trick.

Remarkably, the guards produced an envelope with her Alpina watch, gold ring, and Dutch guilders.

Outside once again, she watched the massive gates swing open. She and others marched numbly back up the hill toward the railroad tracks where she and Betsie had arrived four months earlier. When she reached the crest, she didn't look back. Ravensbrück was a nightmare.

The group of inmates followed the tracks into the village of Furstenburg. Every moment seemed like a dream to Corrie. She waited numbly in the small train station with another Dutch woman, Claire Prins, and other inmates. Corrie was numb all the way on the boxcar into the sprawling train yards of Berlin. Were they really free? It didn't seem possible. Corrie and Claire clambered into another boxcar, this one on a freight train bound west toward Holland. The boxcars were icy cold. And the two Dutch women had to beg food at train stations. They had no food coupons. Nazis weren't going to waste food on foreigners.

She was getting weak again. She did not indulge in self-pity; she was long past that anyway. She saw now how the German people were suffering under the Nazis. Berlin was near the eastern boundary of Germany, and Corrie traveled across what was once the industrial might of Germany. Her boxcar passed one bombed city after another. As the train passed through the broken black shell of Bremen, Corrie couldn't help praying for Lieutenant Rahm's family. Some day she must find out if they survived the bombing.

Magically, one night a man spoke to them in Dutch! She and Claire discovered they were in Nieuweschans in Holland. Not long after that they were rolling into Groningen, where they had to leave the train. The rest of Holland's rail system was destroyed.

She limped with Claire to a Christian hospital called the Deaconess

Home. There Corrie received a strong dose of reality. The young nurse help-ing her asked, "Where are you from?"

"Haarlem."

"Oh, do you know Corrie ten Boom?"

Corrie blinked. "Are you one of my girls?"

"One of *your* girls? I'm Truus Benes."

"Truus! I'm Corrie."

Truus stared hard. Her face paled. "Of course it's you. I can see that now." She tried to hide her shock. Tears welled in her eyes.

Corrie knew now she was just a shadow of her former self. "Jesus will restore me," she assured Truus.

The Dutch in those dark days considered themselves deprived, but Cor-rie thought she had found paradise. Her starved senses were glutted. Corrie lingered in a bath, the first warm water on her crusted flea-bitten skin in a year. The nurses dressed her in different clothes. She was glad to be rid of Nazi clothes she was sure had been confiscated from some poor confused victim. Her first meal seemed a banquet for Queen Wilhemina: brussels sprouts, po-tatoes, gravy, even traces of meat. And dessert was pudding with currant juice and an apple. After supper her head sank into a real pillow on a real mattress in a real bedroom. A nurse even propped her swollen feet up on another pillow. The bedroom was a rainbow of colors. And the air smelled so clean.

When she woke up the next morning in her cradle of bliss, she saw a bookcase. She heard children playing on their way to school. She heard the merry bells of a carillon and a choir. As she shuffled past a nurse's room on her swollen feet, she heard an organist playing Bach! The nurse was listening to her radio. What a feast life was now! Did it take prison to sharpen these wonderful gifts from God?

Ten days later, Corrie got a midnight ride on a food truck. Farmers were trucking their produce illegally all over Holland in darkness. Many Dutch in the cities were starving. Once again the farmers were doing their duty. Finally, she arrived at Hilversum. How good it was to see Willem again. Even he, who considered death a mere step into glory, slumped when he heard Betsie was gone. Betsie made everything around her better. Corrie soon learned how much Willem's own family had suffered. Kik had been caught and hauled away by the Nazis. Willem was yellow-skinned. He had contracted some kind of crippling disease of the spine in the prison at Scheveningen. But he was just like Betsie. He acted as if he were going to live another thirty years.

One February day, almost one year since the Gestapo hauled her away from the Beje, she was back in Haarlem. Even though the Nazis still occupied Haarlem, Pickwick delivered her to the Beje in his limousine. Suddenly, the limousine stopped at the alley door of the Beje. A woman stepped out the door.

"Nollie!" screamed Corrie.

"Corrie!"

Through a flood of tears, the sisters hugged each other, while Nollie's daughters gathered around, chattering like happy larks. Cocky, Aty, and Elske hugged Corrie next. Corrie stumbled inside. Yes, the Beje was fine as long as Nollie and her happy girls were there with her. But after they left that afternoon, it was so lonely. The stolen typewriter, rugs, watches, and clocks nagged at her. But what were they compared to poor Betsie? And poor Papa? Grief overwhelmed her. She had to get busy again.

She tried to occupy herself with the watch shop. And no ten Boom could tolerate a house with empty beds. She took in a retarded child. But Betsie's vision swelled up inside her. Now was the time. Corrie was back in Haarlem. What was her excuse? Betsie's vision could not be neglected. But where would Corrie find the mansion of Betsie's vision? Even Pickwick did not have a house that grand. And who would she talk to? And who would want to listen? The Nazis were still here.

She began speaking anyway—to clubs, to people in their homes, to anyone who would listen anywhere at any time. Often her contact at a garden club or Bible class would be reluctant, even frightened. But Corrie had to get her message out. It took only a few talks, and she felt God had told her exactly what to say. She had to point out that no pit was too deep for someone who was safe in Jesus. She described every degrading detail of imprisonment so people would know how deep the pit was. She described Betsie's vision. The Dutch must care for these poor people who were scarred by prisons and camps. The Dutch must give them a chance to find Jesus. The Lord would take care of their recovery.

Often a woman would approach her after her talk and whisper, "Can't you wait? There are still Nazis here."

So when a woman, dressed in such finery that she appeared untouched by the war, approached her after a talk, Corrie expected the usual warning. But the woman said, "I'm Mrs. Bierens de Haan. I live in a very large house in Bloemendaal. But now I am a widow. All my sons are grown. My son Jan was taken to Germany. A lightning bolt suddenly struck me that if God would return Jan to me, I would have to give up my house for your sister's vision."

Corrie was leery. One does not bargain with God. "Are you sure?"

"It was a revelation, right out of the blue."

Corrie sighed. She didn't want to spurn an offer, but what this woman was doing seemed wrong. Corrie said, "My sister had a very specific place in mind." Corrie hoped she didn't sound like a snob. But she wasn't lying about what Betsie said. "This house of Betsie's has a golden floor of inlaid wood. Beautiful manicured gardens surround it. There must be a gallery around a central hall. The walls must be adorned by bas-relief statues. There is a wonderful gabled roof with tall leaded windows—" She stopped. The woman's mouth was gaping. Corrie hoped the woman didn't say too many bad things about her high and mighty demands, her rude ingratitude.

The woman said, "That's my house!"

It was mystical. Corrie was sure now. The woman certainly had not bargained with God. God was using the woman in His plan, just as He used Betsie in His plan, just as He used Corrie in His plan.

Corrie was not surprised when Mrs. de Haan sent her a note later. "Jan came home!" she had scribbled excitedly.

So they opened a home for those poor unfortunate minds mangled by the prisons and concentration camps. Holland's liberation seemed almost anticlimactic. Suddenly, Corrie realized the Nazis were gone. The streets were full of soldiers from Canada. They were the Canadian First Army, someone told her, under General Crerar. But Corrie was no more interested in details like that than she had been when the German army had arrived. Oh, she knew in her head it was a great day for Holland. But in her heart she knew really great days were when people found the Light.

Corrie seemed to be operating on a new level. Why would God give Betsie such a startling vision if it were not going to come true? This kind of miraculous thing happened in the Bible, of course. But now it had happened to Betsie. Corrie was sure of it. She already believed in angels. Hadn't they protected her at Scheveningen, Vught, and Ravensbrück? Would this miraculous foresight ever come to Corrie herself? And it struck her: If she became part of the vision, surely God would tell her what to do next.

To make sure she was deserving, she studied the Bible as she never had before. She didn't want to make any mistakes. One of the first insights she had was that she had to forgive. Everyone. Even the dreadful Nazis. And there were people in Holland whom the Dutch hated even more than the Nazis. Those were the traitors, the Dutch who helped the Nazis. And it was this step in Corrie's burning desire to do God's will that hurt her the most.

In June of 1945, she wrote a painful letter to a Dutchman from Ermelo:

I heard that most probably you are the one who betrayed me. I went through ten months of concentration camp. My father died after nine days of imprisonment. My sister died in prison, too.

The harm you planned was turned into good for me by God. I came nearer to Him. A severe punishment is waiting for you. I have prayed for you, that the Lord may accept you if you will repent. Think about the fact that the Lord Jesus on the cross also took your sins upon Himself. If you accept this, and want to be His child, you are saved for eternity.

I have forgiven you everything. God will also forgive you everything, if you ask Him. He loves you, and He Himself sent His Son to earth to reconcile your sins. . .to suffer the punishment for you and me. You, on your part, have to give an answer to this. If He says: "Come to Me, give Me your heart," then your answer must be: "Yes, Lord, I come. Make me Your child." If it is difficult for you to pray, then ask if God will give you His Holy Spirit, who works the faith in your heart.

Never doubt the Lord Jesus' love. He is standing with His arms spread out to receive you.

I hope that the path which you will now take may work for your eternal salvation.

That letter was so painful Corrie was nauseated. Would she meet others who turned her stomach? What if she met a guard who had beaten her? How could she ever forgive a guard for beating sweet Betsie when she was so weak? What if she met a guard she saw beat some inmate to death? What would she do? Could she still forgive? God said, "Yes. You must. Or I will not forgive you." It was right there bright as day in the Lord's Prayer. No one could claim ignorance of that.

Corrie soon discovered that her mind was free of the man who betrayed her family. The hatred, the urge to kill, was gone. Once again, God was right. He was always right. Why did people resist Him so? Even Corrie herself resisted Him. She thought long and hard about how she must determine God's will for herself. God did not speak to her directly. She was no saint. He did not make it easy for her. Life is not a cartoon. Doors opened and doors closed, and those who had eyes must look hard; those who have ears must listen hard.

One of the first arrivals at the fifty-six-room mansion in Bloemendaal was Mrs. Kan, the wife of the watchmaker in Barteljorisstraat. Mr. Kan had died while in hiding, and Mrs. Kan was very old and infirm. Soon the great mansion was full of patients and volunteers. Corrie still went out speaking her message, once again the organizer finding volunteers and raising money, this time for the rehabilitation center. She made mistakes, like trying too soon to rehabilitate traitors, but she moved ahead. But even Nollie was not prepared for Corrie's next move.

SEVENTEEN

I'm going to America," said Corrie.

"But what about the watch shop?" asked Nollie.

"I'm giving the business to my helpers. I tried to get back into the business. I really did. I even traveled to Switzerland for watches, which are very hard to get right now. But I know Betsie would be sad if she knew I was using up my precious time for such things when I could be delivering her message about the victory of Jesus in the concentration camps."

"And the Beje?" asked Nollie.

"I'm turning it into a home for victims of the war. The rehabilitation center in Bloemendaal is overflowing."

"But they say it is impossible to get to America. Everyone wants to go. The waiting list for a passenger ship is a year at least. And you need a lot of money to go to America, Corrie."

"I have fifty dollars."

Nollie, always as blunt as the sunrise, laughed. "Oh, Corrie, dear. What will a pitiful fifty dollars do?"

"If God does not want me to go, the gate will be closed for me. But if He does want me to go, the gate will open."

Nollie laughed again. "Few people pound harder on the gate or more persistently than you do, Corrie. Be sure to write me from America."

And in a time when it was possible only for people with money and influence to find passage to America, Corrie found herself on a freighter just a few days later steaming for America! She didn't worry about her lack of money. She trusted God completely. In New York City she got a room at the YWCA, and every morning she went out, bought her one meal of the day: coffee, orange juice, and a donut, then trudged all day long through the long canyons of Manhattan knocking on every church door. She had to move out of the YWCA and drift from room to room. But a woman who had survived the Nazi concentration camps didn't quit but prayed harder. God would provide for her somehow. But she might have to suffer first.

Corrie struggled. She was operating on nickels and dimes. Some Americans treated her like a beggar. Some told her no one wanted to talk about the war anymore. But what were those obstacles to a survivor of the Nazi concentration camps? Corrie began to get a few invitations to speak. Her audiences seemed riveted, especially the Americans who remained at home as civilians. They envisioned the war as battling soldiers, not fifty-year-old ladies. How would they have survived an occupation? Corrie prayed her listeners appreciated that she survived on spiritual power.

She began to meet a few movers and shakers in the American churches. She met a few publishers of Christian books and magazines. She told them she had hundreds of stories to tell. She prayed she radiated the love of Jesus. She got a wrenching letter from Nollie. Willem had died. He had tuberculosis of the spine. And Tine learned Kik had died in a work camp in Germany. So more of Corrie's beautiful family had succumbed to the Nazis!

By the year's end, her first foray into America was complete. She had made some friends she felt she could always rely on, because she intended to came back again. Now it was time to move on. She knew her next move would confound Nollie again. Corrie was going to go to Germany. She and Betsie had talked about it, huddled together in the deadening cold of the barracks. Betsie said they had to go back to Germany and paint the prison barracks bright colors and plant flowers. But that was only the beginning. They had to help the poor, sick guards, the tiny, nasty cogs in the insane Nazi machine, to find new lives through Jesus. Their rehabilitation was important. Any dream of Betsie's was reality to Corrie.

Corrie went to Darmstadt, southeast of Frankfurt, to help a church organization renovate a concentration camp. It was a small but vibrant start. The brightly painted barracks held 160 Germans. Many were women with children. Germany had lost almost four million soldiers in the war. The facts of Hitler's insanity were seeping out, like blood under a closet door, too horrible for the human mind to comprehend. Twenty million Russians and seven million Germans had died. The dead on all sides of the insane war totaled fifty-five million!

The truth about the concentration camps was horrifying, too. In the six years before the war, the Nazis operated camps at Buchenwald, Dachau, Flossenbürg, Mauthausen, Sachsenhausen, and, of course, Ravensbrück. As the war began, these camps held twenty-five thousand political enemies and those Germans the Nazis regarded religious misfits, such as Jews and Jehovah's Witnesses. But during the war, the power-crazed Nazis added camps at Auschwitz-Birkenau, Natzweiler, Neuengamme, Gross Rosen, Stutthof, Lublin-Maidanek, Hinzert, Vught, Dora, and Bergen-Belsen. Nazis then arrested gypsies, homosexuals, and prostitutes, too. Millions, mostly Jews, entered these camps from every occupied country of Europe. The Nazis worked them to death and executed them by gassing or shooting. The final toll was over six million!

Corrie found out Lieutenant Rahm and his family were still alive. Rahm admitted he still suffered enormous guilt. And Corrie knew millions of surviving

Germans carried that guilt. No one needed Jesus more. Once after Corrie talked in a church, the people got up silently, as they always did in Germany, and filed out. But working against the flow was a man coming toward Corrie. He looked familiar.

No! She wanted to scream.

The man stopped in front of her, smiling. "What a fine message, Frau ten Boom. I'm so glad to hear our sins are forgiven." This very man was at Ravensbrück! He was one of the guards who watched coldly as Corrie and Betsie filed past, naked and degraded. She remembered him distinctly. Corrie could not speak. She pretended to be preoccupied. Would he never go away? The man went on confidently, "You mentioned you were at Ravensbrück. You won't believe this, but I was a guard at Ravensbrück. However, after the war I became a Christian. God forgave me. Will you forgive me?" He extended his weathered hairy hand. It was as repulsive as a snake.

Oh, how hard it is to be in Christ at times like this, thought Corrie. She had a thousand reasons to hate this evil man. Poor sweet Betsie. But Betsie would have been first to forgive him. Corrie had to forgive him, or God would not forgive her. It was perfectly clear in the Bible. She looked at the man's repulsive hand. Forgiveness was not an emotion one indulged. It was the will of God.

She extended her hand. "I forgive you."

Warmth flooded over her. It was intense. She felt herself glow with love. But it was not her love. She was powerless. Corrie prayed the world would forgive the Germans, too. She bought a German camera and began snapping slides of everything she saw that interested her. As if she didn't have enough to do, she now carefully inked notes on the paper portion of each slide after it was developed. But she remained much more than a tourist.

Theologians who sat around critiquing the Bible but doing nothing to mend the broken spirits of their flocks angered her. Once in Germany she said to such a group, "If I speak about the Lord's return, as I probably shall, will you label me a sectarian? If I speak about the fullness of the Holy Spirit, does that make me a Pentecostal? Get your labels ready. If I speak about conversion, will you label me a pietist? If my message piques your consciences too much, you can label me and set me aside in a dusty pigeonhole."

The world did forgive the Germans, as Corrie had. Help poured in to rehabilitate them. After a while, Corrie saw her own mission in Germany not complete but well under way. There were other places to go to deliver her message about Jesus. She left Germany to continue her odyssey. She knew she seemed wildly impulsive to Nollie, establishing herself and her message in one country and abruptly leaving to go somewhere else. But she was guided by

God. Mention of another country would sometimes strike her as divine guidance. It was absolutely compelling. Or a country on a map might seem to jump out at her. And she would have to go there. In weak moments, she wondered if her imprisonment didn't make her want to flee, flee, flee. She no longer took money. Money was not always offered for the right reasons. Nollie didn't want her to take money, either. So Corrie became like Paul. She arrived, she worked, she preached the gospel, and she accepted whatever anyone wanted to give her. A bed. A meal. But not money. She proudly called herself a "tramp for the Lord."

For years she traveled alone, brazenly intruding on lives, preaching the gospel: in Cuba, South Africa, Japan, Bermuda, New Zealand, Australia, Spain, England, Denmark, Taiwan, Israel. She returned to America and Germany, too. She wrote books, too. Her anecdotes were becoming very popular. The royalties from the books were pumped into her work. She bought another house in the Bloemendaal district of Haarlem. Of course, the house became a center for rehabilitation. She went there only to rest occasionally. She was no celebrity anywhere, especially in Holland. Too many others had endured the same experience to be awed by her courage.

Nollie's death in 1953 stunned her. Nollie was only sixty-three. Now Corrie's generation of the family was dead except for herself. Corrie grieved a long time. In her own way, Nollie was as saintly as Betsie. Six children were Nollie's life's work. Corrie idolized both her sisters.

By 1957, after twelve years of unrelenting activity, Corrie was being crushed under her own popularity. She was in demand. Her books were known far and wide. She had even stayed as Queen Wilhemina's guest at the palace in Holland. Corrie needed help, and she found a perfect companion: Conny van Hoogstraten, a tall attractive Dutch woman. Conny became Corrie's buffer, making traveling arrangements, filtering invitations for speaking engagements, making guests welcome, but protecting Corrie.

Corrie traveled with Conny now: Cuba, Africa, India, Argentina, Korea, Eastern Europe, Russia, and countries in every continent. In 1964, Corrie was brought down by hepatitis. She was seventy, almost the exact age Papa was when he fell prey to hepatitis. Doctors ordered her to rest one year, so she rested at Lweza, a missionary home in Uganda. Located on the shore of Lake Victoria, it was very peaceful. Corrie slept in the same bed every night. Her clothes hung in a closet. She strolled into nearby Kumpala two or three times a week to show people the way to Jesus. Rest was paradise. At the end of the year, she did not want to leave. Why should she? She was still leading people to Jesus. This must be God's plan for her.

Then she had a visitor.

EIGHTEEN

Her visitor was a minister from Rwanda, a tiny country also on the shore of Lake Victoria. He said, "Five years ago when you visited us and thrilled us with your prison stories, we could not appreciate the hell you went through."

"Yes?" said Corrie suspiciously.

"We have had a terrible civil war in Rwanda. I myself have been in prison two years. Your message about Jesus sustained me."

"Yes?"

"We would be so happy if you came to minister to our poor people when they get out of prison. Who can do it better than you?"

Once again Corrie packed her bags. God surely did not intend for her to slow down yet. After Conny left her in 1967 to get married, Corrie traveled alone again. She was still going strong, even though she was seventy-five years old. She did buy an apartment in Baarn, Holland, where she was supposed to go periodically to rest and write books. But she did far more writing and receiving friends there than resting. Her personal friends seemed to number in the thousands.

Traveling was harder for Corrie. More and more often she was tempted to quit. Didn't she deserve to rest at her age? And how would she ever replace Conny? Then one day Ellen de Kroon, a tall, blond Dutch woman in her late twenties, visited. Although Ellen seemed so much younger than Corrie, she, too, had scars from World War II.

"We were starving in Rotterdam," she told Corrie. "My father was forced to go to a work camp in Germany. So mother took us to a farm."

"God bless those wonderful Dutch farmers," interrupted Corrie. "What would we have done without them?"

"We five children would have starved. Every time the Nazis came to the farm, we all rushed into the woods to hide."

"I must know something, Ellen. Did your father come back after the war ended?"

"Why yes."

"Praise the Lord. I'm looking for a companion, Ellen. And you seem just perfect," enthused Corrie.

"Me! But you don't know me well enough. I can't type. I can't drive a car. I don't speak German or English."

Corrie was beaming. "You cannot do it yourself anyway, Ellen. But God can do it *through* you."

Ellen agreed to try it. She made some changes in Corrie's life, too. Corrie talked a lot, but she did listen to what other people said. Some were too intimidated by her forcefulness to offer suggestions. But Ellen bluntly said Corrie's wardrobe was outdated. So Corrie meekly let Ellen replace her gloomy wardrobe of long dark dresses and heavy black shoes. From now on Corrie would wear beige or brown shoes with colorful print dresses.

"It's a good thing you are a nurse," Corrie told Ellen not long after they teamed up. Corrie had just been in a car accident. She broke not only her shoulder but her right arm in five places.

Ellen helped her rehabilitation. Corrie could not write with her shattered arm, so she practiced until she could write with her left hand. Later she worked with sandbags to build the strength back in her right arm.

But to Corrie the temptation to quit was still strong. Traveling tired her. Speech after speech tired her. And after every speech, she and Ellen sat at a table selling her books and tapes. She still would not ask for money, but earned her way just as Paul had earned his way making tents while he evangelized. Corrie noticed her tired mind drifted into self-pity more and more often. But then she got terrible news that Conny had died of cancer. How could Corrie quit when vivacious Conny had spent so much of her youth to help her spread the gospel?

Years of speaking in public taught Corrie how to assemble a talk in seconds. All she needed to know was how much time her hosts were going to allow her. She had two favorite props for her shorter talks. One was a piece of material she called the "crown." She would begin by holding up what appeared to her audience to be nothing more than rough blue cloth with tangled knots of golden thread hanging from it. She would recite a poem:

My life is like a weaving
between my God and me.
I do not choose the colors
He works steadily.
Sometimes He weaves sorrow
and I in foolish pride
forget He sees the upper,
and I the underside.
Not till the loom is silent
and the shuttles cease to fly

will God unroll the canvas
and explain the reason why
the dark threads are as needful
in the skillful weaver's hand
as the threads of gold and silver
in the pattern He has planned.

Corrie would triumphantly flip the cloth over to show her audience what God sees: a golden crown on a field of blue! That is what the believer will eventually see of God's plan in heaven. Even the most sophisticated listeners seemed stunned by the metaphor.

Then she would unashamedly launch her appeal, "Do you know Jesus? I don't mean do you know *about* Him—but do you *know* Him? I asked the Lord Jesus to come into my heart when I was five years old. He came into my heart, and He has never let me down. . . ."

Another favorite prop of Corrie's was a flashlight. She would throw the switch, and when the light failed to shine, she exclaimed, "Is there no light in your life?" She unscrewed the end of the flashlight. "Invite Jesus into your life!" She pushed a battery into the flashlight. The light still failed to shine. Her audience was startled. "What's wrong?" She unscrewed the end again. "What is this?" She pulled out a rag. "Pride!" She pulled out another rag. "Envy!" She pulled out another. "Love of money!" Finally, she would slide in the battery again. The flashlight beamed brilliant light!

She had hundreds of stories she had polished over many years. Sweet Betsie taught her how to enchant listeners in the beginning. But now Corrie had the powerful story of the concentration camps, too. "No pit is too deep when Jesus is in your heart," she said. And she knew that when she told this story she became more than a peppery old lady telling charming stories. The world now knew the Nazis were devils. How many in her audience could have survived the Nazi camps? How many of them could have shed the bitterness like she did? Surely they knew she got her courage from Jesus just as she said.

But soon Ellen was giving speeches. Sometimes Corrie was simply too exhausted to give another speech. And the speech was already scheduled. They couldn't let an audience down. The message was too important. When Ellen overcame her fear, it was not so difficult. Corrie insisted Ellen need not feel like a fraud. Ellen had truly suffered under the Nazis, too.

NINETEEN

A writing team told Corrie how excited they were by her book about Ravensbrück called *A Prisoner and Yet*. But they were sure there was a bigger story to be told. Soon Corrie was collaborating on a book with them emphasizing her war experiences from 1939 to 1944. The book was to be called *The Hiding Place*. The title referred to two hiding places: the secret room where the ten Boom family hid refugees from the Nazis, and Jesus, in whom Corrie hid when events were crushing her. Published in 1971, the book was no narration of dry facts, but a first person cliff-hanger.

Corrie, still globe-trotting with Ellen, now lugged along dozens of copies of that book on her trips. Any moment was a perfect occasion for Corrie to unashamedly spring her book on any candidate for salvation. That included everyone.

Corrie was relentless with her book. She passed out thousands of copies—free. What were books for? And so what if she paid for the copies herself?

The evangelist Billy Graham told Corrie he was interested in making *The Hiding Place* into a movie. He had a motion picture company called World Wide Pictures to make movies with Christian themes. Corrie prayed that it would come true eventually. But she had too many other activities to think about it much.

Also as a result of the book, she was invited to appear on Robert Schuller's *Hour of Power* television show. After that first appearance on nationwide television, her invitations to speak increased more and more.

By 1974, Corrie had collaborated with another writer on a sequel to *The Hiding Place* called *Tramp for the Lord*. American friends had to incorporate her as "Christians, Inc." to free her of red tape and the necessity to manage her money. Corrie still traveled the globe. Money meant little more to Corrie than buying airfare for Ellen and herself to their next destination. After all these years, she perfectly understood her Papa's total disregard for money.

By 1975, Billy Graham's World Wide Pictures started filming *The Hiding Place*. Locations were in England and Holland. Veteran actors assured a professional effort. Arthur O'Connell, nominated for two Oscars in a long Hollywood career, was to play Papa. Julie Harris, a veteran of Hollywood and Broadway, had the role of sweet Betsie. Eileen Heckart, winner of both an Emmy and an Oscar, would play an older version of the scrounger Mien. Broadway actress Jeannette Clift had the part of Corrie.

That same year, Corrie finished collaborating on a third major book, *In My Father's House*, covering her early years. Billy Graham invited her to speak on his televised crusades. He did convince her that personal appearances were no longer the most effective way for her to spread the gospel. Her impact would be greater through his televised crusades.

But she still wanted to travel the globe and talk to groups, too. Spreading the message "Jesus is Victor" was so personal that way. And in Tel Aviv, she presented the two millionth copy of *The Hiding Place* to another brave woman, Golda Meir, the prime minister of Israel. Early in 1976, Ellen left Corrie to be married. This time Corrie's companion was an English woman, Pam Rosewell. She joined Corrie resting at her new house in a suburb of Haarlem. Shortly after Pam arrived, Corrie had a nostalgic golden reunion with her club girls. Corrie was amused. Pam would soon discover that the work never ended, and just when Pam thought she had everything under control, Corrie would take on something else. Eighty-four-year-old Corrie had planned an eighteen-city tour in America, lasting seven months!

But things had really changed for Corrie, too. Now she had fans. Fans were celebrity worshippers. They would rush up and explode a flashbulb right in her face. And Pam would try to fend off fans who would try to grab the eighty-four-year-old around the neck to hug her.

As much as Corrie enjoyed the warmth of personal appearances, she finally admitted to herself that this new kind of exuberant fan was dangerous to her at her age. She had a troubling dream now, too. She was locked in a room with no way out.

Corrie brushed off the disturbing dream and made her plans. She was convinced now that she must channel her flagging energies into short films and writing books. Personal appearances were too dangerous, and she was not reaching enough people that way.

She told Pam she wanted to move to the Los Angeles area in California, close to the headquarters of Christians, Inc., in Orange and close to Billy Graham's movie studio. Thirty-three years to the day since she was arrested by the Gestapo in 1944, she moved into a ranch-style home in Placentia. She dubbed it "Shalom House," for her desire for peace and quiet, and soon celebrated her eighty-fifth birthday there.

After talking to both World Wide Pictures and Bill Barbour, her publisher, Corrie announced her plans to Pam: five books and five movie shorts. Pam protested. How could Corrie do so much? Was this peace and quiet? But Corrie really did intend to write five books and make five movie shorts. If only Pam could keep her from taking too many other commitments.

But of course Corrie did make other commitments. It was only natural after she finished her short prison film, *One-Way Door*, that she start a neighborhood group praying weekly for prisoners. Naturally she had to be at the prayer meeting herself. And when she got an invitation to the prison at San Quentin, how could she refuse to go? And when people showed up at Shalom House saying God sent them there, how could Corrie refuse to see them? Pam watched helplessly.

By December Corrie had finished the first of her five books, *Each New Day*, and stopped long enough to get a pacemaker. She was proud of her new constant pulse of seventy-two. She was sure the pacemaker would serve the Lord well.

She celebrated her eighty-sixth birthday while making a film with Christian Indians in Arizona. In the summer of 1978, she made a third film, *Jesus Is Victor*, and was honored in Denver on an episode of *This is Your Life* for television. Each venture now required more recuperation. And recovery was difficult at Shalom House where Corrie couldn't refuse to see anyone.

Often Corrie saw fatigue or botched plans as an attack by the devil. Following an unrelenting schedule, Corrie reached her goal of five books and five movie shorts in less than two years. But one morning in August, when she woke up, she couldn't move. Was she only dreaming she woke up? In her heart she knew she was awake. All her memories of Mama's paralysis flooded back. Now here was Corrie sixty years later. Her troubling dream of being locked in a room had come true.

TWENTY

Soon after Corrie was rushed to the hospital, she lost consciousness. How long she drifted in the void she couldn't tell. Gradually, she realized she was awake again. When she tried to speak, she must have been speaking gibberish, because Pam just looked at her blankly. Soon she realized she was saying a few words like "yes" and "Conny." She remembered how she dismissed the importance of her own name sixty years ago when Mama said it after her stroke. Had she been Mama's favorite like Conny was her favorite? Weeks later, back at the Shalom House, Corrie now played the guessing game with Pam, just as Mama had played it with her. Corrie would gesture yes or no to question after question until the answer she sought finally came.

Occasionally she recovered full speech.

But Corrie's life now was mostly a pleasant indulgence. An old friend of Corrie's, Lotte Reimeringer, came to help Pam. The two helpers walked Corrie in the garden behind the house. She watched birds at the bird feeder. She did needlework. She listened to Bach. Her favorite Bible, the English translation by J. B. Phillips, was read to her several times a day. She prayed with Pam and Lotte. She received only a few visitors. She went on drives in a car. She was able to put together another devotional book with Lotte by indicating her choices of many clippings she had saved over the years. But the old peppery evangelizing days were over. And sometimes she wept in frustration. But she would remember Mama's paralysis and her unbound love. Love triumphs over all afflictions. And our earthly sufferings only serve to make that which awaits us an even greater glory. And so she poured out her love to Pam and Lotte and everyone around her.

Then Corrie was struck down again. It was May 1979. And yet, again she lived, more helpless than before. Her hearing was still very sharp. Well-meaning friends discussed her funeral and burial. Pam already knew what Corrie thought of burial. "Oh, just bury me in the backyard," she had said with a wave of the hand. She heard hospital staff say she weighed no more than eighty pounds. She heard it said she showed the first symptoms of kidney failure, a certain precursor of death. That angered Corrie. God would decide when she had to leave her body. She started getting better.

The doctors no longer liked to make predictions about eighty-eight-year-old Corrie ten Boom. She seemed to be getting higher medical help. She returned home again. She was completely bedridden now, her speech almost nonexistent, her arms and hands rags. In the evenings, Lotte and Pam gave her slide shows of the sixty-six countries and hundreds of dear friends she had visited. She had seven thousand slides! How fortunate she had been. She seemed to have lived a dozen lives. But occasionally the futility of her existence overwhelmed her and she wept. *Why keep me here so long, God? Why?* In the fall of 1980, she suffered a third stroke. She became even less responsive. Corrie felt shame. How could she question God's plan? This had happened to Mama. She must not forget the glory that awaited. But still, why did she linger so long?

One day she had a marvelous vision of the Lord. It seemed as rich as Revelation. It had to be the third paradise Paul could not write about. How she wanted to at least tell Pam and Lotte that she glimpsed glory. But could she?

Corrie lived on and on. She experienced visions. She experienced despair. Eventually, Corrie could not open her eyes. She had nothing left but her hearing. She heard Pam reading Psalm 103, a Dutch tradition for birthdays: ". . .who redeems your life from the pit and crowns you with love and compassion." That verse seemed written for Corrie. And it was as if Betsie was reading it to her.

As if God offered her passing as one more proof of His will, Corrie passed away on April 15, 1983—her ninety-first birthday.